SWIFT'S SATIRES
AND
PERSONAL WRITINGS

Oxford University Press, Amen House, London, E.C.4
GLASGOW NEW YORK TORONTO MELBOURNE WELLINGTON
BOMBAY CALCUTTA MADRAS CAPE TOWN
Geoffrey Cumberlege, Publisher to the University

SATIRES
AND
PERSONAL WRITINGS

BY

JONATHAN SWIFT

Edited with Introduction and Notes by

WILLIAM ALFRED EDDY

Geoffrey Cumberlege
OXFORD UNIVERSITY PRESS
London New York Toronto

JONATHAN SWIFT

Born, Dublin	30 November 1667
Died, Dublin	19 October 1745

This edition of Swift's Satires *was first published in 1932 and reprinted in 1937, 1944, 1949, and 1951*

PRINTED IN GREAT BRITAIN

O.S.A.

PREFATORY NOTE

THE purpose of this volume is to provide a generous selection of Swift's best work in prose and verse to supplement the volume containing *Gulliver's Travels*, *A Tale of a Tub*, and *The Battle of the Books*.

Each item is a faithful reproduction of the best text published during the lifetime of Swift and is reprinted from a photostat of the original. Where early editions differed in detail, there has been no emendation and no substitution of variant readings. The best of the contemporary editions is simply reproduced in its entirety, including the original spelling and punctuation. Only obvious printer's errors have been corrected.

The policy of reproducing an edition integrally is abandoned in favour of collation only in the case of Swift's letters and poems, contemporary editions of which were incomplete and unsatisfactory. The source of each text and the method of reproduction are described in the separate prefaces. Limitations of space have necessitated in a very few cases, such as *The Journal to Stella*, *Letters*, and *Poems*, an abbreviated text, but there has been no expurgation.

This edition differs from previous selections from the writings of Swift in favouring his lighter and wittier satires at the expense of his political tracts for the times. If the proportion of *jeux d'esprit* seems excessive it may be borne in mind that the purpose of the editor is to represent faithfully the most significant and readable pages of Swift the writer, rather than to reconstruct the controversies of Swift the party politician. Accordingly, the Introduction deals with Swift's mind and style rather than with his public or private career.

CONTENTS

IRONICAL ESSAYS

SATIRICAL DIVERSIONS

MISCELLANEOUS ESSAYS

INTIMATE AND PERSONAL WRITINGS

INTRODUCTION

I. *The Man and His Times*

WHILE walking with Swift one day in the country, Pope ventured the opinion that chance reflections are often as important as laboured syllogisms, the extemporized 'aside' more to the point than the prepared declamation. Acting upon this theory they produced some of the best pages of their joint *Miscellanies*—pages in which trifles are illumined with the fire of genius.

To Swift this employment of his wit, in conversation and in writing, was ever congenial. In his old age he wrote, 'I love la Bagatelle better than ever'. Trivia was his patron saint, and Lilliput his refuge from the Yahoo. Pregnant with humour as are *Gulliver* and *A Tale of a Tub*, the reader who knows Swift only through his extended and completed satires is in danger of missing the human comedy laid bare in a hundred brief sketches drawn in a merrier mood. Satirical tracts dashed off in haste and published unsigned and unrevised, ideas for later use caught on the wing and assembled incongruously in a common-place book as *Thoughts on Various Subjects*, titles and plots suggested to fellow writers in a letter or over a cup of coffee, bear witness to a gaiety and fertility of imagination which has been overlooked or discarded as inconvenient by the makers of the myth of a pathological misanthrope. The Swift who enlivened the company of Stella, Arbuthnot, Addison, Gay, and Pope is the Swift for modern readers, rather than the monster described by Thackeray, the bloodless rationalist depicted by Leslie Stephen, or the 'neurotic', the exhumed 'skull', and the 'tiger' of more recent biographers. Swift did indeed live a frustrated life, but the intellectual diversions which engaged his liveliest wit and his closest friends are at least as revealing as the melancholia which finally overpowered him. Into the scales must be cast the 'thoughts hardly to be packed, into a narrow act; fancies that broke through language and escaped'. When this is done, we discover the companion known to his comrades as 'the laughter-loving dean', 'the merry yahoo', 'Bickerstaff', and 'Martin Scriblerus'. Too much attention has been riveted upon the last decade of Swift's life (1735–45) when his health was going rapidly to pieces; we are apt to forget that his work was all done between 1696 and 1735—years when poets and wits sought his company, when politicians competed for his assistance, when crowds of grateful Irishmen cheered him in the streets of Dublin. From this period comes no voice to tell us that Swift was an ogre. He lived the greater part of his life amid the diversions of Lilliput, with shorter sojourns among the Yahoos.

Even great and often bitter satires took root in moments of diversion. The adventures of Gulliver were written into the *Memoirs of Scriblerus* in 1714. Pope dedicated the *Dunciad* to Swift, invoking the quixotic air and Rabelaisian laughter which had marked their collaboration on countless trifles. Swift suggested to Gay a Newgate pastoral, and the result was the *Beggar's Opera.* The scattered chapters of Scriblerus writings; the *Directions to Servants*; the manuals of *Genteel Conversation*; the seven years' war with Partridge, the astrologer (which captured the attention of London and gave birth to the *Tatler*); the Manual for Maids of Honour, projected but never written by Swift and Arbuthnot, illustrate the volume of materials for comedy scattered by Swift. Unfortunately, a formidable array of critics has insisted upon Swift's gloom. They have told the truth, but not all nor even the major part. In the final Ordeal by Time, the light often floats while the heavy sinks out of sight. Swift's own epitaph attests the end of his indignation, his Tory controversies, his ecclesiastical disappointments. But when did wit die at his hand? The obscure victims of his satire may be forgotten, but the execution remains to enliven the pages of history. The contents of the present volume alone demonstrate Swift's dexterity in dealing, with one and the same blow, death to dunces and life to la Bagatelle.

By common consent of all who knew him, Swift was an extraordinary man. In extraordinary persons we find more that is mysterious and inexplicable, just as we also find more that is comprehensible and worth noting. There was much that Swift did not understand about himself. Are the visions that come to men of genius the product of inspiration or of indigestion? Is intellectual curiosity a disease of the flesh? May it not be true that 'this is the sublime and refined point of felicity . . . the possession of being well-deceived; the serene peaceful state of being a fool among knaves'? Where Swift failed to explain himself, we may be excused from succeeding. If we do not fit into familiar patterns of conduct his relations with women, his devotion to Christianity coupled perversely with his contempt for mankind, his unique talent for combining on the same page the fury of a moralist and the farce of a harlequin, we must at least avoid the snare of over-simplification into which some commentators have fallen. The definitive biography of Swift has not yet been written.[1] The materials for it

[1] The *Life of Swift* by Leslie Stephen, 1882, remains the most satisfactory biography. For a more complete and fully documented discussion the reader must turn to the two volumes by Henry Craik, 1882. Carl Van Doren's *Swift*, 1930, is a brilliant sketch in the modern manner, presenting Swift (somewhat overcharged with fury and insolence) as a restless tiger

are, to a considerable extent, contained in these two volumes of Selections from Swift which every reader is at liberty to open for himself without prejudice from previous investigations. Few of Swift's contemporaries knew him intimately, while the critics of intervening generations knew nothing that we may not discover for ourselves. Stella and Arbuthnot might have helped us much, for of them alone can it be said that they knew Swift, loved him, and were loved by him. But Stella and Arbuthnot told us nothing. With them lies buried the key, if there be one, to the heart of Swift. But the 'mysteries' are, after all, only a part of what was in the main a most rational life. The opinions that matter and the surmises he was willing to share, Swift put into his writings. That testimony proves the author to have been uncommonly sane—often, in fact, too brutally sane for the reader's comfort. Moreover, much that to us may appear inexplicable is only the normal temper of the early eighteenth century.

The opinions held by Swift, though expressed with uncommon vigour, reflect from the very age and body of the time his form and pressure.[1] A thinker is not advanced beyond his contemporaries by virtue of using an idiom unintelligible to his generation. Milton, whom the schoolboy of to-day may feel inclined to disparage as a man who believed in a personal devil, was actually a theological rebel who could find no pew in any orthodox

captured and caged for the convenience of readers who cannot afford the time to hunt Swift down in his own writings. The best critical work on Swift's life is being done in France by Emile Pons, whose valuable *La Jeunesse de Swift et le Conte du Tonneau*, 1925, is to be followed by two more volumes.

[1] For an introduction to the culture in which Swift lived, the reader is referred to A. S. Turberville, *English Men and Manners in the Eighteenth Century*, Oxford, 1926; and to Leslie Stephen, *English Literature and Society in the Eighteenth Century*, Putnam, 1904.

church. Swift was a Tory. It comes to some as a surprise that the biting satirist, the scourge of society, should have been in so many ways, by twentieth-century standards, a reactionary, an advocate of the established order in Church and State, a friend of hereditary and vested privilege. Swift, however, lived before the hue and cry after Democracy. In his time it was believed (and it was doubtless true) that society could be served best by the *reasonable* administration of power concentrated in the hands of qualified leaders. As a convinced Tory, Swift opposed popular radicalism in politics, philosophy, and religion; when he satirized existing governments, which was often, he attacked not the theory but the abuse of authority. When he castigated bishops and prime ministers it was because they were unintelligent or corrupt. If the Irish felt that their beloved Drapier Dean would like to have brought them popular Home Rule, they were sadly deceived. Swift championed them against unscrupulous exploitation, but he feared the tyranny of anarchy even more than the divine right of kings. With practical realism he looked about him on a world which at best was pretty bad, and he supported the lesser of evils. That his allegiance was never blind his satires prove conclusively. On the whole, he observed, reason is more often the property of the educated few than of the illiterate many. Time alone will determine whether the Tory or the democrat is right, and this time has not yet done. Swift's position is, at any rate, clear: even the civilization of England in 1700 is an advance over the state of nature, because in it man has been subjected to the discipline of ideas. Gulliver is admittedly more intelligent, more useful, and more companionable than the unredeemed Yahoos, though they be of one blood.

More difficult for our generation to accept is Swift's

open contempt for 'Free-thinkers'; but here, as elsewhere, he was ahead of, not behind, his times, and may prove to be the prophet of the twenty-first century. Freedom of thought has been exalted by romanticists until it has ceased to be a subject of dispute and has become an obsession. Without doubt we are free to govern our own thoughts. We are free to expound the Trinity though we do not have a grammar-school education; we may revise the ratio between the diameter and the circumference of the circle to eliminate inconvenient decimals. If it is not to-day good form to assert that the earth is flat, we may yet read in the press of living defenders of that personal privilege of a man born free and equal to the best of scholars! To all of this specious nonsense the exigencies of modern civilization are rapidly putting an end, for Science is a law-giver more intolerant of heresy than the Inquisition. Science is telling us that there is no freedom to think wrong thoughts. The engineer is bound to think of a red light as red, in spite of his preference for green. The surgeon who does not wish to starve is compelled to curb his freedom to think while he is on duty and to accept that anatomy of the human organs which the bodies of his patients invariably present. Freedom of thought, we are discovering, can be purchased too dearly. Swift saw that this was as true of scholarship and of religion as we now know it to be of the physical sciences. Should not one be free to interpret Scripture for himself, even though he be an unlettered cobbler? No, thought Swift, not if it leads the cobbler to set up as a prophetic quack who poisons the minds and bodies of his clients; not if it leads bigots into crusades against cakes and ale, to the torture of 'witches', and to the murder of any neighbour they choose to label a Jebusite. Furthermore, it should be recalled that the self-styled 'Free-thinkers' whom Swift scorned had nothing in common with a Shelley or a Tom Paine. Many of them were irresponsible lechers and notorious though well-born morons to whom free-thinking did not mean freedom to think, but freedom not-to-think —a privilege which might be conceded with impunity to Robinson Crusoe living in splendid isolation, not to men vested with authority over their fellows. To cover naked libertinism with the cloak of Liberty did not appeal to Swift as useful philanthropy. If the Earl of Wharton was a free-thinker, then Swift was content to be a reactionary.

Satire is often the weapon of rebels against authority. As Goldsmith wrote of Dr. Johnson, that here for once mankind would find the exceptional combination of wit *and* piety, so in Swift's writings we seem to have wit, more caustic than Chesterton's, employed to defend orthodoxy. But this is only a half-truth. The fact is that Swift was a rebel of uncommon courage, even for satirists. Instead of rebelling against out-moded traditions (the pastime of pseudo-satirists) he rebelled against the latest idiocies of his own fashionable society. We have to-day adolescent journalistic satirists who solicit our applause for their novels or their parlour-dramas in which they valiantly club to death Victorian conventions and medieval superstitions already moribund. This is not rebellion, but lynching; the odds are a thousand to one; the victory is foreknown and approved by the mob. Children have always ridiculed the fashions of their grandparents; teachers are perennially ready to sneer at undergraduate opinion; students find it easy to be sarcastic about their woolly-headed professors. The quaint customs that prevail in the other camp look absurd when viewed from our side. But the rebel worthy of the name is the one who can turn on his own pack, see the follies of his confederates, the hypocrisies of his own profession, and the superstitions peculiar to his own generation. Swift's satire was up to date. He found himself surrounded by men who considered themselves emancipated: deists, Whigs, and dissenters, who in mad game had burst the manacles of superstitions already rusted through with age; and he informed them coldly that they wore the name of 'Freedom' graven on a heavier chain.

If Swift has been admired and feared more than he has been loved, it is partly because he does not write the language of the heart. Unromantic he was by temperament, but it should be recalled that his age distrusted sentiment and disdained romance. Queen Anne was not Gloriana; nor was Esther Johnson Juliet Capulet. If Swift did not offer sighs and blandishments to ladies, it is not necessary to conclude that he was diseased. Sighs and blandishments were not expected from him nor from his fellow writers. Romeo was not encouraged either in real life or in fiction. It was a masculine society: at its crudest, of four-bottle men who aspired to drink like lords and roar like Mohocks; at its best, of polished gatherings in coffee-houses and salons to discuss literature and politics. Ladies secured public attention, if at all, by adopting the tone of men in their conversation, their letters, and their more ambitious attempts at literature. Susanna Centlivre and Aphra Behn wrote plays no more delicate than the plays of Congreve, and less sentimental than the plays of Steele. Mary Wortley Montagu successfully, Eliza Haywood and Mary Manley unsuccessfully, competed with the Wits for an audience, and adopted the masculine style: urbane, impersonal, cosmopolitan, and well-informed. Stella we know only through Swift and through tributes to her personality recorded by others.

As her tutor in the household of Sir William Temple, Swift taught her to read and write, helped to form her literary tastes, and watched her develop into refined, poiseful womanhood. Whether or not Stella died of a broken heart, starved for romantic affection, we do not know; but we must not be too immoderate in our pity. She enjoyed much that women of her time sought eagerly: the friendship of the leading men of letters; a wide acquaintance among the cultured who year after year frequented her parlour; the gratitude of many unfortunates to whom she was a gracious and open-handed patroness. If she remained in the shadow of a great man, she was one of many women who chose that part. She was Swift's lifelong companion and his closest friend, intensely interested in his career, able to converse with him and to criticize his ideas. He was devoted to her charming person, her uncommon gentility and refinement, her sound opinions and lively conversation, her unfailing generosity and kindliness. That a tragedy lurked beneath this restrained interchange of affection all who read between the lines of the story know well; but Stella died without asking for the world's sympathy. In the absence of information and of any invitation to interfere, common courtesy suggests that we leave the secret of their unfulfilled love where Stella kept it, locked in her heart.

Too much has perhaps been made of the *Journal to Stella* as an intimate revelation of Swift's feelings. To be sure he wrote it nightly, when he was alone in bed, to the friend he trusted above all others. It is indeed confidential, intimate, informal; and it shows us Swift off-stage. But the *Journal* tells us little of his feelings towards Stella that we do not know from other writings. Its chief value lies in the detailed picture of Swift's thoughts and occupations throughout a course of dramatic months: how he handled ministers of state and his servant, Patrick; what he ate and drank, and how he passed his evenings; the secret lobbies he attended; the tracts he wrote and printed anonymously. But as a series of love-letters the *Journal* is not a masterpiece.

Swift's correspondence with his various friends proves that in his social life he was not so abnormal as sometimes has been alleged. Like many strong-minded men, his intimate friends were few; but these few were his for life. Many of his letters are excellent models of the easy familiar style. Some throw light on his literary practice and his moral philosophy. Others are full of glimpses into the petty economy of his domestic life, especially after his exile to Ireland: the weekly round of restful pleasures and inconsequential irritations. But though written to intimate friends in a personal, non-ironic style, we do not find the whimper and sob of a lonely heart any more than we find them in the *Journal*, or in *Gulliver*. Men at that time did not dip their pens in tears—least of all did Jonathan Swift. His reserve was not so much pathological as it was logical, normal, and expected.

The contemporaries of Pope did not cultivate romantic poetry any more than romantic conventions of love; and the reader who turns to Swift's poems to uncover his sentimental side will be disappointed. Swift could not write even the 'poetry of reason' well enough to suit Dryden or Pope. In fact, the shortest way out of a discussion of his poems (though not altogether fair to him) is to avoid the word 'poetry' altogether and refer to Swift's 'verse'. After a few youthful and unhappy attempts at classical odes, after being told by Dryden and shown by Addison that he was no poet, Swift abandoned the Muse. Verses he continued to write, as many do who know they are not great poets: some excellent satires he contributed to periodicals; some compliments to Stella he put into rhyme no worse than similar verses we ourselves may have pinned to birthday presents. Observations on satire, reflections on friendship, and meditations on death he cast into doggerel that is at once terrifying and comic. Of grace and melody there is little. In reading his verses we are assisting at a pastime with which he amused himself and a few friends as he whiled away a vacant hour.

Other poems, unfortunately, were penned under the spell of that revulsion against chivalry which haunted his mind and curdled his regard for love and marriage. Never lascivious, his poems sometimes attain a scatalogical ugliness that is nauseating to the most hardened cynic. The explanation that his realistic mind penetrated beneath the veils of convention is no justification for the distorted and ghoulish focus of attention upon the pathology of physical love. Where the sentimentalist views love through rose-tinted glasses, Swift substitutes equally deceiving spectacles bespattered with mud. In those terrible hours when he verged on the madness which eventually overthrew him, Swift looked upon the bridal chamber as on a whited sepulchre, infested by worms and reeking with putrefaction.

Swift worshipped at the altar of invisible Justice and Charity discerned by his intellect—an altar which, his eyes told him, was obscured from the common view by animal appetites. Man, he declared, though *rationis capax*, is not yet *animal rationale.* Distrusting emotion as irrational, he missed the beauty that lights up the way of a man with a maid. Bitter thoughts contradicted the pulse of his heart, and informed him that the curl he kept in a locket was 'only a woman's hair'—the radiant

Stella, only a bit of chemistry. All that remains of Yorick is a hideous skull! Why may not imagination trace the noble dust of Alexander, till he find it stopping a bung-hole? Your gambols, your songs, your flashes of merriment, your glory and virtue; above all, your dreams of love—may they not be a tale told by an idiot whose quintessence is dust? 'Lovers . . . seem a perfect moral to the story of that philosopher who, while his thoughts and eyes were fixed upon the constellations, found himself seduced by his lower parts into a ditch.' A behaviourist two hundred years before the word was coined, Swift described human sentiment in terms which may be accurate but which are too hard for the normal man to bear. These deeds must not be thought after these ways, so it will make us mad. Shakespeare, wiser than Swift and less inclined to self-slaughter than Hamlet, knew that if romance did not exist we would have to invent it.

II. *The Satirist*

The satirist, who has always been among us with his lantern looking for an honest man, has been eyed with suspicion and disfavour by society. Mrs. Grundy and her numerous brood of patriots, pedagogues, and parents, feel concern when the Younger Generation reads Voltaire, Anatole France, or Aldous Huxley, and pray to whatever gods may be for a conversion to health and normality. Irony, it is held, is a negative attitude, irreverent to ideals, discouraging to good works, harsh and unsympathetic to the amenities of life. Satirists are a bilious breed who void their rheum boorishly over expensive rugs and evening dresses. They retail venom and delight in diseases of the body politic. In any case, it is alleged, their product is second-rate in quality. Crude and violent, satire does not dwell with beauty; it mars rhyme and sours fiction in the same way that caricature distorts the features of a portrait. At best it is candid and corrective; but the moral it teaches is cynical and pessimistic, the laugh it raises is bitter and unkind.

Under effective disguise, to be sure, the satirist sometimes has succeeded in slipping past the butler. Cloaked as comedians, Pudd'nhead Wilson, Don Quixote, and Lemuel Gulliver are admitted even to the nursery. Wearing the mantle of Elijah, Dickens and Thackeray are permitted to mount the pulpit to berate folly and vice in decorous language. Addison may wag his finger and shake his head as much as he pleases because he is polite. If he does step on people's toes they are the toes of other people who live farther down the street. But these are only exceptions to the opinion that satirists as a clan are enemies to health and should be discouraged.

While these charges can be readily confirmed by chapter and verse, they can be refuted in the same way. If Juvenal, Marston, and Samuel Butler of *Erewhon* were dyspeptic citizens, Chaucer, Rabelais, Fielding, and Jane Austen were regular contributors to the gaiety of nations. If it is true that the bulk of satiric writings has been second-rate in form and substance and has lost its appeal with the passing of the political or personal issues that prompted its composition, the same can be said of the bulk of writings in philosophy, theology, and biography. The rudeness of form which for many centuries characterized satire was a reflex of the low esteem in which it was held by polite writers—just as the village atheist of the Puritan hamlet neglected to shave because nobody ever invited him to dinner. From Ennius to Dryden it was widely held that satire is a literary outcast and should wear rags. Spenser, the courtly poet of the *Faerie*

Queene, whose exquisite stanzas to Gloriana were rapt with the rapture of his ravished thought, deliberately debased his style to write *Mother Hubberd's Tale*, because as a satire,

> No Muse's aide me needes heretoo to call;
> Base is the style, and matter mean withall.

Hounded by orthodox critics and deserted by the Muses, satirists long accepted the seat in the kitchen to which they were assigned. In spite of the precedent set by the elegant Horace, they were content to remain unwashed. The highest flights of poetry they did not attempt, but rather, like the author of *Don Juan*, mocked heroics with travesty and laughed at their own bad rhymes.

In the field of poetry, satire was temporarily redeemed and made respectable largely through the prestige of the poet-laureate, Dryden, and his immediate followers. In prose, satire became the peer of other forms of composition in the time of Swift, and largely because of his achievements. The unmeasured, grotesque style of Lucian and Rabelais gave place to sustained irony—sentences with iron in them, clothing logic that was unanswerable, subtlety that left the reader uncertain of his feet and that seduced him into opinions he had recently denounced. Was the *Tale of a Tub* homily or blasphemy? The Queen had her doubts. Was Gulliver a dangerous giant among philosophers, or only a clown among the puppets of Lilliput? Readers could not be sure. If one laughed, might he not prove to be laughing at the wrong time? If one denounced, might he not prove to be traitor to his beloved Whigs? Swift sat in Rabelais' easy chair, toying with the whip of Juvenal.

Reduced to its simplest terms, irony is commonly known as that figure of speech in which words are used to convey the opposite of their literal meaning. A father addresses his small son affectionately as 'you little rogue', or a student leaving a class observes sardonically to his fellow 'fine lecture'. But sarcasm is the easy acquisition of any schoolboy, and can be maintained by any one without great effort throughout a phrase or even a short clause. It does not help us much in understanding the technique of Swift's irony, which courses like a cataract through the paragraphs of *A Modest Proposal* and *A Meditation upon a Broom-stick*, or flows smoothly and without interruption all the way from Lilliput to Houyhnhnmland.

It has been noted, *ad nauseam*, that Swift wrapped his feelings in a lion's hide, that brutal words and gestures were used by him to flay our race for its brutality and heartlessness. Now it is precisely this trait of character which Swift transferred to paper, and which is the key to his ironic style. Once, Swift discharged a servant brutally. Why? Because the servant had been cruel to a beggar-woman at the door of Swift's home. Another time, Swift wrested a whip from a carter and lashed him unmercifully with it. Why? Because he had caught the carter mercilessly flogging his exhausted horse until it bled—with that same whip. Swift's strategy was to lash his victims with their own whip, to innoculate them with their own poison, to deride them with their own sophistries. To their confusion, their favourite weapons were turned against them. Ironically, as though he accepts it for himself, Swift proceeds to state his opponent's case instead of his own. Like Socrates, he pretends to be convinced by the other man's premisses, and carries them out to the logical conclusions, when the absurdity of the original position suddenly appears. Other writers may plead, cajole, or weep over the wrongs of mankind; they may stop to bind up the wounds of him who fell among thieves. Swift pursues the thieves, wounds their vanity, robs them of their defence, and leaves them by the side of the road less enthusiastic over their profession.

The use of this strategy, no matter how effective it prove against oppression, is not applauded by sentimentalists, who assume that unfortunates prefer kind words and bedside sympathy to the paring of the claws that wound. Critics have not been wanting to denounce Swift for lacking compassion; but these critics have been, for the most part, persons in comfortable circumstances who could afford the luxury of preferring smiles to guineas. A better method is to consult the opinions of the oppressed Yahoos of Ireland whom Swift insulted in word and befriended in deed. His charity was unbounded. From 1720 to 1740 he was the idol of the Dublin poor. They advocated erecting a statue of Swift in place of the statue of Marlborough, the 'murderer'. Often Swift gave as much as five pounds to a needy beggar. He conversed with bootblacks in their own lingo. He contributed to the support of old people, poor poets, and young clergymen; and he kept a personal fund of five hundred pounds for loans without interest, with which he started two hundred families in independent livelihoods. He left his fortune to endow a hospital. Crowds cheered him when he rode into Dublin—crowds which he hated as cordially as he loved individuals. We have people enough in all communities who love mankind and hate their individual neighbours to satisfy our sentimentalists and internationalists. We do not lack men and women who, disliking their acquaintances, yet profess a deep concern for the Chinese, the Russians, or the proletariat. In Swift's defence, Pope justly wrote, 'Who can care for 10,000, who never cared for one?'

Throughout the pages of these satires, the reader will find Swift adopting the mentality and the policies of his opponents with devastating effect. These opponents are seldom individuals. Swift 'lash'd the vice but spar'd the name'. Now he is a Free-thinker, arguing that Christianity should be retained, because, forsooth, it lends spice to forbidden sweets of self-indulgence, keeps up the bank-rate, and increases our credit with other nations—sufficient reasons for worshipping the Galilean since these are obviously the objects for which he died on Calvary! Now he is an English patriot in Ireland, respectfully suggesting to Walpole more efficient means for increasing the revenue of the Crown from Ireland. True, these suggestions involve wholesale murder, but, as things now are, Irish babies either die anyway or become a public charge. The proposal, unhappily, does not solve the problem of adult paupers, but these are already dying 'by cold, and famine, and filth, and vermin as fast as can be *reasonably* expected!' So Swift lashes not Walpole the man, but Walpole the incarnation of shortsightedness and greed, which bled Ireland by decree and consumed Irish flesh by taxes to furnish sweetmeats for the tables of absentee landlords.

Unimpressed himself by fanatics who raise their voices, and conscious that his cultivated readers shared his dislike for shouting, Swift wrote at white heat, as though he were a clerk yawning over his weekly accounts. As if rehearsing platitudes, he expounds opinions which, the style implies, are too obvious to raise any question or to cause any surprise. Disgusted with shilling diplomacy, he casually reduces religion and statecraft to a matter of pence. Impatient with Robert Boyle's fatuous four-minute essays, he soberly composes *A Meditation upon a Broom-stick* in the same manner. From the astrologer who grew rich by predicting the death of great men, Swift borrows an illiterate style to predict in the same language the death of the great astrologer himself. The abuse which he attacks, he appears to defend, if indeed it can be said to need defence. Seeming not to sneer himself, he teaches the reader to sneer. His irony moves swiftly, held to its course by the severest logic. It flows around its victim without a wave of hostile emotion or any sign of storm—a river whose surface is smooth and reassuring, as it mirrors the reader's own thoughts and gives back an echo of his own voice in accents familiar, yet strangely disconcerting. Like the ladies in the *Arabian Nights* whose chastity was tested by the magic mirror from which they shrank, Swift's contemporaries learned to shudder at the reflection of themselves which they found in his prose.

The effectiveness of Swift's satire is derived, in the last analysis, from his mastery of the technique of this grim irony, unrolled in pages of closely knit prose without padding or waste of words—pages on which words are welded and sentences are woven into paragraphs that have been the admiration and despair of imitators. Swift and Rabelais, kindred spirits and both master-satirists, are at opposite poles in style. Rabelais broadcasts his words and his exuberant fancies as a thresher disperses chaff, to pile up where they fall. Swift's wit, no less nimble, is ordered and compressed under the influence of a classically trained intellect. The result is a pertinence of style and a fabric of thought seldom equalled by his contemporaries, either in coherence or in the quantity of ideas per square inch. To discover the virtues of English prose, a young writer may still, following the advice of Dr. Johnson, give his days and nights to the study of the volumes of Addison;

but he will do better to substitute the paragraphs of Swift.

The satires are diversified by resort to a hundred and one devices which can be properly studied only in their context. Two features of Swift's satire may be noted here, in passing. The use of fiction as sugar-coating for a pill of bitter philosophy is one of his greatest distinctions. Perhaps it is a human love of narratives, as ancient as the Stone Age and as universal as the nursery; perhaps it is an instinct for drama, a preference for ideas that are embodied in flesh and blood, that makes us prefer the stage to the pulpit or the forum. Swift was skilful in the use of fable and of dramatic technique. In his hands our race dwindles to inches and our Nardacs strut and rant in vain. The respectable practice of killing off a subject people by attrition is translated melodramatically into a visible and succulent cannibal feast. Religious creeds are identified with a coat which a father bequeathes to his three sons, in whose disputes the reader recognizes church history. Fanatic and illiterate preachers, in real life insufferable bores, are tricked out as eccentric members of the ancient and honourable order of expert belchers. Lemuel Gulliver, Isaac Bickerstaff, Simon Wagstaff, M. B. Drapier, and Martin Scriblerus, are among the actors created by Swift by a stroke of his pen, to speak for him to his countrymen, each in his own character. At other times, he employs the equally mystifying disguise of anonymity. These roles are more than the recreations of a witty ventriloquist;[1] they are of the very essence of the dramatic art and of the parable

[1] I merely mention the spectacular appeal of the narrative element in Swift's satire. The philosophical implications of his more important fables, and the skill with which he uses allegory, are ably discussed by H. M. Dargan, 'The Nature of Allegory as used by Swift' (*Studies in Philology*, 1916, xiii, pp. 159–79).

—the happy incarnation of thought. The fable has ever been close to the heart of satire.

Secondly, to this use of fiction must be added Swift's wit and humour—also an ingredient indispensable to good satire everywhere, since the purpose of satire is to ridicule what the writer would demolish. *Ridiculum acri fortius et melius magnas plerumque secat res*,[1] was one of Swift's favourite texts, as it was the text around which Pope wrote the *Rape of the Lock*:

> And trust me, dear, good humour can prevail,
> When airs, and flights, and screams, and scolding fail.

Swift's humour runs the gamut of our rhetorics on the subject: farce at Brobdingnag; grotesque exaggeration in *Directions to Servants*; parody in *Scriblerus*; overstatement and comic juxtaposition of ideas in *Genteel Conversation*; understatement and anti-climax in a score of essays. The reading world was, and still is, diverted; but Swift's deeper purpose is ever one and always the same: to pour contempt on the intellectual dishonesty of foolish and perverse men. His wit is an intellectual weapon aimed at intellects that are deficient or malicious. *An Argument Against Abolishing Christianity* does not ridicule unbelievers. Many of Swift's respected friends, including Bolingbroke, were unbelievers. Swift ridicules the *mentality* of those agnostics who defended their position by insincere sophistry. In the *Modest Proposal* he is not only denouncing cruelty; he is ridiculing the specious and pious euphemisms by which cruel men screen their cruelty from their own eyes. The effect of his satire is to make his victims appear not knaves but fools—a much more serious predicament. One may be a knave with impunity in this world, where clever

[1] Horace, *Sermonum* lib. I. x. 14–15.

racketeers and captains of industry amass wealth and notoriety without damage to their reputation as supermen. All this Swift knew perfectly well, and accordingly he aimed always at man's vanity. Walpole and Wharton, untroubled by the knowledge that they were devils, could not bear the suggestion, which Swift converted into proof, that they were dunces.

It was Swift's fate to walk alone, even when he was in a crowd. Esther Vanhomrigh, a lady who sought in vain to win his affection, wrote what many of his acquaintances must have felt: 'Could I know your thoughts, which no human creature is capable of guessing at, because never any one living thought like you. . . . Sometimes you strike me with that prodigious awe, I tremble with fear; at other times a charming compassion shines through your countenance, which revives my soul.'[1] Swift's mind furnished him with a hunger which meat and drink could not satisfy, and sent him away from afternoon teas out of love with superficial prattle. Conscious of Reason, he looked upon the multitude and was moved to wrath because they were unreasonable. In love with Justice, he attacked the injustices rampant about him. A knight in the train of Truth, he found England to be Errour's den. A churchman who preached and practised charity, he was surrounded by Yahoos who tore their weaker fellows limb from limb out of lust for the yellow metal. We who are, perhaps, conscious of the same discrepancy between the ideals which the mind of man has discovered and the diseases which are his biological heritage are content to shrug our shoulders and to regard the ideals as academic unrealities in an acquisitive society. Swift did not, could not adjust himself to his environment. Unlike his lifelong friend, Congreve,

[1] Letter to Swift, 1720. *Correspondence* (ed. F. E. Ball), iii. 446.

who saw the facts just as clearly, he did not settle down in the lap of a doting duchess to eat chocolates at her expense. As Swift lay dying in Dublin, his illustrious contemporary and admirer, Lord Chesterfield, came to occupy the Residency as Lord-Lieutenant of Ireland. The greater man lay ruined, a wreck all that was left of his career, his health, and his intellect. Yes, but life is like that, Chesterfield would have observed, the prize goes to the diplomat, not to the genius. And lest his godson choose wrong, he later advised the boy, 'Learn to shrink yourself to the size of the company you are in. Take their tone, whatever it may be.' Chesterfield's advice, though cynical, is the gospel truth for him who seeks to prosper. Only when man contracts his ideas and his ideals to the scale of his tribe will he find gratification in the world's applause and satisfaction with his own stature. In the meantime, there will always be a few, like Swift, who cannot shrink,—whose misfortune or whose preference it is to remain giants in Lilliput. It is a vocation that calls for courage and leads to isolation, bitterness, and certain defeat. This Swift knew from experience as he wrote his own epitaph, calling for another to take up, if he dared, the hopeless task of liberating men from the darkness that dwells within.

Abi viator, et imitare, si poteris, strenuum pro virili libertatis vindicem.

1932 W.A.E.

AN ARGUMENT AGAINST ABOLISHING CHRISTIANITY

This masterpiece of prose irony is at points so intricate and double-edged that the superficial reader finds himself uncertain of Swift's real point of view towards Christianity. Is he attacking Christians or unbelievers? The problem is not quite as simple as that. He is attacking unscrupulous agnostics who used Christianity as a social convenience, who favoured the Establishment of the Church with the Gospel left out. To ridicule the absurdity of calling this state of affairs religion, Swift pretends to be himself one of these political Christians, and proceeds to adduce advantages which will result from preserving the name of Christianity without the reality. To restore the latter, he admits, 'would be to dig up foundations; to destroy at one blow all the wit, and half the learning of the kingdom; to break the entire frame and constitution of things; to ruin trade, extinguish arts and sciences, with the professors of them; in short, to turn our courts, exchanges, and shops into deserts'. To prevent such a disaster it is not necessary nor expedient (he pretends) to be an avowed infidel. Nominal Christianity, which omits primitive Christianity's inconvenient claims on the individual, should be kept on the nation's books, to bolster British credit abroad, to add spice to vice, and to furnish a butt for the wit of syphilitic wits! As on so many other pages, Swift would seem to have written this essay for our generation as much as for his own. It suffices that trust in God is stamped on our coins, and that temperance is written into the [American] Constitution.

The *Argument* was written during Swift's visit to London in 1708, when he was still in league with the Whigs, but it foreshadows his desertion of that party two years later too clearly to leave any doubt that his defection to the Tories was a matter of conviction. In fact, Swift always placed his religion before political parties. Among the Whigs he was finding the most obscene examples of the blasphemous hypocrisy he pillories in this tract. Lord Wharton, who polluted Church altars with excrement, was the type of 'free-thinker', too intelligent to be a Christian in private, with whom Swift found himself in political alliance. This character Swift has painted for us in strong colours, in a separate tract as well as in his contributions to the *Examiner*. There was no middle ground on which Swift could honourably stand: either he must betray the Church and violate his own conscience, or else he must part company with the goatish, scrofulous politicians who praised Christianity from the platform and spat upon it in private. Christianity has frequently erred, but neither then nor since has it followed the Whig leaders of 1708 into the sewer.

The text reproduced is that of Swift's *Miscellanies*, 1711, collated with the more carefully printed text of the *Miscellanies*, vol. i, 1728. The essay was originally published in separate form in 1710, but I have not been able to discover a copy.

I AM very sensible what a Weakness and Presumption it is, to reason against the general Humour and Disposition of the World. I remember it was with great Justice, and a due Regard to the Freedom both of the Publick and the Press, forbidden upon several Penalties to write, or discourse, or lay wagers against the [Union] even before it was confirmed by Parliament; because that was look'd upon as a Design to oppose the Current of the People, which besides the Folly of it, is a manifest Breach of the fundamental Law, that makes this Majority of Opinions the Voice of God. In like manner, and for the very same reasons, it may perhaps be neither safe nor prudent to argue against the abolishing of Christianity, at a Juncture when all Parties seem so unanimously determined upon the Point, as we cannot but allow from their Actions, their Discourses, and their Writings. However, I know not how, whether from the Affectation of Singularity, or the Perverseness of human Nature, but so it unhappily falls out, that I cannot be entirely of this Opinion. Nay, though I were sure an Order were issued out for my immediate Prosecution by the Attorney-General, I should still confess, that in the present Posture of our Affairs at home or abroad, I do not yet see the absolute Necessity of extirpating the Christian Religion from among us.

This perhaps may appear too great a Paradox even for our wise and paradoxical Age to endure; therefore I shall handle it with all Tenderness, and with the utmost Deference to that great and profound Majority which is of another Sentiment.

And yet the Curious may please to observe, how much the Genius of a Nation is liable to alter in half an Age: I have heard it affirmed for certain by some very old

People,

People, that the contrary Opinion was even in their Memories as much in vogue as the other is now; and that a Project for the abolishing of Christianity would then have appeared as singular, and been thought as absurd, as it would be at this Time to write or discourse in its Defence.

Therefore I freely own, that all Appearances are against me. The System of the Gospel, after the Fate of other Systems, is generally antiquated and exploded; and the Mass or Body of the common People, among whom it seems to have had its latest Credit, are now grown as much ashamed of it as their Betters; Opinions, like Fashions, always, descending from those of Quality to the middle Sort, and thence to the Vulgar, where at length they are dropp'd and vanish.

But here I would not be mistaken, and must therefore be so bold as to borrow a Distinction from the Writers on the other Side, when they make a Difference betwixt nominal and real Trinitarians. I hope no Reader imagines me so weak to stand up in the Defence of real Christianity, such as used in primitive Times (if we may believe the Authors of those Ages) to have an Influence upon Men's Belief and Actions: To offer at the restoring of that, would indeed be a wild Project, it would be to dig up Foundations; to destroy at one Blow all the Wit, and half the Learning of the Kingdom; to break the entire Frame and Constitution of Things; to ruin Trade, extinguish Arts and Sciences, with the Professors of them; in short, to turn our Courts, Exchanges, and Shops into Desarts; and would be full as absurd as the Proposal of Horace, where he advises the Romans, all in a Body, to leave their City and seek a new Seat in some remote Part of the World, by way of a Cure for the Corruption of their Manners.

Therefore

Therefore I think this Caution was in itself altogether unnecessary, (which I have inserted only to prevent all possibility of Cavilling) since every candid Reader will easily understand my Discourse to be intended only in Defence of nominal Christianity, the other having been for some time wholly laid aside by general Consent, as utterly inconsistent with all our present Schemes of Wealth and Power.

But why we should therefore cast off the Name and Title of Christians, although the general Opinion and Resolution be so violent for it, I confess I cannot (with Submission) apprehend the Consequence necessary. However, since the Undertakers propose such wonderful Advantages to the Nation by this Project, and advance many plausible Objections against the System of Christianity, I shall briefly consider the Strength of both, fairly allow them their greatest Weight, and offer such Answers as I think most reasonable. After which I will beg leave to shew what Inconveniences may possibly happen by such an Innovation, in the present Posture of our Affairs.

First, One great Advantage proposed by the abolishing of Christianity is, That it would very much enlarge and establish Liberty of Conscience, that great Bulwark of our Nation, and of the Protestant Religion, which is still too much limited by Priest-craft, notwithstanding all the good Intentions of the Legislature, as we have lately found by a severe Instance. For it is confidently reported, that two young Gentlemen of real Hopes, bright Wit, and profound Judgment, who, upon a thorough Examination of Causes and Effects, and by the mere Force of natural Abilities, without the least Tincture of Learning, having made a Discovery, that there was no God, and generously communicating their Thoughts for

the

the Good of the Publick, were some Time ago, by an unparallell'd Severity, and upon I know not what obsolete Law, broke for Blasphemy. And as it hath been wisely observed, if Persecution once begins, no Man alive knows how far it may reach, or where it will end.

In answer to all which, with Deference to wiser Judgments, I think this rather shews the Necessity of a nominal Religion among us. Great Wits love to be free with the highest Objects; and if they cannot be allowed a God to revile or renounce, they will speak evil of Dignities, abuse the Government, and reflect upon the Ministry, which I am sure few will deny to be of much more pernicious Consequence, according to the saying of Tiberius, *Deorum Offensa Diis curae.* As to the particular Fact related, I think it is not fair to argue from one Instance, perhaps another cannot be produced: yet (to the Comfort of all those who may be apprehensive of Persecution) Blasphemy we know is freely spoke a Million of Times in every Coffee-house and Tavern, or wherever else good Company meet. It must be allowed indeed, that to break an English Free-born Officer only for Blasphemy, was, to speak the gentlest of such an Action, a very high Strain of absolute Power. Little can be said in excuse for the General; perhaps he was afraid it might give Offence to the Allies, among whom, for ought we know, it may be the Custom of the Country to believe a God. But if he argued, as some have done, upon a mistaken Principle, that an Officer who is guilty of speaking Blasphemy, may some time or other proceed so far as to raise a Mutiny, the Consequence is by no means to be admitted: For, surely the Commander of an English Army is like to be but ill obey'd, whose Soldiers fear and reverence him as little as they do a Deity.

It is further objected against the Gospel System, that it

it obliges men to the Belief of Things too difficult for Free-Thinkers, and such who have shook off the Prejudices that usually cling to a confin'd Education. To which I answer, that Men should be cautious how they raise Objections which reflect upon the Wisdom of the Nation. Is not every Body freely allowed to believe whatever he pleases, and to publish his Belief to the World whenever he thinks fit, especially if it serves to strengthen the Party which is in the Right? Would any indifferent Foreigner, who should read the Trumpery lately written by Asgill, Tindall, Toland, Coward, and forty more, imagine the Gospel to be our Rule of Faith, and to be confirmed by Parliaments? Does any Man either believe, or say he believes, or desire to have it thought that he says he believes one Syllable of the Matter? and is any Man worse received upon that Score, or does he find his Want of nominal Faith a Disadvantage to him in the Pursuit of any Civil or Military Employment? What if there be an old dormant Statute or two against him, are they not now obsolete, to a Degree, that Empson and Dudley themselves, if they were now alive, would find it impossible to put them in execution?

It is likewise urged, that there are, by computation, in this Kingdom, above ten thousand Parsons, whose Revenues, added to those of my Lords the Bishops, would suffice to maintain at least two hundred young Gentlemen of Wit and Pleasure, and Free-thinking Enemies to Priest-craft, narrow Principles, Pedantry, and Prejudices, who might be an Ornament to the Court and Town: And then again, so great a Number of able [bodied] Divines might be a Recruit to our Fleet and Armies. This indeed appears to be a Consideration of some Weight: But then, on the other Side, several Things deserve to be considered likewise: As, First, Whether it may not be thought necessary

necessary that in certain Tracts of Country, like what we call Parishes, there should be one Man at least, of Abilities to read and write. Then it seems a wrong Computation, that the Revenues of the Church throughout this Island would be large enough to maintain two hundred young Gentlemen, or even half that Number, after the present refined Way of Living, that is, to allow each of them such a Rent, as in the modern Form of Speech, would make them easy. But still there is in this Project a greater Mischief behind; and we ought to beware of the Woman's Folly, who killed the Hen that every Morning laid her a golden Egg. For, pray what would become of the Race of Men in the next Age, if we had nothing to trust to besides the scrophulous consumptive Production furnished by our Men of Wit and Pleasure, when having squandered away their Vigour, Health, and Estates, they are forced, by some disagreeable Marriage, to piece up their broken Fortunes, and entail Rottenness and Politeness on their Posterity? Now, here are ten thousand Persons reduced, by the wise Regulations of Henry the Eighth, to the Necessity of a low Diet, and moderate Exercise, who are the only great Restorers of our Breed, without which the Nation would in an Age or two become one great Hospital.

Another Advantage proposed by the abolishing of Christianity, is the clear Gain of one Day in seven, which is now entirely lost, and consequently the Kingdom one seventh less considerable in Trade, Business, and Pleasure; beside the Loss to the Publick of so many stately Structures now in the Hands of the Clergy, which might be converted into Play-houses, Exchanges, Market-houses, common Dormitories, and other publick Edifices.

I hope I shall be forgiven a hard Word if I call this a perfect Cavil. I readily own there hath been an old Custom,

Custom, Time out of mind, for People to assemble in the Churches every Sunday, and that Shops are still frequently shut, in order, as it is conceived, to preserve the Memory of that ancient Practice; but how this can prove a Hindrance to Business or Pleasure, is hard to imagine. What if the Men of Pleasure are forced, one Day in the Week, to game at Home instead of the Chocolate-House? Are not the Taverns and Coffee-Houses open? Can there be a more convenient Season for taking a Dose of Physick? Are fewer Claps got upon Sundays than other Days? Is not that the chief Day for Traders to sum up the Accounts of the Week, and for Lawyers to prepare their Briefs? But I would fain know how it can be pretended that the Churches are misapplied. Where are more Appointments and Rendezvouzes of Gallantry? Where more Care to appear in the foremost Box, with greater Advantage of Dress? Where more Meetings for Business? Where more Bargains driven of all Sorts? and where so many Conveniencies or Incitements to Sleep?

There is one Advantage greater than any of the foregoing, proposed by the Abolishing of Christianity, that it will utterly extinguish Parties among us, by removing those factious Distinctions of High and Low Church, of Whig and Tory, Presbyterian and Church of England, which are now so many mutual Clogs upon Publick proceedings, and are apt to prefer the gratifying themselves or depressing their Adversaries, before the most important Interest of the State.

I Confess, if it were certain that so great an Advantage would redound to the Nation by this Expedient, I would submit, and be silent: But, will any man say, that if the Words Whoring, Drinking, Cheating, Lying, Stealing, were by Act of Parliament ejected out of the English Tongue and Dictionaries, we should all awake next Morning

Morning chaste and temperate, honest and just, and Lovers of Truth. Is this a fair Consequence? Or if the Physicians would forbid us to pronounce the Words Pox, Gout, Rheumatism, and Stone, would that Expedient serve like so many Talismans to destroy the Diseases themselves? Are Party and Faction rooted in Men's Hearts no deeper than Phrases borrowed from Religion, or founded upon no firmer Principles? And is our Language so poor, that we cannot find other Terms to express them? Are Envy, Pride, Avarice and Ambition such ill Nomenclators, that they cannot furnish Appellations for their Owners? Will not Heydukes and Mamalukes, Mandarins, and Patshaws, or any other Words formed at pleasure, serve to distinguish those who are in the Ministry from others, who would be in it if they could? What, for instance, is easier than to vary the Form of Speech, and instead of the Word Church, make it a Question in Politicks, Whether the Monument be in Danger? Because Religion was nearest at hand to furnish a few convenient Phrases, is our Invention so barren, we can find no other? Suppose, for argument sake, that the Tories favoured Margarita, the Whigs Mrs. Tofts, and the Trimmers Valentini, would not Margaritians, Toftians and Valentinians be very tolerable Marks of Distinction? The Prasini and Veneti, two most virulent Factions in Italy, began (if I remember right) by a Distinction of Colours in Ribbons, which we might do with as good a Grace about the Dignity of the Blue and the Green, and serve as properly to divide the Court, the Parliament, and the Kingdom between them, as any Terms of Art whatsoever, borrowed from Religion. And therefore I think there is little Force in this Objection against Christianity, or Prospect of so great an Advantage as is proposed in the abolishing of it.

'Tis

'Tis again objected, as a very absurd ridiculous custom, that a Sett of Men should be suffered, much less employed and hired, to bawl one Day in Seven against the Lawfulness of those Methods most in Use towards the Pursuit of Greatness, Riches, and Pleasure, which are the constant Practice of all Men alive on the other six. But this Objection is, I think, a little unworthy so refined an Age as ours. Let us argue this Matter calmly; I appeal to the Breast of any polite Free-Thinker, whether, in the Pursuit of gratifying a predominant Passion, he hath not always felt a wonderful Incitement, by reflecting it was a Thing forbidden: And therefore we see, in order to cultivate this Test, the Wisdom of the Nation hath taken special Care, that the Ladies should be furnished with prohibited Silks, and the Men with prohibited Wine: And indeed it were to be wished, that some other Prohibitions were promoted, in order to improve the Pleasures of the Town; which, for Want of such Expedients, begin already, as I am told, to flag and grow languid, giving way daily to cruel Inroads from the Spleen.

'Tis likewise proposed, as a great Advantage to the Publick, that if we once discard the System of the Gospel, all Religion will of course be banished for ever, and consequently along with it, those grievous Prejudices of Education, which, under the Names of Virtue, Conscience, Honour, Justice, and the like, are so apt to disturb the Peace of human Minds, and the Notions whereof are so hard to be eradicated by right Reason or Free-Thinking, sometimes during the whole Course of our Lives.

Here first I observe how difficult it is to get rid of a Phrase which the World is once grown fond of, tho' the Occasion that first produced it, be entirely taken away.

For

For some Years past, if a Man had but an ill-favoured Nose, the deep Thinkers of the Age would some Way or other contrive to impute the Cause to the Prejudice of his Education. From this Fountain were said to be derived all our foolish Notions of Justice, Piety, Love of our Country; all our Opinions of God or a future State, Heaven, Hell, and the like: And there might formerly perhaps have been some Pretence for this Charge. But so effectual Care hath been since taken to remove those Prejudices, by an entire Change in the Methods of Education, that (with Honour I mention it to our polite Innovators) the young Gentlemen, who are now on the Scene, seem to have not the least Tincture left of those Infusions, or String of those Weeds, and by consequence the Reason for abolishing nominal Christianity upon that Pretext, is wholly ceas'd.

For the rest, it may perhaps admit a Controversy, whether the banishing all Notions of Religion whatsoever, would be convenient for the Vulgar. Not that I am in the least of opinion with those who hold Religion to have been the Invention of Politicians, to keep the lower Part of the World in Awe by the Fear of invisible Powers; unless Mankind were then very different from what it is now: For I look upon the Mass or Body of our People here in England, to be as Free-Thinkers, that is to say, as stanch Unbelievers, as any of the highest Rank. But I conceive some scattered Notions about a superior Power to be of singular Use for the common People, as furnishing excellent Materials to keep Children quiet when they grow peevish, and providing Topicks of Amusement in a tedious Winter Night.

Lastly, 'Tis proposed as a singular Advantage, that the abolishing of Christianity will very much contribute to the uniting of Protestants, by enlarging the Terms of

Communion

Communion so as to take in all sorts of Dissenters, who are now shut out of the Pale upon Account of a few Ceremonies, which all Sides confess to be Things indifferent: That this alone will effectually answer the great Ends of a Scheme for Comprehension, by opening a large noble Gate, at which all Bodies may enter; whereas the chaffering with Dissenters, and dodging about this or t'other Ceremony, is but like opening a few Wickets, and leaving them at Jar, by which no more than one can get in at a Time, and that not without stooping, and sideling, and squeezing his Body.

To all this I answer, That there is one darling Inclination of Mankind, which usually affects to be a Retainer to Religion, though she be neither its Parent, its Godmother, nor its Friend; I mean the Spirit of Opposition, that lived long before Christianity, and can easily subsist without it. Let us, for instance, examine wherein the Opposition of Sectaries among us consists; we shall find Christianity to have no share in it at all. Does the Gospel any where prescribe a starched squeezed Countenance, a stiff formal Gait, a Singularity of Manners and Habit, or any affected Forms and Modes of Speech different from the reasonable Part of Mankind? Yet, if Christianity did not lend its Name to stand in the Gap, and to employ or divert these Humours, they must of necessity be spent in Contraventions to the Laws of the Land, and Disturbance of the publick Peace. There is a Portion of Enthusiasm assigned to every Nation, which if it hath not proper Objects to work on, will burst out, and set all into a Flame. If the Quiet of a State can be bought by only flinging Men a few Ceremonies to devour, it is a Purchase no wise Man would refuse. Let the Mastiffs amuse themselves about a Sheep's Skin stuff'd with Hay, provided it will keep them from worrying the Flock.

Flock. The Institution of Convents abroad, seems in one point a Strain of great Wisdom, there being few Irregularities in human Passions, which may not have recourse to vent themselves in some of those Orders, which are so many Retreats for the Speculative, the Melancholy, the Proud, the Silent, the Politick, and the Morose, to spend themselves, and evaporate the noxious Particles; for each of whom we in this Island are forced to provide a several Sect of Religion, to keep them quiet; and whenever Christianity shall be abolished, the Legislature must find some other Expedient to employ and entertain them. For what imports it how large a Gate you open, if there will be always left a Number who place a Pride and a Merit in not coming in?

Having thus consider'd the most important Objections against Christianity, and the chief Advantages proposed by the Abolishing thereof; I shall now with equal Deference and Submission to wiser Judgments, as before, proceed to mention a few Inconveniences that may happen, if the Gospel should be repealed; which perhaps the Projectors may not have sufficiently considered.

And first, I am very sensible how much the Gentlemen of Wit and Pleasure are apt to murmur, and be shocked at the Sight of so many daggled-tail Parsons, that happen to fall in their Way, and offend their Eyes; but at the same time these wise Reformers do not consider what an Advantage and Felicity it is, for great Wits to be always provided with Objects of Scorn and Contempt, in order to exercise and improve their Talents, and divert their Spleen from falling on each other, or on themselves, especially when all this may be done without the least imaginable Danger to their Persons.

And to urge another Argument of a parallel Nature: If Christianity were once abolished, how could the Free-Thinkers,

Thinkers, the strong Reasoners, and the Men of profound Learning, be able to find another Subject so calculated in all Points whereon to display their Abilities. What wonderful Productions of Wit should we be deprived of, from those whose Genius, by continual Practice, hath been wholly turn'd upon Raillery and Invectives against Religion, and would therefore never be able to shine or distinguish themselves upon any other Subject. We are daily complaining of the great Decline of Wit among us, and would we take away the greatest, perhaps the only Topick we have left? Who would ever have suspected Asgill for a Wit, or Toland for a Philosopher, if the inexhaustible Stock of Christianity had not been at hand to provide them with Materials? What other Subject through all Art or Nature could have produced Tindall for a profound Author, or furnished him with Readers? It is the wise Choice of the Subject that alone adorns and distinguishes the Writer. For had a Hundred such Pens as these been employed on the side of Religion, they would have immediately sunk into Silence and Oblivion.

Nor do I think it wholly groundless, or my Fears altogether imaginary, that the Abolishing of Christianity may perhaps bring the Church in Danger, or at least put the Senate to the Trouble of another securing Vote. I desire I may not be mistaken; I am far from presuming to affirm or think that the Church is in Danger at present, or as Things now stand; but we know not how soon it may be so, when the Christian Religion is repealed. As plausible as this Project seems, there may a dangerous Design lurk under it: Nothing can be more notorious, than that the Atheists, Deists, Socinians, Anti-Trinitarians, and other Subdivisions of Free-Thinkers, are Persons of little Zeal for the present ecclesiastical Establishment: Their declared Opinion is for repealing the

sacramental

sacramental Test; they are very indifferent with regard to Ceremonies; nor do they hold the *Jus Divinum* of Episcopacy: Therefore this may be intended as one politick Step towards altering the Constitution of the Church established, and setting up Presbytery in the Stead, which I leave to be further considered by those at the Helm.

In the last Place I think nothing can be more plain, than that by this Expedient, we shall run into the Evil we chiefly pretend to avoid; and that the Abolishment of the Christian Religion, will be the readiest Course we can take to introduce Popery. And I am the more inclined to this Opinion, because we know it has been the constant Practice of the Jesuits to send over Emissaries, with Instructions to personate themselves Members of the several prevailing Sects amongst us. So it is recorded, that they have at sundry times appeared in the Guise of Presbyterians, Anabaptists, Independants, and Quakers, according as any of these were most in Credit; so, since the Fashion hath been taken up of exploding Religion, the Popish Missionaries have not been wanting to mix with the Free-Thinkers; among whom Toland, the great Oracle of the Anti-Christians, is an Irish Priest, the Son of an Irish Priest; and the most learned and ingenious Author of a Book called the *Rights of the Christian Church*, was in a proper Juncture reconciled to the Romish Faith, whose true Son, as appears by a hundred Passages in his Treatise, he still continues. Perhaps I could add some others to the Number; but the Fact is beyond Dispute, and the Reasoning they proceed by is right: For supposing Christianity to be extinguished, the People will never be at Ease till they find out some other Method of Worship; which will as infallibly produce Superstition, as this will end in Popery.

And

And therefore, if notwithstanding all I have said, it still be thought necessary to have a Bill brought in for repealing Christianity, I would humbly offer an Amendment, That instead of the Word Christianity, may be put Religion in general, which I conceive will much better answer all the good Ends proposed by the Projectors of it. For, as long as we leave in being, a God and his Providence, with all the necessary Consequences which curious and inquisitive Men will be apt to draw from such Premises, we do not strike at the Root of the Evil, though we should ever so effectually annihilate the present Scheme of the Gospel; For, of what Use is Freedom of Thought, if it will not produce Freedom of Action, which is the sole End, how remote soever in Appearance, of all Objections against Christianity; and therefore, the Free-Thinkers consider it as a Sort of Edifice, wherein all the Parts have such a mutual Dependance on each other, that if you happen to pull out one single Nail, the whole Fabrick must fall to the Ground. This was happily exprest by him who had heard of a Text brought for proof of the Trinity, which in an ancient Manuscript was differently read; he thereupon immediately took the Hint, and by a sudden Deduction of a long Sorites, most Logically concluded: Why, if it be as you say, I may safely whore and drink on, and defy the Parson. From which, and many the like Instances easy to be produced, I think nothing can be more manifest, than that the Quarrel is not against any particular Points of hard Digestion in the Christian System, but against Religion in general, which, by laying Restraints on human Nature, is supposed the great Enemy to the Freedom of Thought and Action.

Upon the whole, if it shall still be thought for the Benefit of Church and State, that Christianity be abolished, I conceive however, it may be more convenient to defer the Execution

Execution to a Time of Peace, and not venture in this Conjuncture to disoblige our Allies, who, as it falls out, are all Christians, and many of them, by the Prejudices of their Education, so bigotted, as to place a sort of Pride in the Appellation. If upon being rejected by them, we are to trust to an Alliance with the Turk, we shall find our selves much deceived: For, as he is too remote, and generally engaged in War with the Persian Emperor, so his People would be more scandalized at our Infidelity, than our Christian Neighbours. For they are not only strict Observers of religious Worship, but, what is worse, believe a God; which is more than is required of us, even while we preserve the Name of Christians.

To conclude: Whatever some may think of the great Advantages to Trade by this favourite Scheme, I do very much apprehend, that in six Months Time after the Act is past for the Extirpation of the Gospel, the Bank and East-India Stock, may fall at least One per Cent. And since that is fifty Times more than ever the Wisdom of our Age thought fit to venture for the Preservation of Christianity, there is no Reason we should be at so great a Loss, merely for the sake of destroying it.

A MODEST PROPOSAL FOR PREVENTING THE CHILDREN OF IRELAND FROM BEING A BURDEN TO THEIR PARENTS OR COUNTRY

The student of Swift can do no better than to begin with this essay which is a touchstone for Swift's style and character as a satirist. The dispassionate, business-like tone in which he unfolds the grotesque proposal is but a thin layer of cooled lava covering a pit of boiling indignation whose depth has never been sounded. This combination of fury and farce, of restraint and passion, has been the admiration and despair of imitators. Walpole, Wood, and absentee English landlords had literally torn the bread from the hands of Irish children, and the flesh from their bones. Now the outraged observer of such brutality has several options. He may shed tears and pass by. He may appeal hysterically to humanitarian sentiment and collect from sympathizers contributions to relieve a handful of people momentarily. He may denounce the Government. But Swift knew that official Yahoodom was not to be reformed by any of these means; empire builders never fail of an apologia disguised as a necessity of statecraft. As usual, Swift employs ridicule as the most effective weapon. He knew that the devil is brave in the face of threats, stony-hearted before tears, vulnerable only in the Achilles' heel of his vanity. So Swift translates England's exploitation of Ireland into the more accurate language of cannibalism, and proceeds to outline a plan whereby the administration can be made more profitable. If revenue from Ireland is to be the only consideration, as it was, then his proposal is logical, and profitable to all concerned. His motive was only in part to expose the brutal facts of Irish suffering. The sentimentalist could have done that. It was also to make ridiculous and contemptibly mean the Irish policy so urbanely phrased by official spokesmen in London.

The text reproduced is that of the original edition, 1729.

IT is a melancholly Object to those, who walk through this great Town or travel in the Country, when they see the Streets, the Roads and Cabbin-doors crowded with Beggers of the Female Sex, followed by three, four, or six Children, all in Rags, and importuning every Passenger for an Alms. These Mothers instead of being able to work for their honest livelyhood, are forced to employ all their time in Stroling to beg Sustenance for their helpless Infants, who, as they grow up, either turn Thieves for want of Work, or leave their dear Native Country, to fight for the Pretender in Spain, or sell themselves to the Barbadoes.

I think it is agreed by all Parties, that this prodigious number of Children in the Arms, or on the Backs, or at the Heels of their Mothers, and frequently of their Fathers, is in the present deplorable state of the Kingdom, a very great additional grievance; and therefore whoever could find out a fair, cheap and easy method of making these Children sound and useful Members of the Common-wealth, would deserve so well of the publick, as to have his Statue set up for a Preserver of the Nation.

But my Intention is very far from being confined to provide only for the Children of professed Beggers, it is of a much greater Extent, and shall take in the whole Number of Infants at a certain Age, who are born of Parents in effect as little able to support them, as those who demand our Charity in the Streets.

As to my own part, having turned my Thoughts, for many Years, upon this important Subject, and maturely weighed the several Schemes of other Projectors, I have always found them grossly mistaken in their computation. It is true, a Child just dropt from its Dam, may be supported by her Milk, for a Solar Year with little other

Nourishment,

Nourishment, at most not above the Value of two Shillings, which the Mother may certainly get, or the Value in Scraps, by her lawful Occupation of Begging; and it is exactly at one Year Old that I propose to provide for them in such a manner, as, instead of being a Charge upon their Parents, or the Parish, or wanting Food and Raiment for the rest of their Lives, they shall, on the Contrary, contribute to the Feeding and partly to the Cloathing of many Thousands.

There is likewise another great Advantage in my Scheme, that it will prevent those voluntary Abortions, and that horrid practice of Women murdering their Bastard Children, alas! too frequent among us, Sacrificing the poor innocent Babes, I doubt, more to avoid the Expence than the Shame, which would move Tears and Pity in the most Savage and inhuman breast.

The number of Souls in this Kingdom being usually reckoned one Million and a half, Of these I calculate there may be about two hundred thousand Couple whose Wives are Breeders; from which number I substract thirty Thousand Couples, who are able to maintain their own Children, although I apprehend there cannot be so many, under the present Distresses of the Kingdom; but this being granted, there will remain an hundred and seventy thousand Breeders. I again Substract fifty Thousand, for those Women who miscarry, or whose Children die by accident, or disease within the Year. There only remain an hundred and twenty thousand Children of poor Parents annually born: The question therefore is, How this number shall be reared, and provided for? which, as I have already said, under the present Situation of Affairs, is utterly impossible by all the Methods hitherto proposed; for we can neither employ them in Handicraft or Agriculture; we neither build Houses, (I mean in the

Country)

Country) nor cultivate Land: They can very seldom pick up a Livelihood by Stealing till they arrive at six years Old; except where they are of towardly parts; although, I confess, they learn the Rudiments much earlier; during which time they can however be properly looked upon only as Probationers; as I have been informed by a principal Gentleman in the County of Cavan, who protested to me, that he never knew above one or two Instances under the Age of six, even in a part of the Kingdom so renowned for the quickest proficiency in that Art.

I am assured by our Merchants, that a Boy or a Girl before twelve years Old, is no saleable Commodity, and even when they come to this Age, they will not yield above three Pounds, or three Pounds and half a Crown at most, on the Exchange; which cannot turn to Account either to the Parents or Kingdom, the Charge of Nutriment and Rags having been at least four times that Value.

I shall now therefore humbly propose my own Thoughts, which I hope will not be liable to the least Objection.

I have been assured by a very knowing American of my acquaintance in London, that a young healthy Child well Nursed is at a year Old a most delicious nourishing and wholesome Food, whether Stewed, Roasted, Baked, or Boiled; and I make no doubt that it will equally serve in a Fricasie, or a Ragoust.

I do therefore humbly offer it to publick consideration, that of the Hundred and twenty thousand Children, already computed, twenty thousand may be reserved for Breed, whereof only one fourth part to be Males; which is more than we allow to Sheep, black Cattle, or Swine, and my Reason is, that these Children are seldom the Fruits of Marriage, a Circumstance not much regarded

by

by our Savages, therefore, one Male will be sufficient to serve four Females. That the remaining Hundred thousand may at a year Old be offered in Sale to the Persons of Quality and Fortune, through the Kingdom, always advising the Mother to let them Suck plentifully in the last Month, so as to render them Plump, and Fat for a good Table. A Child will make two Dishes at an Entertainment for Friends, and when the Family dines alone, the fore or hind Quarter will make a reasonable Dish, and seasoned with a little Pepper or Salt will be very good Boiled on the fourth Day, especially in Winter.

I have reckoned upon a Medium, that a Child just born will weigh 12 pounds, and in a solar Year, if tolerably nursed, encreaseth to 28 Pounds.

I grant this food will be somewhat dear, and therefore very proper for Landlords, who, as they have already devoured most of the Parents seem to have the best Title to the Children.

Infant's flesh will be in Season throughout the Year, but more plentiful in March, and a little before and after; for we are told by a grave Author an eminent French Physician, that Fish being a prolifick Dyet, there are more Children born in Roman Catholick Countries about nine Months after Lent, than at any other Season; therefore reckoning a Year after Lent, the Markets will be more glutted than usual, because the Number of Popish Infants, is at least three to one in this Kingdom, and therefore it will have one other Collateral advantage, by lessening the Number of Papists among us.

I have already computed the Charge of nursing a Begger's Child (in which List I reckon all Cottagers, Labourers, and four fifths of the Farmers) to be about two Shillings per Annum, Rags included; and I believe no Gentleman would repine to give Ten Shillings for the

Carcass

Carcass of a good fat Child, which, as I have said will make four Dishes of excellent Nutritive Meat, when he hath only some particular Friend, or his own Family to dine with him. Thus the Squire will learn to be a good Landlord, and grow popular among his Tenants, the Mother will have Eight Shillings neat Profit, and be fit for Work till she produces another Child.

Those who are more thrifty (as I must confess the Times require) may flay the Carcass; the Skin of which, Artificially dressed, will make admirable Gloves for Ladies, and Summer Boots for fine Gentlemen.

As to our City of Dublin, Shambles may be appointed for this purpose, in the most convenient parts of it, and Butchers we may be assured will not be wanting; although I rather recommend buying the Children alive, and dressing them hot from the Knife, as we do roasting Pigs.

A very worthy Person, a true Lover of his Country, and whose Virtues I highly esteem, was lately pleased, in discoursing on this matter, to offer a refinement upon my Scheme. He said, that many Gentlemen of this Kingdom, having of late destroyed their Deer, he conceived that the Want of Venison might be well supply'd by the Bodies of young Lads and Maidens, not exceeding fourteen Years of Age, nor under twelve; so great a Number of both Sexes in every Country being now ready to Starve, for want of Work and Service: And these to be disposed of by their Parents if alive, or otherwise by their nearest Relations. But with due deference to so excellent a Friend, and so deserving a Patriot, I cannot be altogether in his Sentiments; for as to the Males, my American acquaintance assured me from frequent Experience, that their Flesh was generally Tough and Lean, like that of our Schoolboys, by continual exercise, and their Taste disagreeable,

disagreeable, and to fatten them would not answer the Charge. Then as to the Females, it would, I think with humble Submission, be a Loss to the Publick, because they soon would become Breeders themselves: And besides it is not improbable that some scrupulous People might be apt to Censure such a Practice, (although indeed very unjustly) as a little bordering upon Cruelty, which, I confess, hath always been with me the strongest Objection against any Project, how well soever intended.

But in order to justify my Friend, he confessed, that this expedient was put into his Head by the famous Sallmanaazor, a Native of the Island Formosa, who came from thence to London, above twenty Years ago, and in Conversation told my Friend, that in his Country when any young Person happened to be put to Death, the Executioner sold the Carcass to Persons of Quality, as a prime Dainty, and that, in his Time, the Body of a plump Girl of fifteen, who was crucified for an attempt to poison the Emperor, was sold to his Imperial Majesty's prime Minister of State, and other great Mandarins of the Court, in Joints from the Gibbet, at four hundred Crowns. Neither indeed can I deny, that if the same Use were made of several plump young Girls in this Town, who, without one single Groat to their Fortunes, cannot stir abroad without a Chair, and appear at a Play-house, and Assemblies in Foreign fineries, which they never will pay for; the Kingdom would not be the worse.

Some Persons of a desponding Spirit are in great concern about that vast Number of poor People, who are Aged, Diseased, or Maimed, and I have been desired to imploy my Thoughts what Course may be taken, to ease the Nation of so grievous an Incumbrance. But I am not in the least Pain upon that matter, because it is very well known, that they are every Day dying, and rotting,

by

by cold and famine, and filth, and vermin, as fast as can be reasonably expected. And as to the younger Labourers, they are now in almost as hopeful a Condition. They cannot get Work, and consequently pine away for want of Nourishment, to a degree, that if at any Time they are accidentally hired to common Labour, they have not Strength to perform it, and thus the Country and themselves are happily delivered from the Evils to come.

I have too long digressed, and therefore shall return to my Subject. I think the Advantages by the Proposal which I have made are obvious and many, as well as of the highest Importance.

For *First*, as I have already observed, it would greatly lessen the Number of Papists, with whom we are Yearly over-run, being the principal Breeders of the Nation, as well as our most dangerous Enemies, and who stay at home on purpose with a Design to deliver the Kingdom to the Pretender, hoping to take their Advantage by the Absence of so many good Protestants, who have chosen rather to leave their Country, than stay at home, and pay Tithes against their Conscience, to an Episcopal Curate.

Secondly, The poorer Tenants will have something valuable of their own which by Law may be made lyable to Distress, and help to pay their Landlord's Rent, their Corn and Cattle being already seized, and Money a Thing unknown.

Thirdly, Whereas the Maintenance of an hundred thousand Children, from two Years old, and upwards, cannot be computed at less than Ten Shillings a Piece per Annum, the Nation's Stock will be thereby increased fifty thousand Pounds per Annum, besides the Profit of a new Dish, introduced to the Tables of all Gentlemen of Fortune in the Kingdom, who have any Refinement in Taste,

Taste, and the Money will circulate among our Selves, the Goods being entirely of our own Growth and Manufacture.

Fourthly, The constant Breeders, besides the gain of eight Shillings Sterling per Annum, by the Sale of their Children, will be rid of the Charge of maintaining them after the first Year.

Fifthly, This Food would likewise bring great Custom to Taverns, where the Vintners will certainly be so prudent as to procure the best Receipts for dressing it to Perfection; and consequently have their Houses frequented by all the fine Gentlemen, who justly value themselves upon their Knowledge in good Eating; and a skilful Cook, who understands how to oblige his Guests, will contrive to make it as expensive as they please.

Sixthly, This would be a great Inducement to Marriage, which all wise Nations have either encouraged by Rewards, or enforced by Laws and Penalties. It would encrease the Care and Tenderness of Mothers towards their Children, when they were sure of a Settlement for Life, to the poor Babes, provided in some Sort by the Publick, to their annual Profit instead of Expence; we should soon see an honest Emulation among the married Women, which of them could bring the fattest Child to the Market. Men would become as fond of their Wives, during the Time of their Pregnancy, as they are now of their Mares in Foal, their Cows in Calf, or Sows when they are ready to farrow, nor offer to beat or kick them (as is too frequent a Practice) for fear of a Miscarriage.

Many other Advantages might be enumerated. For Instance, the Addition of some thousand Carcasses in our Exportation of Barrel'd Beef: The Propagation of Swine's Flesh, and Improvement in the Art of making good Bacon, so much wanted among us by the great Destruc-

tion

tion of Pigs, too frequent at our Tables, which are no way comparable in Taste, or Magnificence to a well grown, fat yearling Child, which roasted whole will make a considerable Figure at a Lord Mayor's Feast, or any other Publick Entertainment. But this, and many others, I omit, being studious of Brevity.

Supposing that one thousand Families in this City, would be constant Customers for Infant's Flesh, besides others who might have it at merry Meetings, particularly at Weddings and Christenings, I compute that Dublin would take off Annually about twenty thousand Carcasses, and the rest of the Kingdom (where probably they will be sold somewhat cheaper) the remaining eighty Thousand.

I can think of no one Objection, that will possibly be raised against this Proposal, unless it should be urged, that the Number of People will be thereby much lessened in the Kingdom. This I freely own, and 'twas indeed one principal Design in offering it to the World. I desire the Reader will observe, that I calculate my Remedy for this one individual Kingdom of Ireland, and for no Other that ever was, is, or, I think, ever can be upon Earth. Therefore let no man talk to me of other Expedients: Of taxing our Absentees at five Shillings a Pound: Of using neither Cloaths, nor Household Furniture, except what is of our own Growth and Manufacture: Of utterly rejecting the Materials and Instruments that promote Foreign Luxury: Of curing the Expensiveness of Pride, Vanity, Idleness, and Gaming in our Women: Of introducing a Vein of Parcimony, Prudence and Temperance: Of learning to love our Country, wherein we differ even from Laplanders, and the Inhabitants of Topinamboo: Of quitting our Animosities, and Factions, nor act any longer like the Jews, who were murdering one another at the

the very Moment their City was taken: Of being a little cautious not to sell our Country and Consciences for nothing: Of teaching Landlords to have at least one Degree of Mercy towards their Tenants. Lastly, Of putting a Spirit of Honesty, Industry, and Skill into our Shop-keepers, who, if a Resolution could now be taken to buy only our Native Goods, would immediately unite to cheat and exact upon us in the Price, the Measure, and the Goodness, nor could ever yet be brought to make one fair Proposal of just Dealing, though often and earnestly invited to it.

Therefore I repeat, let no Man talk to me of these and the like Expedients, till he hath at least some Glimpse of Hope, that there will ever be some hearty and sincere Attempt to put them in Practice.

But as to my self, having been wearied out for many Years with offering vain, idle, visionary Thoughts, and at length utterly despairing of Success, I fortunately fell upon this Proposal, which as it is wholly new, so it hath something Solid and Real, of no Expence and little Trouble, full in our own Power, and whereby we can incur no Danger in disobliging England. For this kind of Commodity will not bear Exportation, the Flesh being of too tender a Consistence, to admit a long Continuance in Salt, although perhaps I cou'd name a Country, which wou'd be glad to eat up our whole Nation without it.

After all, I am not so violently bent upon my own Opinion, as to reject any Offer, proposed by wise Men, which shall be found equally Innocent, Cheap, Easy, and Effectual. But before something of that Kind shall be advanced in Contradiction to my Scheme, and offering a better, I desire the Author or Authors, will be pleased maturely to consider two Points. *First*, As Things now stand, how they will be able to find Food and Raiment

for

for a hundred Thousand useless Mouths and Backs. And *Secondly*, There being a round Million of Creatures in Human Figure, throughout this Kingdom, whose whole Subsistence put into a common Stock, would leave them in Debt two Millions of Pounds Sterling, adding those, who are Beggers by Profession, to the Bulk of Farmers, Cottagers and Labourers, with their Wives and Children, who are Beggers in Effect; I desire those Politicians, who dislike my Overture, and may perhaps be so bold to attempt an Answer, that they will first ask the Parents of these Mortals, Whether they would not at this Day think it a great Happiness to have been sold for Food at a Year Old, in the manner I prescribe, and thereby have avoided such a perpetual Scene of Misfortunes, as they have since gone through, by the Oppression of Landlords, the Impossibility of paying Rent without Money or Trade, the Want of common Sustenance, with neither House nor Cloaths to cover them from the Inclemencies of the Weather, and the most inevitable Prospect of intailing the like, or greater Miseries, upon their Breed for ever.

I profess in the Sincerity of my Heart, that I have not the least Personal Interest in endeavouring to promote this necessary Work, having no other Motive than the Publick Good of my Country, by advancing our Trade, providing for Infants, relieving the Poor, and giving some Pleasure to the Rich. I have no Children, by which I can propose to get a single Penny; the youngest being nine Years Old, and my Wife past Child-bearing.

A LETTER OF ADVICE TO A YOUNG POET

To understand something of the commercial battle of the books waged continuously in Grub Street in the time of Pope and Swift it is not necessary to plough through the notes of the *Dunciad*, nor to exhume the bones of Bentley and Curll. In this amusing satire Swift has sketched for us the tricks by which scribblers won publishers and readers without invoking the aid of the Muses. The title might be modernized to read, 'How to write like Homer and Milton by working ten minutes a day. No education necessary. Send for our free booklet of easy rules.'

For other satires on the same subject the reader is referred to the Scriblerus essays of Arbuthnot and Pope and to the delightful essay by Bishop Copleston, 'Advice to a Young Reviewer, with a Specimen of his Art', 1807.

This essay first appeared in Dublin, 1721, and was reprinted in London in the same year. The text reproduced is that of *Lord Somers' Tracts*, 1748 (revised edition by Walter Scott, vol. xiii, 1815), which has been collated with the original edition. It was not included in any of the editions of Swift's collected works in the first half of the eighteenth century.

SIR,

AS I have always profess'd a Friendship for you, and have therefore been more inquisitive into your Conduct and Studies than is usually agreeable to young Men, so I must own I am not a little pleas'd to find, by your last Account, that you have entirely bent your Thoughts to English Poetry, with Design to make it your Profession and Business. Two Reasons incline me to encourage you in this Study; one, the Narrowness of your present Circumstances; the other, the great Use of Poetry to Mankind and Society, and in every Employment of Life. Upon these Views, I cannot but commend your wise Resolution to withdraw so early from other unprofitable and severe Studies, and betake yourself to that, which, if you have good Luck, will advance your Fortune, and make you an Ornament to your Friends and your Country. It may be your Justification, and farther Encouragement, to consider that History, Ancient or Modern, cannot furnish you an Instance of one Person, eminent in any Station, who was not in some Measure vers'd in Poetry, or at least a Well-wisher to the Professors of it; neither would I despair to prove, if legally call'd thereto, that it is impossible to be a good Soldier, Divine, or Lawyer, or even so much as an eminent Bell-Man, or Ballad-Singer, without some Taste of Poetry, and a competent Skill in Versification: But I say the less of this, because the renowned Sir P. Sidney has exhausted the Subject before me, in his Defence of Poesie, on which I shall make no other Remark but this, that he argues there as if he really believed himself.

For my own part, having never made one Verse since I was at School, where I suffered too much for my Blunders in Poetry, to have any Love to it ever since, I am not able,

from

from any Experience of my own, to give you those Instructions you desire: neither will I declare (for I love to conceal my Passions) how much I lament my Neglect of Poetry in those Periods of my Life, which were properest for Improvements in that ornamental Part of Learning; besides, my Age and Infirmities might well excuse me to you, as being unqualify'd to be your Writing-Master, with Spectacles on, and a Shaking Hand. However, that I may not be altogether wanting to you in an Affair of so much importance to your credit and happiness, I shall here give you some scatter'd thoughts upon the Subject, such as I have gather'd by Reading and Observation.

There is a certain little Instrument, the first of those in Use with Scholars, and the meanest, considering the Materials of it, whether it be a joint of Wheaten-Straw (the old Arcadian Pipe), or just three inches of slender Wire, or a stript Feather, or a Corking-Pin. Furthermore, this same diminutive Tool, for the Posture of it, usually reclines its head on the Thumb of the Right Hand, sustains the foremost Finger upon its Breast, and is it self supported by the second. This is commonly known by the Name of a Fescue; I shall here therefore condescend to be this little Elementary Guide, and point out some Particulars which may be of Use to you in your Horn-Book of Poetry.

In the first Place, I am not yet convinc'd, that it is at all necessary for a modern poet to believe in God, or have any serious Sense of Religion; and in this Article you must give me Leave to suspect your Capacities; because Religion being what your Mother taught you, you will hardly find it possible, at least not easy, all at once to get over those early Prejudices, so far as to think it better to be a great Wit than a good Christian, tho' herein the

General

General Practice is against you; so that if, upon Enquiry, you find in your self any such Softnesses, owing to the Nature of your Education, my Advice is, that you forthwith lay down your Pen, as having no farther Business with it in the Way of Poetry, unless you will be content to pass for an Insipid, or will submit to be hooted at by your Fraternity, or can disguise your Religion, as well-bred Men do their Learning, in Complaisance to Company.

For Poetry, as it has been manag'd for some Years past, by such as make a Business of it (and of such only I speak here, for I do not call him a Poet that writes for his Diversion, any more than that Gentleman a Fidler who amuses himself with a Violin) I say, our Poetry of late has been altogether disengag'd from the narrow Notions of Virtue and Piety, because it has been found by Experience of our Professors, that the smallest Quantity of Religion, like a single Drop of Malt-Liquor in Claret, will muddy and discompose the brightest Poetical Genius.

Religion supposes Heaven and Hell, the Word of God, and Sacraments, and twenty other Circumstances, which taken seriously, are a wonderful Check to Wit and Humour, and such as a true poet cannot possibly give into with a saving to his Poetical License; but yet it is necessary for him, that others should believe those Things seriously, that his Wit may be exercised on their Wisdom, for so doing: For tho' a Wit need not have Religion, religion is necessary to a Wit, as an Instrument is to the Hand that plays upon it: And for this the Moderns plead the Example of their great Idol Lucretius, who had not been by half so eminent a Poet (as he truly was), but that he stood tip-toe on Religion, *Religio pedibus subjecta*, and by that rising Ground had the advantage of all the poets of his own or following Times, who were not mounted on the same Pedestal.

Besides,

Besides, it is farther to be observed, that Petronius, another of their Favourites, speaking of the Qualifications of a good Poet, insists chiefly on the *Liber Spiritus*; by which I have been ignorant enough heretofore to suppose he meant, a good Invention, or great Compass of Thought, or a sprightly Imagination: But I have learned a better Construction, from the Opinion and Practice of the Moderns; and taking it literally for a free Spirit, i.e. a Spirit, or Mind, free or disengag'd from all Prejudices concerning God, Religion, and another World, it is to me a plain Account why our present Sett of Poets are, and hold themselves oblig'd to be, Free-Thinkers.

But altho' I cannot recommend Religion upon the practice of some of our most eminent English Poets, yet I can justly advise you, from their Example, to be conversant in the Scriptures, and, if possible, to make yourself entirely Master of them: In which, however, I intend nothing less than imposing upon you a Task of Piety. Far be it from me to desire you to believe them, or lay any great Stress upon their Authority, (in that you may do as you think fit) but to read them as a Piece of necessary Furniture for a wit and a Poet; which is a very different View from that of a Christian. For I have made it my Observation, that the greatest Wits have been the best Textuaries: Our modern Poets are, all to a Man, almost as well read in the Scriptures as some of our Divines, and often abound more with the Phrase. They have read them Historically, Critically, Musically, Comically, Poetically, and every other Way except Religiously, and have found their Account in doing so. For the Scriptures are undoubtedly a Fund of Wit, and a subject for wit. You may, according to the modern Practice, be witty upon them or out of them: And to speak the Truth, but for them, I know not what our Play-wrights

Play-wrights would do for Images, Allusions, Similitudes, Examples, or even Language itself. Shut up the Sacred Books, and I would be bound our Wit would run-down like an Alarm, or fall as the Stocks did, and ruin half the Poets in these Kingdoms. And if that were the Case, how would most of that Tribe, (all, I think, but the immortal Addison, who made a better Use of his Bible, and a few more) who dealt so freely in that Fund, rejoice that they had drawn out in Time, and left the present Generation of Poets to be the Bubbles?

But here I must enter one caution, and desire you to take notice, that in this advice of reading the Scriptures, I had not the least thought concerning your qualifications that way for Poetical Orders; which I mention, because I find a notion of that kind advanc'd by one of our English poets, and is, I suppose, maintain'd by the rest. He says to Spencer, in a pretended Vision,

——With Hands laid on, ordain me fit
For the great Cure and Ministry of Wit.

Which Passage is, in my Opinion, a notable Allusion to the Scriptures, and making (but reasonable) Allowances for the small circumstance of Profaneness, bordering close upon Blasphemy, is inimitably fine; besides some useful Discoveries made in it, as, that there are Bishops in Poetry, that these Bishops must Ordain young poets, and with laying on Hands; and that Poetry is a Cure of Souls; and consequently speaking, those who have such Cures ought to be Poets, and too often are so: And indeed, as of old, Poets and Priests were one and the same Function, the Alliance of those ministerial Offices is to this Day happily maintain'd in the same Persons; and this I take to be the only justifiable Reason for that Appellation which they so much affect, I mean the modest Title of *Divine Poets*. However, having never been present

present at the Ceremony of ordaining to the Priesthood of Poetry, I own I have no Notion of the Thing, and shall say the less of it here.

The Scriptures then being generally both the Fountain and Subject of modern Wit, I could do no less than give them the Preference in your Reading. After a thorough Acquaintance with them, I would advise you to turn your Thoughts to Human Literature, which yet I say more in Compliance with vulgar Opinions, than according to my own Sentiments.

For, indeed, nothing has surpriz'd me more, than to see the Prejudices of Mankind as to this Matter of human Learning, who have generally thought it is necessary to be a good Scholar, in order to be a good Poet, than which nothing is falser in Fact, or more contrary to Practice and Experience. Neither will I dispute the Matter, if any Man will undertake to shew me one professed Poet now in Being, who is any thing of what may be justly called a Scholar; or is the worse Poet for that, but perhaps the better, for being so little encumber'd with the Pedantry of Learning: 'Tis true, the contrary was the Opinion of our Forefathers, which we of this Age have Devotion enough to receive from them on their own Terms, and unexamin'd, but not sense enough to perceive 'twas a gross Mistake in them. So Horace has told us.

Scribendi recte sapere est et principium et fons,
Rem tibi Socraticæ poterunt ostendere chartæ.

But to see the different Casts of Men's Heads, some not inferior to that Poet in Understanding (if you will take their own Word for it), do see no consequence in this rule, and are not ashamed to declare themselves of a contrary opinion. Do not many men write well in common account, who have nothing of that Principle? Many are too Wise to be Poets, and others too much

Poets

Poets to be Wise. Must a man, forsooth, be no less than a philosopher to be a poet, when it is plain, that some of the greatest idiots of the age are our prettiest Performers that Way? And for this, I appeal to the Judgment and observation of Mankind. Sir Ph. Sidney's notable Remark upon this Nation, may not be improper to mention here. He says, "In our Neighbour-Country Ireland, where true learning goes very bare, yet are their poets held in devout Reverence;" which shews, that Learning is no way necessary either to the making a Poet, or judging of him. And farther to see the Fate of Things, notwithstanding our Learning here is as bare as ever, yet are our Poets not held, as formerly, in devout reverence, but are, perhaps, the most contemptible Race of Mortals now in this Kingdom, which is no less to be Wonder'd at than Lamented.

Some of the old Philosophers were Poets (as, according to the forementioned Author, Socrates and Plato were; which, however, is what I did not know before) but that does not say that all Poets are, or that any need be Philosophers, otherwise than as those are so call'd who are a little out at the Elbows. In which sense the great Shakespear might have been a Philosopher; but was no Scholar, yet was an excellent Poet. Neither do I think a late most judicious Critick so much mistaken, as others do, in advancing this Opinion, that Shakespear had been a worse Poet had he been a better Scholar: And Sir W. Davenant is another instance in the same Kind. Nor must it be forgotten, that Plato was an avow'd enemy to Poets, which is, perhaps, the reason why Poets have been always at Enmity with his Profession; and have rejected all Learning and Philosophy for the Sake of that one Philosopher. As I take the Matter, neither Philosophy, nor any Part of Learning, is more necessary to poetry,

(which,

(which, if you will believe the same Author, is the Sum of all Learning) than to know the Theory of Light, and the several Proportions and Diversifications of it in particular Colours, is to a good Painter.

Whereas therefore, a certain Author, call'd Petronius Arbiter, going upon the same Mistake, has confidently declar'd, that one Ingredient of a good Poet is *Mens ingenti literarum flumine inundata*; I do, on the contrary, declare, that this his Assertion (to speak of it in the softest Terms) is no better than an invidious and unhandsome Reflection on all the Gentlemen-Poets of these Times; for, with his good Leave, much less than a Flood, or Inundation, will serve the Turn, and to my certain Knowledge, some of our greatest Wits, in your poetical Way, have not as much real Learning as would cover a Six-Pence in the Bottom of a Bason; nor do I think the worse of them.

For, to speak my private Opinion, I am for every Man's working upon his own Materials, and producing only what he can find within himself, which is commonly a better Stock than the Owner knows it to be. I think Flowers of Wit ought to spring, as those in a Garden do, from their own Root and Stem, without Foreign Assistance. I would have a Man's Wit rather like a Fountain, that feeds itself invisibly, than a River, that is supply'd by several Streams from abroad.

Or if it be necessary, as the Case is with some barren Wits, to take in the Thoughts of others, in order to draw forth their own, as dry Pumps will not play till Water is thrown into them; in that Necessity, I would recommend some of the approv'd Standard-Authors of Antiquity for your Perusal, as a Poet and a Wit; because Maggots being what you look for, as Monkeys do for Vermin in their Keepers Heads, you will find they abound in good old Authors,

Authors, as in rich old Cheese, not in the new; and for that Reason you must have the Classicks, especially the most Worm-eaten of them, often in your Hands.

But with this Caution, that you are not to use those Antients as unlucky Lads do their old Fathers, and make no Conscience of picking their Pockets and pillaging them. Your Business is not to steal from them, but to improve upon them, and make their Sentiments your own; which is an Effect of great Judgment; and tho' difficult, yet very possible, without the scurvy Imputation of Filching: For I humbly conceive, tho' I light my Candle at my Neighbour's Fire, that does not alter the Property, or make the Wyck, the Wax, or the Flame, or the whole Candle, less my own.

Possibly you may think it a very severe Task, to arrive at a competent Knowledge of so many of the Antients, as excel in their Way; and indeed it would be really so, but for the short and easy Method lately found out of Abstracts, Abridgments, Summaries, &c. which are admirable Expedients for being very learned with little or no Reading; and have the same Use with Burning-Glasses, to collect the diffus'd Rays of Wit and Learning in Authors, and make them point with Warmth and Quickness upon the Reader's Imagination. And to this is nearly related that other modern Device of consulting Indexes, which is to read Books Hebraically, and begin where others usually end; and this is a compendious Way of coming to an Acquaintance with Authors: For authors are to be used like Lobsters, you must look for the best Meat in the Tails, and lay the Bodies back again in the Dish. Your cunningest Thieves (and what else are Readers who only read to borrow, i.e. to steal) use to cut off the Portmanteau from behind, without staying to dive into the Pockets of the owner. Lastly, you are taught

taught thus much in the very Elements of Philosophy, for one of the first rules in Logick is, *Finis est primus in intentione.*

The learned World is therefore most highly indebted to a late painful and judicious Editor of the Classicks, who has labour'd in that new Way with exceeding Felicity. Every Author, by his Management, sweats under himself, being over-loaded with his own Index, and carries, like a North-Country Pedlar, all his Substance and Furniture upon his Back, and with as great Variety of Trifles. To him let all young Students make their Compliments for so much Time and Pains sav'd in the Pursuit of useful Knowledge; for whoever shortens a Road is a Benefactor to the Publick, and to every particular Person who has Occasion to travel that Way.

But to proceed. I have lamented nothing more in my Time, than the Disuse of some ingenious little Plays, in Fashion with young Folks, when I was a Boy, and to which the great Facility of that Age, above ours, in composing, was certainly owing; and if any Thing has brought a Damp upon the Versification of these Times, we have no farther than this to go for the Cause of it. Now could these Sports be happily reviv'd, I am of Opinion your wisest Course would be to apply your Thoughts to them, and never fail to make a Party when you can, in those profitable Diversions. For Example, Crambo is of extraordinary Use to good Rhiming, and Rhiming is what I have ever accounted the very Essential of a good Poet: And in that Notion I am not singular; for the aforesaid Sir P. Sidney has declar'd, That the chief Life of modern Versifying consisteth in the like sounding of Words, which we call rhime; which is an Authority, either without Exception or above any Reply. Wherefore, you are ever to try a good Poem as you would a

sound

sound Pipkin, and if it rings well upon the Knuckle, be sure there is no Flaw in it. Verse without Rhime is a Body without a Soul, (for the chief Life consisteth in the Rhime) or a Bell without a Clapper; which, in Strictness, is no Bell, as being neither of Use nor Delight. And the same ever-honoured Knight, with so musical an Ear, had that veneration for the Tuneableness and Chiming of verse, that he speaks of a Poet as one that has the Reverend Title of a Rhimer. Our celebrated Milton has done these Nations great Prejudice in this Particular, having spoil'd as many reverend rhimers, by his example, as he has made real Poets.

For which Reason, I am overjoy'd to hear, that a very ingenious Youth of this Town is now upon the useful Design (for which he is never enough to be commended) of bestowing Rhime upon Milton's *Paradise Lost*, which will make your Poem, in that only defective, more Heroick and Sonorous than it has hitherto been. I wish the Gentleman Success in the Performance; and, as it is a work in which a young Man could not be more happily employ'd, or appear in with greater Advantage to his Character, so I am concern'd that it did not fall out to be your Province.

With much the same View, I would recommend to you the witty Play of Pictures and Motto's, which will furnish your Imagination with great Store of Images and suitable Devices. We of these Kingdoms have found our Account in this Diversion, as little as we consider or acknowledge it. For to this we owe our eminent Felicity in Posies of Rings, Motto's of Snuff-Boxes, the Humours of Sign-Posts, with their elegant inscriptions, &c. in which kind of Productions not any Nation in the World, no, not the Dutch themselves, will presume to rival us.

For much the same Reason it may be proper for you to have

have some Insight into the Play call'd *What is it like?* as of great Use in common Practice, to quicken slow Capacities, and improve the quickest: but the chief End of it is to supply the Fancy with Variety of Similies for all Subjects. It will teach you to bring Things to a Likeness which have not the least Conformity in Nature, which is properly Creation, and the very Business of a Poet, as his Name implies; and let me tell you, a good Poet can no more be without a Stock of Similies by him than a Shoe-Maker without his Lasts. He shou'd have them siz'd, and rang'd, and hung up in order in his Shop, ready for all Customers, and shap'd to the Feet of all sorts of Verse: And here I cou'd more fully (and I long to do it) insist upon the wonderful Harmony and Resemblance between a Poet and a Shoe-Maker, in many Circumstances common to both; such as the Binding of their Temples, the Stuff they work upon, and the Paring-Knife they use, &c. but that I would not digress, nor seem to trifle in so serious a Matter.

Now I say, if you apply yourself to these diminutive Sports (not to mention others of equal Ingenuity, such as Draw-Gloves, Cross-Purposes, Questions and Commands, and the rest) it is not to be conceived what Benefit (of Nature) you will find by them, and how they will open the Body of your Invention. To these devote your Spare Hours, or rather Spare all your Hours to them, and then you will act as becomes a wise Man, and make even Diversions an Improvement; like the inimitable Management of the Bee, which does the whole Business of Life at once, and at the same time both feeds, and works, and diverts itself.

Your own Prudence will, I doubt not, direct you to take a Place every Evening amongst the Ingenious, in the Corner of a certain Coffee-House in this Town, where

you

you will receive a Turn equally right as to Wit, Religion, and Politicks: As likewise to be as frequent at the Play-House as you can afford, without selling your Books. For in our chast Theatre, even Cato himself might sit to the falling of the Curtain: Besides, you will sometimes meet with tolerable Conversation amongst the Players; they are such a kind of Men as may pass, upon the same sort of Capacities, for Wits off the Stage, as they do for fine Gentlemen upon it. Besides that, I have known a Factor deal in as good Ware, and sell as cheap, as the Merchant himself that employs him.

Add to this the Expediency of furnishing out your Shelves with a choice Collection of modern Miscellanies, in the gayest Edition; and of reading all sorts of Plays, especially the New, and above all, those of our own Growth, printed by Subscription, in which Article of Irish Manufacture I readily agree to the late Proposal, and am altogether for rejecting and renouncing every Thing that comes from England; To what Purpose shou'd we go thither for Coals or Poetry when we have a Vein within ourselves equally Good and more Convenient? Lastly,

A common-place-Book is what a provident Poet cannot subsist without for this proverbial Reason, that great Wits have short Memories; and whereas on the other Hand, poets being Lyars by Profession, ought to have good Memories; to reconcile these, a Book of this sort is in the Nature of a Supplemental Memory, or a Record of what occurs remarkable in every Day's Reading or Conversation: There you enter not only your own Original Thoughts, (which, a hundred to one, are few and insignificant) but such of other Men as you think fit to make your own by entering them there. For take this for a Rule, when an Author is in your Books, you have

the

the same Demand upon him for his Wit as a merchant has for your Money when you are in his.

By these few and easy Prescriptions (with the Help of a good Genius) 'tis possible you may in a short time arrive at the Accomplishments of a Poet, and shine in that Character. As for your manner of Composing, and choice of Subjects, I cannot take upon me to be your Director, but I will venture to give you some short Hints, which you may enlarge upon at your Leisure. Let me entreat you then by no Means to lay aside that Notion peculiar to our modern Refiners in Poetry, which is, That a Poet must never Write or Discourse as the ordinary Part of Mankind do, but in Number and Verse, as an Oracle; which I mention the rather, because upon this Principle I have known Heroes brought into the Pulpit, and a whole Sermon compos'd and deliver'd in Blank Verse, to the vast Credit of the Preacher, no less than the real Entertainment and great Edification of the Audience.

The secret of which I take to be this. When the Matter of such Discourses is but mere Clay, or, as we usually call it, sad Stuff, the Preacher, who can afford no better, wisely Moulds, and Polishes, and Drys, and Washes this piece of Earthen-Ware, and then Bakes it with Poetic Fire, after which it will ring like any Pan-crock, and is a good dish to set before common Guests, as every Congregation is that comes so often for Entertainment to one Place.

There was a good old Custom in Use, which our Ancestors had, of Invoking the Muses at the Entrance of their Poems, I suppose, by Way of craving a Blessing: This the graceless Moderns have in a great Measure laid aside, but are not to be followed in that Poetical Impiety; for altho' to nice Ears such Invocations may sound harsh and disagreeable (as tuning instruments is before a Concert)

Concert) they are equally necessary. Again, you must not fail to dress your Muse in a Forehead-cloth of Greek or Latin, I mean, you are always to make use of a quaint Motto to all your Compositions; for, besides that this Artifice bespeaks the Reader's Opinion of the Writer's Learning, it is otherwise useful and commendable. A bright Passage in the Front of a Poem is a good Mark, like a Star in a Horse's Face, and the Piece will certainly go off the better for it. The *Os magna sonaturum*, which, if I remember right, Horace makes one qualification of a good Poet, may teach you not to gagg your Muse, or stint your Self in Words and Epithets (which cost you nothing) contrary to the Practice of some few out-of-the-way Writers, who use a natural and concise Expression, and affect a Stile like unto a Shrewsbury-cake, Short and Sweet upon the Palate; they will not afford you a Word more than is necessary to make them intelligible, which is as poor and niggardly as it would be to set down no more Meat than your Company will be sure to eat up. Words are but Lacquies to Sense, and will dance attendance, without wages or Compulsion; *Verba non invita sequentur.*

Farthermore, when you set about Composing, it may be necessary, for your ease and better Distillation of Wit, to put on your worst Cloaths, and the worse the better; for an Author, like a Limbick, will yield the better for having a Rag about him: Besides that, I have observed a Gardener cut the outward Rind of a Tree (which is the Surtout of it), to make it bear well: And this is a natural Account of the usual Poverty of Poets, and is an Argument why Wits, of all Men living, ought to be ill Clad. I have always a secret Veneration for any one I observe to be a little out of Repair in his Person, as supposing him either a Poet or a Philosopher; because the richest Minerals

Minerals are ever found under the most ragged and withered Surface of Earth.

As for your Choice of Subjects, I have only to give you this Caution, that as a handsome Way of Praising is certainly the most difficult Point in Writing or Speaking, I wou'd by no means advise any young Man to make his first Essay in Panegyrick, besides the Danger of it; for a particular Encomium is ever attended with more Ill-will than any general Invective, for which I need give no Reasons; wherefore, my Counsel is, that you use the Point of your Pen, not the Feather: Let your first Attempt be a *Coup d'Eclat* in the way of Libel, Lampoon or Satyr. Knock down half a score Reputations, and you will infallibly raise your Own; and so it be with Wit, no matter with how little Justice, for Fiction is your Trade.

Every great Genius seems to ride upon Mankind, like Pyrrhus on his Elephant; and the way to have the absolute Ascendant of your resty Nag, and to keep your Seat, is, at your first mounting, to afford him the Whip and Spurs plentifully, after which, you may travel the rest of the Day with great Alacrity. Once kick the world, and the world and you will live together at a reasonable good Understanding. You cannot but know, that these of your Profession have been called *Genus irritabile vatum*, and you will find it necessary to qualify yourself for that whaspish Society, by exerting your Talent of Satyr upon the first Occasion, and to abandon Good-nature, only to prove yourself a true Poet, which you will allow to be a valuable Consideration: In a Word, a young Robber is usually ent'red by a Murder: A young Hound is blooded when he comes first into the Field: A young Bully begins with killing his Man: And a young Poet must shew his Wit, as the other his Courage, by cutting

cutting and slashing, and laying about him, and banging Mankind.

Lastly, it will be your Wisdom to look out betimes for a good Service for your Muse, according to her Skill and Qualifications, whether in the Nature of a Dairy-Maid, a Cook, or Charwoman: I mean to hire out your Pen to a Party which will afford you both Pay and Protection; and when you have to do with the Press (as you will long to be there), take care to bespeak an importunate Friend to extort your Productions with an agreeable Violence; and which, according to the Cue between you, you must surrender *digito male pertinaci*: There is a Decency in this, for it no more becomes an Author in Modesty to have a Hand in publishing his own Works, than a Woman in Labour to lay herself.

I wou'd be very loth to give the least Umbrage of offence by what I have here said, as I may do, if I should be thought to insinuate that these Circumstances of good Writing have been unknown to, or not observed by, the Poets of this Kingdom: I will do my Countrymen the Justice to say, they have written by the foregoing Rules with great Exactness, and so far, as hardly to come behind those of their Profession in England, in Perfection of low Writing. The Sublime, indeed, is not so common with us; but ample Amends is made for that want, in great Abundance of the Admirable and Amazing, which appears in all our Compositions. Our very good Friend (the Knight aforesaid) speaking of the Force of Poetry, mentions "rhiming to Death", which (adds he) is said to be done in Ireland, and truly, to our Honour be it spoken, that Power, in a great Measure, continues with us to this Day.

I would now offer some poor Thoughts of mine for the Encouragement of Poetry in this Kingdom, if I could

hope

hope they would be agreeable. I have had many an aking Heart for the ill Plight of that noble Profession here, and it has been my late and early Study how to bring it into better Circumstances. And surely, considering what Monstrous Wits in the Poetick Way do almost daily start up and surprize us in this Town; what prodigious Genius's we have here (of which I could give Instances without Number) and withal of what great Benefit it may be to our Trade to encourage that Science here, (for it is plain our Linen-Manufacture is advanced by the great Waste of Paper made by our present Sett of Poets, not to mention other necessary Uses of the same to Shop-keepers, especially Grocers, Apothecaries, and Pastry-Cooks; and I might add, but for our Writers, the Nation wou'd in a little time be utterly destitute of Bum-Fodder, and must of Necessity import the same from England and Holland, where they have it in great abundance, by the indefatigable Labour of their own Wits:) I say, these things consider'd, I am humbly of Opinion, it would be worth the Care of our Governours to cherish Gentlemen of the Quill, and give them all proper Encouragements here. And since I am upon the Subject, I shall speak my mind very freely, and if I added, saucily, it is no more than my Birth-right as a Briton.

Seriously then, I have many Years lamented the want of a Grub-Street in this our large and polite City, unless the whole may be called one. And this I have accounted an unpardonable Defect in our Constitution, ever since I had any Opinions I could call my own. Every one knows Grub-Street is a Market for Small-Ware in Wit, and as necessary, considering the usual Purgings of the human Brain, as the Nose is upon a Man's Face: And for the same Reasons we have here a Court, a College, a Play-

house,

house, and beautiful Ladies, and fine Gentlemen, and good Claret, and abundance of Pens, Ink, and Paper, (clear of Taxes) and every other Circumstance to provoke Wit; and yet those whose Province it is have not yet thought fit to appoint a Place for Evacuations of it, which is a very hard Case, as may be judg'd by Comparisons.

And truly this Defect has been attended with unspeakable Inconveniences; for, not to mention the Prejudice done to the Commonwealth of Letters, I am of opinion we suffer in our Health by it: I believe our corrupted Air, and frequent thick Fogs, are in a great measure owing to the common exposal of our Wit, and that with good Management our poetical Vapours might be carry'd off in a common Drain, and fall into one Quarter of the Town, without infecting the whole, as the Case is at present, to the great Offence of our Nobility and Gentry, and others of nice Noses. When Writers of all Sizes, like Freemen of the City, are at liberty to throw out their Filth and excrementitious Productions in every Street as they please, what can the Consequence be, but that the Town must be poyson'd, and become such another Jakes, as by report of our great Travellers, Edinburgh is at Night, a thing well to be consider'd in these pestilential Times.

I am not of the Society for Reformation of Manners, but, without that pragmatical Title, I would be glad to see some Amendment in the matter before us: Wherefore I humbly bespeak the Favour of the Lord Mayor, the Court of Aldermen and Common Council, together with the whole Circle of Arts in this Town, and do recommend this Affair to their most political Consideration; and I persuade myself they will not be wanting in their best Endeavours, when they can serve two such good Ends

at

at once, as both to keep the Town sweet, and encourage Poetry in it. Neither do I make any Exceptions as to Satyrical Poets and Lampoon Writers, in Consideration of their Office: For though indeed their Business is to rake into Kennels, and gather up the Filth of Streets and Families, (in which respect they may be, for aught I know, as necessary to the Town as Scavengers or Chimney sweeps) yet I have observed they too have themselves at the same Time very foul cloaths, and, like dirty Persons, leave more Filth and Nastiness than they sweep away.

In a Word, what I would be at (for I love to be plain in Matters of Importance to my Country) is, That some private Street, or blind Alley, of this Town may be fitted up at the Charge of the Publick, as an apartment for the Muses, (like those at Rome and Amsterdam, for their Female Relations) and be wholly consign'd to the Uses of our Wits, furnish'd compleatly with all Appurtenances, such as Authors, Supervisors, Presses, Printers, Hawkers, Shops, and Ware-Houses, abundance of Garrets, and every other Implement and Circumstance of Wit; the Benefit of which would obviously be this, viz. That we should then have a safe Repository for our best Productions, which at present are handed about in Single Sheets or Manuscripts, and may be altogether lost, (which were a Pity) or at the best are subject, in that loose Dress, like handsome Women, to great Abuses.

Another Point, that has cost me some melancholy Reflections, is the present State of the Play-House, the Encouragement of which hath an immediate Influence upon the Poetry of the Kingdom; As a good Market improves the Tillage of the neighbouring Country, and enriches the Ploughman; neither do we of this Town seem enough to know or consider the vast Benefit of a

Play-House

Play-House to our City and Nation; that Single House is the Fountain of all our Love, Wit, Dress, and Gallantry. It is the school of Wisdom, for there we learn to know What's what; which, however, I cannot say is always in that Place sound Knowledge. There our young Folks drop their Childish Mistakes, and come first to perceive their Mothers Cheat of the Parsely-Bed; there too they get rid of Natural Prejudices, especially those of Religion and Modesty, which are great Restraints to a Free People. The same is a Remedy for the Spleen and Blushing, and several distempers occasion'd by the Stagnation of the Blood. It is likewise a School of Common Swearing; my young Master, who at first but minc'd an Oath, is taught there to mouth it gracefully, and to swear as he reads French, *ore rotundo*. Prophaneness was before to him in the Nature of his best Suit or holiday-cloathes; but upon frequenting the Play-house, Swearing, Cursing, and Lying, become like his Every-day coat, wastecoat, and Breeches. Now I say, common Swearing, a produce of this Country as plentiful as our Corn, thus cultivated by the Play-House, might, with Management, be of wonderful Advantage to the Nation, as a Projector of the Swearers Bank has prov'd at large. Lastly, the Stage in great Measure supports the Pulpit; for I know not what our Divines cou'd have to say there against the corruptions of the Age, but for the Play-house, which is the Seminary of them. From which it is plain, the Publick is a Gainer by the Play-House, and consequently ought to countenance it; and were I worthy to put in my Word, or prescribe to my Betters, I could say in what Manner.

I have heard that a certain Gentleman has great designs to serve the Publick in the Way of their Diversions, with due Encouragement; that is, if he can obtain

some

some Concordatum-Money, or Yearly Salary, and handsome Contributions: And well he deserves the Favours of the Nation; for, to do him Justice, he has an uncommon Skill in Pastimes, having altogether apply'd his Studies that Way, and travell'd full many a League, by Sea and Land, for this his profound Knowledge. With that View alone he has visited all the Courts and Cities in Europe, and has been at more Pains than I shall speak of to take an exact Draught of the Play-House at the Hague, as a Model for a new one here. But what can a private Man do by himself in so publick an Undertaking? It is not to be doubted, but by his Care and Industry vast Improvements may be made, not only in our Play-House, (which is his immediate Province) but in our Gaming-Ordinaries Groom-Porter's, Lotteries, Bowling-Greens, Nine-pin Allies, Bear-Gardens, Cock-pits, Prizes, Puppet and Raree-shows, and whatever else concerns the elegant Divertisements of this Town. He is truly an Original Genius, and I felicitate this our Capital City on his Residence here, where I wish him long to live and flourish for the Good of the Commonwealth.

Once more: If any farther Applications shall be made on t'other Side, to obtain a Charter for a Bank here, I presume to make a Request, that Poetry may be a Sharer in that Privilege, being a Fund as real, and to the full as well grounded, as our Stocks; but I fear our Neighbours, who envy our Wit, as much as they do our Wealth or Trade, will give no Encouragement to either. I believe also, it might be proper to erect a Corporation of Poets in this City. I have been Idle enough in my Time, to make a Computation of Wits here, and do find we have three hundred performing Poets and upwards, in and about this Town, reckoning six Score to the Hundred, and allowing for Demi's like Pint Bottles; including

including also the several Denominations of Imitators, Translators, and Familiar-Letter-Writers, &c. One of these last has lately entertain'd the town with an original Piece, and such a one as, I dare say, the late British Spectator, in his Decline, would have call'd, An excellent Specimen of the true Sublime; or, A noble Poem; or, a fine Copy of Verses, on a Subject perfectly new, (the Author himself) and had given it a Place amongst his latest Lucubrations.

But, as I was saying, so many Poets, I am confident, are sufficient to furnish out a Corporation in point of Number. Then for the several Degrces of subordinate Members requisite to such a Body, there can be no Want; for altho' we have not one Masterly Poet, yet we abound with Wardens and Beadles, having a Multitude of Poetasters, Poetito's, Parcel-Poets, Poet-Apes, and Philo-Poets, and many of inferior Attainments in Wit, but strong Inclinations to it, which are by Odds more than all the rest. Nor shall I ever be at Ease, 'till this project of mine (for which I am heartily thankful to myself) shall be reduced to Practice. I long to see the Day, when our Poets will be a regular and distinct Body, and wait upon our Lord-mayor on publick Days, like other good Citizens, in Gowns turn'd up with Green instead of lawrels; and when I myself, who make this Proposal, shall be free of their Company.

To conclude, what if our Government had a Poet-Laureat here, as in England? What if our University had a Professor of Poetry here as in England? What if our Lord-Mayor had a City Bard here, as in England? And, to refine upon England, What if every Corporation, Parish, and Ward in this Town, had a Poet in Fee, as they have not in England? Lastly, What if every one so qualify'd were obliged to add one more than usual to

the

the Number of his Domesticks, and besides a fool and a Chaplain, (which are often united in one Person) would retain a Poet in his Family; for, perhaps, a Rhimer is as necessary amongst Servants of a House, as a Dobben with his Bells, at the Head of a Team: But these Things I leave to the Wisdom of my Superiors.

While I have been directing your Pen, I should not forget to govern my own, which has already exceeded the Bounds of a Letter: I must therefore take my Leave abruptly, and desire you, without farther Ceremony, to believe that I am, Sir,

Your most humble Servant.

Dec. 1. 1720.

A LETTER TO A YOUNG LADY ON HER MARRIAGE

According to the *Memoirs* of the gossipy Mrs. Pilkington, this letter was addressed to Miss Betty Moore (at the time of her marriage to Mr. George Rochfort), who was not amused by its contents. Editors of Swift have debated among themselves with no little feeling the question of Swift's lack of chivalry towards Lady Betty, and towards ladies in general. The displeasure of Lady Betty is surely immaterial to us now, and we may concede the discourtesy to the fair sex, if that will help. Swift's age, profession, and position as adviser to the very young girl gave him the opportunity to tell her some homely truths, candidly and rudely—truths which the amenities of social life would have prevented others from disclosing. Most men readers (and perhaps some ladies) will conclude in private what they may or may not be willing to admit to others: that Swift has here stated the case for husbands with commendable vigour. It is, of course, true that romance is utterly lacking in the married state he represents here, as elsewhere in his writings. Swift knew he was not a poet, and he was sensible enough to leave to others the task of rendering homage to love.

The text reproduced is that of the earliest known edition, Swift's *Miscellanies*, vol. ii, 1727.

MADAM,

THE hurry and impertinence of receiving and paying Visits on account of your Marriage, being now over, you are beginning to enter into a Course of Life, where you will want much Advice to divert you from falling into many Errors, Fopperies, and Follies to which your Sex is subject. I have always borne an entire Friendship to your Father and Mother; and the Person they have chosen for your Husband, hath been for some Years past my particular Favorite; I have long wished you might come together, because I hoped, that from the goodness of your Disposition, and by following the Council of wise Friends, you might in time make your self worthy of him. Your Parents were so far in the right, that they did not produce you much into the World, whereby you avoided many wrong Steps which others have taken; and have fewer ill Impressions to be removed: But they failed, as it is generally the Case, in too much neglecting to cultivate your Mind; without which it is impossible to acquire or preserve the Friendship and Esteem of a Wise Man, who soon grows weary of acting the Lover and treating his Wife like a Mistress, but wants a reasonable Companion, and a true Friend through every Stage of his Life. It must be therefore your Business to qualify your self for those Offices, wherein I will not fail to be your Director as long as I shall think you deserve it, by letting you know how you are to act, and what you ought to avoid.

And beware of despising or neglecting my Instructions, whereon will depend, not only your making a good figure in the World, but your own real Happiness, as well as that of the Person who ought to be the Dearest to you.

I must therefore desire you in the first place to be very slow in changing the modest behaviour of a Virgin: It is

usual

usual in young wives before they have been many Weeks married, to assume a bold, forward Look and manner of Talking; as if they intended to signify in all Companies, that they were no longer Girls, and consequently that their whole Demeanor, before they got a Husband, was all but a Countenance and Constraint upon their Nature: Whereas, I suppose, if the Votes of wise Men were gathered, a very great Majority would be in favour of those Ladies, who after they were entered into that State, rather chose to double their portion of Modesty and Reservedness.

I must likewise warn you strictly against the least degree of Fondness to your Husband before any Witness whatsoever, even before your nearest Relations, or the very Maids of your Chamber. This proceeding is so exceeding odious and disgustful to all who have either good Breeding or good Sense, that they assign two very unamiable Reasons for it; the one is gross Hypocrisy, and the other has too bad a Name to mention. If there is any difference to be made, your Husband is the lowest Person in Company, either at Home or Abroad, and every Gentleman present has a better claim to all marks of Civility and Distinction from you. Conceal your Esteem and Love in your own Breast, and reserve your kind Looks and Language for Private hours, which are so many in the Four and Twenty, that they will afford time to employ a Passion as exalted as any that was ever described in a French Romance.

Upon this Head, I should likewise advise you to differ in Practice from those Ladies who affect abundance of Uneasiness while their Husbands are abroad, start with every Knock at the Door, and ring the Bell incessantly for the Servants to let in their Master; will not eat a bit at Dinner or Supper if the Husband happens to stay out, and

and receive him at his return with such a Medly of chiding and kindness, and catechising him where he has been, that a Shrew from Billingsgate would be a more easy and eligible Companion.

Of the same leaven are those Wives, who when their Husbands are gone a Journey, must have a Letter every Post, upon pain of Fits and Hystericks, and a day must be fixed for their return home without the least allowance for Business, or Sickness, or Accidents, or Weather: Upon which, I can only say that in my observation, those Ladies who were apt to make the greatest clutter upon such occasions, would liberally have paid a Messenger for bringing them news that their Husbands had broken their Necks upon the Road.

You will perhaps be offended when I advise you to abate a little of that violent Passion for fine Cloaths, so predominant in your Sex. It is a little hard, that ours, for whose sake you wear them, are not admitted to be of your Council: I may venture to assure you that we will make an abatement at any time of Four Pounds a yard in a Brocade, if the Ladies will but allow a suitable addition of care in the Cleanliness and Sweetness of their Persons: For, the satyrical part of mankind will needs believe, that it is not impossible, to be very fine and very filthy; and that the Capacities of a Lady are sometimes apt to fall short in cultivating Cleanliness and Finery together. I shall only add, upon so tender a subject, what a pleasant Gentleman said concerning a silly Woman of quality; that nothing could make her supportable but cutting off her Head, for his Ears were offended by her Tongue, and his Nose by her Hair and Teeth.

I am wholly at a loss how to advise you in the choice of Company, which, however, is a point of as great importance as any in your life. If your general acquaintance be

among

among Ladies who are your equals or superiors, provided they have nothing of what is commonly called an ill Reputation, you think you are safe; and this in the style of the world will pass for Good company. Whereas I am afraid it will be hard for you to pick out one Female-acquaintance in this town, from whom you will not be in manifest danger of contracting some foppery, affectation, vanity, folly, or vice. Your only safe way of conversing with them, is by a firm Resolution to proceed in your practice and behaviour directly contrary to whatever they shall say or do: And this I take to be a good General Rule, with very few exceptions. For instance, In the doctrines they usually deliver to young-married-women for managing their Husbands; their several accounts of their own Conduct in that particular to recommend it to your imitation; the Reflections they make upon others of their Sex for acting differently; their directions how to come off with Victory upon any dispute or quarrel you may have with your Husband; the Arts by which you may discover and practice upon his Weak sides; when to work by flattery and insinuation, when to melt him with tears, and when to engage with a high hand. In these, and a thousand other cases, it will be prudent to retain as many of their lectures in your Memory as you can, and then determine to act in full Opposition to them all.

I hope your Husband will interpose his authority to limit you in the trade of Visiting: Half a dozen fools are in all conscience as many as you should require; and it will be sufficient for you to see them twice a year: For I think the fashion does not exact, that Visits should be paid to Friends.

I advise that your company at home should consist of Men, rather than Women. To say the truth, I never yet knew a tolerable Woman to be fond of her own Sex: I
confess,

confess, when both are mixt and well chosen, and put their best qualities forward, there may be an intercourse of civility and good-will; which, with the addition of some degree of sense, can make conversation or any amusement agreeable. But a Knot of Ladies, got together by themselves, is a very school of Impertinence and Detraction, and it is well if those be the worst.

Let your Men-acquaintance be of your Husband's choice, and not recommended to you by any She-companions; because they will certainly fix a Coxcomb upon you, and it will cost you some time and pains before you can arrive at the knowledge of distinguishing such a one from a Man of Sense.

Never take a Favourite-waiting-maid into your Cabinet-Council, to entertain you with Histories of those Ladies whom she hath formerly served, of their Diversions and their Dresses; to insinuate how great a Fortune you brought, and how little you are allowed to squander; to appeal to her from your Husband, and to be determined by her Judgment, because you are sure it will be always for you; to receive and discard Servants by her approbation or dislike; to engage you by her insinuations into misunderstandings with your best Friends; to represent all things in false colours, and to be the common Emissary of Scandal.

But the Grand affair of your life will be to gain and preserve the Friendship and Esteem of your Husband. You are married to a Man of good education and learning, of an excellent understanding, and an exact taste. It is true, and it is happy for you, that these Qualities in him are adorned with great Modesty, a most amiable Sweetness of Temper, and an unusual disposition to Sobriety and Virtue: But neither Good-Nature nor Virtue will suffer him to esteem you against his Judgment; and

 although

although he is not capable of using you ill, yet you will in time grow a thing indifferent, and perhaps, contemptible; unless you can supply the loss of Youth and Beauty with more durable Qualities. You have but a very few years to be young and handsome in the eyes of the World; and as few months to be so in the eyes of a Husband, who is not a Fool; for I hope you do not still dream of Charms and Raptures, which Marriage ever did, and ever will, put a sudden end to. Besides yours was a match of Prudence and common Good-liking, without any mixture of that ridiculous Passion which has no Being but in Play-Books and Romances.

You must therefore use all endeavours to attain to some degree of those Accomplishments which your Husband most values in other People, and for which he is most valued himself. You must improve your Mind, by closely pursuing such a Method of Study as I shall direct or approve of. You must get a collection of History and Travels which I will recommend to you, and spend some hours every day in reading them, and making extracts from them if your Memory be weak. You must invite Persons of knowledge and understanding to an acquaintance with you, by whose Conversation you may learn to correct your Taste and Judgment; and when you can bring yourself to comprehend and relish the good Sense of others, you will arrive in time to think rightly yourself, and to become a Reasonable and Agreeable Companion. This must produce in your Husband a true Rational Love and Esteem for you, which old Age will not diminish. He will have a regard for your Judgment and Opinion in matters of the greatest weight; you will be able to entertain each other without a Third Person to relieve you by finding Discourse. The endowments of your Mind will even make your Person more agreeable to him; and when

you

you are alone, your Time will not lie heavy upon your hands for want of some trifling Amusement.

As little respect as I have for the generality of your Sex, it hath sometimes moved me with pity, to see the Lady of the House forced to withdraw immediately after Dinner, and this in Families where there is not much drinking; as if it were an established Maxim, that Women are uncapable of all Conversation. In a Room where both Sexes meet, if the Men are discoursing upon any general Subject, the Ladies never think it their business to partake in what passes, but in a separate Club entertain each other, with the price and choice of Lace and Silk, and what Dresses they liked or disapproved at the Church or the Play-house. And when you are among yourselves, how naturally, after the first Complements, do you apply your hands to each other's Lappets and Ruffles and Mantua's, as if the whole business of your Lives, and the publick concern of the World, depended upon the Cut or Colour of your Dresses. As Divines say, that some People take more pains to be Damned, than it would cost them to be Saved; so your Sex employs more thought, memory, and application to be Fools, than would serve to make them wise and useful. When I reflect on this, I cannot conceive you to be Human Creatures, but a sort of Species hardly a degree above a Monkey; who has more diverting Tricks than any of you; is an Animal less mischievous and expensive, might in time be a tolerable Critick in Velvet and Brocade, and for ought I know wou'd equally become them.

I would have you look upon Finery as a necessary Folly, as all great Ladies did whom I have ever known: I do not desire you to be out of the fashion, but to be the last and least in it: I expect that your Dress shall be one degree lower than your Fortune can afford; and in your own

own heart I would wish you to be an utter Contemner of all Distinctions which a finer Petticoat can give you; because it will neither make you richer, handsomer, younger, better natur'd, more vertuous, or wise, than if it hung upon a Peg.

If you are in company with Men of learning, though they happen to discourse of Arts and Sciences out of your compass, yet you will gather more advantage by list'ning to them, than from all the nonsense and frippery of your own Sex; but, if they be Men of Breeding as well as Learning, they will seldom engage in any Conversation where you ought not to be a hearer, and in time have your part. If they talk of the Manners and Customs of the several Kingdoms of Europe, of Travels into remoter Nations, of the state of their own Country, or of the great Men and Actions of Greece and Rome; if they give their judgment upon English and French Writers, either in Verse or Prose, or of the nature and limits of Virtue and Vice, it is a shame for an English Lady not to relish such Discourses, not to improve by them, and endeavour by Reading and Information, to have her share in those Entertainments; rather than turn aside, as it is the usual custom, and consult with the Woman who sits next her, about a new Cargo of Fans.

It is a little hard that not one Gentleman's daughter in a thousand should be brought to read or understand her own natural tongue, or be judge of the easiest Books that are written in it: As any one may find, who can have the patience to hear them, when they are disposed to mangle a Play or Novel, where the least word out of the common road is sure to disconcert them; and it is no wonder, when they are not so much as taught to spell in their childhood, nor can ever attain to it in their whole lives. I advise you therefore to read aloud, more or less, every day to your

Husband,

Husband, if he will permit you, or to any other friend, (but not a Female one) who is able to set you right; and as for spelling, you may compass it in time by making Collections from the Books you read.

I know very well that those who are commonly called Learned Women, have lost all manner of Credit by their impertinent Talkativeness and Conceit of themselves; but there is an easy remedy for this, if you once consider, that after all the pains you may be at, you never can arrive in point of learning to the perfection of a School-boy. But the Reading I would advise you to, is only for improvement of your own good Sense, which will never fail of being Mended by Discretion. It is a wrong method, and ill choice of Books, that makes those Learned Ladies just so much worse for what they have read. And therefore it shall be my care to direct you better, a task for which I take my self to be not ill qualified; because I have spent more time, and have had more opportunities than many others, to observe and discover from what sources the various follies of Women are derived.

Pray observe how insignificant things are the common race of Ladies, when they have passed their Youth and Beauty; how contemptible they appear to the Men, and yet more contemptible to the younger part of their own Sex; and have no relief but in passing their afternoons in visits, where they are never acceptable; and their evenings at cards among each other; while the former part of the day is spent in spleen and envy, or in vain endeavours to repair by art and dress the ruins of Time: Whereas I have known Ladies at Sixty, to whom all the polite part of the Court and Town paid their addresses, without any further view than that of enjoying the pleasure of their conversation.

I am ignorant of any one quality that is amiable in a

Man,

Man, which is not equally so in a Woman: I do not except even Modesty and Gentleness of nature. Nor do I know one vice or folly which is not equally detestable in both. There is indeed one infirmity which seems to be generally allowed you, I mean that of Cowardice. Yet there should seem to be something very capricious, that when Women profess their admiration for a Colonel or a Captain on account of his Valour, they should fancy it a very graceful becoming quality in themselves to be afraid of their own shadows; to scream in a Barge when the weather is calmest, or in a Coach at the Ring; to run from a Cow at a hundred yards' distance; to fall into fits at the sight of a Spider, an Earwig, or a Frog. At least, if Cowardice be a sign of Cruelty, (as it is generally granted) I can hardly think it an accomplishment so desirable as to be thought worth improving by Affectation.

And as the same Virtues equally become both Sexes, so there is no quality whereby Women endeavour to distinguish themselves from Men, for which they are not just so much the worse; except that only of Reservedness; which, however, as you generally manage it, is nothing else but Affectation or Hypocrisy. For as you cannot too much discountenance those of our Sex, who presume to take unbecoming liberty before you; so you ought to be wholly unconstrain'd in the company of Deserving Men, when you have had sufficient experience of their discretion.

There is never wanting in this Town, a tribe of bold, swaggering, rattling Ladies, whose Talents pass among Coxcombs for Wit and Humour; their excellency lies in rude choquing Expressions, and what they call running a Man down. If a Gentleman in their Company happens to have any Blemish in his Birth or Person, if any misfortune hath befallen his Family or himself, for which he is ashamed,

ashamed, they will be sure to give him broad Hints of it without any Provocation. I would recommend you to the acquaintance of a common Prostitute, rather than to that of such Termagants as these. I have often thought that no Man is obliged to suppose such Creatures to be Women; but to treat them like insolent Rascals disguised in Female Habits, who ought to be stripp'd and kick'd down Stairs.

I will add one thing although it be a little out of place, which is to desire that you will learn to value and esteem your Husband for those good Qualities which he really possesseth, and not to fancy others in him which he certainly hath not. For although this latter is generally understood to be a mark of Love, yet it is indeed nothing but Affectation or ill Judgment. It is true, he wants so very few Accomplishments, that you are in no great danger of erring on this side: But my Caution is occasion'd by a Lady of your Acquaintance, married to a very valuable Person, whom yet she is so unfortunate as to be always commending for those Perfections to which he can least pretend.

I can give you no Advice upon the Article of Expence, only I think you ought to be well informed how much your Husband's Revenue amounts to, and be so good a Computer as to keep within it, in that part of the Management which falls to your share; and not to put yourself in the number of those Politick Ladies, who think they gain a great Point when they have teazed their Husbands to buy them a new Equipage, a lac'd Head, or a fine Petticoat, without once considering what long Scores remain unpaid to the Butcher.

I desire you will keep this Letter in your Cabinet, and often examine impartially your whole Conduct by it: And so God bless you, and make you a fair Example to your

Sex,

Sex, and a perpetual Comfort to your Husband and your Parents.

I am, with great Truth and Affection,

Madam,

Your most faithful Friend

and humble Servant.

AN ESSAY ON MODERN EDUCATION

In this essay we have a sample of Swift's occasional contributions to periodicals, in which his incisive wit affords a sharp contrast to the conservative pleading of Addison and Steele. Swift was not so fearful of colliding with the opinions of his coffee-house readers as were the editors of the *Tatler* and the *Spectator*. Education to-day has lost some of the features with which the essay is concerned, but by no means all.

The essay first appeared in the Irish *Intelligencer*, No. IX, 1728. The text reproduced is that of the reprint of the nineteen numbers of the *Intelligencer* in one volume, Dublin, 1729. In the original issue the title of No. IX read, 'The Foolish Methods of Education among the Nobility.

FROM frequently reflecting upon the Course and Method of educating Youth in this and a neighbouring Kingdom, with the general Success and Consequence thereof, I am come to this Determination, That Education is always the worse in Proportion to the Wealth of and Grandeur of the Parents; nor do I doubt in the least, that if the whole World were now under the Dominion of one Monarch (provided I might be allowed to chuse where he should fix the Seat of his Empire) the only Son and Heir of that Monarch, would be the worst educated Mortal, that ever was born since the Creation; and I doubt, the same Proportion will hold through all Degrees and Titles, from an Emperor downwards, to the common Gentry.

I do not say, that this hath been always the Case; for in better Times it was directly otherwise, and a Scholar may fill half his Greek and Roman shelves with Authors of the noblest Birth, as well as highest Virtue: Nor, do I tax all Nations at present with this Defect, for I know there are some to be excepted, and particularly Scotland, under all the Disadvantages of its Climate and Soil, if that Happiness be not rather owing even to those very Disadvantages. What is then to be done, if this Reflection must fix on two Countries, which will be most ready to take Offence, and which of all others it will be least prudent or safe to offend?

But there is one Circumstance yet more dangerous and lamentable: For if, according to the *Postulatum* already laid down, the higher Quality any Youth is of, he is in greater Likelyhood to be worse educated; it behoves me to dread, and keep far from the Verge of *Scandalum Magnatum*.

Retracting therefore that hazardous *Postulatum*, I shall venture no further at present than to say, that perhaps some

some additional Care in educating the Sons of Nobility and principal Gentry, might not be ill employed. If this be not delivered with Softness enough, I must for the future be silent.

In the mean time, let me ask only two Questions, which relate to England. I ask first, how it comes about, that for above sixty Years past, the chief Conduct of Affairs hath been generally placed in the Hands of New-men, with very few Exceptions? The Noblest Blood of England having been shed in the grand Rebellion, many great Families became extinct, or supported only by Minors. When the King was restored, very few of those Lords remained, who began, or at least had improved their Education, under the happy Reign of King James, or King Charles I. of which Lords the two principal were the Marquis of Ormond, and the Earl of Southampton. The Minors have, or had, during the Rebellion and Usurpation, either received too much Tincture of bad Principles from those fanatick Times, or coming to Age at the Restoration, fell into the Vices of that dissolute Reign.

I date from this Æra, the corrupt Method of Education among us, and the Consequence thereof, in the Necessity the Crown lay under of introducing New-men into the chief Conduct of publick Affairs, or to the Office of what we now call Prime Ministers, Men of Art, Knowledge, Application and Insinuation, merely for Want of a Supply among the Nobility. They were generally (though not always) of good Birth, sometimes younger Brothers, at other Times such, who although inheriting good Estates, yet happened to be well educated, and provided with Learning; such under that King, were Hyde, Bridgeman, Clifford, Osborn, Godolphin, Ashley-Cooper: Few or none under the short Reign of King James II. Under King William; Sommers, Mountague, Churchil, Vernon, Boyle,

and

and many others: Under the Queen; Harley, St. John, Harcourt, Trevor, who indeed were Persons of the best private Families, but unadorn'd with Titles. So in the following Reign, Mr. Robert Walpole, was for many Years Prime Minister, in which Post he still happily continues: His Brother Horace is Ambassador Extraordinary to France. Mr. Addison and Mr. Craggs, without the least Allowance to support them, have been Secretaries of State.

If the Facts have been thus for above sixty Years past (whereof I could with a little further Recollection produce many more Instances) I would ask again, how it hath happened, that in a Nation plentifully abounding with Nobility, so great Share in the most competent Parts of publick Management, hath been for so long a Period chiefly entrusted to Commoners, unless some Omissions or Defects of the highest Import, may be charged upon those, to whom the Care of educating our Noble Youth hath been committed? For, if there be any Difference between human Creatures in the Point of natural Parts, as we usually call them, it should seem that the Advantage lies on the Side of Children, born from noble and wealthy Parents; the same traditional Sloth and Luxury which render their Body weak and effeminate, perhaps refining and giving a freer Motion to the Spirits, beyond what can be expected from the gross, robust Issue of meaner Mortals. Add to this, the peculiar Advantages, which all young Noblemen possess, by the Privileges of their Birth. Such as a free Access to Courts, and a universal Deference paid to their Persons.

But as my Lord Bacon chargeth it for a Fault on Princes, that they are impatient to compass Ends, without giving themselves the Trouble of consulting or executing the Means: So perhaps it may be the Disposition

tion of young Nobles, either from the Indulgence of Parents, Tutors and Governors, or their own Inactivity, that they expect the Accomplishments of a good Education, without the least Expence of Time or Study, to acquire them.

What I said last, I am ready to retract; for the Case is infinitely worse; and the very Maxims set up to direct modern Education, are enough to destroy all the Seeds of Knowledge, Honour, Wisdom and Virtue among us. The current Opinion prevails, that the Study of Greek and Latin is Loss of Time; that publick Schools by mingling the Sons of Noblemen with those of the Vulgar, engage the former in bad Company; that Whipping breaks the Spirits of Lads well born; that Universities make young Men Pedants; that to dance, fence, speak French, and know how to behave your self among great Persons of both Sexes, comprehends the whole Duty of a Gentleman.

I cannot but think this wise System of Education, hath been much cultivated among us by those Worthies of the Army, who during the last War, returning from Flanders at the Close of each Campaign, became the Dictators of Behaviour, Dress, and Politeness, to all those Youngsters, who frequent Chocolate-Coffee-Gaming-Houses, Drawing-Rooms, Operas, Levees and Assemblies; where a Colonel by his Pay, Perquisites and Plunder, was qualified to outshine many Peers of the Realm; and by the Influence of an exotick Habit and Demeanor, added to other foreign Accomplishments, gave the Law to the whole Town, and was copyed as the Standard-Pattern of whatever was refined in Dress, Equipage, Conversation, or Diversions.

I remember in those Times, an admired Original of that Vocation, sitting in a Coffee-house near two Gentlemen, whereof one was of the Clergy, who were engag'd in some Discourse

Discourse that savoured of Learning; this Officer thought fit to interpose, and professing to deliver the Sentiments of his Fraternity, as well as his own (and probably did so of too many among them) turning to the Clergy-Man, spoke in the following Manner, 'D——n me, Doctor, say what you will, the Army is the only School for Gentlemen. Do you think my Lord Marlborough beat the French with Greek and Latin. D——n me, a Scholar when he comes into good Company, what is he but an Ass? D——n me, I would be glad by G-d to see any of your Scholars with his Nouns, and his Verbs, and his Philosophy, and Trigonometry, what a Figure he would make at a Siege or Blockade, or rencountring——D——n me,' &c. After which he proceeded with a Volley of Military Terms, less significant, sounding worse, and harder to be understood than any that were ever coined by the Commentators upon Aristotle. I would not here be thought to charge the Soldiery with Ignorance and Contempt of Learning, without allowing Exceptions, of which I have known many; but however, the worse Example, especially in a great Majority, will certainly prevail.

I have heard, that the late Earl of Oxford, in the Time of his Ministry, never pass'd by White's Chocolate-House (the common Rendezvous of infamous Sharpers, and noble Cullies) without bestowing a Curse upon that famous Academy, as the Bane of half the English Nobility. I have likewise been told another Passage concerning that great Minister, which, because it gives a humorous Idea of one principal Ingredient in modern Education, take as followeth. Le-Sack, the famous French Dancing-master, in great Admiration, asked a Friend, whether it were true, that Mr. Harley was made an Earl and Lord-Treasurer? And finding it confirmed, said; 'Well, I wonder what the Devil the Queen could see in him; for I attended him

two

two Years, and he was the greatest Dunce that ever I taught.'

Another Hindrance to good Education, and I think the greatest of any, is that pernicious Custom in rich and noble Families, of entertaining French Tutors in their Houses. These wretched Pedagogues are enjoyned by the Father, to take special Care that the Boy shall be perfect in his French; by the Mother, that Master must not walk till he is hot, nor be suffered to play with other Boys, nor be wet in his Feet, nor daub his Cloaths, and to see that Dancing-master attends constantly, and does his Duty; she further insists, that the Child be not kept too long poring on his Book, because he is subject to sore eyes, and of a weakly Constitution.

By these Methods, the young Gentleman is in every Article as fully accomplished at eight Years old as at eight and twenty, Age adding only to the Growth of his Person and his Vice; so that if you should look at him in his Boy-hood thro' the magnifying End of a Perspective, and in his Manhood through the other, it would be impossible to spy any Difference; the same Airs, the same Strutt, the same Cock of his Hat, and Posture of his Sword (as far as the Change of Fashions will allow) the same Understanding, the same Compass of Knowledge, with the very same Absurdity, Impudence and Impertinence of Tongue.

He is taught from the Nursery, that he must inherit a great Estate, and hath no need to mind his Book, which is a Lesson he never forgets to the End of his Life. His chief Solace is to steal down, and play at Span-farthing with the Page, or young Black-a-moor, or little favourite Foot-boy, one of which is his principal Confident and Bosom-Friend.

There is one young Lord in this Town, who, by an unexampled

exampled Piece of good Fortune, was miraculously snatched out of the Gulph of Ignorance, confined to a publick School for a due Term of Years, well whipped when he deserved it, clad no better than his Comrades, and always their Play-fellow on the same Foot, had no Precedence in the School, but what was given him by his Merit, and lost it whenever he was negligent. It is well known how many Mutinies were bred at this unprecedented Treatment, what Complaints among his Relations, and other Great Ones of both Sexes; that his Stockings with silver Clocks were ravish'd from him; that he wore his own Hair; that his Dress was undistinguished; that he was not fit to appear at a Ball or Assembly, nor suffered to go to either: And it was with the utmost Difficulty, that he became qualified for his present Removal, where he may probably be farther persecuted, and possibly with Success, if the Firmness of a very worthy Governor, and his own good Dispositions will not preserve him. I confess, I cannot but wish he may go on in the Way he began, because I have a Curiosity to know by so singular an Experiment, whether Truth, Honour, Justice, Temperance, Courage, and good Sense, acquired by a School and College Education, may not produce a very tolerable Lad, although he should happen to fail in one or two of those Accomplishments, which in the general Vogue are held so important to the finishing of a Gentleman.

It is true, I have known an Academical Education to have been exploded in publick Assemblies; and have heard more than one or two Persons of high Rank declare, they could learn nothing more at Oxford and Cambridge, than to drink Ale and smoke Tobacco; wherein I firmly believed them, and could have added some hundred Examples from my own Observation in one of those Universities; but they all were of young Heirs sent thither, only

only for Form; either from Schools, where they were not suffered by their careful Parents to stay above three Months in the Year; or from under the Management of French Family-Tutors, who yet often attended them to their College, to prevent all Possibility of their Improvement: But, I never yet knew any one Person of Quality, who followed his Studies at the University, and carryed away his just Proportion of Learning, that was not ready upon all Occasions to celebrate and defend that Course of Education, and to prove a Patron of learned Men.

There is one Circumstance in a learned Education, which ought to have much Weight, even with those who have no Learning at all. The Books read at School and Colleges, are full of Incitements to Virtue, and Discouragements from Vice, drawn from the wisest Reasons, the strongest Motives, and the most influencing Examples. Thus, young Minds are filled early with an Inclination to Good, and an Abhorrence of Evil, both which encrease in them, according to the Advances they make in Literature; and, although they may be, and too often are, drawn by the Temptations of Youth, and the Opportunities of a large Fortune, into some Irregularities, when they come forward into the great World, it is ever with Reluctance and Compunction of Mind, because their Byass to Virtue still continues. They may stray sometimes out of Infirmity or Complyance, but they will soon return to the right Road, and keep it always in view. I speak only of those Excesses, which are too much the Attendants of Youth and warmer Blood; for, as to the Points of Honour, Truth, Justice, and other noble Gifts of the Mind, wherein the Temperature of the Body hath no Concern, they are seldom or ever known to be wild.

I have engaged my self very unwarily in too copious a Subject for so short a Paper. The present Scope I would

aim

aim at is to prove, that some Proportion of human Knowledge appears requisite to those, who, by their Birth or Fortune, are called to the making of Laws, and in a subordinate Way to the Execution of them; and that such Knowledge is not to be obtained without a Miracle, under the frequent, corrupt, and sottish Methods, of educating those, who are born to Wealth or Titles. For, I would have it remembered, that I do by no Means confine these Remarks to young Persons of Noble Birth; the same Errors running through all Families, where there is Wealth enough to afford, that their Sons (at least the Eldest) may be good for nothing. Why should my Son be a Scholar, when it is not intended that he should live by his Learning? By this Rule, if what is commonly said be true, that Money answereth all Things, why should my Son be honest, temperate, just, or charitable, since he hath no Intention to depend upon any of these Qualities for a Maintenance?

When all is done, perhaps upon the Whole, the Matter is not so bad as I would make it; and God, who worketh Good out of Evil, acting only by the ordinary Cause and Rule of Nature, permits this continual Circulation of human Things for his own unsearchable Ends. The Father grows rich by Avarice, Injustice, Oppression; he is a Tyrant in the Neighbourhood over Slaves and Beggars, whom he calls his Tenants. Why should he desire to have Qualities infused into his Son, which himself never possessed, or knew, or found the Want of in the Acquisition of his Wealth? The Son bred in Sloth and Idleness, becomes a Spendthrift, a Cully, a Profligate, and goes out of the World a Beggar, as his Father came in: Thus the former is punished for his own Sins, as well as for those of the latter. The Dunghil having raised a huge Mushroom of short Duration, is now spread to enrich other Mens

Lands

Lands. It is indeed of worse Consequence, where noble Families are gone to Decay; because their Titles and Privileges outlive their Estates: And, Politicians tell us, that nothing is more dangerous to the Publick, than a numerous Nobility without Merit or Fortune. But even here, God hath likewise prescribed some Remedy in the Order of Nature, so many great Families coming to an End by the Sloth, Luxury, and abandoned Lusts, which enervated their Breed through every Succession, producing gradually a more effeminate Race, wholly unfit for Propagation.

A TRUE AND FAITHFUL NARRATIVE OF WHAT PASSED IN LONDON

Seldom did Swift write genial, good-natured satire to better effect than in this little-known tract. The superstitious fears spread abroad by astrologers, the absurdities of dissenting 'fanatics' who announce the approaching end of the world, the hypocrisies of eleventh-hour penitents, the private morals of free-thinkers and maids-of-honour, are all touched in his happiest vein.

The immediate subject of ridicule was the self-anointed prophet, William Whiston (1667–1752), who founded a freak religious society in 1717, who wrote his own autobiography as well as a score of books expounding Biblical prophecies, who carried up and down England a model of the Tabernacle of Israel as he lectured on the rebuilding of Solomon's Temple, the restoration of Palestine to the Jews, and the Second Coming of Christ in 1766.

In the early miscellanies, this essay was variously ascribed to Swift, Pope, and Gay. Sir Walter Scott rightly assigned it to Swift. The internal evidence is almost conclusive, in the absence of other data. The text reproduced is that of Swift's *Miscellanies*, vol. iii, 1732.

ON Tuesday the 13th of October, Mr. Whiston held his Lecture near the Royal Exchange, to an Audience of Fourteen worthy Citizens, his Subscribers and constant Hearers. Besides these, there were five chance Auditors for that Night only, who had paid their Shillings a piece I think my self oblig'd to be very particular in this Relation, lest my Veracity should be suspected; which makes me appeal to the Men who were Present; of which number, I myself was one. Their Names are

Henry Watson, *Haberdasher.*
George Hancock, *Druggist.*
John Lewis, *Dry-Salter.*
William Jones, *Corn-Chandler.*
Henry Theobald, *Watchmaker.*
James Peters, *Draper.*
Thomas Floyer, *Silver-Smith.*
John Wells, *Brewer.*
Samuel Gregg, *Soap-Boyler.*
William Cooley, *Fish-monger.*
James Harper, *Hosier.*
Robert Tucker, *Stationer.*
George Ford, *Iron-monger.*
Daniel Lynch, *Apothecary.*

William Bennet,
David Somers,
Charles Lock, } *Apprentices.*
Leonard Daval,
Henry Croft,

Mr. Whiston began by acquainting us, that (contrary to his Advertisement) he thought himself in duty and conscience, oblig'd to change the subject Matter of his intended discourse.—Here he paus'd, and seem'd for a

short

short space as it were lost in Devotion and mental Prayer; after which, with great earnestness and vehemence he spake as follows.

'Friends and Fellow-Citizens, all speculative Science is at an end; the Period of all things is at Hand; on Friday next this World shall be no more. Put not your confidence in me, Brethren, for to-morrow Morning five Minutes after Five the Truth will be Evident; in that instant the Comet shall appear, of which I have heretofore warn'd you. As ye have heard, believe. Go hence, and prepare your Wives, your Families and Friends, for the universal Change.'

At this solemn and dreadful Prediction, the whole Society appear'd in the utmost Astonishment: but it would be unjust not to remember, that Mr. Whiston himself was in so calm a Temper, as to return a Shilling a piece to the Youths who had been disappointed of their Lecture, which I thought from a Man of his Integrity a convincing Proof of his own Faith in the Prediction.

As we thought it a Duty, in Charity to warn all Men; in two or three Hours the News had spread through the City. At first indeed, our report met with but little Credit, it being by our greatest dealers in Stocks, thought only a Court-Artifice to sink them, that some choice Favourites might purchase at a lower Rate; for the South-Sea, that very Evening fell five per Cent. the India, eleven; and all the other Funds in Proportion. But at the Court-end of the Town, our Attestations were intirely disbeliev'd or turn'd into ridicule; yet nevertheless the News spread every where, and was the subject-matter of all Conversation.

That very Night, (as I was credibly inform'd) Mr. Whiston was sent for to a great Lady, who is very curious in the Learned Sciences, and addicted to all the Specula-

tive

tive Doubts of the most able Philosophers; but he was not now to be found: and since at other times, he has been known not to decline that Honour, I make no doubt he conceal'd himself to attend to the great Business of his Soul: But whether it was the Lady's Faith, or Inquisitiveness, that occasion'd her to send, is a Point I shall not presume to determine. As for his being sent for to the Secretary's Office by a Messenger, it is now known to be a Matter notoriously false, and indeed at first it had little credit with me, that so Zealous and Honest a Man should be ordered into Custody, as a Seditious Preacher, who is known to be so well affected to the present happy Establishment.

'Twas now I reflected with exceeding trouble and sorrow, that I had disus'd Family Prayers for above five Years, and (though it hath been a Custom of late intirely neglected by Men of any Business or Station) I determin'd within myself no longer to omit so reasonable and religious a Duty. I acquainted my Wife with my Intentions: But two or three Neighbours having been engaged to Sup with us that Night, and many Hours being unwarily spent at Cards, I was prevail'd upon by her, to put it off till the next Day; she reasoning, that it would be time enough to take off the Servants from their Business (which this practice must infallibly occasion for an Hour or two every Day) after the Comet had made its appearance.

Zachary Bowen, a Quaker, and my next Neighbour, had no sooner heard of the Prophecy but he made me a Visit. I informed him of every thing I had heard, but found him quite obstinate in his unbelief; for, said he, be comforted, Friend, thy tidings are Impossibilities, for were these things to happen, they must have been foreseen by some of our Brethren. This indeed (as in all other spiritual

Cases

Cases with this set of People) was his only reason against believing me; and, as he was fully persuaded that the Prediction was erroneous, he in a very neighbourly Manner admonished me against selling my Stock, at the present low Price; which, he said, beyond dispute must have a Rise before Monday, when this unreasonable Consternation should be over.

But on Wednesday Morning (I believe to the exact Calculation of Mr. Whiston) the Comet appear'd: For at three Minutes after five by my own Watch, I saw it. He indeed, foretold that it would be seen at five Minutes after Five, but as the best Watches may be a Minute or too slow, I am apt to think his Calculation Just to a Minute.

In less than a quarter of an Hour, all Cheap-side was crouded with a vast concourse of People, and notwithstanding it was so early, 'tis thought that through all that part of the Town, there was not Man, Woman or Child, except the Sick, or Infirm, left in their Beds. From my own Balcony, I am confident, I saw several Thousands in the Street, and counted at least seventeen who were upon their Knees, and seem'd in actual Devotion. Eleven of them indeed appear'd to be old Women of about Fourscore; The Six others, were Men in an advanc'd Life, but (as I could guess) two of them might be under Seventy.

It is highly probable, that an event of this Nature, may be pass'd over by the greater Historians of our Times, as conducing very little or nothing to the unravelling and laying open the deep Schemes of Politicians and Mysterys of State; for which reason, I thought it might not be unacceptable to record the Facts, which in the Space of three Days came to my Knowledge, either as an Eye-witness, or from unquestionable Authorities; nor can I think this Narrative will be intirely

without

without its Use, as it may enable us to form a more just Idea of our Countrymen in general, particularly in regard to their Faith, Religion, Morals and Politicks.

Before Wednesday Noon, the Belief was universal that the Day of Judgment was at Hand, insomuch, that a Waterman of my acquaintance told me he counted no less than one Hundred and twenty Three Clergymen, who had been Ferry'd over to Lambeth before twelve a-Clock: these, 'tis said, went thither, to Petition, that a short Prayer might be Penn'd and Order'd, there being none in the Service upon that occasion. But as in things of this Nature, it is necessary that the Comet be consulted, their request was not immediately comply'd with; and this I affirm to be the true and only Reason that the Churches were not that Morning so well attended; and is in no ways to be imputed to the Fears and Consternation of the Clergy, with which the Free-thinkers have since very unjustly reproach'd them.

My Wife and I went to Church (where we had not been for many Years on a Week-day) and, with a very large Congregation, were disappointed of the Service. But (what will be scarce credible) by the carelessness of a 'Prentice, in our abscence, we had a Piece of fine Cambric carried off by a Shop-lifter, so little impression was yet made on the minds of those wicked Women!

I cannot omit the care of a particular Director of the Bank; I hope the worthy and wealthy Knight will forgive me that I endeavour to do him Justice; for it was unquestionably owing to Sir G— H—'s sagacity that all the Fire-Offices were requir'd to have a particular Eye upon the Bank of England. Let it be recorded to his Praise that in the general hurry, this struck him as his nearest and tenderest concern; but the next Day in the Evening, after having taken due care of all his Books, Bills and Bonds,

Bonds, I was inform'd, his mind was wholly turn'd upon Spiritual Matters; yet, ever and anon, he could not help expressing his resentment against the Tories and Jacobites, to whom he imputed that sudden Run upon the Bank which happen'd on this occasion.

A Great Man (whom at this time it may not be prudent to name) employ'd all the Wednesday Morning, to make up such an Account as might appear fair, in case he should be call'd upon to produce it on the Friday; but was forced to desist, after having for several Hours together attempted it, not being able to bring himself to a resolution to trust the many hundred Articles of his secret Transactions upon Paper.

Another seem'd to be very melancholy, which his flatterers imputed to his dread of losing his Power in a Day or two; but I rather take it, that his chief concern was, the Terror of being try'd in a Court that could not be influenc'd, and where a Majority of Voices could avail him nothing. It was observ'd too, that he had few Visiters that Day; this added so much to his Mortification, that he read thro' the first Chapter of the Book of Job, and wept over it bitterly; in short, he seem'd a true Penitent in every thing but in Charity to his Neighbour. No business was that Day done in his Compting-House; 'tis said too, that he was advis'd to Restitution, but I never heard that he comply'd with it any farther than in giving half a Crown a Piece to several craz'd, and starving Creditors, who attended in the outward Room.

Three of the Maids of Honour sent to countermand their Birth-day Cloaths; two of them burnt all their Collections of Novels and Romances, and sent to a Bookseller's in Pall-mall to buy each of them a Bible, and Taylor's *Holy Living and Dying*. But I must do all of them the Justice to acknowledge, that they shew'd a very

decent

decent Behaviour in the drawing-Room, and restrain'd themselves from those innocent Freedoms and little Levities so commonly incident to young Ladies of their Profession. So many Birth-day Suits were countermanded the next Day, that most of the Taylors and Mantua-makers discharg'd all their Journey-Men and Women. A grave elderly Lady of great Erudition and Modesty who visits these young Ladies, seem'd to be extreamly shock'd, by the Apprehensions that She was to appear naked before the whole World; and no less so, that all Mankind was to appear naked before her; which might so much divert her Thoughts, as to incapacitate her to give ready and apt Answers to the Interrogatories that might be made her. The Maids of Honour who had both Modesty and Curiosity, could not imagine the Sight so disagreeable as was represented; nay, one of them went so far as to say, she perfectly long'd to see it; for it could not be so indecent, when every body was to be alike: and they had a Day or two to prepare themselves, to be seen in that condition. Upon this reflection, each of them order'd a Bathing-Tub to be got ready that Evening, and a Looking-Glass to be set by it. So much are these young Ladies both by Nature and Custom addicted to cleanly appearance.

A West-Country Gentleman told me, he got a Church-Lease fill'd up that Morning, for the same Sum which had been refus'd for three Years successively. I must impute this meerly to accident; for I cannot imagine that any Divine could take the advantage of his Tenant, in so unhandsome a Manner; or that the shortness of the Life was in the least his Consideration; though I have heard the same worthy Prelate aspers'd and malign'd since upon this very Account.

The Term being so near, the alarm among the Lawyers was

was inexpressible, though some of them, I was told, were so vain as to promise themselves some advantages in making their defence, by being vers'd in the Practice of our earthly Courts. It is said too, that some of the chief Pleaders were heard to express great satisfaction, that there had been but few State-Tryals of late Years. Several Attorneys demanded the return of Fees that had been given the Lawyers: but it was answered, that the Fee was undoubtedly charg'd to their Client, and that they could not connive at such Injustice, as to suffer it to be sunk in the Attorney's Pockets. Our sage and learned Judges had great consolation, insomuch as they had not pleaded at the Bar for several Years; the Barristers rejoyced in that they were not Attornies, and the Attornies felt no less satisfaction that they were not Petti-foggers, Scriveners, and other meaner Officers of the Law.

As to the Army, far be it from me to conceal the Truth. Every Soldier's behaviour was as undismayed, and undaunted, as if nothing was to happen: I impute not this to their want of Faith, but to their martial Disposition; though I cannot help thinking they commonly accompany their commands with more Oaths than are requisite, of which there was no remarkable diminution this Morning on the Parade in St. James's Park. But possibly it was by choice, and on consideration, that they continued this way of Expression, not to intimidate the common Soldiers, or give occasion to suspect that even the Fear of Damnation could make any impression upon their Superior Officers. A Duel was fought the same Morning between two Colonels, not occasion'd, (as was reported) because the one was put over the other's Head; that being a Point which might at such a Juncture have been accommodated by the Mediation of Friends; but as this

was

was upon the account of a Lady, 'twas judg'd it could not be put off at this Time, above all others, but demanded immediate Satisfaction. I am apt to believe, that a young Officer who desir'd his Surgeon to defer putting him into a Salivation till Saturday, might make this request out of some Opinion he had of the truth of the Prophecy; for the apprehensions of any danger in the Operation could not be his Motive, the Surgeon himself having assured me that he had before undergone three severe Operations of the like Nature, with great resignation and fortitude.

There was an Order issued, that the Chaplains of the several Regiments should attend their Duty; but as they were dispers'd about in several parts of England, it was believ'd, that most of them could not be found, or so much as heard of, till the great Day was over.

Most of the considerable Physicians by their outward demeanor seem'd to be Unbelievers; but at the same time, they every where insinuated, that there might be a Pestilential Malignancy in the Air, occasion'd by the Comet, which might be arm'd against by proper and timely Medicines. This caution had but little effect; for as the time approach'd, the Christian Resignation of the People increas'd, and most of them (which was never before known) had their Souls more at Heart, than their Bodies.

If the Reverend Clergy show'd more Concern than others, I charitably impute it to their great charge of Souls; and what confirm'd me in this Opinion was, that the Degrees of Apprehension and Terror could be distinguish'd to be greater or less, according to their Ranks and Degrees in the Church.

The like might be observ'd in all sorts of Ministers, though not of the Church of England; the higher their Rank, the more was their Fear.

I speak not of the Court, for fear of offence; and I forbear

bear inserting the Names of particular Persons, to avoid the imputation of Slander, so that the Reader will allow this Narrative must be deficient, and is therefore desir'd to accept hereof rather as a Sketch, than a regular circumstantial History.

I was not inform'd of any Persons who shew'd the least Joy, except three Malefactors who were to be executed the Monday following, and one Old Man, a constant Church-goer, who being at the point of Death, exprest some satisfaction at the News.

On Thursday Morning there was little or nothing transacted in Change-Alley; there were a Multitude of Sellers, but so few Buyers, that one cannot affirm the Stocks bore any certain Price except among the Jews; who this Day, reap'd great Profit by their Infidelity. There were many who call'd themselves Christians, who offer'd to buy for time, but as these were People of great Distinction, I chuse not to mention them, because in effect it would seem to accuse them both of Avarice, and Infidelity.

The Run upon the Bank is too well known to need a particular Relation; for it never can be forgotten that no one Person whatever (except the Directors themselves, and some of their particular Friends and Associates) could convert a Bill all that Day into Specie; all hands being employ'd to serve them.

In the several Churches of the City and Suburbs, there were seven Thousand two Hundred and Forty Five, who publickly and solemnly declar'd before the Congregation, that they took to Wife their several kept Mistresses, which was allow'd as valid Marriage, the Priests not having time to pronounce the Ceremony in Form.

At St. Bride's Church in Fleetstreet, Mr. Woolston (who writ against the Miracles of our Saviour) in the utmost Terrors of Conscience, made a publick Recantation. Dr. Mandevil,

Mandevil, (who had been groundlessly reported formerly to have done the same) did it now in good earnest at St. James's Gate; as did also at the Temple Church several Gentlemen, who frequent the Coffee-Houses near the Bar. So great was the Faith and Fear of two of them, that they dropt Dead on the Spot; but I will not record their Names, lest I should be thought invidiously to lay an Odium on their Families and Posterity.

Most of the Players who had very little Faith before, were now desirous of having as much as they cou'd, and therefore embrac'd the Roman Catholick Religion; the same thing was observ'd of some Bawds, and Ladies of Pleasure.

An Irish Gentleman out of pure Friendship came to make me a Visit, and advis'd me to hire a Boat for the ensuing Day, and told me, that unless I gave earnest for one immediately, he fear'd it might be too late; for his Country-Men had secured almost every Boat upon the River, as judging that, in the general Conflagration, to be upon the Water would be the safest Place.

There were two Lords, and three Commoners, who, out of a scruple of Conscience, very hastily threw up their Pensions, as imagining a Pension was only an annual retaining Bribe. All the other great Pensioners, I was told, had their Scruples quieted by a Clergyman or two of distinction, whom they happily consulted.

It was remarkable that several of our very richest Tradesmen of the City, in common Charity, gave away Shillings and Six-pences to the Beggers, who ply'd about the Church Doors; and at a particular Church in the City, a Wealthy Church-warden with his own Hands distributed Fifty twelve-penny Loaves to the Poor, by way of Restitution for the many great and costly Feasts, which he had eaten of at their expence.

Three great Ladies, a *Valet de Chamber*, two Lords, a Custom-House-Officer, five Half-pay Captains, and a Baronet, (all noted Gamesters) came publickly into a Church at Westminster, and deposited a very considerable Sum of Money in the Minister's Hands; the Parties whom they had defrauded, being either out of Town, or not to be found. But so great is the Hardness of Heart of this Fraternity, that among either the Noble, or Vulgar Gamesters, (though the Profession is so general) I did not hear of any other restitution of this Sort. At the same time I must observe that (in comparison of these) through all parts of the Town, the Justice and Penitence of the High-way-Men, House-breakers, and common Pick-Pockets was very remarkable.

The Directors of our Publick Companies were in such dreadful apprehensions, that one would have thought a Parliamentary Enquiry was at hand; yet so great was their presence of Mind, that all the Thursday Morning was taken up in private Transfers, which by malicious People was thought to be done with design to conceal their Effects.

I forbear mentioning the private Confessions of particular Ladies to their Husbands; for as their children were born in Wedlock, and of consequence are Legitimate, it would be an invidious Task to record them as Bastards; and particularly, after their several Husbands have so charitably forgiven them.

The Evening and Night, through the whole Town, were spent in Devotions both Publick and Private; the Churches for this one Day, were so crouded by the Nobility and Gentry, that Thousands of common People were seen praying in the publick Streets. In short, one would have thought the whole Town had been really and seriously religious. But what was very remarkable, all

the

the different Persuasions kept by themselves, for as each thought the other would be damned, not one would join in Prayer with the other.

At length Friday came, and the People cover'd all the Streets; Expecting, Watching and Praying. But as the Day wore away, their Fears first began to abate, then lessen'd every hour, at Night they were almost extinct, till the total Darkness, that hitherto us'd to terrify, now comforted every Free-thinker and Atheist. Great numbers went together to the Taverns, bespoke Suppers, and broke up whole Hogsheads for joy. The subject of all Wit and Conversation was to ridicule the Prophecy, and railly each other. All the Quality and Gentry were perfectly asham'd, nay, some utterly disown'd that they had manifested any Signs of Religion.

But the next Day, even the Common People, as well as their Betters, appear'd in their usual state of Indifference. They Drank, they Whor'd, they Swore, they Ly'd, they Cheated, they Plunder'd, they Gam'd, they Quarrell'd, they Murder'd. In short, the World went on in the old Channel.

I need not give any Instances of what will so easily be credited, but I cannot omit relating, that Mr. Woolston advertis'd, in that very Saturday's *Evening-Post*, a new Treatise against the Miracles of our Saviour; and that the few, who had given up their Pensions the Day before, solicited to have them continued; which, as they had not been thrown up upon any Ministerial Point, I am inform'd was readily granted.

THE MEMOIRS OF MARTIN SCRIBLERUS

In the *Journal to Stella* (21 June 1711) we read first of the Tory Club, or Society, in which Swift was for three years the moving spirit, and to which he refers so frequently. 'We made some laws today, which I am to digest, and add to, against next meeting. Our meetings are to be every Thursday: we are yet but twelve. . . . We take in none but men of wit and interest; and if we go on as we begin, no other club in this town will be worth talking of.'

In February 1713–14, Swift converted the group into the famous Scriblerus Club, whose members included Pope, Gay, Oxford, Parnell, and above all, Arbuthnot, in whose apartments in St. James's Palace the Club met frequently till the members were dispersed after the death of Queen Anne five months later. The avowed purpose was to compose in collaboration a comprehensive satire on abuses in learning—centred in the life and works of Martinus Scriblerus. As early as 11 October 1711 (*Journal to Stella*), Oxford had nicknamed Swift 'Dr. Martin, because martin is a sort of swallow, and so is a swift'. Martin also stood for Swift in *A Tale of a Tub*.

In this project, undertaken during the months of highest political excitement, when Swift's career was at the cross-roads, we find his characteristic form of relaxation. While it is impossible to distinguish with any certainty the several authors of the chapters, it would seem fairly clear that most of them as finally published came from the pen of Arbuthnot, certainly the chapters which satirize the various arts and sciences of rhetoric, logic, metaphysics, anatomy, and physic. It is indeed probable that he inspired more passages in the works of Pope and Swift than are claimed for him by his editors. The chapters here reproduced are those which most clearly point to the style of Swift, or which contain the suggestions for other and later writings of Swift, to be found elsewhere in these volumes, including *Gulliver's Travels, A Modest Proposal,* and *Memoirs of the Life of Scriblerus.*

Whether or not these chapters are altogether from the pen of Swift is a secondary consideration. That he was regarded as the principal author by Pope and Arbuthnot, we know from their letters. That these *Memoirs* are the most readable product of his activity as promoter and collaborator in the Scriblerus Club is beyond question. Here is Swift in Rabelais's easy chair, composing a satiric biography that will always rank with the histories of Panurge, Quixote, and Tristram Shandy—'a learned phantom which is to be immortal'.

The Memoirs of Martinus Scriblerus were first published in Pope's *Prose Works,* vol. ii, 1741. They have been reproduced here from Pope's *Works*, vol. vii, 1754, and collated carefully with the first edition.

BOOK I

CHAPTER I

Of the Parentage and Family of Scriblerus, how he was begot, what Care was taken of him before he was born, and what Prodigies attended his Birth.

IN the City of Munster in Germany, lived a grave and learned Gentleman, by profession an Antiquary; who among all his invaluable Curiosities, esteemed none more highly than a Skin of the true Pergamenian Parchment, which hung at the upper end of his hall. On this was curiously traced the ancient Pedigree of the *Scribleri*, with all their Alliances and collateral Relations (among which were reckoned Albertus Magnus, Paracelsus Bombastus, and the famous Scaligers in old time Princes of Verona) and deduced even from the Times of the Elder Pliny to Cornelius Scriblerus; for such was the name of this venerable Personage, whose glory it was, that, by the singular Virtue of the women, not one had a Head of a different Cast from his family.

His wife was a Lady of singular beauty, whom not for that reason only he espoused, but because she was undoubted daughter either of the great Scriverius, or of Gaspar Barthius. It happen'd on a time the said Gaspar made a visit to Scriverius at Harlem, taking with him a comely Lady of his acquaintance, who was skilful in the Greek Tongue, of whom the learned Scriverius became so enamour'd, as to inebriate his friend, and be familiar with his Mistress. I am not ignorant of what Columesius[1] affirms, that the learned Barthius was not so overtaken,

[1] Columesius relates this from Isaac Vossius, in his Opuscula, p. 102. (Pope).

but

but he perceiv'd it; and in Revenge suffer'd this unfortunate Gentlewoman to be drowned in the Rhine at her return. But Mrs. Scriblerus (the issue of that Amour) was a living proof of the falsehood of this Report. Dr. Cornelius was farther induced to his marriage, from the certain information that the aforesaid Lady, the mother of his wife, was related to Cardan on the father's side, and to Aldrovandus on the mother's: Besides which, her Ancestors had been professors of Physik, Astrology, or Chymistry, in German Universities, from generation to generation.

With this fair Gentlewoman had our Doctor lived in a comfortable Union for about ten years; But this our sober and orderly pair, without any natural infirmity, and with a constant and frequent compliance to the chief duty of conjugal life, were yet unhappy, in that Heaven had not blessed them with any issue. This was the utmost grief to the good man; especially considering what exact Precautions and Methods he had used to procure that Blessing: for he never had cohabitation with his spouse, but he ponder'd on the rules of the Ancients, for the generation of Children of Wit. He ordered his diet according to the prescription of Galen, confining himself and his wife for almost the whole first year to Goat's[1] Milk and Honey. It unfortunately befel her, when she was about four months gone with child, to long for somewhat, which that author inveighs against as prejudicial to the understanding of the Infant: This her husband thought fit to deny her, affirming, it was better to be childless, than to become the Parent of a Fool. His Wife miscarried; but as the Abortion proved only a female Foetus, he comforted himself, that, had it arrived to perfection, it would not have answer'd his

[1] Galen. Lib. de Cibis boni et mali succi, cap. 3. (Pope.)

account

account; his heart being wholly fixed upon the learned Sex. However he disdained not to treasure up the Embryo in a Vial, among the curiosities of his family.

Having discovered that Galen's prescription could not determine the sex, he forthwith betook himself to Aristotle. Accordingly he with-held the nuptial embrace when the wind was in any point of the South; this Author[1] asserting that the grossness and moisture of the southerly winds occasion the procreation of females, and not of males. But he redoubled his diligence when the wind was at West, a wind on which that great Philosopher bestowed the Encomiums of Fatner of the earth, Breath of the Elysian Fields, and other glorious Elogies. For our learned man was clearly of opinion, that the Semina out of which animals are produced, are Animalcula ready formed, and received in with the Air.

Under these regulations, his wife, to his unexpressible joy, grew pregnant a second time; and (what was no small addition to his happiness) he just then came to the possession of a considerable Estate by the death of her Uncle, a wealthy Jew, who resided at London. This made it necessary for him to take a journey to England; nor would the care of his posterity let him suffer his Wife to remain behind him. During the voyage, he was perpetually taken up on the one hand how to employ his great Riches, and on the other, how to educate his Child. He had already determin'd to set apart several Sums, for the recovery of Manuscripts, the effossion of Coins, the procuring of Mummies; and for all those curious discoveries by which he hoped to become (as himself was wont to say) a second Peireskius. He had already chalked out all possible schemes for the improvement of a male child, yet was so far prepar'd for the worst that

[1] Arist. xiv. Sect. Prob. 5. (Pope.)

could

could happen, that before the nine months were expired, he had composed two Treatises of Education; the one he called, *A Daughter's Mirror*, and the other *A Son's Monitor*.

This is all we can find relating to Martinus, while he was in his Mother's womb, excepting that he was entertained there with a Consort of Musick once in twenty-four Hours, according to the Custom of the Magi; and that on a particular day,[1] he was observed to leap and kick exceedingly, which was on the first of April, the birth-day of the great Basilius Valentinus.

The truth of this, and every preceding fact, may be depended upon, being taken literally from the Memoirs. But I must be so ingenuous as to own, that the accounts are not so certain of the exact time and place of his birth. As to the first, he had the common frailty of old men, to conceal his age: as to the second, I only remember to have heard him say, that he first saw the light in St. Giles's parish. But in the investigation of this point Fortune has favoured our diligence. For one day as I was passing by the Seven Dials, I overheard a dispute concerning the place of Nativity of a great Astrologer, which each man alleged to have been in his own street. The circumstances of the time, and the description of the person, made me imagine it might be that universal Genius whose life I am writing. I returned home, and having maturely considered their several arguments, which I found to be of equal weight, I quieted my curiosity with this natural conclusion, that he was born in some point common to all the seven streets; which must be that on which the Column is now erected. And it

[1] Ramsey's Cyrus. (Pope.) It was with judgment, that the Authors chose rather to ridicule the modern relator of this ridiculous practice, than the Ancients from whence he took it; as it is a sure instance of folly, when amongst the many excellent things which may be learned from antiquity, we find a modern writer only picking out their absurdities. (Warburton.)

it is with infinite pleasure that I since find my Conjecture confirmed, by the following passage in the Codicil to Mr. Neale's Will.

I appoint my Executors to engrave the following Inscription on the Column in the centre of the seven streets which I erected.

LOC. NAT. INCLVT. PHILOS. MAR. SCR.

But Mr. Neale's order was never performed, because the Executors durst not administer.

Nor was the Birth of this great man unattended with Prodigies: He himself has often told me, that on the night before he was born, Mrs. Scriblerus dream'd she was brought to bed of a huge Ink-horn, out of which issued several large streams of Ink, as it had been a fountain. This dream was by her husband thought to signify that the child should prove a very voluminous Writer. Likewise a Crab-tree[1] that had been hitherto barren, appeared on a sudden laden with a vast quantity of Crabs: this sign also the old gentleman imagined to be a prognostic of the acuteness of his Wit. A great swarm of Wasps[2] play'd round his Cradle without hurting him, but were very troublesome to all in the room besides: This seemed a certain presage of the effects of his Satire. A Dunghill was seen within the space of one night to be covered all over with Mushrooms: This some interpreted to promise the infant great fertility of fancy, but no long duration to his works; but the Father was of another opinion.

But what was of all most wonderful was a thing that seemed a monstrous Fowl, which just then dropt through the sky-light, near his wife's apartment. It had a large body, two little disproportioned wings, a prodigious tail, but no head. As its colour was white, he took it at first

[1] Virgil's Laurel. Donat. (Pope).

[2] Plato, Lucan, &c. (Pope).

sight

sight for a Swan, and was concluding his son would be a Poet: but on a nearer view, he perceived it to be speckled with black, in the form of letters; and that it was indeed a Paper-kite which had broke its leash by the impetuosity of the wind. His back was armed with the Art Military, his belly was filled with Physic, his wings were the wings of Quarles and Withers, the several Nodes of his voluminous tail were diversify'd with several branches of Science; where the Doctor beheld with great joy a knot of Logick, a knot of Metaphysick, a knot of Casuistry, a knot of Polemical Divinity, and a knot of Common Law, with a Lanthorn of Jacob Behmen.

There went a Report in the family that, as soon as he was born, he uttered the voice of nine several animals; he cry'd like a Calf, bleated like a Sheep, chattered like a Mag-pye, grunted like a Hog, neighed like a Foal, croaked like a Raven, mewed like a Cat, gabbled like a Goose, and bray'd like an Ass. And the next morning he was found playing in his bed with two Owls, which came down the chimney. His father greatly rejoiced at all these signs, which betokened the variety of his Eloquence, and the extent of his Learning; but he was more particularly pleased with the last, as it nearly resembled what happen'd at the birth of Homer.[1]

CHAPTER II

The Speech of Cornelius over his Son, at the hour of his Birth.

No sooner was the cry of the Infant heard, but the old gentleman rushed into the Room, and snatching it into his arms, examin'd every limb with attention. He was

[1] Vid. Eustath. in Odyss. l. xii. ex Alex. Paphio, et Leo. Allat. de patr. Hom. pag. 45. (Pope.)

infinitely

infinitely pleas'd to find that the Child had the Wart of Cicero, the wry Neck of Alexander, knots upon his legs like Marius, and one of them shorter than the other, like Agesilaus. The good Cornelius also hoped he would come to stammer like Demosthenes, in order to be as eloquent; and in time arrive at many other Defects of famous men. He held the child so long, that the Midwife, grown out of all patience, snatch'd it from his arms, in order to swaddle it. 'Swaddle him?' quoth he, 'far be it from me to submit to such a pernicious Custom! Is not my son a Man, and is not Man the Lord of the Universe? Is it thus you use this Monarch at his first arrival in his dominions, to manacle and shackle him hand and foot? Is this what you call to be free-born? If you have no regard to his natural Liberty, at least have some to his natural Faculties. Behold with what agility he spreadeth his Toes, and moveth them with as great variety as his Fingers! a power which, in the small circle of a year, may be totally abolish'd, by the enormous confinement of shoes and stockings. His Ears (which other animals turn with great advantage towards the sonorous object) may, by the ministry of some accursed Nurse, for ever lie flat and immoveable. Not so the Ancients, they could move them at pleasure, and accordingly are often describ'd *arrectis auribus*.' 'What a devil,' quoth the Midwife, 'would you have your son move his Ears like a Drill?' 'Yes, fool,' said he, 'why should he not have the perfection of a Drill, or of any other animal?' Mrs. Scriblerus, who lay all this while fretting at her husband's discourse, at last broke out to this purpose: 'My dear, I have had many disputes with you upon this subject before I was a month gone; we have but one child, and cannot afford to throw him away upon experiments. I'll have my boy bred up like other gentlemen, at home, and always under my own eye.'

eye.' All the Gossips with one voice, cry'd Ay, ay; but Cornelius broke out in this manner: 'What, bred at home? Have I taken all this pains for a creature that is to live the inglorious life of a Cabbage, to suck the nutritious juices from the spot where he was first planted? No; to perambulate this terraqueous Globe is too small a Range; were it permitted, he should at least make the Tour of the whole System of the Sun. Let other mortals pore upon maps, and swallow the legends of lying travellers: the son of Cornelius shall make his own legs his compasses; with those he shall measure Continents, Islands, Capes, Bays, Streights, and Isthmuses. He shall himself take the altitude of the highest mountains, from the Peak of Derby to the Peak of Tenariff; when he has visited the top of Taurus, Imaus, Caucasus, and the famous Ararat, where Noah's Ark first moor'd, he may take a slight view of the snowy Riphæans, nor would I have him neglect Athos and Olympus, renowned for poetical fictions. Those that vomit fire will deserve a more particular attention; I will therefore have him observe with great care Vesuvius, Ætna, the burning mountain of Java, but chiefly Hecla, the greatest rarity in the Northern Regions. Then he may likewise contemplate the wonders of the Mephitick cave. When he has div'd into the bowels of the earth, and survey'd the works of nature under ground, and instructed himself fully in the nature of Vulcanos, Earthquakes, Thunders, Tempests, and Hurricanes, I hope he will bless the world with a more exact survey of the deserts of Arabia and Tartary than as yet we are able to obtain: Then will I have him cross the seven Gulphs, measure the currents in the fifteen famous Streights, and search for those fountains of fresh water that are at the bottom of the Ocean.'—At these last words Mrs. Scriblerus fell into a trembling: the descrip-

tion

tion of this terrible scene made too violent an impression upon a woman in her condition, and threw her into a strong hysteric Fit, which might have proved dangerous, if Cornelius had not been pushed out of the room by the united force of the women.

CHAPTER III

Showing what befel the Doctor's Son and his Shield, on the day of the Christ'ning.

The day of the Christ'ning being come, and the house filled with Gossips, the Levity of whose Conversation suited but ill with the Gravity of Dr. Cornelius, he cast about how to pass this day more agreeably to his Character; that is to say, not without some Profitable Conference, nor wholly without observance of some Ancient Custom.

He remembered to have read in Theocritus, that the cradle of Hercules was a Shield; and being possess'd of an antique Buckler, which he held as a most inestimable Relick, he determined to have the infant laid therein, and in that manner brought into the Study, to be shown to certain learned men of his acquaintance.

The regard he had for this Shield had caused him formerly to compile a Dissertation concerning it, proving from the several properties, and particularly the colour of the Rust, the exact chronology thereof.

With this Treatise, and a moderate supper, he proposed to entertain his Guests; though he had also another design, to have their assistance in the calculation of his Son's Nativity.

He therefore took the Buckler out of a Case (in which he always kept it, lest it might contract any modern rust), and entrusted it to his House-maid, with orders that, when

when the company was come, she should lay the Child carefully in it, covered with a mantle of blue Sattin.

The Guests were no sooner seated, but they entered into a warm Debate about the *Triclinium*, and the namner of *Decubitus* of the Ancients, which Cornelius broke off in this manner:—

'This day, my Friends, I purpose to exhibit my son before you; a Child not wholly unworthy of Inspection, as he is descended from a Race of Virtuosi. Let the Physiognomists examine his features; let the Chirographists behold his Palm; but above all, let us consult for the calculation of his Nativity. To this end, as the child is not vulgar, I will not present him unto you in a vulgar manner. He shall be cradled in my Ancient Shield, so famous through the Universities of Europe. You all know how I purchas'd that invaluable piece of Antiquity, at the great (though indeed inadequate) expence of all the Plate of our family, how happily I carry'd it off, and how triumphantly I transported it hither, to the inexpressible grief of all Germany. Happy in every circumstance, but that it broke the heart of the great Melchior Insipidus!'

Here he stopped his Speech, upon sight of the Maid, who entered the room with the child; he took it in his arms, and proceeded.

'Behold then my Child, but first behold the Shield; Behold this Rust,—or rather let me call it this precious ærugo,—behold this beautiful Varnish of Time,—this venerable Verdure of so many Ages—'

In speaking these words, he slowly lifted up the Mantle which cover'd it, inch by inch; but at every inch he uncovered his cheeks grew paler, his hand trembled, his nerves failed, till on sight of the whole, the Tremor became universal; The Shield and the Infant both dropt

to

to the ground, and he had only strength enough to cry out, 'O God! my Shield, my Shield!'

The Truth was, the Maid (extremely concerned for the reputation of her own cleanliness, and her young master's honour) had scoured it as clean as her Andirons.

Cornelius sunk back on a chair, the Guests stood astonished, the infant squalled, the maid ran in, snatched it up again in her arms, flew into her mistress's room, and told what had happened. Down stairs in an instant hurried all the Gossips, where they found the Doctor in a Trance: Hungary water, Hartshorn, and the confused noise of shrill voices, at length awakened him: when, opening his eyes, he saw the Shield in the hands of the Housemaid. 'O Woman! Woman!' he cry'd (and snatch'd it violently from her), 'was it to thy ignorance that this Relick owes its ruin? Where, where is the beautiful Crust that covered thee so long? where those Traces of Time and fingers as it were of Antiquity? Where all those beautiful obscurities, the cause of much delightful disputation, where doubt and curiosity went hand in hand, and eternally exercised the speculations of the learned! All this the rude Touch of an ignorant woman hath done away! The curious Prominence at the belly of that figure, which some taking for the *Cuspis* of a sword, denominated a Roman Soldier; others accounting the *Insignia Virilia*, pronounced to be one of the *Dii Termini*; behold she hath cleaned it in like shameful sort, and shown to be the head of a Nail. O my Shield! my Shield! well may I say with Horace, *non bene relicta Parmula.*'

The Gossips, not at all inquiring into the cause of his sorrow, only asked if the Child had no hurt? and cry'd, Come, come, all is well; what has the woman done but her duty? a tight cleanly wench I warrant her; what a

stir

stir a man makes about a Bason, that, an hour ago, before this labour was bestowed upon it, a Country Barber would not have hung at his shop door. 'A Bason! (cry'd another), no such matter, 'tis nothing but a paltry old Sconce, with the nozzle broke off.' The learned Gentlemen, who till now had stood speechless, hereupon looking narrowly on the Shield, declared their assent to this latter opinion; and desir'd Cornelius to be comforted, assuring him it was a Sconce and no other. But this, instead of comforting, threw the Doctor into such a violent Fit of passion that he was carried off groaning and speechless to bed; where, being quite spent, he fell into a kind of slumber.

CHAPTER IV

Of the Suction and Nutrition of the Great Scriblerus in his Infancy, and of the first Rudiments of his Learning.

As soon as Cornelius awaked, he rais'd himself on his elbow, and casting his eye on Mrs. Scriblerus, spoke as follows. 'Wisely was it said by Homer, that in the Cellar of Jupiter are two barrels, the one of good, the other of evil, which he never bestows on mortals separately, but constantly mingles them together. Thus at the same time hath Heav'n blessed me with the birth of a Son, and afflicted me with the scouring of my Shield. Yet let us not repine at His Dispensations, who gives and who takes away; but rather join in prayer, that the Rust of Antiquity which He hath been pleas'd to take from my Shield, may be added to my Son; and that so much of it as it is my purpose he shall contract in his Education may never be destroy'd by any Modern Polishing.'

He cou'd no longer bear the sight of the Shield, but order'd it should be remov'd for ever from his eyes. It

was

was not long after purchas'd by Dr. Woodward, who, by the assistance of Mr. Kemp incrusted it with a new Rust, and is the same whereof a Cut has been engraved, and exhibited to the great Contentation of the learned.

Cornelius now began to regulate the Suction of his Child. Seldom did there pass a day without disputes between him and the Mother, or the Nurse, concerning the nature of Aliment. The poor woman never dined but he denied her some dish or other, which he judg'd prejudicial to her milk. One day she had a longing desire to a piece of beef, and as she stretch'd her hand towards it the old gentleman drew it away, and spoke to this effect. 'Had'st thou read the Ancients, O Nurse, thou would'st prefer the welfare of the Infant which thou nourishest, to the indulging of an irregular and voracious Appetite. Beef, it is true, may confer a Robustness on the limbs of my son, but will hebetate and clogg his Intellectuals.' While he spoke this, the Nurse look'd upon him with much anger, and now and then cast a wishful eye upon the Beef.—'Passion (continu'd the Doctor, still holding the dish) throws the mind into too violent a fermentation; it is a kind of Fever of the soul, or, as Horace expresses it, a Short Madness. Consider Woman, that this day's Suction of my son may cause him to imbibe many ungovernable Passions, and in a manner spoil him for the temper of a Philosopher. Romulus, by sucking a Wolf, became of a fierce and savage disposition; and were I to breed some Ottoman Emperor, or Founder of a Military Commonwealth, perhaps I might indulge thee in this carnivorous Appetite.'—'What,' interrupted the Nurse, 'Beef spoil the understanding? that's find indeed—how then could our Parson preach as he does upon Beef, and Pudding too if you go to that? Don't tell me of your Ancients, had not

you

you almost killed the poor babe with a dish of dæmonial black broth?'—'Lacedemonian black Broth, thou would'st say, (reply'd Cornelius) but I cannot allow the surfeit to have been occasioned by that diet, since it was recommended by the Divine Lycurgus. No, Nurse, thou must certainly have eaten some meats of ill digestion the day before, and that was the real cause of his disorder. Consider, Woman, the different Temperaments of different Nations: What makes the English Phlegmatick and melancholy but Beef? What renders the Welch so hot and cholerick, but cheese and leeks? The French derive their levity from their Soups, Frogs, and Mushrooms: I would not let my Son dine like an Italian, lest like an Italian he should be jealous and revengeful: The warm and solid diet of Spain may be more beneficial, as it might endow him with a profound Gravity, but at the same time, he might suck in with their food their intolerable Vice of Pride. Therefore Nurse, in short, I hold it requisite to deny you at present, not only Beef, but likewise whatsoever any of those Nations eat.' During this speech, the nurse remain'd pouting, and marking her plate with the knife, nor would she touch a bit during the whole dinner. This the old gentleman observing, order'd that the child, to avoid the risque of imbibing ill humours, should be kept from her breast all that day, and be fed with Butter mix'd with Honey, according to a Prescription he had met with somewhere in Eustathius upon Homer. This indeed gave the child a great looseness, but he was not concern'd at it, in the opinion that whatever harm it might do his body would be amply recompenced by the improvements of his understanding. But from thenceforth he insisted every day upon a particular Diet to be observed by the Nurse; under which having been long uneasy, she at last parted

from

from the family, on his ordering her for dinner the Paps of a Sow with pig; taking it as the highest indignity, and a direct Insult upon her Sex and Calling.

Four years of young Martin's life pass'd away in squabbles of this nature. Mrs. Scriblerus consider'd it was now time to instruct him in the fundamentals of Religion, and to that end took no small pains in teaching him his Catechism: But Cornelius look'd upon this as a tedious way of instruction, and therefore employ'd his head to find out more pleasing methods, the better to induce him to be fond of learning. He would frequently carry him to the Puppet-show of the Creation of the world, where the Child, with exceeding delight, gain'd a notion of the History of the Bible. His first rudiments in profane history were acquired by seeing of Raree-shows, where he was brought acquainted with all the Princes of Europe. In short, the old Gentleman so contriv'd it to make every thing contribute to the improvement of his knowledge, even to his very Dress. He invented for him a Geographical suit of cloaths, which might give him some hints of that Science, and likewise some knowledge of the Commerce of different Nations. He had a French Hat with an African Feather, Holland Shirts and Flanders Lace, English Cloth lin'd with Indian Silk, his Gloves were Italian, and his Shoes were Spanish: He was made to observe this, and daily catechis'd thereupon, which his Father was wont to call 'Travelling at home.' He never gave him a Fig or an Orange but he obliged him to give an account from what Country it came. In Natural history he was much assisted by his Curiosity in Sign-Posts, in so much that he hath often confess'd he owed to them the knowledge of many Creatures which he never found since in any Author, such as White Lions, Golden Dragons, &c. He once thought the same of Green

Green Men, but had since found them mention'd by Kercherus, and verify'd in the history of William of Newbury.[1]

His disposition to the Mathematicks was discovered very early, by his drawing parallel lines on his bread and butter, and intersecting them at equal Angles, so as to form the whole Superficies into squares. But in the midst of all these Improvements a stop was put to his learning the Alphabet, nor would he let him proceed to letter D, till he could truly and distinctly pronounce C in the ancient manner, at which the Child unhappily boggled for near three months. He was also oblig'd to delay his learning to write, having turned away the Writing-Master because he knew nothing of Fabius's Waxen Tables.

Cornelius having read, and seriously weigh'd the methods by which the famous Montaigne was educated, and resolving in some degree to exceed them, resolv'd he should speak and learn nothing but the learned Languages, and especially the Greek; in which he constantly eat and drank, according to Homer. But what most conduced to his easy attainment of this Language was his love of Gingerbread; which his Father observing, caused to be stamped with the letters of the Greek Alphabet; and the child the very first day eat as far as Iota. By his particular application to this language above the rest, he attain'd so great a proficiency therein, that Gronovius ingenuously confesses he durst not confer with this child in Greek at eight years old; and at fourteen he composed a Tragedy in the same language, as the younger Pliny[2] had done before him.

He learn'd the Oriental languages of Erpenius, who

[1] Gul. Neubrig. Book i. ch. 27 (Pope).
[2] Plin. Epist. lib. vii (Pope).

resided

resided some time with his father for that purpose. He had so early a Relish for the Eastern way of writing, that even at this time he composed (in imitation of it) the *Thousand and One Arabian Tales*, and also the *Persian Tales*, which have been since translated into several languages, and lately into our own with particular elegance by Mr. Ambrose Philips. In this work of his Childhood he was not a little assisted by the historical Traditions of his Nurse.

CHAPTER V

A Dissertation upon Play-things.

Here follow the Instructions of Cornelius Scriblerus concerning the Plays and Play-things to be used by his son Martin.

'Play was invented by the Lydians as a remedy against Hunger. Sophocles says of Palamedes, that he invented Dice to serve sometimes instead of a dinner. It is therefore wisely contrived by Nature, that children, as they have the keenest Appetites, are most addicted to Plays. From the same cause, and from the unprejudic'd and incorrupt simplicity of their minds it proceeds, that the plays of the ancient children are preserv'd more entire than any other of their customs. In this matter I would recommend to all who have any concern in my Son's Education that they deviate not in the least from the primitive and simple Antiquity.

'To speak first of the Whistle, as it is the first of all Play-things. I will have it exactly to correspond with the ancient *Fistula*, and accordingly to be compos'd *septem paribus disjuncta cicutis*.

'I heartily wish a diligent search may be made after the true *Crepitaculum*, or Rattle of the Ancients, for that (as Archytus

Archytus Tarentinus was of opinion) kept the children from breaking Earthen Ware. The China cups in these days are not at all the safer for the modern Rattles; which is an evident proof how far their *Crepitacula* exceeded ours.

'I would not have Martin as yet to scourge a Top, till I am better informed whether the *Trochus*, which was recommended by Cato, be really our present Top or rather the Hoop, which the boys drive with a stick. Neither Cross and Pile, nor Ducks and Drakes are quite so ancient as Handy-dandy, tho' Macrobius and St. Augustine take notice of the first, and Minutius Fœlix describes the latter; but Handy-dandy is mention'd by Aristotle, Plato, and Aristophanes.

'The Play which the Italians call *Cinque*, and the French *Mourre*, is extremely ancient; it was played at by Hymen and Cupid at the marriage of Psyche, and term'd by the Latins, *digitis micare.*

'Julius Pollux describes the *Omilla* or Chuck-Farthing: though some will have our modern Chuck-farthing to be nearer the *Aphelinda* of the Ancients. He also mentions the *Basilinda*, or king I am; and *Myinda*, or Hoopers-hide.

'But the *Chytrindra* described by the same Author is certainly not our Hot-cockle; for that was by pinching and not by striking; though there are good authors who affirm the *Rathapygismus* to be yet nearer the modern Hot-cockle. My son Martin may use either of them indifferently, they being Equally antique.

'Building of Houses and Riding upon Sticks have been used by children in all ages, *Ædificare casas, equitare in arundine longa.* Yet I much doubt whether the Riding upon Sticks did not come into use after the age of the Centaurs.

'There

'There is one Play which shows the gravity of ancient Education, call'd the *Acinetinda*, in which children contended who could longest stand still. This we have suffer'd to perish entirely; and, if I might be allowed to guess, it was certainly first lost among the French.

'I will permit my Son to play at *Apodidrascinda*, which can be no other than our Puss in a Corner.

'Julius Pollux, in his ninth book, speaks of the *Melolonthe* or the Kite; but I question whether the Kite of Antiquity was the same with ours; and tho' the *'Ορτυγοκοπία* or Quail-fighting is what is most taken notice of, they had doubtless Cock-matches also, as is evident from certain ancient Gems and Relievos.

'In a word, let my son Martin disport himself at any Game truly Antique, except one, which was invented by a people among the Thracians, who hung up one of their Companions in a Rope, and gave him a Knife to cut himself down; which if he fail'd in, he was suffer'd to hang till he was dead; and this was only reckon'd a sort of joke. I am utterly against this, as barbarous and cruel.

'I cannot conclude, without taking notice of the beauty of the Greek names, whose Etymologies acquaint us with the nature of the sports; and how infinitely, both in sense and sound, they excel our barbarous names of Plays.'

Notwithstanding the foregoing Injunctions of Dr. Cornelius, he yet condescended to allow the Child the use of some few modern Play-things; such as might prove of any benefit to his mind, by instilling an early notion of the sciences. For example, he found that Marbles taught him Percussion and the Laws of Motion; Nut-crackers the use of the Leaver; swinging on the ends of a Board, the Balance; Bottle-screws, the Vice; Whirligigs, the Axis and Peritrochia; Bird-cages, the Pulley; and Tops, the Centrifugal motion.

Others of his sports were farther carry'd to improve his tender soul even in Virtue and Morality. We shall only instance one of the most useful and instructive, Bob-cherry, which teaches at once two noble Virtues, Patience and Constancy; the first in adhering to the pursuit of one end, the latter in bearing a disappointment.

Besides all these, he taught him as a diversion, an odd and secret manner of Stealing, according to the custom of the Lacedæmonians; wherein he succeeded so well, that he practised it to the day of his death.

CHAPTER VI

Of the Gymnasticks, in what Exercises Martinus was educated; something concerning Musick, and what sort of a Man his Uncle was.

Nor was Cornelius less careful in adhering to the rules of the purest Antiquity, in relation to the Exercises of his Son. He was stript, powder'd, and anointed, but not constantly bath'd, which occasion'd many heavy complaints of the Laundress about dirtying his linnen. When he play'd at Quoits, he was allow'd his Breeches and Stockings; because the *Discoboli* (as Cornelius well knew) were naked to the middle only. The Mother often contended for modern Sports and common Customs, but this was his constant reply, 'Let a Daughter be the care of her Mother, but the Education of a Son should be the delight of his Father.'

It was about this time, he heard to his exceeding content, that the *Harpastus* of the Ancients was yet in use in Cornwall, and known there by the name of Hurling. He was sensible the common Foot-ball was a very imperfect imitation of that exercise, and thought it necessary to send Martin into the West, to be initiated in in that truly ancient and manly part of the Gymnasticks. The poor boy was so unfortunate as to return with a broken leg. This Cornelius look'd upon but as a slight ailment, and promis'd his mother he would instantly cure it: He slit a green Reed, and cast the knife upward, then tying the two parts of the Reed to the disjointed place, pronounced these words,[1] *Daries, daries, astataries, dissunapiter; huat, hanat, huat, ista, pista, fista, domi abo, damnaustra.* But finding to his no small astonishment, that this had no effect, in five days he condescended to have it set by a modern Surgeon.

Mrs. Scriblerus, to prevent him from exposing her Son to the like dangerous exercises for the future, propos'd to send for a dancing master, and to have him taught the Minuet and Rigadoon. (Dancing) quoth Cornelius, 'I much approve, for Socrates said the best Dancers were the best Warriors; but not those species of Dancing which you mention: They are certainly corruptions of the Comic and Satyric Dance, which were utterly disliked by the sounder Ancients. Martin shall learn the Tragic Dance only, and I will send all over Europe, till I find an Antiquary able to instruct him in the *Saltatio Pyrrhica.* Scaliger,[2] from whom my son is lineally descended, boasts to have performed this warlike Dance in the Presence of the Emperor, to the great admiration of all Germany. What would he say, could he look down and see one of his posterity so ignorant as not to know the least step of that noble kind of saltation?'

[1] Plin. *Hist. Nat.* lib. xvii in fine. 'Carmen contra luxata membra, cujus verba inserere non equidem serio ausim, quanquam a Catone prodita.' Vid. Caton. *de re rust.* c. 160 (Pope).

[2] Scalig. *Poetic.* l. x. c. 9. 'Hanc saltationem Pyrrhicam, nos sæpe et diu, jussu Bonifacii patrui, coram Divo Maximiliano, non sine stupore totius Germaniæ, repræsentavimus. Quo tempore vox illa Imperatoris, Hic puer aut thoracem pro pelle aut pro cunis habuit' (Pope).

The

The poor Lady was at last enur'd to bear all these things with a laudable patience, till one day her husband was seized with a new thought. He had met with a saying, that 'Spleen, Garter, and Girdle are the three impediments to the *Cursus*.' Therefore Pliny (lib. xi. cap. 37) says, that such as excel in that exercise have their Spleen cauteriz'd. 'My son (quoth Cornelius) runs but heavily; therefore I will have this operation performed upon him immediately. Moreover it will cure that immoderate Laughter to which I perceive he is addicted: for laughter (as the same author hath it, *ibid.*) is caused by the bigness of the Spleen.' This design was no sooner hinted to Mrs. Scriblerus, but she burst into tears, wrung her hands, and instantly sent to his Brother Albertus, begging him for the love of God to make haste to her husband.

Albertus was a discreet man, sober in his opinions, clear of Pedantry, and knowing enough both in books and in the world, to preserve a due regard for whatever was useful or excellent, whether ancient or modern: If he had not always the authority, he had at least the art, to divert Cornelius from many extravagancies. It was well he came speedily, or Martin could not have boasted the entire Quota of his Viscera. What does it signify (quoth Albertus) whether my Nephew excels in the *cursus* or not? Speed is often a symptom of Cowardice, witness Hares and Deer.—Do not forget Achilles (quoth Cornelius) I know that running has been condemn'd by the proud Spartans, as useless in war; and yet Demosthenes could say *'Ανὴρ ὁ φεύγων καὶ πάλιν μαχήσεται,* a thought which the English Hudibras has well rendered,

> For he that runs may fight again,
> Which he can never do that's slain.

That's true (quoth Albertus) but pray consider on the other

other side that Animals spleened[1] grow extremely salacious, an experiment well known in dogs. Cornelius was struck with this, and reply'd gravely: 'If it be so, I will defer the Operation, for I will not Increase the powers of my son's body at the expence of those of his mind. I am indeed disappointed in most of my projects, and fear I must sit down at last contented with such methods of Education as modern barbarity affords. Happy had it been for us all, had we lived in the age of Augustus! Then my son might have heard the Philosophers dispute in the Porticos of the Palæstra, and at the same time form'd his Body and his Understanding. It is true (reply'd Albertus) we have no *Exedra* for the Philosophers adjoining to our Tennis-courts; but there are Ale-houses where he will hear very notable argumentations: Tho' we come not up to the Ancients in the Tragic-dance, we excel them in the κυβιστική, or the art of Tumbling. The Ancients would have beat us at Quoits, but not so much at the *Jaculum*, or pitching the Bar. The *Pugilalus*[2] is in as great perfection in England as in old Rome, and the Cornish-Hug in the *Luctus*[3] is equal to the *volutaloria* of the Ancients. You could not (answer'd Cornelius) have produc'd a more unlucky instance of modern folly and barbarity, than what you say of the *Jaculum*. The Cretans[4] wisely forbid their servants Gymnastics, as well as Arms; and yet your modern Footmen exercise themselves daily in the *jaculum* at the corner of Hyde-Park, whilst their enervated Lords are lolling in their chariots (a species of Vectitation seldom used among the Ancients, except by old men.) You say well (quoth Albertus) and we have several other kinds of Vectitation unknown

[1] Blackmore's *Essay on Spleen* (Pope).
[2] Fisticuffs (Pope).
[3] Wrestling (Pope).
[4] Aristot. *Politic.* lib. ii. cap. 3 (Pope).

to

to the ancients; particularly flying Chariots, where the people may have the benefit of this exercise at the small expense of a farthing. But suppose (which I readily grant) that the ancients excelled us almost in everything, yet why this singularity? Your son must take up with such masters as the present age affords; we have Dancing-masters, Writing-masters, and Music-masters.'

The bare mention of Music threw Cornelius into a passion. How can you dignify (quoth he) this modern fidling with the name of Musick? Will any of your best Hautboys encounter a Wolf now a-days with no other arms but their instruments, as did that ancient piper Pythocaris? Have ever wild Boars, Elephants, Deer, Dolphins, Whales or Turbotts, shew'd the least emotion at the most elaborate strains of your modern Scrapers, all which have been, as it were, tam'd and humaniz'd by ancient Musicians? Does not Ælian[1] tell us how the Libian mares were excited to horsing by Musick? (which ought in truth to be a caution to modest women against frequenting Operas; and consider, brother, you are brought to this dilemma, either to give up the virtue of the Ladies, or the power of your Musick.) Whence proceeds the degeneracy of our Morals? Is it not from the loss of ancient musick, by which (says Aristotle) they taught all the Virtues? Else might we turn Newgate into a College of Dorian musicians, who should teach moral Virtues to those People. Whence comes it that our present diseases are so stubborn? Whence is it that I daily deplore my Sciatical pains? Alas! because we have lost their true cure, by the melody of the Pipe. All this was well known to the Ancients, as Theophrastus[2]

[1] Ælian. *Hist. Animal.* lib. xi. cap. 18. and lib. xii. cap. 44 (Pope).

[2] Athenæus, lib. xiv (Pope).

assures

assures us (whence Cælius[1] calls it *loca dolentia decantare*) only indeed some small remains of this skill are preserved in the cure of the Tarantula. Did not Pythagoras[2] stop a company of drunken Bullies from storming a civil house by changing the strain of the Pipe to a sober Spondæus? and yet your modern musicians want art to defend their windows from common Nickers. It is well known that when the Lacedæmonian Mob were up they commonly[3] sent for a Lesbian Musician to appease them, and they immediately grew calm as soon as they heard Terpander sing; Yet I don't believe that the Pope's whole band of music, though the best of this age, could keep his Holiness's Image from being burnt on a fifth of November. Nor would Terpander himself (replyed Albertus) at Billingsgate, nor Timotheus at Hockley-in-the-Hole have any manner of effect, nor both of 'em together bring Horneck[4] to common civility. That's a gross mistake (said Cornelius very warmly) and to prove it so, I have here a small Lyra of my own, fram'd, strung, and tun'd after the ancient manner. I can play some fragments of Lesbian tunes, and I wish I were to try them upon the most passionate creatures alive.—You never had a better opportunity (says Albertus) for yonder are two apple-women scolding, and just ready to uncoif one another. With that Cornelius, undress'd as he was, jumps out into his Balcony, his Lyra in hand, in his slippers, with his breeches hanging down to his ankles, a stocking upon his head, and waistcoat of murrey-colour'd sattin upon his body: He touch'd his Lyra with a very unusual sort of an Harpegiatura, nor were his

[1] Lib. de Sanitate Tuenda, cap. 2 (Pope).

[2] Quintilian. lib. i. cap. 10 (Pope).

[3] Suidas in Timotheo (Pope).

[4] Horneck, a scurrilous scribbler, who wrote a weekly paper, called *The High German Doctor*. See *Dunciad*, III. 152.

hopes

hopes frustrated. The odd Equipage, the uncouth Instrument, the strangeness of the Man and of the Musick, drew the ears and eyes of the whole Mob that were got about the two female Champions, and at last of the Combatants themselves. They approach'd the Balcony, in as close attention as Orpheus's first Audience of Cattle, or that of an Italian Opera, when some favourite Air is just awaken'd. This sudden effect of his Musick encouraged him mightily, and it was observ'd he never touched his Lyre in such a truly chromatick and unharmonick manner as upon that occasion. The mob laugh'd, sung, jump'd, danc'd, and us'd many odd gestures, all which he judg'd to be caused by the various strains and modulations. 'Mark (quoth he) in this the power of the Ionian, in that you see the effect of the Æolian.' But in a little time they began to grow riotous, and throw stones: Cornelius then withdrew, but with the greatest air of Triumph in the world. Brother (said he) do you observe I have mixed unawares too much of the Phrygian; I might change it to the Lydian, and soften their riotous tempers: But it is enough: learn from this Sample to speak with veneration of ancient Musick. If this Lyre in my unskilful hands can perform such wonders, what must it not have done in those of a Timotheus or a Terpander? Having said this, he retir'd with the utmost Exultation in himself, and Contempt of his Brother; and, it is said, behav'd that night with such unusual haughtiness to his family, that they all had reason to wish for some ancient Tibicen to calm his Temper. . . .

CHAPTER XI

The Case of a young Nobleman at Court, with the Doctor's Prescription for the same.

An eminent Instance of Martinus's Sagacity in discovering the Distempers of the Mind, appear'd in the case of a young Nobleman at Court, who was observ'd to grow extremely affected in his speech, and whimsical in all his behaviour. He began to ask odd questions, talk in verse to himself, shut himself up from his friends, and be accessible to none but Flatterers, Poets, and Pickpockets; till his Relations and old Acquaintance judged him to be so far gone, as to be a fit patient for the Doctor.

As soon as he had heard and examined all the symptoms, he pronounced his distemper to be Love.

His friends assured him that they had with great care observ'd all his motions, and were perfectly satisfy'd there was no Woman in the case. Scriblerus was as positive that he was desperately in love with some person or other. 'How can that be?' (said his Aunt, who came to ask the advice) 'when he converses almost with none but himself?' 'Say you so?' he replied, 'why then he is in love with Himself, one of the most common cases in the world. I am astonish'd people do not enough attend this Disease, which has the same causes and symptoms, and admits of the same cure, with the other: especially since here the case of the Patient is the more helpless and deplorable of the two, as this unfortunate passion is more blind than the other. There are people who discover from their very youth, a most amorous inclination to themselves; which is unhappily nurs'd by such Mothers, as with their good will, would never suffer their children to be cross'd in love. Ease, luxury, and idleness, blow up this flame as well as the other: Constant opportunities of conversation with the person beloved (the greatest of incentives) are here impossible to be prevented. Bawds and Pimps in the other love, will be perpetually doing kind offices, speaking a good word for the party, and carrying about Billet doux. Therefore I ask you, Madam, if this Gentleman has not been much frequented by Flatterers, and a sort of people who bring him dedications and verses?' 'O Lord! Sir', (quoth the aunt) 'the house is haunted with them.' 'There it is' (reply'd Scriblerus), 'those are the bawds and pimps that go between a man and himself. Are there no civil Ladies, that tell him he dresses well, has a gentlemanly air, and the like?' 'Why truly, Sir, my nephew is not aukward'—'Look you, Madam, this is a misfortune to him: In former days these sort of lovers were happy in one respect, that they never had any Rivals, but of late they have all the ladies so—Be pleased to answer a few questions more. Whom does he generally talk of?'—'Himself,' quoth the Aunt.—'Whose wit and breeding does he most commend?'—'His own,' quoth the Aunt.—'Whom does he write letters to?'—'Himself.'—'Whom does he dream of?'—'All the dreams I ever heard were of himself.'—'Whom is he ogling yonder?'—'Himself in his looking-glass.'—'Why does he throw back his head in that languishing posture?'—'Only to be blest with a smile of himself as he passes by.'—'Does he ever steal a kiss from himself, by biting his lips?'—'Oh continually, till they are perfect vermilion.'—'Have you observ'd him to use Familiarities with any body?'—'With none but himself: he often embraces himself with folded arms, he claps his hand often upon his hip, nay sometimes thrusts it into—his breast.'

'Madam,' said the Doctor, 'all these are strong symptoms,

symptoms, but there remain a few more. Has this amorous gentleman presented himself with any Love-toys; such as gold Snuff-boxes, repeating-Watches, or Tweezer-cases? those are things that in time will soften the most obdurate heart.'—'Not only so' (said the Aunt), 'but he bought the other day a very fine brilliant diamond Ring for his own wearing.'—'Nay, if he has accepted of this Ring, the intrigue is very forward indeed, and it is high time for friends to interpose. Pray, Madam, a word or two more—Is he jealous that his acquaintance do not behave themselves with respect enough? will he bear jokes and innocent freedoms?'—'By no means; a familiar appellation makes him angry; if you shake him a little roughly by the hand, he is in a rage; but if you chuck him under the chin, he will return you a box on the ear.'—'Then the case is plain: he has the true Pathognomick sign of Love, Jealousy; for no body will suffer his mistress to be treated at that rate. Madam, upon the whole, this Case is extreamly dangerous. There are some people who are far gone in this passion of self-love; but then they keep a very secret Intrigue with themselves, and hide it from all the world besides. But this Patient has not the least care of the Reputation of his Beloved, he is downright scandalous in his behaviour with himself; he is enchanted, bewitch'd, and almost past cure. However, let the following methods be try'd upon him.

'First, let him * * * *Hiatus.* * * * Secondly, let him wear a Bob-wig. Thirdly, shun the company of flatterers, nay of ceremonious people, and of all Frenchmen in general. It would not be amiss if he travel'd over England in a Stage-coach, and made the tour of Holland in a Track-scoute. Let him return the Snuff-boxes, Tweezer-cases (and particularly the Diamond Ring), which

which he has receiv'd from himself. Let some knowing friend represent to him the many vile Qualities of this Mistress of his: let him be shown that her Extravagance, Pride, and Prodigality, will infallibly bring him to a morsel of bread: Let it be prov'd, that he has been false to himself, and if Treachery is not a sufficient cause to discard a Mistress, what is? In short, let him be made to see that no mortal besides himself either loves or can suffer this Creature. Let all Looking-glasses, polish'd Toys, and even clean Plates be removed from him, for fear of bringing back the admired object. Let him be taught to put off all those tender airs, affected smiles, languishing looks, wanton tosses of the head, coy motions of the body, that mincing gait, soft tone of voice, and all that enchanting womanlike behaviour, that has made him the charm of his own eyes, and the object of his own adoration. Let him surprize the Beauty he adores at a disadvantage, survey himself naked, divested of artificial charms, and he will find himself a forked stradling Animal, with bandy legs, a short neck, a dun hide, and a pot-belly. It would be yet better if he took a strong purge once a week, in order to contemplate himself in that condition: at which time it will be convenient to make use of the Letters, Dedications, &c., abovesaid. Something like this has been observ'd, by Lucretius and others, to be a powerful remedy in the case of Women. If all this will not do, I must e'en leave the poor man to his destiny. Let him marry himself, and when he is condemn'd eternally to himself, perhaps he may run to the next pond to get rid of himself, the Fate of most violent Self-lovers.' . . .

CHAPTER XIII[1]

OF THE SECESSION OF MARTINUS, AND SOME HINTS OF HIS TRAVELS.

It was in the year 1699 that Martin set out on his Travels. Thou wilt certainly be very curious to know what they were? It is not yet time to inform thee. But what hints I am at liberty to give, I will.

Thou shalt know then, that in his first Voyage he was carry'd by a prosperous Storm, to a Discovery of the Remains of the ancient Pygmæan Empire.

That in his second, he was as happily shipwreck'd on the land of the Giants, now the most humane people in the world.

That in his third Voyage, he discover'd a whole Kingdom of Philosophers, who govern by the Mathematicks; with whose admirable Schemes and Projects he return'd to benefit his own dear Country; but had the misfortune to find them rejected by the envious Ministers of Queen Anne, and himself sent treacherously away.

And hence it is, that in his fourth Voyage he discovered a Vein of Melancholy, proceeding almost to a Disgust of

[1] Chap. XVI, as originally printed. In the first edition of the *Memoirs* there was no Chap. XIII; and Chaps. XIV ('The Double Mistress') and XV ('Of the strange and never to be paralleled Process at Law upon the marriage of Scriblerus, and the Pleadings of the Advocates') have been omitted by all editors since Warburton, except Bowles. These chapters, though very coarse, describe with much wit the troubles that came upon Martin through falling in love with one of two sisters whom he saw at a show, who were inseparably joined together. Even greater than his love was his admiration of her as a charming monster. Opportunity for satire upon the lawyers and their endless pleadings and appeals from court to court is found in a trial on the question whether the marriage could be dissolved. When the *Memoirs* appeared, a note was prefixed to Chap. XIV, apparently by Pope, in which reference was made to the difference of style in that chapter compared with the rest of the book. It seemed probable, however, that this chapter was written by the Philosopher himself, because he expressly directed that not one word of it should be altered. (Aitken.)

his

his Species; but, above all, a mortal Detestation to the whole flagitious Race of Ministers, and a final Resolution not to give in any Memorial to the Secretary of State, in order to subject the Lands he discover'd to the Crown of Great Britain.

Now if, by these hints, the Reader can help himself to a further discovery of the Nature and Contents of these Travels, he is welcome to as much light as they afford him; I am oblig'd, by all the tyes of honour, not to speak more openly.

But if any man shall ever see such very extraordinary Voyages, into such very extraordinary Nations, which manifest the most distinguishing marks of a Philosopher, a Politician, and a Legislator; and can imagine them to belong to a Surgeon of a Ship, or a Captain of a Merchant-man, let him remain in his Ignorance.

And whoever he be, that shall further observe, in every page of such a book, that cordial Love of Mankind, that inviolable Regard to Truth, that Passion for his dear Country, and that particular attachment to the excellent Princess Queen Anne; surely that man deserves to be pity'd, if by all those visible Signs and Characters, he cannot distinguish and acknowledge the Great Scriblerus.[1]

CHAPTER XIV

Of the Discoveries and Works of the great Scriblerus, made and to be made, written and to be written, known and unknown.

Here therefore, at this great Period, we end our first Book. And here, O Reader, we entreat thee utterly to forget all thou hast hitherto read, and to cast thy eyes only for-

[1] *Gulliver's Travels*, here described in brief, were first intended to form part of Scriblerus' Memoirs.

ward

ward, to that boundless Field the next shall open unto thee; the fruits of which (if thine, or our sins do not prevent) are to spread and multiply over this our work, and over all the face of the Earth.

In the mean time, know what thou owest, and what thou yet may'st owe, to this excellent Person, this Prodigy of our Age; who may well be called The Philosopher of Ultimate Causes, since by a Sagacity peculiar to himself, he hath discover'd Effects in their very Cause; and without the trivial helps of Experiments, or Observations, hath been the Inventor of most of the modern Systems and Hypotheses.

He hath enrich'd Mathematicks with many precise and Geometrical Quadratures of the Circle. He first discover'd the Cause of Gravity, and the intestine Motion of Fluids.

To him we owe all the observations on the Parallax of the Pole-Star, and all the new Theories of the Deluge.

He it was, that first taught the right use sometimes of the *Fuga Vacui*, and sometimes the *Materia Subtilis*, in resolving the grand Phœnomena of Nature.

He it was that first found out the Palpability of Colours; and by the delicacy of his Touch, could distinguish the different Vibrations of the heterogeneous Rays of Light.

His were the Projects of *Perpetuum Mobiles*, Flying Engines, and Pacing Saddles; the Method of discovering the longitude, by Bomb-Vessels, and of increasing the Trade-Wind by vast plantations of Reeds and Sedges.

I shall mention only a few of his Philosophical and Mathematical Works.

1. A compleat Digest of the Laws of Nature, with a Review of those that are obsolete or repealed, and of those that are ready to be renew'd and put in force.

2. A Mechanical

2. A Mechanical Explication of the Formation of the Universe, according to the Epicurean Hypothesis.

3. An Investigation of the Quantity of real Matter in the Universe, with the proportion of the specific Gravity of solid Matter to that of fluid.

4. Microscopical Observations of the Figure and Bulk of the constituent Parts of all fluids. A Calculation of the proportion in which the Fluids of the earth decrease, and of the period in which they will be totally exhausted.

5. A Computation of the Duration of the Sun, and how long it will last before it be burn'd out.

6. A method to apply the Force arising from the immense Velocity of Light to mechanical purposes.

7. An answer to the question of a curious Gentleman; How long a New Star was lighted up before its appearance to the Inhabitants of our earth? To which is subjoin'd a Calculation, how much the Inhabitants of the Moon eat for Supper, considering that they pass a Night equal to fifteen of our natural days.

8. A Demonstration of the natural Dominion of the Inhabitants of the Earth over those of the Moon, if ever an intercourse should be open'd between them. With a Proposal of a Partition-Treaty, among the earthly Potentates, in case of such discovery.

9. Tide-Tables, for a Comet, that is to approximate towards the Earth.

10. The Number of the Inhabitants of London determin'd by the Reports of the Gold-finders, and the tonnage of their Carriages; with allowance for the extraordinary quantity of the *Ingesta* and *Egesta* of the people of England, and a deduction of what is left under dead walls, and dry ditches.

It will from hence be evident, how much all his Studies

were

were directed to the universal Benefit of Mankind. Numerous have been his Projects to this end, of which Two alone will be sufficient to show the amazing Grandeur of his Genius. The first was a Proposal, by a general contribution of all Princes, to pierce the first crust or *Nucleus* of this our Earth quite through, to the next concentrical Sphere: The advantage he propos'd from it was, to find the *Parallax* of the Fixt Stars; but chiefly to refute Sir Isaac Newton's Theory of Gravity, and Mr. Halley's of the Variations. The second was, to build Two Poles to the Meridian, with immense Light-houses on the top of them; to supply the defect of Nature, and to make the longitude as easy to be calculated as the latitude. Both these he could not but think very practicable, by the Power of all the Potentates of the world.

May we presume after these to mention, how he descended from the sublime to the beneficial parts of Knowledge, and particularly his extraordinary practice of physick? From the Age, Complexion, or Weight of the person given, he contrived to prescribe at a distance, as well as at a Patient's bed-side. He taught the way to many modern Physicians to cure their patients by Intuition, and to others to cure without looking on them at all. He projected a Menstruum to dissolve the Stone, made of Dr. Woodward's *Universal Deluge-water*. His also was the device to relieve consumptive or asthmatic persons by bringing fresh Air out of the Country to Town, by pipes of the nature of the Recipients of Air-pumps: And to introduce the Native air of a man's country into any other in which he should travel, with a seasonable Intromission of such Steams as were most familiar to him; to the inexpressible comfort of many Scotsmen, Laplanders, and white Bears.

In Physiognomy, his penetration is such, that from the

Picture

Picture only of any person he can write his Life; and from the features of the Parents, draw the Portrait of any Child that is to be born.

Nor hath he been so enrapt in these Studies as to neglect the Polite Arts of Painting, Architecture, Musick, Poetry, &c. It was he that gave the first hints to our modern Painters, to improve the Likeness of their Portraits by the use of such Colours as would faithfully and constantly accompany the Life, not only in its present state, but in all its alterations, decays, age, and death itself.

In Architecture, he builds not with so much regard to present symmetry or conveniency, as with a Thought well worthy of the lover of Antiquity, to wit, the noble effect the Building will have to posterity, when it shall fall and become a Ruin.

As to Musick, I think Heidegger has not the face to deny that he has been much beholden to his Scores.

In Poetry, he hath appear'd under a hundred different names, of which we may one day give a Catalogue.

In Politicks, his Writings are of a peculiar Cast, for the most part Ironical, and the Drift of them often so delicate and refin'd, as to be mistaken by the vulgar. He once went so far as to write a Persuasive to people to eat their own Children, which was so little understood as to be taken in ill part.[1] He has often written against Liberty in the name of Freemen and Algernon Sydney, in vindication of the Measures of Spain under that of Raleigh, and in praise of Corruption under those of Cato and Publicola.

It is true, that at his last departure from England, in the Reign of Queen Anne, apprehending lest any of these might be perverted to the Scandal of the weak, or

[1] Swift's *Modest Proposal*, published in 1729.

Encouragement

Encouragement of the flagitious, he cast them all, without mercy, into a Bog-house near St. James's. Some however have been with great diligence recover'd, and fish'd up with a hook and line, by the Ministerial Writers, which make at present the great Ornaments of their works.

Whatever he judg'd beneficial to Mankind, he constantly communicated (not only during his stay among us, but ever since his absence) by some method or other in which Ostentation had no part. With what incredible Modesty he conceal'd himself, is known to numbers of those to whom he address'd sometimes Epistles, sometimes Hints, sometimes whole Treatises, Advices to Friends, Projects to First Ministers, Letters to Members of Parliament, Accounts to the Royal Society, and innumerable others.

All these will be vindicated to the true Author, in the course of these Memoirs. I may venture to say they cannot be unacceptable to any, but to those, who will appear too much concern'd as Plagiaries, to be admitted as Judges. Wherefore we warn the publick, to take particular notice of all such as manifest any indecent Passion at the appearance of this Work, as Persons most certainly involved in the Guilt.

MEMOIRS OF THE LIFE OF SCRIBLERUS

The Memoirs of Martinus Scriblerus, printed above, are the only portion of the assorted Scriblerus writings which we can feel certain was composed in collaboration before 1715. Other fragments of the projected cyclopedia of pedantry appeared later in miscellanies, where they were attributed variously to Swift, Pope, or Arbuthnot. Several of these repay the reader well, notably Pope's *Bathos, or Treatise on the Art of Sinking in Poetry,* and Arbuthnot's *Essay Concerning the Origin of the Sciences.* All were reluctant to abandon the subject, and Swift in particular was urged by the others, after his retirement, 'to attend . . . to the life and adventures of Scriblerus', but Swift refused. Pope, he knew, was better qualified to ridicule the poetasters and verse-pedants; to Arbuthnot he resigned the whip with which to lash pseudo-science. Besides, Martinus would never discover the Yahoos! Swift cast about for a more intelligent hero, and fell upon Gulliver.

Scriblerus remained for him a bagatelle, useful to divert the world but not to vex it. Either Swift himself or some one who had access to his manuscript notes (the parallel in narrative detail admits of no other hypothesis) wrote these abbreviated *Memoirs of the Life of Scriblerus,* a *jeu d'esprit* in which the satirist scores his own literary activities. Here, at any rate, is an alternative biography of the Grub-Street hero created by Swift, the 'few hints which I design one day to extend into a sizeable volume', and the final decision to abandon the enterprise because of 'the incapacity I have all along discovered to do justice to my friend'.

These *Memoirs* have never been reprinted, and remain all but unknown. Professor R. F. Jones, of Washington University, St. Louis, Mo., first called my attention to them and expressed his conviction that they were written by Swift, an opinion in which I concur.

The text reproduced is that of the first and only edition, 1723.

AS I have a tender Regard to Men of great Merit, and small Fortunes, I shall let slip no Opportunity of bringing them to Light, when either through a peculiar Modesty, or some Unhappiness in their Personal Appearance, they have been unwilling to present themselves to the World, and have been consequently no otherwise remarkable in it, than by the Number or Size of their Performances. This Piece of Humanity was instilled into me by an accidental Turn in my own Fortunes, which was owing to the Discovery a Man of great Penetration and Power made of the Excellence and Superiority of my Genius; and reflecting how much it was obscur'd by a Thread-bare Coat, very graciously advanc'd me to a Station of good Profit and little Trouble, any farther than to provide others to do my Business. This gave me an Opportunity of cultivating my Person, which had lain long unregarded, in which Branch of my Profession I am so considerably advanced, that I often over-hear the Good Women, as I pass by, cry out, L—d! how sleek our D——r is. This Piece of Flattery, with some other private Reasons, not very material to insert here, makes me advance twice a Year to shew my Person and Parts, for the Sake and Improvement of my Male and Female Auditors; this generally occasions Matter of mutual compliment, and is the Support of a civil Correspondence the Year round.

Here you see an Instance of the Grand Foible in human Nature, for which I will not make any Apology, though I have the greatest Authority of my Side; my Design being at present to celebrate a Person, whose Merit will employ all the Stock of Genius I have collected, so that begging the gentle Reader to excuse these few Hints which I design one Day to extend into a sizeable Volume, I shall,

without

without farther Ceremony, conduct him out of the Entry to the Place of Entertainment.

I say, proceeding upon this Principle,

Haud ignara mali miseris succurrere disco.

I have, in Justice to this worthy Gentleman, who (notwithstanding his Writings have furnish'd this our noble City with its politest Conversation for ten Years past) might otherwise have remain'd in Obscurity, collected some remarkable Circumstances of his Life, which I assure the Reader are related with all imaginable Truth and Accuracy.

The first of this antient Family that distinguish'd himself in the World was Joachim Scriblerus, a very learned Divine; he flourished in the Thirteenth and Fourteenth Centuries, and wrote an immense Quantity of very valuable Books in Divinity, of which there remain Thirty Two compleat Bodies, Seventy Six Commentaries, besides Two Thousand Dissertations and separate Treatises; of which, a great Part were to be seen in a curious Collection of most rare Books, set forth in a neighbouring Metropolis, by that Ingenious Gentleman, T——— R———.

This Joachim had Seven Sons, who were all educated under the Father till they came of Age, but were then turned out to the wide World with a sufficient Quantity of Quills, and other Implements, to get a Livelihood. But as the Father was to portion out his Stock into so many equal Parts, neither of these young Gentlemen were able to make any great Figure among the *Literati*; so that not one of the Family broke out in any remarkable Manner till the last Century, when the scattered Genius[1] of the

[1] Here it may not be improper to remark the near Relation of Quills and Genius. When a Man makes any bold Stroke in Rhime, don't we cry,—

Family

Family was collected into the Hands of the only Male Heir, to whose Life and History the curious Reader is desired to attend.

Timothy Scriblerus was the Son of an eminent Stationer, who for several Years after Marriage was in Expectation of a Male Heir; Daughters he had in Abundance, but his chief Concern was, least the Fame of the Family should dwindle for Want of a Son, and the World should not know he was any Relative of Old Joachim. This made him frequently very pensive, and one Day when he was more than ordinary so, an elderly Woman observing the Concern in his Countenance, came up to the Shop Door, and shaking her Head, accosted him in the following Manner: I am very sorry for your Misfortune, my good Master, but if you will cross my Hand with a small Spill, and follow my Advice, you shall have a Son to your Wish before the Year is out. The Mention of a Circumstance that he could not imagine how she came acquainted with, encouraged him to gratify her in any Request, whereupon he desired her to sit down and proceed. You are to know then, Sir, said she, that from my Acquaintance with the Stars I came by the Knowledge of your Wants; and by my great Skill in Natural Magick, to understand the Method of supplying them; provided you do your Part and follow this Direction: He promis'd strict Observance, and received the following Prescript: Take Seven of the fairest Sheets of Paper, and upon each of them you must have Seven Alphabets of Seven different Languages varied Seventy Seven times, so that no one Letter stand twice in the same Posture;

That's a fine Flight,—he soars;—that's a lofty Expression;—or,—his Fancy is upon the Wing; finding the Sentence always dignify'd by an Allusion to a Goose-Wing, which shews the Preeminence, tho' I compliment my Friend by making them signify the same.

when

when you have done this, clip all these Letters asunder, and sew them up in a Pillowbier, and upon a certain critical Conjuncture . . . .

. . . .

During this Operation the Pillow must be placed so, that she may incline herself towards the Right Side, I suppose from that Hint of the Poet's,

Virgam Dextra tenet——

The Good Man communicated this to his Wife, and they took the first Opportunity of following her Advice: Accordingly in Nine Months Time they were in daily Expectation of Success. It happen'd one Evening they were amusing themselves with the Prospect of their Bliss, and laying Schemes for the Education and Advancement of their promis'd Heir; the Conversation made such an Impression upon the Woman that she dreamt that Night the following Dream: She thought the Pains of Childbearing were coming upon her, and order'd the Midwife to be sent for, who no sooner enter'd the Room but ran to her Assistance, and immediately, with one dreadful Pang, out came a monstrous Thing, which the Midwife taking to the Light, in a great Fright, cry'd out, L—d! what is this? And laying it down upon the Table there issued from it a great Stream of Liquid, that divided itself into ten thousand little Branches, that spread themselves over the whole Room: This alarm'd the Company, which by this Time she thought was grown very numerous from the Flock of good Women that came to assist at her Labour; every body crowded to see the young Progeny, when, to their horrid Amasement, they found it was a great black Inkhorn sending out innumerable Streams of ink; this so alarm'd her that she awaked.

In dreadful Consternation she continued the remaining

Part

Part of the Night, to think what could be the Event of so uncouth a Dream; but in the Morning advising with her Husband, they determined to go to a Man in the next Street, who had great Skill in Dreams, and other Misteries of Nature; accordingly up they got, and were heying to the Expounder, when they were met at the Door, by the same good Woman, whose advise they had followed with such Success; and immediately taking her by the Arm drew her in, and desired her Opinion of the Dream that had created in them so many Fears, which they related as above, not omitting the least Circumstance. Here the Sallow Sorceress paus'd a while, then with a chearful Countenance, that dispersed half their Fears, began: The Inkhorn with those innumerable Streams issuing from it, are the Types, or Symbols of his Genius, and the Extent of it; by them are signify'd the great Variety of Productions in human Learning, that will render him the Admiration and Surprize of all the Universe; as to that Spout, it betokens the Sex, and that it will be a Son. Overjoy'd at this Interpretation they dismis'd her with a Reward, determining to wait the Event with Patience. In a few Days the Woman was brought to Bed of a Son, which assur'd them of the remaining Part; and now all their Hearts were set upon, was the proper Method of educating it, least by any false Step they should mar the great Genius that was to be the Light of future Ages. Long Time they consulted together, at last determin'd to watch the little Motions of his Infancy, and learn from them how best to humour his Genius. They observ'd no Diversion took so much with him as the ratling of Paper, and dabling in Ink, and that young Tim was never better pleased than when up to the Elbows in it; this they look'd upon as an Earnest of what was promised in the Dream, and resolv'd to encourage him as far as their Stock would permit.

permit. One Day the Nurse, with great Joy, came running to the Father to tell him Master Tim call'd Papa, but the Father soon found the Mistake, and that the first Word Tim utter'd was, Paper. As Tim advanc'd in Years, the manifest bent of his Genius determin'd the Father to put him Apprentice to a Scrivener, where he might learn to write a legible and swift Hand, that his Invention might not wait for his Pen; which was well judged, for I myself must acknowledge that in the Heat of my Imagination, I have had such a quick Succession of beautiful Thoughts, that for Want of Speed to reduce them to Pen, Ink, and Paper, the World has lost, I sigh to repeat it, a most valuable Treasure, both of Instruction and Entertainment. This was prudently avoided, for, by incessant Practice, Tim, in a little Time, wrote as fast as he could think. The Father propos'd to him Accounts, but Tim prudently told him, he was resolv'd not to deal with this World any more than from Hand to Mouth, and begg'd that he might not interrupt his Progress in Affairs of greater Moment. Thus Tim sally'd out, and in the two first Years of his Apprenticeship he apply'd himself so diligently to his Improvement, that, without interrupting his Master's Business, he had transcrib'd 70 Volumes in Folio, of different Languages; he could repeat by Heart all the Seven Wise Masters had said, he knew all the Seven Champions Conquer'd, and the History of the Seven Wonders of the World. He had dipp'd into 7 Sciences, and began now to be in Vogue among the People of Letters. The distress'd of all Kinds came to him to have their Cases drawn up, preferring Tim before his Master. He had such an easy Knack in the Epistolary Way, that he could dress up the Complaint of a forsaken Chamber Maid in the most affecting Terms, describe the Case of a poor Invalid, whether directed to a General, or a Surgeon;

Surgeon; in short, all Cases came before him, and he grew intimate with the Town Intrigues, and learn'd behind the Desk, in a low Way, what he afterwards treated of in the sublime. Tim now began to think that Servitude was an Enemy to Great Minds, that they should not be cramp'd by low Indentures, left his Master, and returned to his Father, who gave him Entertainment in his House, and, to keep his Genius in Play, allow'd him a Rheam of Paper, and a Quartern of Ink every Day: Tho' this was an expensive Article, he was resolv'd to improve his Son's Talents at the Hazzard of his own Fortunes. So unbounded was the Genius of our young Student that he would one Day write a System of Physick; the next, a Comedy, or Copy of Verses; a third, would make a Sermon; the next, a Tale of a Tub, or Romance; but had this peculiar Turn in his Temper (whether it proceeded from natural Modesty, or Policy, I will not venture to determine) that he never would own his Productions, but always father'd them upon some body or other: I remember a Copy of his that appear'd under the Name of P——e, wherein he compliments a musical Lady, but the World found him out here, and tho' they look'd upon it as one of his Juvenile Performances, every body said it was prettily done for one of his Bigness. Tim now apply'd himself to his Studies so strictly that his Father was forced to encrease his Allowance: This fell so heavy upon him, and the Stock wasted so fast, that in a short Time he had no Paper to serve his Customers; his Trade fell off, he run to Decay, and was forc'd to turn himself and his Wife upon their Son for a Support from that Genius they had so carefully indulg'd. Tim soon got him an Appartment, any thing contented him so he had no Noise over his Head; but the Alteration in the Method of Life had such Effect upon the good old Couple, that they were both

seiz'd

seiz'd with an Atrophy, and languishing a few Days, dyed. Now the young Man being more at large than before, began to keep a little Company, and it was soon buzz'd about that Tim was the greatest Genius of the Age, and the Booksellers began to hunt after him; some offer'd Money, but he was so great a Contemner of Mammon that he was never known to keep Company with more than a Tester at once: They attack'd him different Ways to no Purpose, Tim was resolv'd to stand upon his own Bottom, knowing his Capacity would allow him to imitate the sublimest Wits of his Time, and that a Title Page well countenanced would not fail of selling Three Editions at least. It happen'd unluckily about this Time that Tim fell sick of a Fever that settled in his Head, and he would run up and down in Alleys and Corners affronting every Body: In this Mood a Friend of mine met him one Day, and Tim accosted him with an great Oath, Z——ds, Sir, Don't you know me? Not I indeed, Sir, quoth my Friend, very civilly. No, Sir, I am J——n D——s Sir, the only Man alive that has a true Taste of the Sublime. Sir, your most humble Servant, says my Friend, then you are not the Man I took you for. To convince you that I am, quoth Tim, stooping down to the Kennel, take that, and throws a great Handful of Mud all over his Cloaths. My Friend acknowledg'd his Mistake, and got out of his Reach as fast as he could. Another Time he collected a great Mob about him, and was telling them that those Letters the World call'd Mr. Bull's were not Mr. Bull's, and that he could prove they were wrote Two Thousand Years before Mr. Bull was ever thought of. Three or Four Gentlemen passing by over-heard Tim talk in this extravagant Manner, and desired him to keep his Temper a Minute and they wou'd convince him Mr. Bull was the Man that wrote those Letters. How! says Tim, do you pretend to contradict

contradict a Master of a College, (for in those Vagaries he kept to his Humour of personating some Great Man) I tell you, you are a Parcel of ignorant blockheadly Dunces: Here he fell a kicking, and flouncing, and splashing, that the Company was glad to make the best of their Way, for fear of worse Usage. In these Reveries he continued a good while, till Somebody put him into a Course of Physick, and recovered him perfectly. Now he set himself to Work once more, very gravely, for the Improvement of Mankind; and fell upon Two Things. The first was, to wipe out a Flaw in History that the World had passed by for near 1700 Years; and, as a Matter of great Importance, he studied Night and Day to find Proofs to countenance this new and useful Invention. Having settled the Thing to his Mind, he took an Opportunity to tell the World of what Importance it was to be set right in the Affair under his Consideration; and after opening the Mistake to them, began to Reason with them after this Manner: Look ye, Gentlemen, at the Time he lived, the Places he dwell'd in were under the Roman Jurisdiction, and were governed by Lord Lieutenants, so that he could have no Kingdom under them; and if he had a Mind to one by himself, he must have travelled a great Way, Three Parts of the known World being then in their Dominions: But why stand I to prove this! Gentlemen, here is my Hand upon it, I have considered the Thing seriously, and I protest to you solemnly, *in verbo Sacerdotis*, as I hope to change this troublesome —— Life for a better, he was so far from having a Kingdom, that he had not one Foot of Land in all the World; and if either of us had been alive then, and in the same Street, he would have had no more to do with us than the Emperor of Russia has at this Moment. Here Tim made his Bow, and left them to consider of it. Now, thinks he, I have made Way for a fine Argument; and observing

observing he had set the People all agog, he thought this the critical Time to try the Extent of his Genius by managing this whole Argument himself, *Pro* and *Con.* Immediately he publish'd an Answer to his former Assertion, proving that he was a King, and had great Authority upon Earth; and if he attempted to assert the Contrary, he would put him in the C——s, and convince him to his Cost. And now the Storm began to thicken; one Day he would publish, *A Vindication of, &c.* Another, *A Letter to, &c.* A Third, *A Defence of, &c.* Sometimes calling himself[1] ——, or ——, or ——, or ——, or ——, or ——, giving a new Name to every Treatise, and the whole Town began to be in an Uproar for Fear of Daggers drawing, for he would give the Lye again and again, and appeal to three or four at a Time, of each Side, to prove each lied. And tho' he frequently used Language below a Porter, yet he reason'd so much like a Divine, produc'd so many strong Arguments, and couch'd so much Artifice on each Side the Question, that not one of them all refused to own his Productions; but every body swore their Adversaries were ——. The Town continu'd in the Mistake, and least they should any longer, and in Honour to my Friend, I take this Opportunity of assuring them they were every one wrote with his own Hand.

The Second was, he having run through all Universal Systems of Phylosophy, and traced Nature in all her Intricacies, was so familiar with every Operation she was Mistress of, knew the Necessity of her acting in the regular Manner she does, that he had convinc'd himself there was no Occasion for a superior Power; and that this Piece of useful Knowledge should not be kept a Secret from the World, he oblig'd them with his Reasons in several very

[1] Here was a List of **Rt. Rds. Rds.** and **M. As.** which the Bookseller thinks fit to leave out.

elaborate

elaborate Discourses, under the Names of T——d, C——s, C——o, to which the *Beau Monde* are vastly beholden for the most agreeable Set of Morals they ever put in Practice.

I have not been able to collect all the scatter'd Pieces of his, for Want of Time and proper Correspondents, tho' I must not omit three curious little Tracts of P—ns, F——ts, and D—d——ns, all surprizing Pieces of Wit and Ingenuity; with these he complimented Dr. S——ft, which, tho' they were too gay for one of his Cloth, might have set him up for a Wit, had not the World known that his Talent lay more in sound Divinity than Repartee.

I shall take my Leave of the Reader, intreating him, First, not to consider these Memorandums as a perfect History; that was not what I promised, but only look upon it as the Token of a Heart full of Gratitude towards a Man I acknowledge myself, to the last Degree, beholden to. That I could not write for Fame he will be assur'd, when he reflects upon the Incapacity I have all along discover'd to do Justice to my Friend, and I hope no body will descend to suspect me of any Thing else.

I must obviate one Reflection I am aware of, viz. That there is not one Word in the whole Book in different Character, by saying, that in true History there is no Room for Humour or Wit; and I must own I have stifled several very pretty Turns, for no other Reason than that they were below the Dignity of the Subject.

A MEDITATION UPON A BROOM-STICK

The occasion for this famous parody has been described once and for all by Thomas Sheridan as follows:

'In the yearly visits which he made to London, during his stay there, he passed much of his time at Lord Berkeley's, officiating as chaplain to the family, and attending Lady Berkeley in her private devotions. After which, the doctor, by her desire, used to read to her some moral or religious discourse. The countess had at this time taken a great liking to Mr. Boyle's Meditations, and was determined to go through them in that manner; but as Swift had by no means the same relish for that kind of writing which her ladyship had, he soon grew weary of the task. . . . The next time he was employed in reading one of these Meditations, he took an opportunity of conveying away the book, and dexterously inserted a leaf, on which he had written his own 'Meditation on a Broomstick'; after which, he took care to have the book restored to its proper place, and in his next attendance on my lady, when he was desired to proceed to the next Meditation, Swift . . . with an inflexible gravity of countenance, proceeded to read the Meditation, in the same solemn tone he had used in delivering the former. . . . Soon after, some company coming in, Swift pretended business, and withdrew, foreseeing what was to follow. Lady Berkeley, full of the subject, soon entered upon the praises of those heavenly Meditations of Mr. Boyle. "But," said she, "the doctor has been just reading one to me, which has surprised me more than all the rest . . . I mean, that excellent Meditation on a Broomstick." The company looked at each other with some surprise, and could scarce refrain from laughing. . . . One of them opened the book, and found it there indeed, but in Swift's handwriting; upon which a general burst of laughter ensued; and my lady, when the first surprise was over, enjoyed the joke as much as any of them, saying, "What a vile trick that rogue played me. But it is his way, he never balks his humour in any thing." The affair ended in a great deal of harmless mirth, and Swift, you may be sure, was not asked to proceed any farther in the Meditations.' [1]

In this trifle, Swift proves the truth which he states explicitly in the verses in which he refuses to write to a lady in the heroic style—that laughter will cure affectation more effectively than reproof. The *Meditation* was written in 1704, and was first printed in 1710 in the original edition here reproduced.

[1] Thomas Sheridan, *Life of Swift*, prefixed to his edition of Swift's *Works*, re-edited by John Nichols, vol. i, 1812, pp. 113–14.

THIS single Stick, which you now behold ingloriously lying in that neglected Corner, I once knew in a flourishing State in a Forest: It was full of Sap, full of Leaves, and full of Boughs: But now, in vain does the busy Art of Man pretend to vye with Nature, by tying that wither'd Bundle of Twigs to its sapless Trunk: 'Tis now at best but the Reverse of what it was, a Tree turned upside down, the Branches on the Earth, and the Root in the Air: 'Tis now handled by every dirty Wench, condemned to do her Drudgery, and, by a capricious kind of Fate, destin'd to make other Things Clean, and be Nasty itself: At length, worn to the Stumps in the Service of the Maids, 'tis either thrown out of Doors, or condemned to the last Use of kindling a Fire. When I beheld this, I sigh'd, and said within my self, Surely mortal Man is a Broom-stick; Nature sent him into the World strong and lusty in a thriving Condition, wearing his own Hair on his Head, the proper Branches of this Reasoning Vegetable, till the Axe of Intemperance has lopp'd off his green Boughs, and left him a wither'd Trunk: He then flies to Art, and puts on a Periwig, valuing himself upon an unnatural Bundle of Hairs, all covered with Powder that never grew on his Head; but now should this our Broom-stick pretend to enter the Scene, proud of those Birchen Spoils it never bore, and all covered with Dust, though the Sweepings of the finest Lady's Chamber, we should be apt to ridicule and despise its Vanity. Partial Judges that we are of our own Excellencies, and other Men's Defaults!

But a Broom-stick, perhaps you will say, is an Emblem of a Tree standing on its Head; and pray what is Man, but a topsy-turvy Creature, his Animal Faculties perpetually mounted on his Rational, his Head where his Heels

should

should be, groveling on the Earth! And yet, with all his Faults, he sets up to be an universal Reformer and Corrector of Abuses, a Remover of Grievances, rakes into every Slut's Corner of Nature, bringing hidden Corruptions to the Light, and raises a mighty Dust where there was none before, sharing deeply all the while in the very same Pollutions he pretends to sweep away: His last Days are spent in Slavery to Women, and generally the least deserving; till worn to the Stumps, like his Brother Bezom, he is either kick'd out of Doors, or made use of to kindle Flames, for others to warm themselves by.

THE PARTRIDGE-BICKERSTAFF PAPERS

John Partridge, originally John Hewson, an obscure cobbler, had come to London and set up as an astrologer in 1678. The ignorant who patronized him made him rich, and King William, grateful for his vile and continued denunciations of Popery, made him court physician without salary. By 1700, Partridge, though a dunce, had become the professional heir of Lilly, the leading astrologer in London; and the object of frequent ridicule by the Wits, including Ned Ward and Tom Brown. He throve in spite of persecution. In 1708 Swift unaccountably decided to continue Tom Brown's parodies of Partridge's predictions, under the name of a fictitious, rival astrologer, Bickerstaff, in which he predicted the death of Partridge on 29 March. On the morning of 30 March, newsboys hawked about the streets Swift's *Elegy* on the death of Partridge; and a few days later appeared the second pamphlet here reprinted, *An Account of the Death of Partridge.* The joke would no doubt have ended here had not Partridge been such an idiot as to argue that he was alive, and had been alive also on the preceding 29 March. To this Swift replied in his *Vindication.*

The hoax became famous. Congreve, Gay, Pope, Steele, and many others took part in the flood of squibs and announcements which were published to prove to Partridge that he was dead. The Company of Stationers struck Partridge's name from their rolls, making it impossible for him to continue the publication of his almanac, *Merlinus Liberatus.* He appeared in court to contest the action, but the Lord Chamberlain decided against him. When Steele started the *Tatler*, in 1709, he took the surest means of attracting attention, by capitalizing popular interest in the Partridge affair, and entitled his periodical, *The Lucubrations of Isaac Bickerstaff.*

The best account of Partridge, and of the attacks upon him, is given by John Nichols in the additional notes to his valuable edition of the *Tatler*, vol. v, 1786.

The Bickerstaff papers are here reproduced for the first time from the original editions.

PREDICTIONS FOR THE YEAR 1708.
By ISAAC BICKERSTAFF

I HAVE consider'd the gross Abuse of Astrology in this Kingdom, and upon debating the Matter with my self, I could not possibly lay the Fault upon the Art, but upon those gross Impostors who set up to be the Artists. I know several learned Men have contended that the whole is a Cheat; that it is absurd and ridiculous to imagine, the Stars can have any Influence at all upon humane Actions, Thoughts or Inclinations; And whoever has not bent his Studies that Way, may be excused for thinking so, when he sees in how wretched a manner that noble Art is treated by a few mean illiterate Traders between us and the Stars; who import a yearly Stock of Nonsense, Lyes, Folly, and Impertinence, which they offer to the World as genuine from the Planets, tho' they descend from no greater a Height than their own Brains.

I intend in a short Time to publish a large and rational Defence of this Art, and therefore shall say no more in its Justification at present, than that it hath been in all Ages defended by many learned Men, and among the rest by Socrates himself, whom I look upon as undoubtedly the wisest of uninspired Mortals: To which if we add, that those who have condemned this Art, tho' otherwise Learn'd, having been such as either did not apply their Studies this way, or at least did not succeed in their Applications: Their Testimony will not be of much weight to its Disadvantage, since they are liable to the common Objection of Condemning what they did not understand.

Nor am I at all offended, or think it an Injury to the Art, when I see the common Dealers in it, the Students in Astrology,

Astrology, the Philomaths, and the rest of that Tribe, treated by wise Men with the utmost Scorn and Contempt; but rather wonder, when I observe Gentlemen in the Country, rich enough to serve the Nation in Parliament, poring in Partridge's Almanack, to find out the Events of the Year at Home and Abroad; nor dare to propose a Hunting Match, till Gadbury or he have fix'd the Weather.

I will allow either of the Two I have mention'd, or any others of the Fraternity, to be not only Astrologers, but Conjurers too, if I do not produce a hundred Instances in all their Almanacks, to convince any reasonable Man, that they do not so much as understand common Grammar and Syntax; that they are not able to spell any Word out of the usual road, nor even in their Prefaces correct common Sense or intelligible English. Then for their Observations and Predictions, they are such as will equally suit any Age or Country in the World. 'This Month a certain great Person will be threatned with Death or Sickness.' This the News Paper will tell them, for there we find at the End of the Year, that no Month passes without the Death of some Person of Note; and it would be hard if it should be otherwise, when there are at least Two thousand Persons of Note in this Kingdom, many of them old, and the Almanack-maker has the liberty of chusing the sickliest Season of the Year where he may fix his Prediction; Again, 'This Month an Eminent Clergyman will be preferr'd'; of which there may be some Hundreds, half of them with one Foot in the Grave. Then, 'Such a Planet in such a House shews great Machinations, Plots and Conspiracies, that may in time be brought to Light': After which; if we hear of any Discovery, the Astrologer gets the Honour, if not, his Prediction still stands good. And at last, 'God preserve K. William from

all

all his open and secret Enemies, Amen.' When, if the King should happen to have died, the Astrologer plainly foretold it; otherwise it passes but for the pious Ejaculation of a Loyal Subject: Tho' it unluckily happen'd in some of their Almanacks, that poor K. William was pray'd for many Months after he was dead, because it fell out that he died about the beginning of the Year.

To mention no more of their impertinent Predictions; What have we to do with their Advertisements about Pills and Drinks for the Venereal Disease, or their mutual Quarrels in Verse and Prose of Whig and Tory, wherewith the Stars have little to do.

Having long observ'd and lamented these, and a hundred other Abuses of this Art, too tedious to repeat, I resolv'd to proceed in a new Way, which I doubt not will be to the general Satisfaction of the Kingdom: I can this Year produce but a Specimen of what I design for the future: Having employ'd most part of my Time in adjusting and correcting the Calculations I made for some Years past, because I would offer nothing to the World of which I am not as fully satisfied, as that I am now alive. For these last two Years I have not fail'd in above one or two Particulars, and those of no very great Moment. I exactly foretold the Miscarriage at Toulon, with all its Particulars; and the loss of Admiral Shovell, tho' I was mistaken as to the Day, placing that Accident about 36 Hours sooner than it happen'd; but upon reviewing my Schemes, I quickly found the Cause of that Error. I likewise foretold the Battle at Almanza to the very Day and Hour, with the Loss on both Sides, and the Consequences thereof. All which I shew'd to some Friends many Months before they happen'd. That is, I gave them Papers sealed up, to open in such a Time, after which they were at liberty to read them; and there they found my Predictions

Predictions true in every Article, except one or two very minute.

As for the few following Predictions I now offer to the World, I forbore to publish them till I had perused the several Almanacks for the Year we are now entred on. I find them all in the usual Strain, and I beg the Reader will compare their Manner with mine: And here I make bold to tell the World, that I lay the whole Credit of my Art upon the Truth of these Predictions; And I will be content, that Partridge, and the rest of his Clan, may hoot me for a Cheat and Impostor if I fail in any single particular of Moment. I believe, any Man who reads this Paper will look upon me to be at least a Person of as much Honesty and Understanding, as a common Maker of Almanacks. I do not lurk in the Dark; I am not wholly unknown in the World; I have set my Name at length, to be a Mark of Infamy to Mankind, if they shall find I deceive them.

In one thing I must desire to be forgiven, that I talk more sparingly of Home Affairs; As it would be Imprudence to discover Secrets of State, so it would be dangerous to my Person, but in smaller Matters, and that are not of publick Consequence, I shall be very free; and the Truth of my Conjectures will as much appear from these as the other. As for the most signal Events abroad in France, Flanders, Italy and Spain, I shall make no Scruple to Predict them in plain Terms: Some of them are of Importance, and I hope I shall seldom mistake the Day they will happen; therefore I think good to inform the Reader, that I all along make use of the Old Style observ'd in England, which I desire he will compare with that of the News-Papers, at the time they relate the Actions I mention.

I must add one Word more; I know it hath been the Opinion

Opinion of several Learned, who think well enough of the true Art of Astrology, That the Stars do only incline, and not force, the Actions or Wills of Men: And therefore, however, I may proceed by right Rules, yet I cannot in Prudence so confidently assure the Events will follow exactly as I predict them.

I hope I have maturely consider'd this Objection, which in some Cases is of no little Weight: For Example; A Man may by the Influence of an over-ruling Planet be disposed or inclined to Lust, Rage, or Avarice, and yet by the force of Reason overcome that bad Influence; and this was the Case of Socrates; But the great Events of the World usually depending upon Numbers of Men, it cannot be expected they should all unite to cross their Inclinations, from pursuing a general Design, wherein they unanimously agree. Besides, the Influence of the Stars reaches to many Actions and Events, which are not any way in the Power of Reason; as Sickness, Death, and what we commonly call Accidents, with many more, needless to repeat.

But it is now time to proceed to my Predictions, which I have begun to calculate from the time that the Sun enters into Aries. And this I take to be properly the Beginning of the natural Year. I persue them to the Time that he enters Libra, or somewhat more, which is the busy Period of the Year. The Remainder I have not yet adjusted, upon Account of several Impediments needless here to mention. Besides, I must remind the Reader again, that this is but a Specimen of what I design in succeeding Years to treat more at large, if I may have Liberty and Encouragement.

My first Prediction is but a Trifle, yet I will mention it, to shew how ignorant these Sottish Pretenders to Astrology are in their own Concerns: It relates to Par-

tridge

tridge the Almanack-maker; I have consulted the Star of his Nativity by my own Rules, and find he will infallibly dye upon the 29th of March next, about Eleven at Night, of a raging Feaver; therefore I advise him to consider of it, and settle his Affairs in time.

The Month of APRIL will be observable for the Death of many great Persons. On the 4th, will dye the Cardinal de Noailles Archbishop of Paris: On the 11th, the young Prince of Asturias, Son to the Duke of Anjou: On the 14th, a great Peer of this Realm will dye at his Country House: On the 19th, an old Layman of great Fame for Learning: And on the 23rd, an Eminent Goldsmith in Lombard-Street. I could mention others, both at home and abroad, if I did not consider it is of very little use or Instruction to the Reader, or to the World.

As to Publick affairs: On the 7th of this Month, there will be an Insurrection in Dauphiné, occasion'd by the Oppressions of the People, which will not be quieted in some Months.

On the 15th, will be a violent Storm on the South-East-Coast of France, which will destroy many of their Ships, and some in the very Harbour.

The 19th, will be famous for the Revolt of a whole Province or Kingdom, excepting one City, by which the Affairs of a certain Prince in the Alliance will take a better Face.

MAY, against common Conjectures, will be no very busy Month in Europe, but very signal for the Death of the Dauphin, which will happen on the 7th, after a short Sickness, and grievous Torments with the Strangury. He dies less lamented by the Court, than the Kingdom.

On the 9th, a Mareschal of France will break his Leg by a Fall from his Horse. I have not been able to discover whether he will then dye or not.

On

On the 11th, will begin a most important Siege, which the Eyes of all Europe will be upon: I cannot be more Particular, for in relating Affairs that so nearly concern the Confederates, and consequently this Kingdom, I am forc'd to confine my self, for several Reasons very obvious to the Reader.

On the 15th, News will arrive of a very Surprizing Event, than which nothing could be more unexpected.

On the 19th, three noble Ladies of this Kingdom will against all Expectation, prove with Child, to the great Joy of their Husbands.

On the 23th, a famous Buffoon of the Play-house will dye of a ridiculous Death suitable to his Vocation.

JUNE. This Month will be distinguish'd at home by the utter dispersing of those ridiculous deluded Enthusiasts, commonly call'd the Prophets; occasion'd chiefly by seeing the Time come that many of their Prophesies should be fulfill'd, and then finding themselves deceiv'd by contrary Events. It is indeed to be admir'd how any Deceiver can be so weak to foretell Things near at hand, when a very few Months must of necessity discover the Imposture to all the World; in this Point less Prudent than common Almanack-makers, who are so wise to wander in general, and talk dubiously, and leave to the Reader the Business of interpreting.

On the 1st of this Month, a French General will be kill'd by a random Shot of a Cannon Ball.

On the 6th, a Fire will break out in the Suburbs of Paris, which will destroy above a thousand Houses; and seems to be the foreboding of what will happen, to the Surprise of all Europe, about the End of the following Month.

On the 10th, a great Battle will be fought which will begin at Four of the Clock in the Afternoon, and last till

9 at

9 at Night with great Obstinacy, but no very decisive Event. I shall not name the Place, for the Reasons aforesaid; but the Commanders on each Left Wing will be kill'd.——I see Bonfires, and hear the Noise of Guns, for a Victory.

On the 14th, there will be a false Report of the French King's Death:

On the 20th, the Cardinal Portocarero will dye of a Dissentery, with great Suspicion; but the Report of his Intentions to revolt to King Charles will prove false.

July. The 6th of this Month, a certain General will, by a Glorious Action recover the Reputation he lost by former Misfortunes.

On the 12th, a Great Commander will dye a Prisoner in the Hands of his Enemies.

On the 14th, a shameful Discovery will be made, of a French Jesuit giving Poison to a great Foreign General, and when he is put to the Torture, will make wonderful Discoveries.

In short, this will prove a Month of great Action, if I might have Liberty to relate the Particulars.

At home, the Death of an old famous Senator will happen on the 15th, at his County-House, worn out with Age and Diseases.

But that which will make this Month memorable to all Posterity, is the Death of the French King Lewis XIV. after a Week's Sickness at Marli, which will happen on the 29th about six a Clock in the Evening. It seems to be an effect of the Gout in his Stomach, follow'd by a Flux. And in three Days after Monsieur Chamillard will follow his Master, dying suddenly of an Apoplexy.

In this Month likewise an Ambassador will dye in London, but I cannot assign the day.

August. The Affairs of France will seem to suffer no

change

change for a while under the Duke of Burgundy's Administration; but the Genius that animated the whole Machine being gone, will be the Cause of mighty turns and Revolutions in the following year. The new King makes yet little Change either in the Army or Ministry, but the Libels against his Father that fly about his very Court, give him uneasiness.

I see an Express in mighty haste, with Joy and Wonder in his Looks, arriving by break of day on the 26th of this Month, having travell'd in 3 days a prodigious Journey by Land and Sea. In the Evening I hear Bells and Guns, and see the Blazing of a thousand Bonfires.

A young Admiral of noble Birth does likewise this Month gain immortal Honour by a great Atchievement.

The Affairs of Poland are this Month entirely settled: Augustus resigns his pretensions, which he had again taken up for some time: Stanislaus is peaceably posses'd of the Throne: And the King of Sweden declares for the Emperor.

I cannot omit one particular Accident here at home, and near the end of this Month much Mischief will be done at Bartholomew Fair by the fall of a Booth.

September. This Month begins with a very surprising Fit of Frosty weather, which will last near 12 days.

The Pope having long languish'd last Month the Swellings in his Legs breaking, and the Flesh mortifying, will die on the 11th Instant, and in Three Weeks time after a mighty Contest, be succeeded by a Cardinal of the Imperial Faction but Native of Tuscany, who is now about 61 Years old.

The French Army acts now wholly on the defensive, strongly fortified in their Trenches; and the young French King sends Overtures for a Treaty of Peace, by the Duke of Mantua; which, because it is a matter of State that

concerns

concerns us here at home, I shall speak no further of it.

I shall add but one Prediction more, and that in mystical Terms, which shall be included in a Verse out of Virgil.

Alter erit jam Tethys, & altera quæ vehat Argo
Dilectas Heroas.

Upon the 25th day of this Month, the fulfilling of this Prediction will be manifest to every body.

This is the furthest I have proceeded in my Calculations for the present year. I do not pretend that these are all the great Events which will happen in this Period, but that those that I have set down will infallibly come to pass. It will perhaps still be objected, why I have not spoke more particularly of Affairs at home, or of the Success of our Armies abroad, which I might add could very largely have done; but those in Power have wisely discourag'd Men from meddling in publick Concerns, and I was resolv'd by no means to give the least Offence. This I will venture to say, That it will be a Glorious Campaign for the Allies, wherein the English Forces both by Sea and Land, will have their full share of Honour; That Her Majesty Queen Anne will continue in Health and Prosperity; And that no ill Accident will arrive to any in the Chief Ministry.

As to the particular Events I have mention'd, the Readers may judge by the fulfilling of them, whether I am of the Level with common Astrologers; who with an old paultry Cant, and a few Pot-hooks for Planets to amuse the Vulgar, have, in my Opinion, too long been suffer'd to abuse the World: But an honest Physician ought not to be despis'd, because there are such things as Mountebanks. I hope I have some share of Reputation, which

I would

I would not willingly forfeit for a Frolick of Humour; And I believe no Gentleman, who reads this Paper, will look upon it to be of the same Last or Mould with the common Scribbles that are every Day hawk'd about. My Fortune has plac'd me above the little regards of Scribbling for a few pence, which I neither value nor want: Therefore let not wise Men too hastily Condemn this Essay, intended for a good design to cultivate and improve an Ancient Art long in Disgrace by having fallen into mean and unskilful Hands. A little time will determine, whether I have deceived others, or my self; and I think it no very unreasonable Request, that Men would please to suspend their Judgments till then. I was once of the Opinion with those who despise all Predictions from the Stars, till in the year 1686, a Man of Quality shew'd me written his Album, That the most Learned Astronomer Captain H. assur'd him, he would never believe any thing of the Stars Influence, if there were not a great Revolution in England in the year 1688. Since that time I began to have other Thoughts, and after eighteen years diligent Study and Application, I think I have no Reason to repent of my Pains. I shall detain the Reader no longer than to let him know that the Account I design to give of next years Events shall take in the Principal Affairs that happen in Europe; and if I be denied the Liberty of offering it to my own Country, I shall appeal to the Learn'd World, by publishing it in Latin, and giving Order to have it Printed in Holland.

THE ACCOMPLISHMENT OF THE FIRST OF MR. BICKERSTAFF'S PREDICTIONS, BEING AN ACCOUNT OF THE DEATH OF MR. PARTRIDGE

My LORD,

IN Obedience to your Lordship's Commands, as well as to satisfy my own Curiosity, I have for some Days past enquired constantly after Partrige, the Almanack-maker, of whom it was foretold in Mr. Bickerstaff's Predictions, publish'd about a Month ago, that he should die the 29th Instant about 11 at Night, of a Raging Fever. I had some sort of Knowledge of him when I was employ'd in the Revenue, because he used every Year to present me with his Almanack, as he did other Gentlemen, upon the Score of some little Gratuity we gave him: I saw him accidentally once or twice about 10 Days before he died, and observed he began very much to Droop and Languish, tho' I hear his Friends did not seem to apprehend him in any Danger. About Two or Three Days ago he grew Ill, was confin'd first to his Chamber, and in a few Hours after to his Bed, where Dr. Case and Mrs. Kirleus were sent for to Visit and to Prescribe to him. Upon this Intelligence I sent thrice every Day one Servant or other to enquire after his Health; and yesterday, about Four in the Afternoon, Word was brought me that he was past Hopes; upon which I prevailed with my self to go and see him, partly out of Commiseration, and, I confess, partly out of Curiosity. He knew me very well, seem'd surprized at my Condescention, and made me Complements upon it as well as he could in the Condition he was. The People about him said he had been for some Hours delirious; but when I saw him he had his Understanding

standing as well as ever I knew, and spoke Strong and Hearty, without any seeming Uneasiness or Constraint. After I had told him how sorry I was to see him in those Melancholy Circumstances, and said some other Civilities, suitable to the Occasion, I desired him to tell me freely and ingeniously whether the Predictions Mr. Bickerstaff had publish'd relating to his Death had not too much affected and work'd on his Imagination. He confess'd he had often had it in his Head, but never with much Apprehension till about a Fortnight before; since which Time it had the perpetual Possession of his Mind and Thoughts, and he did verily believe was the true Natural Cause of his present Distemper: For, said he, I am throughly perswaded, and I think I have very good Reasons, that Mr. Bickerstaff spoke altogether by Guess, and knew no more what will happen this Year than I did my self. I told him his Discourse surprized me, and I would be glad he were in a State of Health to be able to tell me what Reason he had to be convinced of Mr. Bickerstaff's Ignorance. He reply'd, I am a Poor Ignorant Fellow, Bred to a Mean Trade, yet I have Sense enough to know that all Pretences of foretelling by Astrology are Deceits, for this manifest Reason, because the Wise and the Learned, who can only know whether there be any Truth in this Science, do all unanimously agree to laugh at and despise it; and none but the Poor, Ignorant, Vulgar, give it any Credit, and that only upon the Word of such silly Wretches as I and my Fellows, who can hardly Write or Read. I then ask'd him why he had not Calculated his own Nativity, to see whether it agreed with Bickerstaff's Prediction? At which he shook his Head, and said, O! Sir, this is no Time for Jesting, but for Repenting those Fooleries, as I do now from the very Bottom of my Heart. By what I can gather from you, said

said I, the Observations and Predictions you printed with your Almanacks were meer Impositions upon the People. He reply'd, If it were otherwise I should have the less to answer for. We have a Common Form for all those Things; as to foretelling the Weather, we never meddle with that, but leave it to the Printer, who takes it out of any Old Almanack as he thinks fit; the rest was my own Invention, to make my Almanack Sell, having a Wife to Maintain, and no other Way to get my Bread, for mending Old Shoes is a Poor Livelihood: And (added he, sighing,) I wish I may not have done more Mischief by my Physick than my Astrology, tho' I had some good Receits from my Grandmother, and my own Compositions were such as I thought could at least do no Hurt.

I had some other Discourses with him, which now I cannot call to mind; and I fear I have already tired your Lordship. I shall only add One Circumstance, that on his Death-bed he declar'd himself a Nonconformist, and had a Fanatick Preacher to be his Spiritual Guide. After Half an Hour's Conversation I took my Leave, being half stifled by the Closeness of the Room. I imagined he could not hold out long, and therefore withdrew to a little Coffee-house hard by, leaving a Servant at the House with Orders to come immediately, and tell me as near as he could the Minute when Partrige should expire, which was not above Two Hours after; when looking upon my Watch, I found it to be above Five Minutes after Seven; by which it is clear that Mr. Bickerstaff was mistaken almost Four Hours in his Calculation. In the other Circumstances he was exact enough; but whether he has not been the Cause of this Poor Man's Death, as well as the Predictor, may be very reasonably disputed. However, it must be confess'd the Matter is odd enough, whether we should endeavour to account for it by Chance,

or

or the Effect of Imagination: For my own Part, tho' I believe no Man has less Faith in these, yet I shall wait with some Impatience, and not without Expectation, the fulfilling of Mr. Bickerstaff's Second Prediction, That the Cardinal de Noailles is to die upon the 4th of April; and if that should be verified as exactly as this of Poor Partrige, I must own I should be wholly surprized, and at a loss, and should infallibly expect the Accomplishment of all the rest.

SQUIRE BICKERSTAFF DETECTED[1]
BY JOHN PARTRIDGE

IT is hard, my dear Country-men of these United Nations: It is very hard, that a Briton born, a Protestant Astrologer, a Man of Revolution-Principles, an Asserter of the Liberty and Property of the People, should cry out, in vain, for Justice against a Frenchman, a Papist, and an illiterate Pretender to Science; that would blast my Reputation, most inhumanly bury me alive, and defraud my Native Country of those Services, that, in my double Capacity, I daily offer the Publick.

What great Provocations I have receiv'd, let the impartial Reader judge, and how unwillingly, even in my own Defence, I now enter the Lists against Falshood, ignorance and Envy: But I am exasperated at length to drag out this Cacus from the Den of Obscurity where he Lurks, detect him by the Light of those Stars he has so impudently traduced, and show there's not a Monster in the Skyes so pernicious and malevolent to Mankind, as an ignorant Pretender to Physick and Astrology. I shall not directly fall on the many gross Errors, nor expose the notorious Absurdities of this prostituted Libeller, till I have let the learned World fairly into the Controversy depending, and then leave the Unprejudic'd to judge of the Merits and Justice of my Cause.

It was towards the Conclusion of the Year, 1707, when an impudent Pamphlet crept into the World, intituled, *Predictions*, &c. by Isaac Bickerstaff, Esq.;—Amongst the many arrogant Assertions laid down by that lying Spirit

[1] Written by Swift with the help of Congreve, this essay was given by Thomas Yalden to Partridge, who published it in good faith as a 'defence' against his tormentors!

of

of Divination, he was pleas'd to pitch on the Cardinal de Noailles, and myself, among many other eminent and illustrious Persons, that were to dye within the compass of the ensuing Year; and peremptorily fixes the Month, Day, and Hour of our Deaths: This, I think, is sporting with Great Men, and Publick Spirits, to the Scandal of Religion, and Reproach of Power; and if Sovereign Princes and Astrologers must make Diversion for the Vulgar——— Why, then farewell, say I, to all Governments, Ecclesiastical and Civil. But, I thank my better Stars, I am alive to confront this false and audacious Predictor, and to make him rue the Hour he ever affronted a Man of Science and Resentment. The Cardinal may take what Measures he pleases with him, as his Excellency is a Foreigner, and a Papist, he has no reason to rely on me for his Justification; I shall only assure the World he is alive, —— but as he was bred to Letters, and is Master of a Pen, let him use it in his own Defence. In the mean time, I shall present the Publick with a faithful Narrative of the ungenerous Treatment and hard Usage I have receiv'd from the virulent Papers and malicious Practices of this pretended Astrologer.

AN ACCOUNT OF THE PROCEEDINGS OF ISAAC BICKERSTAFF, ESQ.

THE 29th of March, Anno Dom. 1708. being the Night this Sham-Prophet had so impudently fix'd for my last, which made little Impression on my Self; but I cannot answer for my whole Family; for my Wife, with a Concern more than usual, prevailed on me to take somewhat to sweat for a Cold; and, between the Hours of 8 and 9, to go to bed: The Maid as she was warming my Bed, with a Curiosity Natural to young Wenches, runs to the Window, and asks of one passing the Street, Who the Bell told for? Dr. Partridge says he, the famous Almanack-maker, who died suddenly, this Evening: The poor Girl, provok'd, told him, He ly'd like a Rascal, the other very sedately replied, The Sexton had so inform'd him, and if false, he was to blame for imposing upon a Stranger. She ask'd a second, and a third, as they pass'd, and every one was in the same Tone. Now I don't say these were Accomplices to a certain Astrological 'Squire, and that one Bickerstaff might be Sauntring thereabouts; because I will assert nothing here but what I dare attest, and plain Matter of Fact. My Wife at this fell into a violent Disorder; and I must own, I was a little discompos'd at the Oddness of the Accident. In the mean time, one knocks at my Door, Betty runs down, and opening, finds a sober, grave Person, who modestly inquires, If this was Dr. Partridge's? She taking him for some cautious City-Patient that came at that Time, for Privacy, shews him into the Dining-Room. As soon as I could compose my self, I went to him, and was surpriz'd to find my Gentleman mounted on a Table with a 2-Foot Rule in his Hand, measuring my Walls, and taking the Dimensions of the

Room.

Room. Pray, Sir, says I, not to interrupt you, have you any Business with me? Only, Sir, replies he, Order the Girl to bring me a better Light, for this is but a very dim one. Sir, says I, my Name is Partridge: Oh! the Doctors Brother, belike, crys he; the Stair-Case, I believe, and these two Apartments hung in close Mourning, will be sufficient, and only a Strip of Bayes round the other Rooms. The Dr. must needs die Rich, he had great Dealings, in his Way, for many Years; if he had no Family-Coat, you had as good use the 'Scutcheons of the Company, they are as Showish, and will look as Magnificent as if he was descended from the Blood-Royal. With that, I assumed a greater Air of Authority, and demand who employ'd him, or how he came there? Why, I was sent, Sir, by the Company of Undertakers, says he, and they were employ'd by the honest Gentleman, who is Executor to the good Dr. departed; and our rascally Porter, I believe is fallen fast asleep with the Black Cloath, and Sconces, or he had been here, and we might have been tacking up by this Time. Sir, says I, pray be advised by a Friend, and make the best of your Speed out of my Doors, for I hear my Wife's Voice (which, by the by, is pretty distinguishable) and in that Corner of the Room stands a good Cudgel, which somebody has felt ere-now; if that light in her Hands, and she know the Business you came about, without consulting the Stars, I can assure you it will be employ'd very much to the Detriment of your Person. Sir, crys he, bowing, with great Civility, I perceive Extreem Grief for the Loss of the Doctor disorders you a little at present, but early in the Morning i'll wait on you, with all necessary Materials. Now I mention no Mr. Bickerstaff, nor do I say, that a certain Star-gazing Squire has been a playing my Executor before his Time; but I leave the World to judge, and if it puts Things

and

and Things fairly together, it won't be much wide of the Mark.

Well once more I get my Doors clos'd, and prepare for Bed, in hopes of a little Repose after so many ruffling Adventures; just as I was putting out my Light in order to it, another bounces as hard as he can knock; I open the Window, and ask who's there, and what he wants? I am Ned, the Sexton, replies he, and come to know whether the Doctor left any Orders for a Funeral Sermon, and where he is to be laid, and whether his Grave is to be Plain or Brickt? Why, Sirrah, says I, you know me well enough, you know I am not dead; and how dare you affront me, after this manner? Alack a day, Sir, replies the Fellow, why, 'tis in Print, and the whole Town knows you are dead; why, there's Mr. White, the Joyner, is but fitting Screws to your Coffin, he'll be here with it in an instant, he was afraid you wou'd have wanted it before this Time. Sirrah, Sarrah, says I, you shall know to morrow, to your Cost, that I am alive, and alive like to be. Why, 'tis strange, Sir, says he, you should make such a Secret of your Death, to us that are your Neighbours; it looks as if you had a Design to defraud the Church of its Dues; and, let me tell you, for one that has lived so long by the Heavens, that's unhandsomely done. Hist, hist, says another Rogue that stood by him, away Doctor into your Flannel Gear as fast as you can, for here's a whole Pack of Dismals coming to you with their black Equipage; and how indecent will it look for you to stand frightning Folks at your Window, when you should have been in your Coffin this Three Hours? In short, what with Undertakers, Embalmers, Joyners, Sextons, and your damn'd Elegy-Hawkers, upon a late Practitioner in Physick and Astrology, I got not one Wink of Sleep that Night, nor scarce a Moments Rest ever since. Now, I doubt not but this

this Villanous Esq; has the Impudence to assert, that these are intirely Strangers to him; He, good Man, knows nothing of the Matter, and Honest Isaac Bickerstaff, I warrant you, is more a Man of Honour, than to be an Accomplice with a Pack of Rascals, that walk the Streets on Nights, and disturb good People in their Beds; but he is out, if he thinks the whole World is Blind; for there is one John Partridge can smell a Knave as far as Grubstreet —— tho' he lies in the most exalted Garret, and writes himself, Esq; ——— But I'll keep my Temper, and proceed in the Narration.

I could not stir out of Doors for the space of 3 Months after this, but presently one comes up to me in the Street, Mr. Partridge, that Coffin you was last buried in, I have not been yet paid for: Dr. cries another Dog, How d'ye think People can live by making of Graves for Nothing? Next time you die, you may e'en toll out the Bell your Self, for Ned. A Third Rogue tips me by the Elbow, and wonders how I have the Conscience to sneak abroad, without paying my Funeral Expences. Lord, says one, I durst have swore that was honest Dr. Partridge, my old Friend; but poor Man he is gone. I beg your pardon says another, you look so like my old Acquaintance that I us'd to consult on some private Occasions; but alack he's gone the way of all Flesh.—Look, look, look crys a Third, after a competent space of staring at me; wou'd not one think our Neighbour the Almanack-maker, was crept out of his Grave, to take to'ther Peep at the Stars in this World, and shew how much he is improv'd in Fortune-telling, by having taken a Journey to the Other?

Nay, the very Reader of our Parish, a good sober discreet Person, has sent 2 or 3 Times for me to come and be buried decently, or send him sufficient Reasons to the Contrary; or, if I have been interr'd in any other Parish,

to

to produce my Certificate as the Act requires. My poor Wife is almost run distracted with being call'd Widdow Partridge, when she knows it's false; and once a Term she is cited into the Court, to take out Letters of Administration. But the greatest Grievance, is a paultry Quack, that takes up my Calling just under my Nose; and in his printed Directions with N.B. Says, ☞ He lives in the House of the late ingenious Mr. John Partridge, an Eminent Practitioner in Leather, Physick, and Astrology.

But to shew how far the wicked Spirit of Envy, Malice, and Resentment can hurry some Men, my Nameless old Persecutor, had provided me a Monument at the Stone-Cutters, and would have erected it in the Parish-Church; and this Piece of Notorious and Expensive Villany had actually succeeded, had I not used my utmost Interest with the Vestry, where it was carry'd, at last, but by Two Voices, that I am still alive. That Stratagem failing, out comes a long Sable Elegy, bedeck'd with Hour-glasses, Mattocks, Sculls, Spades and Skelletons, with an Epitaph as confidently written to abuse me, and my Profession, as if I had been under-ground these Twenty Years.

And after such barbarous Treatment as this, can the World blame me, when I ask, What is become of the Freedom of an English Man? And where is the Liberty and Property, that my old glorious Friend came over to assert? We have drove Popery out of the Nation, and sent Slavery to foreign Climes. The Arts only remain in Bondage, when a Man of Science and Character shall be openly insulted in the midst of the many useful Services he is daily paying the Publick. Was it ever heard, even in Turky or Algiers, that a State-Astrologer was banter'd out of his Life by an ignorant Impostor, or bawl'd out of the World by a pack of Villainous deep-mouth'd Hawkers? Tho' I print Almanacks and publish Advertisements; tho'

I produce

I produce Certificates under the Minister and Church-Wardens Hands, I am alive, and attest the same on Oath at Quarter-Sessions; out-comes, a Full and True Relation of the Death and Interment of John Partridge; Truth is bore down, Attestations neglected, the Testimony of sober Persons despised, and a Man is look'd upon by his Neighbours, as if he had been Seven Years dead, and is buried alive in the midst of his Friends and Acquaintance.

Now, can any Man of Common Sense think it consistent with the Honour of my Profession, and not much beneath the Dignity of a Philosopher, to stand bawling before his own Dore ——— Alive! Alive! Hoa! The famous Dr. Partridge! No Counterfeit, but all Alive ——— As if I had the 12 Celestial Monsters of the Zodiack to shew within, or was forced for a Livelihood to turn Retailer to May and Bartholomew-Fairs. Therefore, if her Majesty would but graciously be pleas'd to think a Hardship of this Nature worthy her Royal Consideration; and the next Parl—m—t, in their great Wisdom, cast but an Eye towards the deplorable Case of their old Philomath, that annually bestows his Poetical good Wishes on them; I am sure, there is one Isaac Bickerstaff, Esq; would soon be truss'd up for his bloody Predictions, and putting good Subjects in terrour of their Lives: And that henceforward to murder a Man by way of Prophecy, and bury him in a printed Letter, either to a Lord or Commoner, shall as legaly entitle him to the present Possession of Tyburn, as if he rob'd on the High-way, or cut your Throat in Bed.

Advertisement

N.B. ☞ *There is now in the Press, my Appeal to the Learned; Or, my general Invitation to all Astrologers, Divines, Physicians, Lawyers, Mathematicians, Philologers, and*

and to the Literati *of the whole World, to come and take their Places in the Common Court of Knowledge, and receive the Charge given in by me, against* Isaac Bickerstaff, *Esq; that most notorious Imposter in Science, and illiterate Pretender to the Stars; where I shall openly Convict him of Ignorance in his Profession, Impudence and Falshood in every Assertion, to the great Detriment and Scandal of Astrology. I shall farther demonstrate to the Judicious, that* France *and* Rome *are at the bottom of this horrid Conspiracy against me; and that* Culprit, *aforesaid, is a Popish Emissary, has paid his Visits to* St. Germains, *and is now in the Measures of* Lewis *the* XIV. *That in attempting my Reputation, there is a general Massacre of Learning design'd in these Realms: And thro' my Sides, there is a Wound given to all the Protestant Almanack-Makers in the Universe.*

Vivat Regina.

A VINDICATION OF ISAAC BICKERSTAFF, ESQ.

MR. PARTRIDGE hath been lately pleased to treat me after a very rough Manner in that which is called, His Almanack for the present Year: Such Usage is very undecent from one Gentleman to another, and does not at all contribute to the Discovery of Truth, which ought to be the great End in all Disputes of the Learned. To call a Man Fool and Villain, and impudent Fellow, only for differing from him in a Point meerly Speculative, is in my humble Opinion a very improper Style for a Person of his Education. I appeal to the Learned World, whether in my last Year's Predictions, I gave him the least Provocation for such unworthy Treatment. Philosophers have differed in all Ages, but the discreetest among them have always differed as became Philosophers. Scurrility and Passion, in a Controversy among Scholars, is just so much of nothing to the purpose; and at best, a tacit Confession of a weak Cause: My Concern is not so much for my own Reputation, as that of the Republick of Letters, which Mr. Partridge hath endeavoured to wound thro' my Sides. If Men of publick Spirit must be superciliously treated for their ingenuous Attempts, how will true useful Knowledge be ever advanced? I wish Mr. Partridge knew the Thoughts which Foreign Universities have conceived of his ungenerous Proceeding with me; but I am too tender of his Reputation to publish them to the World. That Spirit of Envy and Pride, which blasts so many rising Genius's in our Nation, is yet unknown among Professors abroad; The Necessity of justifying my self, will excuse my Vanity, when I tell the Reader, that I have received near a hundred honorary Letters from several Parts of

Europe.

Europe, (some as far as Muscovy) in Praise of my Performance. Beside several others which, as I have been credibly informed, were open'd in the P—— Office, and never sent me. 'Tis true, the Inquisition in P——l was pleased to burn my Predictions, and condemn the Author and Readers of them; but I hope at the same time, it will be considered in how deplorable a State Learning lies at present in that Kingdom: And with the profoundest Veneration for Crown'd Heads, I will presume to add, That it a little concerned his Majesty of P——l, to interpose his Authority in behalf of a Scholar and a Gentleman, the Subject of a Nation with which he is now in so strict an Alliance. But the other Kingdoms and States of Europe have treated me with more Candor and Generosity. If I had Leave to print the Latin Letters transmitted to me from Foreign Parts, they would fill a Volume, and be a full Defence against all that Mr. Partridge, or his Accomplices of the P——l Inquisition, will be ever able to Object; who, by the Way, are the only Enemies my Predictions have ever met with at Home or Abroad. But I hope I know better what is due to the Honour of a learned Correspondence, in so tender a Point. Yet some of those illustrious Persons will perhaps excuse me for transcribing a Passage or two in my own Vindication. The most Learned Monsieur Leibnitz thus addresses to me his Third Letter: *Illustrissimo Bickerstaffio Astrologico instauratori*, &c. Monsieur le Clerc quoting my Predictions in a Treatise he published last Year, is pleased to say, *Ità nuperrimè Bickerstaffius magnum illud Angliæ fidus.* Another great Professor writing of me, has these Words: *Bickerstaffius, nobilis Anglus, Astrologorum hujusce Seculi facilè Princeps.* Signior Magliabecchi, the Great Duke's famous Library-Keeper, spends almost his whole Letter in Compliments and Praises. 'Tis true, the renowned Professor of Astronomy

nomy at Utrecht, seems to differ from me in one Article; but it is after the modest manner that becomes a Philosopher; as, *Pace tanti viri dixerim*: And, Pag. 55. he seems to lay the Error upon the Printer, (as indeed it ought) and says, *Vel forsan error Typographi, sum alioquin Bickerstaffius vir doctissimus*, &c.

If Mr. Partridge had followed this Example in the Controversy between us, he might have spared me the Trouble of justifying my self in so publick a Manner. I believe few Men are readier to own their Errors than I, or more thankful to those who will please to inform him of them. But it seems, this Gentleman, instead of encouraging the Progress of his own Art, is pleased to look upon all Attempts of that Kind as an Invasion of his Province. He has been indeed so wise, to make no Objection against the Truth of my Predictions, except in one single Point, relating to himself: And to demonstrate how much Men are blinded by their own Partiality, I do solemnly assure the Reader, that he is the only Person from whom I ever heard that Objection offer'd; which Consideration alone, I think will take off all its Weight.

With my utmost Endeavours, I have not been able to trace above Two Objections ever made against the Truth of my last Year's Prophecies: The First was of a French Man, who was pleased to publish to the World, That the Cardinal de Noailles was still alive, notwithstanding the pretended Prophecy of Monsieur Biquerstaffe: But how far a Frenchman, a Papist, and an Enemy, is to be believed in his own Case, against an English Protestant, who is true to the Government, I shall leave to the candid and impartial Reader.

The other Objection is the unhappy Occasion of this Discourse, and relates to an Article in my Predictions, which foretold the Death of Mr. Partridge to happen on

March

March 29. 1708. This he is pleased to contradict absolutely in the Almanack he has publish'd for the present Year, and in that ungentlemanly Manner, (pardon the Expression) as I have above related. In that Work, he very roundly asserts, That he is not only now alive, but was likewise alive upon that very 29th of March, when I had foretold he should die. This is the Subject of the present Controversie between us; which I design to handle with all Brevity, Perspicuity and Calmness: In this Dispute, I am sensible, the Eyes not only of England, but of all Europe, will be upon us: And the Learned in every Country will, I doubt not, take Part on that Side where they find most Appearance of Reason and Truth.

Without entring into Criticisms of Chronology about the Hour of his Death, I shall only prove, that Mr. Partridge is not alive. And my First Argument is thus: Above a Thousand Gentlemen having bought his Almanack for this Year, meerly to find what he said against me; at every Line they read, they would lift up their Eyes, and cry out, betwixt Rage and Laughter, They were sure no Man alive ever writ such damn'd Stuff as this. Neither did I ever hear that Opinion disputed. So that Mr. Partridge lies under a Dilemma, either of disowning his Almanack, or allowing himself to be, No Man alive. Secondly, Death is defined by all Philosophers, a Separation of the Soul and Body. Now it is certain, that the poor Woman, who has best Reason to know, has gone about for some time to every Alley in the Neighbourhood, and swore to the Gossips, that Her Husband had neither Life nor Soul in Him. Therefore if an uninformed Carcass walks still about, and is pleased to call it self Partridge, Mr. Bickerstaff does not think himself any way answerable for that. Neither had the said Carcass any Right to beat the poor Boy, who happen'd to pass by it in the Street,

Street, crying, A full and true Account of Dr. Partridge's Death, &c.

Thirdly, Mr. Partridge pretends to tell Fortunes, and recover stolen Goods; which all the Parish says he must do by conversing with the Devil, and other evil Spirits: And no wise Men will ever allow he could converse personally with either, till after he was dead.

Fourthly, I will plainly prove him to be dead, out of his own Almanack for this Year, and from the very Passage which he produces to make us think him alive. He there says, He is not only now alive, but was also alive upon that very 29th of March, which I foretold he should die on: By this, he declares his Opinion, That a Man may be alive now, who was not alive a Twelvemonth ago. And indeed, there lies the Sophistry of his Argument. He dares not assert he was alive but since that 29th of March, but that he is now alive, and was so on that day: I grant the latter; for he did not die till night; as appears by the printed Account of his Death, in *a Letter to a Lord*; and whether he is since revived, I leave the World to judge. This indeed is perfect cavilling, and I am ashamed to dwell any longer upon it.

Fifthly, I will appeal to Mr. Partridge himself, whether it be probable I could have been so indiscreet, to begin my Predictions with the only Falshood that ever was pretended to be in them; and this in an Affair at Home, where I had so many Opportunities to be exact; and must have given such Advantages against me to a Person of Mr. Partridge's Wit and Learning, who, if he could possibly have rais'd one single Objection more against the Truth of my Prophecies, would hardly have spared me.

And here I must take Occasion to reprove the abovementioned Writer of the Relation of Mr. Partridge's Death, in a *Letter to a Lord*; who was pleased to tax me

with

with a Mistake of Two whole Hours in my Calculation of that Event. I must confess, this Censure pronounced with an Air of Certainty, in a Matter that so nearly concerned me, and by a grave judicious Author, moved me not a little. But tho' I was at that Time out of Town, yet several of my Friends, whose Curiosity had led them to be exactly informed, (for as to my own Part, having no Doubt at all in the Matter, I never once thought of it) assured me I computed to something under half an Hour; which (I speak my private Opinion) is an Error of no very great Magnitude, that Men should raise Clamour about it. I shall only say, it would not be amiss, if that Author would henceforth be more tender of other Men's Reputation as well as his own. It is well there were no more Mistakes of that kind; if there had, I presume he would have told me of them with as little Ceremony.

There is one Objection against Mr. Partridge's Death, which I have sometimes met with, tho' indeed very slightly offered; That he still continues to write Almanacks. But this is no more than what is common to all of that Profession; Gadbury, Poor Robin, Dove, Wing, and several others, do yearly publish their Almanacks, tho' several of them have been dead since before the Revolution. Now the Natural Reason of this, I take to be, That whereas it is the Priviledge of other Authors, to live after their Deaths; Almanack-makers are alone excluded, because their Dissertations treating only upon the Minutes as they pass, became useless as those go off. In Consideration of which, Time, whose Registers they are, gives them a Lease in Reversion, to continue their Works after their Death: Or, perhaps, a Name can make an Almanack, as well as it can sell one. And to strengthen this Conjecture, I have heard the Booksellers affirm, That they have desired Mr. Partridge to spare himself further Trouble, and

and only lend them his Name, which could make Almanacks much better than himself.

I should not have given the Publick, or my self, the Trouble of this Vindication, if my Name had not been made use of by several Persons, to whom I never lent it; one of which, a few days ago, was pleased to father on me a new Set of Predictions. But I think those are Things too Serious to be trifled with. It grieved me to the Heart, when I saw my Labours, which had cost me so much Thought and Watching, bawl'd about by the common Hawkers of Grubstreet, which I only intended for the weighty Consideration of the gravest Persons. This prejudiced the World so much at first, that several of my Friends had the Assurance to ask me, Whether I were in Jest? To which I only answered coldly, That the Event would shew. But it is the Talent of our Age and Nation, to turn Things of the greatest Importance into Ridicule. When the End of the Year had verified all my Predictions, out comes Mr. Partridge's Almanack, disputing the Point of his Death; so that I am employed, like the General, who was forced to kill his Enemies twice over, whom a Necromancer had raised to Life. If Mr. Partridge has practiced the same Experiment upon himself, and be again alive, long may he continue so; that does not in the least contradict my Veracity: But I think I have clearly proved, by invincible Demonstration, that he died at furthest within half an Hour of the Time I foretold.

A COMPLEAT COLLECTION OF GENTEEL AND INGENIOUS CONVERSATION

Swift's *Hints toward an Essay on Conversation*, 1709, which contains the ideas of this treatise in briefer form, and allusions to the project in his letters, prove that he had the subject in mind for over thirty years. It was set aside for other tasks till after the death of Stella. In a letter to Gay, 28 August 1731, he wrote that he was again at work 'to reduce the whole politeness, wit, humour, and style of England into one short system, for the use of all persons of quality, and particularly the maids of honour'. The best part is the *Introduction*, about four-fifths of which is here reprinted. The three dialogues are represented by the opening pages of the first dialogue, which are ample to illustrate the vapid *clichés* of conversation, many of which remain to this day the currency of what the world is pleased to call polite society.

In reponse to an appeal for financial aid, Swift gave the manuscript to Mrs. Barber (wife of an impoverished Dublin tailor, who had been the object of his charity before) to raise what money she could with it. It was published with great success, and the *Dialogues* were acted in a Dublin theatre, the proceeds of sale at the bookshops and of production on the stage yielding more than enough to relieve the poor woman's needs. From Swift's last years of activity, when his mind was about to fail, comes this proof that his wit and his philanthropy were active and unimpaired.

The text reproduced is that of the original Dublin edition, 1738.

AN

INTRODUCTION[1]

AS my life hath been chiefly spent in consulting the honour and welfare of my country for more than forty years past, not without answerable success, if the world and my friends have not flattered me; so there is no point wherein I have so much laboured, as that of improving and polishing all parts of conversation between persons of quality, whether they meet by accident or invitation, at meals, tea, or visits, mornings, noons, or evenings.

I have passed, perhaps, more time than any other man of my age and country in visits and assemblies, where the polite persons of both sexes distinguish themselves; and could not, without much grief, observe how frequently both gentlemen and ladies are at a loss for questions, answers, replies, and rejoinders. However, my concern was much abated, when I found that these defects were not occasioned by any want of materials, but because those materials were not in every hand: for instance, one lady can give an answer better than ask a question: one gentleman is happy at a reply; another excels in a rejoinder: one can revive a languishing conversation by a sudden surprizing sentence; another is more dextrous in seconding; a third can fill the gap with laughing, or commending what has been said: thus fresh hints may be started, and the ball of the discourse kept up.

[1] This treatise appears to have been written with the same view, as the critical essay on the faculties of the mind, but upon a more general plan: the ridicule, which is there confined to literary composition, is here extended to conversation, but its object is the same in both; the repetition of quaint phrases picked up by rote either from the living or the dead, and applied upon every occasion to conceal ignorance or stupidity, or to prevent the labour of thoughts to produce native sentiment, and combine such words as will precisely express it.

But,

But, alas! this is too seldom the case, even in the most select companies. How often do we see at court, at publick visiting-days, at great men's levees, and other places of general meeting, that the conversation falls and drops to nothing, like a fire without supply of fuel. This is what we all ought to lament; and against this dangerous evil I take upon me to affirm, that I have, in the following papers, provided an infallible remedy.

It was in the year 1695, and the sixth of his late majesty King William the Third, of ever glorious and immortal memory, who rescued three kingdoms from popery and slavery, when, being about the age of six-and-thirty, my judgment mature, of good reputation in the world, and well acquainted with the best families in town, I determined to spend five mornings, to dine four times, pass three afternoons, and six evenings every week, in the houses of the most polite families, of which I would confine myself to fifty; only changing as the masters or ladies died, or left the town, or grew out of vogue, or sunk in their fortunes, or (which to me was of the highest moment) became disaffected to the government; which practice I have followed ever since to this very day; except when I happened to be sick, or in the spleen upon cloudy weather; and except when I entertained four of each sex at my own lodgings once in a month, by way of retaliation.

I always kept a large table-book in my pocket; and as soon as I left the company, I immediately entered the choicest expressions that passed during the visit; which, returning home, I transcribed in a fair hand, but somewhat enlarged; and had made the greatest part of my collection in twelve years, but not digested into any method; for this I found was a work of infinite labour, and what required the nicest judgment, and consequently could

could not be brought to any degree of perfection in less than sixteen years more.

Herein I resolved to exceed the advice of Horace, a Roman poet, which I have read in Mr. Creech's admirable translation; that an author should keep his works nine years in his closet, before he ventured to publish them; and finding that I still received some additional flowers of wit and language, although, in a very small number, I determined to defer the publication, to pursue my design, and exhaust, if possible, the whole subject, that I might present a complete system to the world; for I am convinced, by long experience, that the criticks will be as severe as their old envy against me can make them: I foresee they will object, that I have inserted many answers and replies which are neither witty, humorous, polite, nor authentic; and have omitted others that would have been highly useful, as well as entertaining. But let them come to particulars, and I will boldly engage to confute their malice.

For these last six or seven years I have not been able to add above nine valuable sentences to enrich my collection: from whence I conclude, that what remains will amount only to a trifle. However, if, after the publication of this work, any lady or gentleman, when they have read it, shall find the least thing of importance omitted, I desire they will please to supply my defects by communicating to me their discoveries; and their letters may be directed to Simon Wagstaff, Esq. at his lodgings next door to the Gloucester-head in St. James's-street (they paying the postage). In return of which favour, I shall make honourable mention of their names in a short preface to the second edition.

In the mean time, I cannot, but with some pride, and pleasure, congratulate with my dear country, which hath

outdone

outdone all the nations of Europe, in advancing the whole art of conversation to the greatest heighth it is capable of reaching; and therefore, being entirely convinced that the collection I now offer to the publick is full and complete, I may, at the same time, boldly affirm, that the whole genius, humour, politeness, and eloquence of England are summed up in it: nor is the treasure small, wherein are to be found at least a thousand shining questions, answers, repartees, replies, and rejoinders, fitted to adorn every kind of discourse that an assembly of English ladies and gentlemen, met together for their mutual entertainment, can possibly want: especially when the several flowers shall be set off and improved by the speakers, with every circumstance of preface and circumlocution, in proper terms; and attended with praise, laughter, or admiration.

There is a natural, involuntary distortion of the muscles, which is the anatomical cause of laughter: but there is another cause of laughter which decency requires, and is the undoubted mark of a good taste, as well as of a polite obliging behaviour; neither is this to be acquired without much observation, long practice, and a sound judgment; I did therefore once intend, for the ease of the learner, to set down in all parts of the following dialogues certain marks, asterisks, or *notabene's* (in English markwell's) after most questions, and every reply or answer; directing exactly the moment when one, two, or all the company are to laugh: but having duly considered, that this expedient would too much enlarge the bulk of the volume, and consequently the price; and likewise that something ought to be left for ingenious readers to find out, I have determined to leave that whole affair, although of great importance, to their own discretion.

The reader must learn, by all means, to distinguish between proverbs and those polite speeches which beautify

conversation:

conversation: for, as to the former, I utterly reject them out of all ingenious discourse. I acknowledge indeed, that there may possibly be found in this treatise a few sayings, among so great a number of smart turns of wit and humour as I have produced, which have a proverbial air: however, I hope it will be considered, that even these were not originally proverbs, but the genuine productions of superior wits to embellish and support conversation; from whence, with great impropriety, as well as plagiarism (if you will forgive a hard word), they have most injuriously been transferred into proverbial maxims; and therefore, in justice, ought to be resumed out of vulgar hands to adorn the drawing-rooms of princes both male and female, the levees of great ministers, as well as the toilet and tea-table of the ladies.

I can faithfully assure the reader, that there is not one single witty phrase in this whole collection, which hath not received the stamp and approbation of at least one hundred years, and how much longer it is hard to determine; he may therefore be secure to find them all genuine, sterling, and authentic.

But before this elaborate treatise can become of universal use and ornament to my native country, two points, that will require time and much application, are absolutely necessary.

For, first, whatever person would aspire to be completely witty, smart, humourous, and polite, must, by hard labour, be able to retain in his memory every single sentence contained in this work, so as never to be once at a loss in applying the right answers, questions, repartees, and the like, immediately, and without study or hesitation.

And, secondly, after a lady or gentleman hath so well overcome this difficulty, as never to be at a loss upon any emergency, the true management of every feature, and

almost

almost of every limb, is equally necessary; without which, an infinite number of absurdities will inevitably ensue. For instance, there is hardly a polite sentence, in the following dialogues, which doth not absolutely require some peculiar graceful motion in the eyes, or nose, or mouth, or forehead, or chin, or suitable toss of the head, with certain offices assigned to each hand; and in ladies, the whole exercise of the fan, fitted to the energy of every word they deliver; by no means omitting the various turns and cadence of the voice; the twistings, and movements, and different postures of the body; the several kinds and gradations of laughter, which the ladies must daily practice by the looking-glass, and consult upon with their waiting-maids.

My readers will soon observe what a great compass of real and useful knowledge this science includes; wherein, although nature, assisted by a genius, may be very instrumental, yet a strong memory and constant application, together with example and precept, will be highly necessary. For these reasons I have often wished, that certain male and female instructors, perfectly versed in this science, would set up schools for the instruction of young ladies and gentlemen therein.

I remember, about thirty years ago, there was a Bohemian woman, of that species commonly known by the name of gypsies, who came over hither from France, and generally attended Isaac the dancing master, when he was teaching his art to misses of quality; and while the young ladies were thus employed, the Bohemian, standing at some distance, but full in their sight, acted before them all proper airs, and heavings of the head, and motions of the hands, and twistings of the body; whereof you may still observe the good effects in several of our eldest ladies.

After

After the same manner, it were much to be desired, that some expert gentlewomen gone to decay would set up publick schools, wherein young girls of quality, or great fortunes, might first be taught to repeat this following system of conversation, which I have been at so much pains to compile; and then to adapt every feature of their countenances, every turn of their hands, every screwing of their bodies, every exercise of their fans, to the humour of the sentences they hear or deliver in conversation. But above all to instruct them in every species and degree of laughing, in the proper seasons, at their own wit, or that of the company. And, if the sons of the nobility and gentry, instead of being sent to common schools, or put into the hands of tutors at home, to learn nothing but words, were consigned to able instructors in the same art, I cannot find what use there could be of books, except in the hands of those who are to make Learning their trade, which is below the dignity of persons born to titles or estates.

It would be another infinite advantage, that, by cultivating this science, we should wholly avoid the vexations and impertinence of pedants, who affect to talk in a language not to be understood; and whenever a polite person offers accidentally to use any of their jargon-terms, have the presumption to laugh at us for pronouncing those words in a genteeler manner. Whereas, I do here affirm, that, whenever any fine gentleman or lady condescends to let a hard word pass out of their mouths, every syllable is smoothed and polished in the passage; and it is a true mark of politeness, both in writing and reading, to vary the orthography as well as the sound; because we are infinitely better judges of what will please a distinguishing ear than those who call themselves scholars, can possibly be: who, consequently, ought to correct their books, and manner of pronouncing, by the authority of our example, from whose lips they proceed with infinitely more beauty and significancy.

But, in the mean time, until so great, so useful, and so necessary a design can be put in execution (which, considering the good disposition of our country at present, I shall not despair of living to see), let me recommend the following treatise to be carried about as a pocket-companion, by all gentlemen and ladies, when they are going to visit, or dine, or drink tea; or, where they happen to pass the evening without cards (as I have sometimes known it to be the case upon disappointments or accidents unforeseen), desiring they would read their several parts in their chairs or coaches, to prepare themselves for every kind of conversation that can possibly happen.

Although I have, in justice to my country, allowed the genius of our people to excel that of any other nation upon earth, and have confirmed this truth by an argument not to be controuled, I mean, by producing so great a number of witty sentences in the ensuing dialogues, all of undoubted authority, as well as of our own production, yet I must confess at the same time, that we are wholly indebted for them to our ancestors; at least, for as long as my memory reacheth, I do not recollect one new phrase of importance to have been added; which defect in us moderns I take to have been occasioned by the introduction of cant-words in the reign of King Charles the Second. And those have so often varied, that hardly one of them, above a year's standing, is now intelligible; nor any where to be found, excepting a small number strewed here and there in the comedies and other fantastick writings of that age. . . .

I have likewise, for some reasons of equal weight, been very sparing in *double entendres*: because they often put

ladies

ladies upon affected constraints, and affected ignorance. In short, they break, or very much entangle the thread of discourse; neither am I master of any rules to settle the disconcerted countenances of the females in such a juncture; I can, therefore, only allow *inuendoes* of this kind to be delivered in whispers, and only to young ladies under twenty, who being, in honour, obliged to blush, may produce a new subject for discourse.

Perhaps the criticks may accuse me of a defect in my following system of Polite Conversation; that there is one great ornament of discourse, whereof I have not produced a single example; which, indeed, I purposely omitted for some reasons that I shall immediately offer; and, if those reasons will not satisfy the male part of my gentle readers, the defect may be supplied, in some manner, by an appendix to the second edition; which appendix shall be printed by itself, and sold for six-pence, stitched, and with a marble cover, that my readers may have no occasion to complain of being defrauded.

The defect I mean is, my not having inserted, into the body of my book, all the oaths now most in fashion for embellishing a discourse; especially since it could give no offence to the clergy, who are seldom or never admitted to these polite assemblies. And it must be allowed, that oaths, well chosen, are not only very useful expletives to matter, but great ornaments of style.

What I shall here offer in my own defence upon this important article will, I hope, be some extenuation of my fault.

First, I reasoned with myself, that a just collection of oaths, repeated as often as the fashion requires, must have enlarged this volume at least to double the bulk; whereby it would not only double the charge, but likewise make the volume less commodious for pocket-carriage.

Secondly,

Secondly, I have been assured, by some judicious friends, that themselves have known certain ladies to take offence (whether seriously or no) at too great a profusion of cursing and swearing, even when that kind of ornament was not improperly introduced; which, I confess, did startle me not a little, having never observed the like in the compass of my own several acquaintance, at least for twenty years past. However, I was forced to submit to wiser judgments than my own.

Thirdly, As this most useful treatise is calculated for all future times, I considered, in this maturity of my age, how great a variety of oaths I have heard since I began to study the world, and to know men and manners. And here I found it to be true, what I have read in an ancient poet:

For now-a-days men change their oaths,
As often as they change their cloaths.

In short, oaths are the children of fashion; they are, in some sense, almost annuals, like what I observed before of cant-words; and I myself can remember about forty different sets. The old stock-oaths, I am confident, do not amount to above forty-five, or fifty at most; but the way of mingling and compounding them is almost as various as that of the alphabet.

Sir John Perrot was the first man of quality, whom I find upon record to have sworn by God's wounds. He lived in the reign of Q. Elizabeth, and was supposed to have been a natural son of Henry the Eighth, who might also, probably, have been his instructor. This oath indeed still continues, and is a stock-oath to this day; so do several others that have kept their natural simplicity: but infinitely the greater number hath been so frequently changed and dislocated, that, if the inventors were now alive, they could hardly understand them.

Upon

Upon these considerations I began to apprehend, that, if I should insert all the oaths that are now current, my book would be out of vogue with the first change of fashion, and grow as useless as an old dictionary: whereas, the case is quite otherwise with my collection of polite discourse; which, as I before observed, hath descended by tradition for at least an hundred years without any change in the phraseology. I therefore determined with myself to leave out the whole system of swearing; because both the male and female oaths are all perfectly well known and distinguished; new ones are easily learnt, and, with a moderate share of discretion, may be properly applied on every fit occasion. However, I must here, upon this article of swearing, most earnestly recommend to my male readers, that they would please a little to study variety. For it is the opinion of our most refined swearers, that the same oath, or curse, cannot, consistently with true politeness, be repeated above nine times, in the same company, by the same person, and at one sitting.

I am far from desiring, or expecting, that all the polite and ingenious speeches contained in this work, should, in the general conversation between ladies and gentlemen, come in so quick and so close, as I have here delivered them. By no means: on the contrary, they ought to be husbanded better, and spread much thinner. Nor do I make the least question, but that, by a discreet and thrifty management, they may serve for the entertainment of a whole year to any person, who does not make too long or too frequent visits in the same family. The flowers of wit, fancy, wisdom, humour, and politeness, scattered in this volume, amount to one thousand seventy and four. Allowing then to every gentleman and lady thirty visiting families (not insisting upon fractions) there will want but little of an hundred polite questions, answers,

answers, replies, rejoinders, repartees, and remarks, to be daily delivered fresh in every company for twelve solar months; and even this is a higher pitch of delicacy than the world insists on, or hath reason to expect. But I am altogether for exalting this science to its utmost perfection.

It may be objected, that the publication of my book may, in a long course of time, prostitute this noble art to mean and vulgar people; but I answer, that it is not so easy an acquirement as a few ignorant pretenders may imagine. A footman can swear, but he cannot swear like a lord. He can swear as often; but, can he swear with equal delicacy, propriety, and judgment? No, certainly, unless he be a lad of superior parts, of good memory, a diligent observer, one who hath a skilful ear, some knowledge in musick, and an exact taste; which hardly fall to the share of one in a thousand among that fraternity, in as high favour as they now stand with their ladies. Neither hath one footman in six so fine a genius as to relish and apply those exalted sentences comprized in this volume, which I offer to the world. It is true, I cannot see that the same ill consequences would follow from the waiting-woman, who, if she had been bred to read romances, may have some small subaltern or second-hand politeness; and, if she constantly attends the tea, and be a good listner, may, in some years, make a tolerable figure, which will serve, perhaps, to draw in the young chaplain, or the old steward. But alas! after all, how can she acquire those hundred graces and motions, and airs, the whole military management of the fan, the contortions of every muscular motion in the face, the risings and fallings, the quickness and slowness of the voice, with the several turns and cadences; the proper juncture of smiling and frowning, how often and how loud to laugh, when to

jibe,

jibe, and when to flout, with all the other branches of doctrine and discipline above recited?

I am therefore not under the least apprehension, that this art will ever be in danger of falling into common hands, which requires so much time, study, practice, and genius, before it arrives to perfection; and therefore I must repeat my proposal for erecting publick schools, provided with the best and ablest masters and mistresses, at the charge of the nation.

I have drawn this work into the form of a dialogue, after the pattern of other famous writers in history, law, politicks, and most other arts and sciences, and, I hope, it will have the same success: for, who can contest it to be of greater consequence to the happiness of these kingdoms, than all human knowledge put together? Dialogue is held the best method of inculcating any part of knowledge; and I am confident, that publick schools will soon be founded for teaching wit and politeness after my scheme to young people of quality and fortune. I have determined next sessions to deliver a petition to the House of Lords, for an act of parliament to establish my book as the standard Grammar in all the principal cities of the kingdom, where this art is to be taught by able masters, who are to be approved and recommended by me; which is no more than Lilly obtained, only for teaching words in a language wholly useless. Neither shall I be so far wanting to myself as not to desire a patent, granted of course to all useful projectors; I mean, that I may have the sole profit of giving a licence to every school to read my Grammar for fourteen years.

The reader cannot but observe what pains I have been at in polishing the style of my book to the greatest exactness: nor have I been less diligent in refining the orthography by spelling the words in the very same manner as they

they are pronounced by the chief patterns of politeness at court, at levees, at assemblies, at play-houses, at the prime visiting places, by young templars, and by gentlemen-commoners of both universities, who have lived at least a twelvemonth in town, and kept the best company. Of these spellings the publick will meet with many examples in the following book. For instance, *can't*, *han't*, *shan't*, *didn't*, *wouldn't*, *isn't*, *e'nt*, with many more; besides several words which scholars pretend are derived from Greek and Latin, but now pared into a polite sound by ladies, officers of the army, courtiers and templars, such as *jommetry* for *geometry*, *verdi* for *verdict*, *lard* for *lord*, *larnen* for *learning*; together with some abbreviations exquisitely refined; as, *pozz* for *positive*; *mobb* for *mobile*; *phizz* for *physiognomy*; *rep* for *reputation*; *plenipo* for *plenipotentiary*; *incog* for *incognito*; *hypps*, or *hippo*, for *hypochondriacs*; *bam* for *bamboozle*; and *bamboozle* for *God knows what*; whereby much time is saved, and the high road to conversation cut short by many a mile.

I have, as it will be apparent, laboured very much, and, I hope, with felicity enough, to make every character in the dialogue agreeable with itself to a degree, that, whenever any judicious person shall read my book aloud for the entertainment and instruction of a select company, he need not so much as name the particular speakers; because all the persons, throughout the several subjects of conversation, strictly observe a different manner peculiar to their characters, which are of different kinds: but this I leave entirely to the prudent and impartial reader's discernment.

Perhaps the very manner of introducing the several points of wit and humour may not be less entertaining and instructing than the matter itself. In the latter I can pretend to little merit; because it entirely depends upon memory

memory and the happiness of having kept polite company: but the art of contriving that those speeches should be introduced naturally, as the most proper sentiments to be delivered upon so great a variety of subjects, I take to be a talent somewhat uncommon, and a labour that few people could hope to succeed in, unless they had a genius particularly turned that way, added to a sincere disinterested love of the publick.

Although every curious question, smart answer, and witty reply, be little known to many people, yet there is not one single sentence in the whole collection, for which I cannot bring most authentick vouchers, whenever I shall be called: and even for some expressions, which, to a few nice ears, may perhaps appear somewhat gross, I can produce the stamp of authority from courts, chocolate-houses, theatres, assemblies, drawing-rooms, levees, card-meetings, balls and masquerades, from persons of both sexes, and of the highest titles next to royal. However, to say the truth, I have been very sparing in my quotations of such sentiments as seem to be over free; because, when I began my collection, such kind of converse was almost in its infancy, till it was taken into the protection of my honoured patronesses at court, by whose countenance and sanction it hath become a choice flower in the nosegay of wit and politeness.

Some will perhaps object, that when I bring my company to dinner, I mention too great a variety of dishes, not always consistent with the art of cookery, or proper for the season of the year, and part of the first course mingled with the second, besides a failure in politeness by introducing a black pudden to a lord's table, and at a great entertainment: but, if I had omitted the black pudden, I desire to know what would have become of that exquisite reason, given by Miss Notable, for not eating it; the

the world perhaps might have lost it for ever, and I should have been justly answerable for having left it out of my collection. I therefore cannot but hope, that such hyper-critical readers will please to consider, my business was to make so full and complete a body of refined sayings as compact as I could; only taking care to produce them in the most natural and probable manner, in order to allure my readers into the very substance and marrow of this most admirable and necessary art.

I am heartily sorry, and was much disappointed to find, that so universal and polite an entertainment as Cards hath hitherto contributed very little to the enlargement of my work. I have sate by many hundred times with the utmost vigilance, and my table-book ready, without being able, in eight hours, to gather matter for one single phrase in my book. But this, I think, may be easily accounted for by the turbulence and justling of passions upon the various and surprizing turns, incidents, revolutions, and events of good and evil fortune, that arrive in the course of a long evening at play; the mind being wholly taken up, and the consequences of non-attention so fatal.

Play is supported upon the two great pillars of deliberation and action. The terms of art are few, prescribed by law and custom; no time allowed for digressions or trials of wit. Quadrille in particular bears some resemblance to a state of nature, which, we are told, is a state of war, wherein every woman is against every woman; the unions short, inconstant, and soon broke; the league made this minute without knowing the ally, and dissolved in the next. Thus, at the game of quadrille, female brains are always employed in stratagem, or their hands in action. Neither can I find, that our art hath gained much by the happy revival of masquerading among us; the whole dialogue, in those meetings, being summed up in one

(sprightly,

(sprightly, I confess, but) single question, and as sprightly an answer. 'Do you know me? Yes, I do.' And, 'Do you know me? Yes, I do.' For this reason, I did not think it proper to give my readers the trouble of introducing a masquerade, merely for the sake of a single question, and a single answer. Especially, when to perform this in a proper manner, I must have brought in a hundred persons together, of both sexes, dressed in fantastick habits for one minute, and dismiss them the next.

Neither is it reasonable to conceive, that our science can be much improved by masquerades, where the wit of both sexes is altogether taken up in contriving singular and humoursome disguises; and their thoughts entirely employed in bringing intrigues and assignations of gallantry to an happy conclusion.

The judicious reader will readily discover, that I make Miss Notable my heroine, and Mr. Thomas Neverout my hero. I have laboured both their characters with my utmost ability. It is into their mouths that I have put the liveliest questions, answers, repartees, and rejoinders; because my design was to propose them both as patterns for all young batchelors and single ladies to copy after. By which, I hope, very soon, to see polite conversation flourish between both sexes in a more consummate degree of perfection, than these kingdoms have yet ever known.

I have drawn some lines of Sir John Linger's character, the Derbyshire knight, on purpose to place it in counterview or contrast with that of the other company; wherein I can assure the reader, that I intended not the least reflexion upon Derbyshire, the place of my nativity. But my intention was only to shew the misfortune of those persons, who have the disadvantage to be bred out of the circle of politeness, whereof I take the present limits to extend no further than London, and ten miles round;

although

although others are pleased to confine it within the bills of mortality. If you compare the discourses of my gentlemen and ladies with those of Sir John, you will hardly conceive him to have been bred in the same climate, or under the same laws, language, religion, or government: and, accordingly, I have introduced him speaking in his own rude dialect, for no other reason than to teach my scholars how to avoid it.

The curious reader will observe, that, when conversation appears in danger to flag, which, in some places, I have artfully contrived, I took care to invent some sudden question, or turn of wit to revive it; such as these that follow: 'What? I think here's a silent meeting! Come, madam, a penny for your thought'; with several other of the like sort. I have rejected all provincial or country turns of wit and fancy; because I am acquainted with very few; but indeed chiefly, because I found them so much inferior to those at court, especially among the gentlemen ushers, the ladies of the bed-chamber, and the maids of honour; I must also add the hither end of our noble metropolis.

When this happy art of polite conversing shall be throughly improved, good company will be no longer pestered with dull, dry, tedious story-tellers, nor brangling disputers: for a right scholar of either sex, in our science, will perpetually interrupt them with some sudden surprizing piece of wit, that shall engage all the company in a loud laugh; and if, after a pause, the grave companion resumes his thread in the following manner, 'Well, but to go on with my story', new interruptions come from the left and right, till he is forced to give over. . . .

I shall conclude this long, but necessary introduction with a request, or indeed rather a just and reasonable demand, from all lords, ladies, and gentlemen, that while they

they are entertaining and improving each other with those polite questions, answers, repartees, replies, and rejoinders, which I have, with infinite labour, and close application during the space of thirty-six years, been collecting for their service and improvement, they shall, as an instance of gratitude, on every proper occasion, quote my name after this or the like manner: 'Madam, as our master Wagstaff says.' 'My Lord, as our friend Wagstaff has it.' I do likewise expect, that all my pupils shall drink my health every day at dinner and supper during my life; and that they, or their posterity, shall continue the same ceremony to my not inglorious memory, after my decease, for ever.

The MEN

Lord SPARKISH.
Lord SMART.
Sir JOHN LINGER.
Mr. NEVEROUT.
Col. ATWITT.

The LADIES

Lady SMART.
Miss NOTABLE.
Lady ANSWERALL.

ARGUMENT

Lord Sparkish *and Colonel* Atwitt *meet in the morning upon the* Mall. *Mr.* Neverout *joins them; they all go to breakfast at Lady* Smart's. *Their conversation over their tea: after which they part; but my lord and the two gentlemen are invited to dinner. Sir* John Linger *invited likewise, and comes a little too late. The whole conversation at dinner: after which the ladies retire to their tea. The conversation of the ladies without the men, who are supposed to stay and drink a bottle; but, in some time, go to the ladies and drink tea with them. The conversation there. After which, a party at Quadrille until three in the morning; but no conversation set down. They all take leave, and go home.*

Polite Conversation, *etc.*

St. JAMES's PARK

Lord Sparkish *meeting Col.* Atwitt.

Col. WELL met, my lord.

Ld. Sparkish. Thank ye, colonel. A parson would have said, I hope we shall meet in heaven. When did you see Tom Neverout?

Col. He's just coming towards us. Talk of the devil——

Neverout *comes up.*

Col. How do you do, Tom?

Neverout. Never the better for you.

Col. I hope you're never the worse: but pray where's your manners? don't you see my Lord Sparkish?

Neverout. My lord, I beg your lordship's pardon.

Ld. Sparkish. Tom, how is it, that you can't see the wood for trees? What wind blew you hither?

Neverout. Why, my lord, it is an ill wind blows no body good; for it gives me the honour of seeing your lordship.

Col. Tom, you must go with us to Lady Smart's to breakfast.

Neverout. Must! why, colonel, must's for the king.

[*Col. offering in jest to draw his sword.*

Col. Have you spoke with all your friends?

Neverout. Colonel, as you're stout, be merciful.

Ld. Sparkish. Come, agree; the law's costly.

[*Col. taking his hand from his hilt.*

Col. Well, Tom, you are never the worse man to be afraid of me. Come along.

Neverout. What! do you think I was born in a wood, to be afraid of an owl?

I'll

I'll wait on you. I hope Miss Notable will be there; egad she's very handsome, and has wit at will.

Col. Why every one as they like, as the good woman said when she kiss'd her cow.

Lord Smart's *house; they knock at the door; the* Porter *comes out.*

Lord Sparkish. Pray, are you the porter?

Porter. Yes, for want of a better.

Ld. Sparkish. Is your lady at home?

Porter. She was at home just now; but she's not gone out yet.

Neverout. I warrant this rogue's tongue is well hung.

Lady Smart's *antichamber.*

Lady Smart, *Lady* Answerall, *and Miss* Notable *at the tea-table.*

Lady Smart. My Lord, your lordship's most humble servant.

Ld. Sparkish. Madam, you spoke too late; I was your ladyship's before.

Lady Smart. O! Colonel, are you here?

Col. As sure as you're there, madam.

Lady Smart. Oh, Mr. Neverout! What such a man alive!

Neverout. Ay, madam, alive, and alive like to be, at your ladyship's service.

Lady Smart. Well, I'll get a knife, and nick it down that Mr. Neverout came to our house. And pray what news, Mr. Neverout?

Neverout. Why, madam, Queen Elizabeth's dead.

Lady Smart. Well: Mr. Neverout, I see you are no changeling.

Miss

Miss Notable *comes in.*

Neverout. Miss, your slave: I hope your early rising will do you no harm. I find you are but just come out of the cloth market.

Miss. I always rise at eleven, whether it be day or no.

Col. Miss, I hope you are up for all day.

Miss. Yes, if I don't get a fall before night.

Col. Miss, I heard you were out of order; pray how are you now?

Miss. Pretty well, Colonel, I thank you.

Col. Pretty and well, miss! that's two very good things.

Miss. I mean I am better than I was.

Neverout. Why then, 'tis well you were sick.

Miss. What! Mr. Neverout, you take me up before I'am down.

Lady Smart. Come, let us leave off children's play, and go to push-pin.

Miss [*To Lady Smart*]. Pray, madam, give me some more sugar to my tea.

Col. Oh! Miss, you must needs be very good-humour'd, you love sweet things so well.

Neverout. Stir it up with the spoon, miss; for the deeper the sweeter.

Lady Smart. I assure you, miss, the colonel has made you a great compliment.

Miss. I am sorry for it; for I have heard say, complimenting is lying.

Lady Smart [*To Lord Sparkish*]. My lord, methinks the sight of you is good for sore eyes; if we had known of your coming, we would have strown rushes for you: how has your lordship done this long time?

Col. Faith, madam, he's better in health than in good conditions.

Ld.

Ld. Sparkish. Well; I see there's no worse friend than one brings from home with one; and I am not the first man has carried a rod to whip himself.

Neverout. Here's poor miss has not a word to throw at a dog. Come, a penny for your thought.

Miss. It is not worth a farthing; for I was thinking of you.

Col. rising up.

Lady Smart. Colonel, where are you going so soon? I hope you did not come to fetch fire.

Col. Madam, I must needs go home for half an hour.

Miss. Why, colonel, they say, the devil's at home.

Lady Answ. Well, but sit while you stay; 'tis as cheap sitting as standing.

Col. No, madam, while I'm standing I'm going.

Miss. Nay, let him go; I promise him we wont tear his cloaths to hold him.

Lady Smart. I suppose colonel, we keep you from better company, I mean only as to myself.

Col. Madam, I am all obedience.

Col. sits down.

Lady Smart. Lord, miss, how can you drink your tea so hot? sure your mouth's paved.

How do you like this tea, colonel?

Col. Well enough, madam; but methinks it is a little more-ish.

Lady Smart. Oh colonel! I understand you. Betty bring the canister; I have but very little of this tea left; but I don't love to make two wants of one; want when I have it, and want when I have it not. He, he, he, he.

[*Laughs.*

Lady Answ. [*to the maid*]. Why, sure, Betty, you are bewitched, the cream is burnt too.

Betty. Why, madam, the bishop has set his foot in it.

Lady

Lady Smart. Go, run, girl, and warm fresh cream.

Betty. Indeed, madam, there's none left; for the cat has eaten it all.

Lady Smart. I doubt it was a cat with two legs.

Miss. Colonel, don't you love bread and butter with your tea?

Col. Yes, in a morning, miss: for they say, butter is gold in the morning, silver at noon, but it is lead at night.

Neverout. Miss, the weather is so hot, that my butter melts on my bread.

Lady Answ. Why, butter, I've heard 'em say, is mad twice a year.

Ld. Sparkish [*to the maid*]. Mrs. Betty, how does your body politick?

Col. Fie, my lord, you'll make Mrs. Betty blush.

Lady Smart. Blush! ay, blush like a blue dog.

Neverout. Pray, Mrs. Betty, are you not Tom Jonson's daughter?

Betty. So my mother tells me, Sir.

Ld. Sparkish. But, Mrs. Betty, I hear you are in love.

Betty. My lord, I thank God, I hate nobody; I am in charity with all the world.

Lady Smart. Why, wench, I think thy tongue runs upon wheels this morning: how came you by that scratch upon your nose? have you been fighting with the cats?

Col. [*to Miss*]. Miss, when will you be married?

Miss. One of these odd-come-shortly's, colonel.

Neverout. Yes; they say the match is half made, the spark is willing, but miss is not.

Miss. I suppose the gentleman has got his own consent for it.

Lady Answ. Pray, my Lord, did you walk through the Park in the rain?

Ld. Sparkish. Yes, madam, we were neither sugar nor salt,

salt, we were not afraid the rain would melt us. He, he, he.

Col. It rain'd, and the sun shone at the same time.

Neverout. Why, the devil was beating his wife behind the door with a shoulder of mutton. [*Laugh.*

Col. A blind man would be glad to see that.

Lady Smart. Mr. Neverout, methinks you stand in your own light.

Neverout. Ah! Madam, I have done so all my life.

Ld. Sparkish. I'm sure he sits in mine: Prithee, Tom, sit a little farther: I believe your father was no glazier.

Lady Smart. Miss, dear Girl, fill me out a dish of tea, for I'm very lazy.

Miss fills a dish of tea, sweetens it, and then tastes it.

Lady Smart. What, miss, will you be my taster?

Miss. No, madam; but they say 'tis an ill cook that can't lick her own fingers.

Neverout. Pray, miss, fill me another.

Miss. Will you have it now, or stay till you get it?

Lady Answ. But, colonel, they say you went to court last night very drunk: nay, I'm told for certain, you had been among the Philistines: no wonder the cat winked, when both her eyes were out.

Col. Indeed, madam, that's a lye.

Lady Answ. 'Tis better I should lye than you should lose your good manners: besides, I don't lie, I sit.

Neverout. O faith, colonel, you must own you had a drop in your eye: when I left you, you were half seas over.

Ld. Sparkish. Well, I fear Lady Answerall can't live long, she has so much wit.

Neverout. No; she can't live, that's certain; but she may linger thirty or forty years.

Miss. Live long! ay, longer than a cat or a dog, or a better thing.

Lady

Lady Answ. Oh! miss, you must give your vardi too!

Ld. Sparkish. Miss, shall I fill you another dish of tea?

Miss. Indeed, my lord, I have drank enough.

Ld. Sparkish. Come, it will do you more good than a month's fasting; here, take it.

Miss. No, I thank your lordship; enough's as good as a feast.

Ld. Sparkish. Well; but if you always say so, you'll never be married.

Lady Answ. Do, my lord, give her a dish; for, they say, maids will say no and take it.

Ld. Sparkish. Well; and I dare say, miss is a maid in thought, word, and deed.

Neverout. I would not take my oath of that.

Miss. Pray, Sir, speak for yourself.

Lady Smart. Fie, miss; they say maids should be seen, and not heard.

Lady Answ. Good miss, stir the fire, that the tea-kettle may boil.—You have done it very well; now it burns purely. Well, miss, you'll have a chearful husband.

Miss. Indeed, your ladyship could have stirred it much better.

Lady Answ. I know that very well, hussy; but I won't keep a dog and bark myself.

Neverout. What! you are sick, miss?

Miss. Not at all; for her ladyship meant you.

Neverout. Oh! faith, miss, you are in Lob's-pound; get out as you can.

Miss. I won't quarrel with my bread and butter for all that; I know when I'm well.

Lady Answ. Well; but miss—

Neverout. Ah! dear madam, let the matter fall; take pity on poor miss; don't throw water on a drowned rat.

Miss.

Miss. Indeed, Mr. Neverout, you should be cut for the simples this morning; say a word more, and you had as good eat your nails.

Ld. Sparkish. Pray, miss, will you be so good as to favour us with a song?

Miss. Indeed, my lord, I can't; for I have a great cold.

Col. Oh! miss, they say all good singers have colds.

Ld. Sparkish. Pray, madam, does not miss sing very well?

Lady Answ. She sings, as one may say, my lord.

Miss. I hear Mr. Neverout has a very good voice.

Col. Yes, Tom sings well, but his luck 's naught.

Neverout. Faith, colonel, you hit yourself a devilish box on the ear.

Col. Miss, will you take a pinch of snuff?

Miss. No, colonel, you must know that I never take snuff but when I'm angry.

Lady Answ. Yes, yes, she can take snuff; but she has never a box to put it in.

Miss. Pray, colonel, let me see that box.

Col. Madam, there's never a C upon it.

Miss. May be there is, colonel.

Col. Ay, but May-Bees don't fly now, miss.

Neverout. Colonel, why so hard upon poor miss? Don't set your wit against a child; miss, give me a blow, and I'll beat him.

Miss. So she pray'd me to tell you.

Ld. Sparkish. Pray, my lady Smart, what kin are you to lord Pozz?

Lady Smart. Why, his grandmother and mine had four elbows.

Lady Answ. Well, methinks here's a silent meeting. Come, miss, hold up your head, girl; there's money bid for you. [*Miss starts.*

Miss.

Miss. Lord, madam, you frighten me out of my seven senses!

Ld. Sparkish. Well, I must be going.

Lady Answ. I have seen hastier people than you stay all night.

Col. [*to Lady Smart*]. Tom Neverout and I are to leap to morrow for a guinea.

Miss. I believe, colonel, Mr. Neverout can leap at a crust better than you.

Neverout. Miss, your tongue runs before your wit; nothing can tame you but a husband.

Miss. Peace! I think I hear the church clock.

Neverout. Why you know, as the fool thinks——

Lady Smart. Mr. Neverout, your handkerchief's fallen.

Miss. Let him set his foot on it, that it may'nt fly in his face.

Neverout. Well, miss——

Miss. Ay, ay! many a one says well that thinks ill.

Neverout. Well, miss, I'll think on this.

Miss. That's rhime, if you take it in time.

Neverout. What! I see you are a poet.

Miss. Yes; if I had but the wit to shew it.

Neverout. Miss, will you be so kind as to fill me a dish of tea?

Miss. Pray let your betters be served before you; I'm just going to fill one for myself; and, you know, the parson always christens his own child first.

Neverout. But I saw you fill one just now for the colonel; well, I find kissing goes by favour.

Miss. But pray, Mr. Neverout, what lady was that you were talking with in the side-box last Tuesday?

Neverout. Miss, can you keep a secret?

Miss. Yes, I can.

Neverout.

Neverout. Well, miss, and so can I.

Col. Odd-so! I have cut my thumb with this cursed knife!

Lady Answ. Ay; that was your mother's fault, because she only warn'd you not to cut your fingers.

Lady Smart. No, no; 'tis only fools cut their fingers, but wise folks cut their thumbs.——

Miss. I'm sorry for it, but I can't cry.

Col. Don't you think miss is grown?

Lady Answ. Ay, ill weeds grow apace.

A puff of smoke comes down the chimney.

Lady Answ. Lord, madam, does your ladyship's chimney smoke?

Col. No, madam; but, they say, smoke always pursues the fair, and your ladyship sat nearest.

Lady Smart. Madam, do you love Bohea tea?

Lady Answ. Why, madam, I must confess I do love it, but it does not love me.

Miss [*to Lady Smart*]. Indeed, madam, your ladyship is very sparing of your tea: I protest, the last I took was no more than water bewitch'd.

Col. Pray, miss, if I may be so bold, what lover gave you that fine etui?

Miss. Don't you know? then keep counsel.

Lady Answ. I'll tell you, colonel, who gave it her; it was the best lover she will ever have while she lives, her own dear papa.

Neverout. Methinks, miss, I don't much like the colour of that ribbon.

Miss. Why then, Mr. Neverout, do you see, if you don't much like it, you may look off of it.

Ld. Sparkish. I don't doubt, madam, but your ladyship has heard that Sir John Brisk has got an employment at court.

Lady

Lady Smart. Yes, yes; and I warrant he thinks himself no small fool now.

Neverout. Yet, madam, I have heard some people take him for a wise man.

Lady Smart. Ay, ay; some are wise, and some are otherwise.

Lady Smart. Do you know him, Mr. Neverout?

Neverout. Know him! ay, as well as the beggar knows his dish.

Col. Well; I can only say that he has better luck than honester folks: but pray, how came he to get this employment?

Ld. Sparkish. Why, by chance, as the man kill'd the devil.

Neverout. Why, miss, you are in a brown study; what's the matter? methinks you look like mum-chance, that was hang'd for saying nothing.

Miss. I'd have you to know, I scorn your words.

Neverout. Well; but scornful dogs will eat dirty puddings.

Miss. Well; my comfort is, your tongue is no slander. What! you would not have one be always on the high grin?

Neverout. Cry map-sticks, madam; no offence I hope.

[*Lady Smart breaks a tea-cup.*

Lady Answ. Lord, madam, how came you to break your cup.

Lady Smart. I can't help it, if I would cry my eyes out.

Miss. Why sell it, madam, and buy a new one with some of the money.

Col. 'Tis a folly to cry for spilt milk.

Lady Smart. Why, if things did not break or wear out, how would tradesmen live?

Miss. Well; I am very sick, if any body car'd for it.

Neverout.

Neverout. Come, then, miss, e'en make a die of it, and then we shall have a burying of our own.

Miss. The devil take you, Neverout, besides all small curses.

Lady Answ. Marry come up, what, plain Neverout! methinks you might have an M under your girdle, miss.

Lady Smart. Well, well, naught 's never in danger; I warrant, miss will spit in her hand, and hold fast. Colonel, do you like this bisket?

Col. I'm like all fools; I love every thing that's good.

Lady Smart. Well, and isn't it pure good?

Col. 'Tis better than a worse.

Footman brings the colonel a letter.

Lady Answ. I suppose, colonel, that's a billet-doux from your mistress.

Col. Egad, I don't know whence it comes; but whoe'er writ it, writes a hand like a foot.

Miss. Well, you may make a secret of it, but we can spell, and put together.

Neverout. Miss, what spells b double uzzard?

Miss. Buzzard in your teeth, Mr. Neverout.

Lady Smart. Now you are up, Mr. Neverout, will you do me the favour, to do me the kindness, to take off the tea-kettle?

Ld. Sparkish. I wonder what makes these bells ring.

Lady Answ. Why, my lord, I suppose, because they pull the ropes. [*Here all laugh.*

Neverout plays with a tea-cup.

Miss. Now a child would have cried half an hour before it would have found out such a pretty play-thing.

Lady Smart. Well said, miss: I vow, Mr. Neverout, the girl is too hard for you.

Neverout.

Neverout. Ay, miss will say any thing but her prayers, and those she whistles.

Miss. Pray, colonel, make me a present of that pretty penknife.

Ld. Sparkish. Ay, miss, catch him at that and hang him.

Col. Not for the world, dear miss; it will cut love.

Ld. Sparkish. Colonel, you shall be married first, I was just going to say that.

Lady Smart. Well, but for all that, I can tell who is a great admirer of miss: pray, miss, how do you like Mr. Spruce? I swear I have often seen him cast a sheep's eye out of a calf's head at you: deny it if you can.

Miss. Oh! madam; all the world knows that Mr. Spruce is a general lover.

Col. Come, miss, 'tis too true to make a jest on.

[*Miss blushes.*

Lady Answ. Well, however, blushing is some sign of grace.

Neverout. Miss says nothing; but I warrant she pays it off with thinking.

Miss. Well, ladies and gentlemen, you are pleas'd to divert yourselves; but, as I hope to be sav'd, there's nothing in it.

Lady Smart. Touch a gall'd horse, and he'll wince: love will creep where it dare not go: I'd hold a hundred pound Mr. Neverout was the inventor of that story; and, colonel, I doubt you had a finger in the pye.

Lady Answ. But, Colonel, you forgot to salute miss when you came in; she said you had not been here a long time.

Miss. Fie, madam! I vow, colonel, I said no such thing; I wonder at your ladyship!

Col.

Col. Miss, I beg your pardon——

Goes to salute her, she struggles a little.

Miss. Well, I'd rather give a knave a kiss for once than be troubled with him; but, upon my word, you are more bold than welcome.

Lady Smart. Fie, fie, miss! for shame of the world, and speech of good people.

Neverout to Miss, who is cooking her tea and bread and butter.

Neverout. Come, come, miss, make much of naught; good folks are scarce.

Miss. What! and you must come in with your two eggs a penny, and three of them rotten.

Col. [*to Ld. Sparkish*]. But, my lord, I forgot to ask you, how you like my new cloaths?

Ld. Sparkish. Why, very well, colonel; only, to deal plainly with you, methinks the worst piece is in the middle. [*Here a loud laugh, often repeated. . . .*

DIRECTIONS TO SERVANTS IN GENERAL

These pages include about one-third of the curious treatise on which Swift worked from time to time between 1730 and 1740. Only his lighter mood has been represented. Other pages are marred by the bitter irony and unconcealed disgust with human personality, which disfigure so many of the soiled 'ropes of sand' made during his last years.

The text reproduced is that of Faulkner's edition of Swift's *Works*, vol. viii, 1751.

CHAP. III

Directions to the FOOTMAN

YOUR employment, being of a mixt nature, extends to a great variety of business, and you stand in a fair-way of being the favourite of your master or mistress, or of the young masters and misses; you are the fine gentleman of the family, with whom all the maids are in love. You are sometimes a pattern of dress to your master, and sometimes he is so to you. You wait at table in all companies, and consequently have the opportunity to see and know the world, and to understand men and manners: I confess your vails are but few, unless you are sent with a present, or attend the tea in the country; but you are called Mr. in the neighbourhood, and sometimes pick up a fortune, perhaps your master's daughter; and I have known many of your tribe to have good commands in the army. In town you have a seat reserved for you in the playhouse, where you have an opportunity of becoming wits and criticks: you have no professed enemy, except the rabble and my lady's waiting-woman, who are sometimes apt to call you skip-kennel. I have a true veneration for your office, because I had once the honour to be one of your order, which I foolishly left, by demeaning myself with accepting an employment in the custom-house. But that you, my brethren, may come to better fortunes, I shall here deliver my instructions, which have been the fruits of much thought and observation, as well as of seven years experience.

In order to learn the secrets of other families, tell them those of your master's; thus you will grow a favourite both at home and abroad, and be regarded as a person of importance.

Never

Never be seen in the streets with a basket or bundle in your hands, and carry nothing but what you can hide in your pocket, otherwise you will disgrace your calling: to prevent which, always retain a black-guard boy to carry your loads; and if you want farthings, pay him with a good slice of bread, or scrap of meat.

Let your shoe-boy clean your own shoes first, for fear of fouling the chamber, then let him clean your master's; keep him on purpose for that use, and to run of errands, and pay him with scraps. When you are sent on an errand, be sure to edge in some business of your own, either to see your sweetheart, or drink a pot of ale with some brother-servants, which is so much time clear gained.

There is a great controversy about the most convenient and genteel way of holding your plate at meals; some stick it between the frame and the back of the chair, which is an excellent expedient, where the make of the chair will allow it: others, for fear the plate should fall, grasp it so firmly, that their thumb reacheth to the middle of the hollow; which however, if your thumb be dry, is no secure method; and therefore in that case, I advise your wetting the ball of it with your tongue. As to that absurd practice of letting the back of the plate lye leaning on the hollow of your hand, which some ladies recommend, it is universally exploded, being liable to so many accidents. Others again are so refined, that they hold their plate directly under the left arm-pit, which is the best situation for keeping it warm; but this may be dangerous in the article of taking away a dish, where your plate may happen to fall upon some of the company's heads. I confess myself to have objected against all these ways, which I have frequently tried; and therefore I recommend a fourth, which is to stick your plate, up to the

the rim inclusive, in the left side between your waistcoat and your shirt: this will keep it at least as warm as under your arm-pit, or ockster (as the Scots call it); this will hide it, so as strangers may take you for a better servant, too good to hold a plate; this will secure it from falling; and, thus disposed, it lies ready for you to whip out in a moment ready warmed, to any guest within your reach, who may want it. And lastly, there is another convenience in this method, that if, any time during your waiting, you find yourself going to cough or sneeze, you can immediately snatch out the plate, and hold the hollow part close to your nose or mouth, and thus prevent spirting any moisture from either, upon the dishes or the ladies head-dress: you see gentlemen and ladies observe a like practice on such an occasion, with a hat or handkerchief; yet a plate is less fouled and sooner cleaned than either of these; for when your cough or sneeze is over, it is but returning your plate to the same position, and your shirt will clean it in the passage.

Take off the largest dishes and set them on with one hand, to shew the ladies your vigour and strength of back; but always do it between two ladies, that, if the dish happens to slip, the soup or sauce may fall on their cloaths, and not daub the floor: by this practice, two of our brethren, my worthy friends, got considerable fortunes.

Learn all the new-fashion words, and oaths, and songs, and scraps of plays, that your memory can hold. Thus you will become the delight of nine ladies in ten, and the envy of ninety nine beaux in a hundred.

Take care, that at certain periods, during dinner especially, when persons of quality are there, you and your bretheren be all out of the room together, by which you will give yourselves some ease from the fatigue of

waiting,

waiting, and, at the same time, leave the company to converse more freely without being constrained by your presence.

When you are sent on a message, deliver it in your own words, although it be to a duke or duchess, and not in the words of your master or lady; for how can they understand what belongs to a message as well as you, who have been bred to the employment? But never deliver the answer till it is called for, and then adorn it with your own style.

When dinner is done, carry down a great heap of plates to the kitchen; and when you come to the head of the stairs, trundle them all before you; there is not a more agreeable sight or sound, especially if they be silver, besides the trouble they save you; and there they will lie ready near the kitchen door for the scullion to wash them.

If you are bringing up a joint of meat in a dish, and it falls out of your hand before you get into the dining-room, with the meat on the ground and the sauce spilled, take up the meat gently, wipe it with the flap of your coat, then put it again into the dish, and serve it up; and when your lady misses the sauce, tell her, it is to be sent up in a plate by itself.

When you carry up a dish of meat, dip your fingers in the sauce, or lick it with your tongue, to try whether it be good, and fit for your master's table.

You are the best judge of what acquaintance your lady ought to have; and therefore, if she sends you on a message of compliment or business to a family you do not like, deliver the answer in such a manner as may breed a quarrel between them not to be reconciled: or, if a footman comes from the same family on the like errand, turn the answer she orders you to deliver in such a manner, as the other family may take it for an affront.

When

When you are in lodgings, and no shoe-boy to be got, clean your master's shoes with the bottom of the curtains, a clean napkin, or your landlady's apron.

Ever wear your hat in the house, but when your master calls; and as soon as you come into his presence, pull it off to shew your manners.

Never clean your shoes on the scraper, but in the entry or at the foot of the stairs, by which you will have the credit of being at home almost a minute sooner, and the scraper will last longer.

Never ask leave to go abroad, for then it will be always known that you are absent, and you will be thought an idle rambling fellow; whereas, if you go out and nobody observes, you have a chance of coming home without being missed, and you need not tell your fellow-servants where you are gone, for they will be sure to say, you were in the house but two minutes ago, which is the duty of all servants.

Snuff the candles with your fingers, and throw the snuff on the floor; then tread it out to prevent stinking: this method will very much save the snuffers from wearing out. You ought also to snuff them close to the tallow, which will make them run, and so encrease the perquisite of the cook's kitchen-stuff; for she is the person you ought, in prudence, to be well with.

While grace is saying after meat, do you and your brethren take the chairs from behind the company, so that when they go to sit again, they may fall backwards, which will make them all merry; but be you so discreet as to hold your laughter till you get to the kitchen, and then divert your fellow-servants.

When you know your master is most busy in company, come in, and pretend to fettle about the room; and if he chides, say, you thought he rung the bell. This will

divert

divert him from plodding on business too much, or spending himself in talk, or racking his thoughts, all which are hurtful to his constitution.

If you are ordered to break the claw of a crab or a lobster, clap it between the sides of the dining-room-door between the hinges: thus you can do it gradually without mashing the meat, which is often the fate of the street-door key, or the pestle.

When you take a foul plate from any of the guests, and observe the foul knife and fork lying on the plate, shew your dexterity; take up the plate, and throw off the knife and fork on the table, without shaking off the bones or broken meat that are left: then the guest, who hath more time than you, will wipe the fork and knife already used.

When you carry a glass of liquor to any person who hath called for it, do not bob him on the shoulder, or cry, Sir, or madam, here's the glass; that would be unmannerly, as if you had a mind to force it down one's throat; but stand at the person's left shoulder and wait his time; and if he strikes it down with his elbow by forgetfulness, that was his fault and not yours.

When your mistress sends you for a hackney coach in a wet day, come back in the coach to save your cloaths and the trouble of walking; it is better the bottom of her petticoats should be daggled with your dirty shoes, than your livery be spoiled, and yourself get a cold.

There is no indignity so great to one of your station, as that of lighting your master in the streets with a lanthorn; and therefore it is very honest policy to try all arts how to evade it: besides, it shews your master to be either poor or covetous, which are the two worst qualities you can meet with in any service. When I was under these circumstances, I made use of several wise expedients, which I here recommend to you: sometimes I took a

candle

candle so long, that it reached to the very top of the lanthorn and burned it: but my master, after a good beating, ordered me to paste it over with paper. I then used a middling candle, but stuck it so loose in the socket, that it leaned towards one side, and burned a whole quarter of the horn. Then I used a bit of candle of half an inch, which sunk in the socket, and melted the solder, and forced my master to walk half the way in the dark. Then he made me stick two inches of candle in the place where the socket was; after which I pretended to stumble, put out the candle, and broke all the tin part to pieces: at last, he was forced to make use of a lanthorn-boy out of perfect good husbandry.

It is much to be lamented, that gentlemen of our employment have but two hands to carry plates, dishes, bottles, and the like, out of the room at meals; and the misfortune is still the greater, because one of those hands is required to open the door, while you are encumbered with your load: therefore I advise, that the door may be always left at jarr, so as to open it with your foot, and then you may carry out plates and dishes from your belly up to your chin, besides a good quantity of things under your arms, which will save you many a weary step; but take care that none of the burden falls till you are out of the room, and, if possible, out of hearing.

If you are sent to the post-office with a letter in a cold rainy night, step to the alehouse and take a pot, until it is supposed you have done your errand; but take the next fair opportunity to put the letter in carefully, as becomes an honest servant.

If you are ordered to make coffee for the ladies after dinner, and the pot happens to boil over while you are running up for a spoon to stir it, or thinking of something else, or struggling with the chamber-maid for a kiss, wipe the

the sides of the pot clean with a dishclout, carry up your coffee boldly, and when your lady finds it too weak, and examines you whether it has not run over, deny the fact absolutely; swear you put in more coffee than ordinary; that you never stirred an inch from it; that you strove to make it better than usual, because your mistress had ladies with her; that the servants in the kitchen will justify what you say: upon this, you will find that the other ladies will pronounce your coffee to be very good, and your mistress will confess that her mouth is out of taste, and she will, for the future, suspect herself, and be more cautious in finding fault. This I would have you do from a principle of conscience, for coffee is very unwholesome; and, out of affection to your lady, you ought to give it her as weak as possible: and, upon this argument, when you have a mind to treat any of the maids with a dish of fresh coffee, you may and ought to subtract a third part of the powder, on account of your lady's health, and getting her maid's good-will.

If your master sends you with a small trifling present to one of his friends, be as careful of it as you would be of a diamond ring; therefore, if the present be only half a dozen pippins, send up the servant, who received the message, to say, that you were ordered to deliver them with your own hands. This will shew your exactness and care to prevent accidents or mistakes; and the gentleman or lady cannot do less than give you a shilling: so, when your master receives the like present, teach the messenger who brings it to do the same, and give your master hints that may stir up his generosity; for brother servants should assist one another, since it is all for their master's honour, which is the chief point to be consulted by every good servant, and of which he is the best judge.

When

When you step but a few doors off, to tattle with a wench, or take a running pot of ale, or to see a brother footman going to be hanged, leave the street door open, that you may not be forced to knock, and your master discover you are gone out; for a quarter of an hour's time can do his service no injury.

When you take away the remaining pieces of bread after dinner, put them on foul plates, and press them down with other plates over them, so as no body can touch them; and so they will be a good perquisite to the black-guard boy in ordinary.

When you are forced to clean your master's shoes with your own hand, use the edge of the sharpest case-knife, and dry them with the toes an inch from the fire, because wet shoes are dangerous, and besides, by these arts, you will get them the sooner for yourself.

In some families the master often sends to the tavern for a bottle of wine, and you are the messenger: I advise you, therefore, to take the smallest bottle you can find; but, however, make the drawer give you a full quart, then you will get a good sup for yourself, and your bottle will be filled. As for a cork to stop it, you need be at no trouble for the thumb will do as well, or a bit of dirty chewed paper.

In all disputes with chairmen and coachmen for demanding too much, when your master sends you down to chaffer with them, take pity of the poor fellows, and tell your master that they will not take a farthing less: it is more for your interest to get a share of a pot of ale, than to save a shilling for your master, to whom it is a trifle.

When you attend your lady in a dark night, if she useth her coach, do not walk by the coach side, so as to tire and dirt yourself, but get up into your proper place

behind

behind it, and so hold the flambeau sloping forward over the coach roof; and when it wants snuffing, dash it against the corners.

When you leave your lady at church on Sundays, you have two hours safe to spend with your companions at the alehouse, or over a beef-stake and a pot of beer at home with the cook and the maids; and, indeed, poor servants have so few opportunities to be happy, that they ought not to lose any.

Never wear socks when you wait at meals, on account of your own health as well as of them who sit at table; because as most ladies like the smell of young men's toes, so it is a sovereign remedy against the vapours.

Chuse a service, if you can, where your livery colours are least tawdry and distinguishing: green and yellow immediately betray your office, and so do all kinds of lace, except silver, which will hardly fall to your share, unless with a duke or some prodigal just come to his estate. The colours you ought to wish for, are blue, or filemot turned up with red; which, with a borrowed sword, a borrowed air, your master's linen, and a natural and improved confidence, will give you what title you please, where you are not known.

When you carry dishes or other things out of the room at meals, fill both your hands as full as possible; for, although you may sometimes spill, and sometimes let fall, yet you will find, at the year's end, you have made great dispatch, and saved abundance of time.

If your master or mistress happens to walk the streets, keep on one side, and as much on the level with them as you can, which people observing, will either think you do not belong to them, or that you are one of their companions; but, if either of them happen to turn back and speak to you, so that you are under the necessity to take

off

off your hat, use but your thumb and one finger, and scratch your head with the rest.

In winter time light the dining-room fire but two minutes before dinner is served up, that your master may see how saving you are of his coals.

When you are ordered to stir up the fire, clean away the ashes from betwixt the bars with the fire-brush.

When you are ordered to call a coach, although it be midnight, go no farther than the door, for fear of being out of the way when you are wanted; and there stand bawling, Coach, coach, for half an hour.

Although you gentlemen in livery have the misfortune to be treated scurvily by all mankind, yet you make a shift to keep up your spirits, and sometimes arrive at considerable fortunes. I was an intimate friend to one of our brethren, who was footman to a court lady: she had an honourable employment, was sister to an earl, and the widow of a man of quality. She observed something so polite in my friend, the gracefulness with which he tript before her chair and put his hair under his hat, that she made him many advances; and one day taking the air in her coach with Tom behind it, the coachman mistook the way, and stopt at a privileged chapel, where the couple were married, and Tom came home in the chariot by his lady's side: but he unfortunately taught her to drink brandy, of which she died, after having pawned all her plate to purchase it; and Tom is now a journeyman maltster.

Boucher, the famous gamester, was another of our fraternity, and when he was worth 50,000 *l.* he dunned the duke of Buckingham for an arrear of wages in his service; and I could instance many more, particularly another, whose son had one of the chief employments at court; and it is sufficient to give you the following advice,

which

which is to be pert and saucy to all mankind, especially to the chaplain, the waiting-woman, and the better sort of servants in a person of quality's family, and value not now and then a kicking, or a caning; for your insolence will at last turn to good account; and from wearing a livery, you may probably soon carry a pair of colours.

When you wait behind a chair at meals, keep constantly wriggling the back of the chair, that the person behind whom you stand may know you are ready to attend him.

When you carry a parcel of china plates, if they chance to fall, as it is a frequent misfortune, your excuse must be, that a dog ran across you in the hall; that the chambermaid accidentally pushed the door against you; that a mop stood across the entry, and tript you up; that your sleeve stuck against the key, or button of the lock.

When your master and lady are talking together in their bed-chamber, and you have some suspicion that you or your fellow-servants are concerned in what they say, listen at the door, for the publick good of all the servants; and join all to take proper measures for preventing any innovations that may hurt the community.

Be not proud in prosperity: you have heard that fortune turns on a wheel; if you have a good place, you are at the top of the wheel. Remember how often you have been stripped and kicked out of doors, your wages all taken up beforehand, and spent in translated red-heeled shoes, second-hand toupees, and repaired lace ruffles, besides a swinging debt to the ale-wife and the brandy-shop. The neighbouring tapster, who before would beckon you over to a savoury bit of ox-cheek in the morning, give it you gratis, and only score you up for the liquor, immediately after you were packed off in disgrace, carried a petition to your master to be paid out of your wages, whereof not a farthing was due, and then pursued you

you with bailiffs into every blind cellar. Remember how soon you grew shabby, thread-bare, and out-at-heels; were forced to borrow an old livery coat, to make your appearance while you were looking for a place; and sneak to every house where you have an old acquaintance to steal you a scrap to keep life and soul together; and, upon the whole, were in the lowest station of human life, which, as the old ballad says, is that of a skipkennel turned out of place; I say, remember all this now in your flourishing condition. Pay your contributions duly to your late brothers the cadets, who are left to the wide world: take one of them as your dependant, to send on your lady's messages when you have a mind to go to the ale-house; slip him out privately now and then a slice of bread and a bit of cold meat; your master can afford it; and, if he be not yet put upon the establishment for a lodging, let him lie in the stable, or the coach-house, or under the back-stairs, and recommend him to all the gentlemen who frequent your house as an excellent servant.

To grow old in the office of a footman, is the highest of all indignities: therefore when you find years coming on without hopes of a place at court, a command in the army, a succession to the stewardship, an employment in the revenue (which two last you cannot obtain without reading and writing), or running away with your master's neice or daughter; I directly advise you to go upon the road, which is the only post of honour left you: there you will meet many of your old comrades, and live a short life and a merry one, and make a figure at your exit, wherein I will give you some instructions.

The last advice I give you, relates to your behaviour when you are going to be hanged; which, either for robbing your master, for house-breaking, or going upon the highway, or in a drunken quarrel by killing the first

man

man you meet, may very probably be your lot, and is owing to one of these three qualities; either a love of good fellowship, a generosity of mind, or too much vivacity of spirits. Your good behaviour on this article will concern your whole community: At your trial deny the fact with all solemnity of imprecations: a hundred of your brethren, if they can be admitted, will attend about the bar, and be ready upon demand to give you a good character before the court: let nothing prevail on you to confess, but the promise of a pardon for discovering your comrades: but I suppose all this to be in vain, for if you escape now, your fate will be the same another day. Get a speech to be written by the best author of Newgate, some of your kind wenches will provide you with a Holland shirt, and white cap, crowned with a crimson or black ribbon: take leave chearfully of all your friends in Newgate; mount the cart with courage; fall on your knees; lift up your eyes: hold a book in your hands, although you cannot read a word; deny the fact at the gallows; kiss and forgive the hangman, and so farewel: you shall be buried in pomp at the charge of the fraternity: the surgeons shall not touch a limb of you; and your fame shall continue until a successor of equal renown succeeds in your place.

CHAP. IX

Directions to the WAITING-MAID

TWO accidents have happened to lessen the comforts and profits of your employment; first, that execrable custom got among ladies of trucking their old cloaths for china, or turning them to cover easy chairs, or making them into patch-work for screens, stools, cushions, and the like. The second is, the invention of small chests and trunks with lock and key, wherein they keep the tea and sugar,

sugar, without which it is impossible for a waiting-maid to live: for by this means you are forced to buy brown sugar, and pour water upon the leaves, when they have lost all their spirit and taste. I cannot contrive any perfect remedy against either of these two evils. As to the former, I think there should be a general confederacy of all the servants in every family, for the publick good, to drive those china hucksters from the doors; and as to the latter, there is no other method to relieve yourselves, but by a false key, which is a point both difficult and dangerous to compass; but, as to the circumstances of honesty in procuring one I am under no doubt, when your mistress gives you so just a provocation by refusing you an antient and legal perquisite. The mistress of the tea-shop may now and then give you half an ounce, but that will be only a drop in the bucket: therefore I fear you must be forced, like the rest of your sisters, to run in trust, and pay for it out of your wages, as far as they will go, which you can easily make up other ways, if your lady be handsome, or her daughters have good fortunes.

If you are in a great family, and my lady's woman, my lord may probably like you, although you are not half so handsome as his own lady. In this case, take care to get as much out of him as you can; and never allow him the smallest liberty, not the squeezing of your hand, unless he puts a guinea into it; so by degrees make him pay accordingly for every new attempt, doubling upon him in proportion to the concessions you allow, and always struggling, and threatening to cry out, or tell your lady, although you receive his money: five guineas for handling your breasts is a cheap pennyworth, although you seem to resist with all your might; but never allow him the last favour under a hundred guineas, or a settlement of twenty pounds a year for life.

In

In such a family, if you are handsome, you will have the choice of three lovers; the chaplain, the steward, and my lord's gentleman. I would first advise you to chuse the steward; but if you happen to be young with child by my lord, you must take up with the chaplain. I like my lord's gentleman the least of the three, for he is usually vain and saucy from the time he throws off his livery: and if he misseth a pair of colours, or a tide-waiter's place, he hath no remedy but the highway.

I must caution you particularly against my lord's eldest son: if you are dextrous enough, it is odds that you may draw him in to marry you, and make you a lady: if he be a common rake (and he must be one or t'other) avoid him like Satan; for he stands less in awe of a mother than my lord doth of a wife; and, after ten thousand promises, you will get nothing from him, but a big belly or a clap, and probably both together.

When your lady is ill, and after a very bad night is getting a little nap in the morning, if a footman comes with a message to enquire how she doth, do not let the compliment be lost, but shake her gently until she awakes; then deliver the message, receive her answer, and leave her to sleep.

If you are so happy as to wait on a young lady with a great fortune, you must be an ill manager if you cannot get five or six hundred pounds for the disposing of her. Put her often in mind, that she is rich enough to make any man happy; that there is no real happiness but in love; that she hath liberty to chuse wherever she pleaseth, and not by the directions of parents, who never give allowances for an innocent passion; that there are a world of handsome, fine, sweet young gentleman in town, who would be glad to die at her feet; that the conversation of two lovers is a heaven upon earth; that love, like death, equals

equals all conditions; that, if she should cast her eyes upon a young fellow below her in birth and estate, his marrying her would make him a gentleman; that you saw yesterday on the Mall the prettiest ensign; and that if you had forty thousand pounds it should be at his service. Take care that every body should know what lady you live with; how great a favourite you are; and that she always takes your advice. Go often to St. James's park; the fine fellows will soon discover you, and contrive to slip a letter into your bosom: pull it out in a fury, and throw it on the ground, unless you find at least two guineas along with it; but in that case, seem not to find it, and to think he was only playing the wag with you: when you come home, drop the letter carelessly in your lady's chamber; she finds it, is angry; protest you knew nothing of it, only you remember, that a gentleman in the park struggled to kiss you, and you believe it was he that put the letter into your sleeve or petticoat; and indeed he was as pretty a man as ever she saw: that she may burn the letter if she pleaseth. If your lady be wise, she will burn some other paper before you, and read the letter when you are gone down. You must follow this practice as often as you safely can; but let him who pays you best with every letter, be the handsomest man. If a footman presumes to bring a letter to the house to be delivered to you for your lady, although it come from your best customer, throw it at his head; call him impudent rogue and villain, and shut the door in his face: run up to your lady, and, as a proof of your fidelity, tell her what you have done.

I could enlarge very much upon this subject, but I trust to your own discretion.

If you serve a lady who is a little disposed to gallantries, you will find it a point of great prudence how to manage. Three

Three things are necessary: first, how to please your lady; secondly, how to prevent suspicion in the husband, or among the family; and lastly, but principally, how to make it most for your own advantage. To give you full directions in this important affair, would require a large volume. All assignations at home are dangerous both to your lady and yourself, and therefore contrive as much as possible to have them in a third place; especially if your lady, as it is a hundred odds, entertains more lovers than one, each of whom is often more jealous than a thousand husbands; and very unlucky rencounters may often happen under the best management. I need not warn you to employ your good offices chiefly in favour of those whom you find most liberal; yet, if your lady should happen to cast an eye upon a handsome footman, you should be generous enough to bear with her humour, which is no singularity, but a very natural appetite: it is still the safest of all home intrigues, and was formerly the least suspected, until of late years it hath grown more common. The great danger is, lest this kind of gentry, dealing too often in bad ware, may happen not to be found; and then your lady and you are in a very bad way, although not altogether desperate.

But to say the truth, I confess it is a great presumption in me to offer you any instructions in the conduct of your lady's amours, wherein your whole sisterhood is already so expert, and deeply learned; although it be much more difficult to compass, than that assistance which my brother footmen give their masters on the like occasion; and therefore I leave this affair to be treated by some abler pen.

When you lock up a silk mantua or laced head in a trunk or chest, leave a piece out, that, when you open the trunk again, you may know where to find it.

CHAP.

CHAP. XIII

Directions to the NURSE

IF you happen to let the child fall, and lame it, be sure never confess it; and if it dies, all is safe.

Contrive to be with child as soon as you can, while you are giving suck, that you may be ready for another service, when the child you nurse dies, or is weaned.

CHAP. XIV

Directions to the LAUNDRESS

IF you singe the linen with the iron, rub the place with flour, chalk, or white powder; and if nothing will do, wash it so long till it be either not to be seen, or torn to rags.

About tearing linen in washing.

When your linen is pinned on the line, or on a hedge, and it rains, whip it off, although you tear it, &c. But the place for hanging them, is on young fruit trees, especially in blossom; the linen cannot be torn, and the trees give them a fine smell.

CHAP. XV

Directions to the HOUSE-KEEPER

YOU must always have a favourite footman whom you can depend upon; and order him to be very watchful, when the second course is taken off, that it be brought safely to your office, that you and the steward may have a tit-bit together.

CHAP. XVI

Directions to the TUTORESS, *or* GOVERNESS

SAY the children have sore eyes; miss Betty won't take to her book, &c.

Make the misses read French and English novels, and French romances, and all the comedies writ in King Charles II. and King William's reigns, to soften their nature, and make them tender-hearted, &c.

ON CORRUPTIONS OF STYLE

Swift wrote a number of essays dealing directly with corruptions of style: *A Proposal for Correcting the English Tongue; Hints toward an Essay on Conversation; A Complete Collection of Genteel Conversation;* and *A Letter to a Young Gentleman Lately Entered into Holy Orders;* besides the present one. They constitute a valuable but very partial key to the strength and purity of his own prose style. Some of the lapses from good taste which he held up for ridicule are coming back into fashion again in our own country. Swift's classical loyalty to clear logical discourse, his contempt for bizarre eccentricities in idiom and vocabulary, and his impatience with 'wit' that does not make sense, are of permanent significance to any one who undertakes to write English prose.

This essay on barbarisms in writing was contributed to the *Tatler*, No. 230, 26 September, 1710. It has been reproduced from the original *Tatler*, a single sheet folio.

From my own Apartment, September 27.

THE following Letter has laid before me many great and manifest Evils in the World of Letters which I had overlooked; but they open to me a very busie Scene, and it will require no small Care and Application to amend Errors which are become so universal. The Affectation of Politeness is exposed in this Epistle with a great deal of Wit and Discernment; so that whatever Discourses I may fall into hereafter upon the Subjects the Writer treats of, I shall at present lay the Matter before the World without the least Alteration from the Words of my Correspondent.

To Isaac Bickerstaff *Esq;*

SIR,

THERE are some Abuses among us of great Consequence, the Reformation of which is properly your Province, tho', as far as I have been conversant in your Papers, you have not yet considered them. These are, the deplorable Ignorance that for some Years hath reigned among our English Writers, the great Depravity of our Taste, and the continual Corruption of our Style. I say nothing here of those who handle particular Sciences, Divinity, Law, Physick, and the like; I mean, the Traders in History and Politicks, and the Belles Lettres; together with those by whom Books are not translated, but (as the common Expressions are) Done out of French, Latin, or other Language, and Made English. I cannot but observe to you, That till of late Years a Grub-street Book was always bound in Sheep-skin, with suitable Print and Paper, the Price never above a Shilling, and taken off wholly by common Tradesmen, or Country Pedlars. But now they appear in all Sizes and Shapes,

and

and in all Places. They are handed about from Lapfulls in every Coffee-house to Persons of Quality, are shewn in Westminster-Hall and the Court of Requests. You may see them gilt, and in Royal Paper, of Five or Six hundred Pages, and rated accordingly. I would engage to furnish you with a Catalogue of English Books published within the Compass of Seven Years past, which at the first Hand would cost you a Hundred Pounds, wherein you shall not be able to find Ten Lines together of common Grammar or common Sense.

These Two Evils, Ignorance and Want of Taste, have produced a Third; I mean, the continual Corruption of our English Tongue, which, without some timely Remedy, will suffer more by the false Refinements of Twenty Years past, than it hath been improved in the foregoing Hundred: And this is what I design chiefly to enlarge upon, leaving the former Evils to your Animadversion.

But instead of giving you a List of the late Refinements crept into our Language, I here send you the Copy of a Letter I received some Time ago from a most accomplished Person in this Way of Writing, upon which I shall make some Remarks. It is in these Terms.

SIR,

'I *Cou'dn't* get the Things you sent for all *about Town*. ... I *thôt* to *ha'* come down my self, and then *I'd ha' brôut 'um*; but I *han't don't*, and I believe I *can't do't*, that's *Pozz*. ... *Tom* begins to *gi'mself Airs* because *he's* going with the *Plenipo's*. ... 'Tis said, the *French* King will *bamboozl' us agen*, which *causes many Speculations*. The *Jacks*, and others of that *Kidney*, are very *uppish*, and *alert upon't*, as you may see by their *Phizz's*. ... *Will Hazzard* has got the *Hipps*, having lost *to the Tune of* Five hundr'd Pound, *thô* he understands Play very well,

well, *no body better.* He has promis't me upon *Rep*, to leave off Play; but you know 'tis a Weakness *he's* too apt to *give into*, *thô* he has as much Wit as any Man, *no body more.* He has lain *incog* ever since. . . . The *Mobb's* very quiet with us now. . . . I believe you *thot* I *banter'd* you in my Last like a *Country Put.* . . . I *sha'n't* leave Town this Month, &c.

This Letter is in every Point an admirable Pattern of the present polite Way of Writing; nor is it of less Authority for being an Epistle. You may gather every Flower in it, with a Thousand more of equal Sweetness, from the Books, Pamphlets, and single Papers, offered us every Day in the Coffee-houses: And these are the Beauties introduced to supply the Want of Wit, Sense, Humour, and Learning, which formerly were looked upon as Qualifications for a Writer. If a Man of Wit, who died Forty Years ago, were to rise from the Grave on Purpose, How would he be able to read this Letter? And after he had got through that Difficulty, How would he be able to understand it? The first Thing that strikes your Eye is the Breaks at the End of almost every Sentence; of which I know not the Use, only that it is a Refinement, and very frequently practised. Then you will observe the Abbreviations and Elisions, by which Consonants of most obdurate Sound are joined together, without one softening Vowel to intervene; and all this only to make one Syllable of two, directly contrary to the Example of the Greeks and Romans; altogether of the Gothick Strain, and a natural Tendency towards relapsing into Barbarity, which delights in Monosyllables, and uniting of Mute Consonants; as it is observable in all the Northern Languages. And this is still more visible in the next Refinement, which consists in pronouncing the

the first Syllable in a Word that has many, and dismissing the rest; such as *Phizz*, *Hipps*, *Mobb*, *Poz. Rep.* and many more; when we are already overloaded with Monosyllables, which are the Disgrace of our Language. Thus we cram one Syllable, and cut off the rest; as the Owl fatten'd her Mice, after she had bit off their Legs to prevent their running away; and if ours be the same Reason for maiming our Words, it will certainly answer the End; for I am sure no other Nation will desire to borrow them. Some Words are hitherto but fairly split, and therefore only in their Way to Perfection, as *Incog* and *Plenipo*: But in a short Time 'tis to be hoped they will be further dock'd to *Inc* and *Plen.* This Reflexion has made me of late Years very impatient for a Peace, which I believe would save the Lives of many brave Words, as well as Men. The War has introduced Abundance of Polysyllables, which will never be able to live many more Campagnes; *Speculations*, *Operations*, *Preliminaries*, *Ambassadors*, *Pallisadoes*, *Communication*, *Circumvallation*, *Battalions*, as numerous as they are, if they attack us too frequently in our Coffee-houses, we shall certainly put them to Flight, and cut off the Rear.

The Third Refinement observable in the Letter I send you, consists in the Choice of certain Words invented by some Pretty Fellows; such as *Banter*, *Bamboozle*, *Country Put*, and *Kidney*, as it is there applied; some of which are now struggling for the Vogue, and others are in Possession of it. I have done my utmost for some Years past to stop the Progress of *Mobb* and *Banter*, but have been plainly borne down by Numbers, and betrayed by those who promised to assist me.

In the last Place, you are to take Notice of certain choice Phrases scattered through the Letter; some of them tolerable enough, till they were worn to Rags by

servile

servile Imitators. You might easily find them, though they were not in a different Print, and therefore I need not disturb them.

These are the false Refinements in our Style which you ought to correct: First, by Argument and fair Means; but if those fail, I think you are to make Use of your Authority as Censor, and by an Annual *Index Expurgatorius* expunge all Words and Phrases that are offensive to good Sense, and condemn those barbarous Mutilations of Vowels and Syllables. In this last Point the usual Pretence is, that they spell as they speak; A noble Standard for Language! to depend upon the Caprice of every Coxcomb, who, because Words are the Cloathing of our Thoughts, cuts them out, and shapes them as he pleases, and changes them oftner than his Dress. I believe, all reasonable People would be content that such Refiners were more sparing in their Words, and liberal in their Syllables: And upon this Head I should be glad you would bestow some Advice upon several young Readers in our Churches, who coming up from the University, full fraught with Admiration of our Town Politeness, will needs correct the Style of their Prayer Books. In reading the Absolution, they are very careful to say *pardons* and *absolves*; and in the Prayer for the Royal Family, it must be, *endue 'um*, *enrich 'um*, *prosper 'um*, and *bring 'um*. Then in their Sermons they use all the modern Terms of Art, *Sham*, *Banter*, *Mob*, *Bubble*, *Bully*, *Cutting*, *Shuffling*, and *Palming*, all which, and many more of the like Stamp, as I have heard them often in the Pulpit from such young Sophisters, so I have read them in some of those Sermons that have made most Noise of late. The Design, it seems, is to avoid the dreadful Imputation of Pedantry, to shew us, that they know the Town, understand Men and Manners, and have not

 been

been poring upon old unfashionable Books in the University.

I should be glad to see you the Instrument of introducing into our Style that Simplicity which is the best and truest Ornament of most Things in Life, which the politer Ages always aimed at in their Building and Dress, (*Simplex munditiis*) as well as their Productions of Wit. 'Tis manifest, that all new, affected Modes of Speech, whether borrowed from the Court, the Town, or the Theatre, are the first perishing Parts in any Language, and, as I could prove by many Hundred Instances, have been so in ours. The Writings of Hooker, who was a Country Clergyman, and of Parsons the Jesuit, both in the Reign of Queen Elizabeth, are in a Style that, with very few Allowances, would not offend any present Reader; much more clear and intelligible than those of Sir H. Wotton, Sir Robert Naunton, Osborn, Daniel the Historian, and several others who writ later; but being Men of the Court, and affecting the Phrases then in Fashion, they are often either not to be understood, or appear perfectly ridiculous.

What Remedies are to be applied to these Evils I have not Room to consider, having, I fear, already taken up most of your Paper. Besides, I think it is our Office only to represent Abuses, and yours to redress them. I am, with great Respect,

SIR,

Your, &c.

A VINDICATION OF MR. GAY, AND THE BEGGAR'S OPERA

Swift here gives us some ideas of his own about humour and satire, as well as his impressions of *The Beggar's Opera* which Gay undertook to write originally, following a suggestion from Swift that he try his hand at a Newgate pastoral.

The essay first appeared in the Irish *Intelligencer*, No. III, 1728, where it bore the title, 'A Vindication of Mr. Gay, and the Beggar's Opera'. The text reproduced is that of the Dublin reprint of the nineteen numbers of the *Intelligencer*, in one volume, 1729.

Number III.

——Ipse per omnes
Ibit personas, & turbam reddet in unam.

THE Players having now almost done with the Comedy, called the *Beggars Opera* for this Season, it may be no unpleasant Speculation, to reflect a little upon this Dramatick Piece, so singular in the Subject, and the Manner so much an Original, and which hath frequently given so very agreeable an Entertainment.

Although an evil Taste be very apt to prevail, both here and in London, yet there is a Point, which whoever can rightly touch, will never fail of pleasing a very great Majority; so great, that the Dislikers, out of Dulness or Affectation will be silent, and forced to fall in with the Herd: The Point I mean, is what we call Humour, which in its Perfection is allowed to be much preferable to Wit, if it be not rather the most useful, and agreeable Species of it.

I agree with Sir William Temple, that the Word is peculiar to our English Tongue; but I differ from him in the Opinion, that the Thing it self is peculiar to the English Nation, because the contrary may be found in many Spanish, Italian and French Productions, and particularly, whoever hath a Taste for True Humour, will find a hundred Instances of it in those Volumes printed in France, under the Name of Le Theatre Italien, to say nothing of Rabelais, Cervantes, and many others.

Now I take the Comedy or Farce, (or whatever Name the Criticks will allow it) called the *Beggars Opera*, to excel in this Article of Humour, and upon that Merit to have met with such prodigious Success both here and in England.

As

As to Poetry, Eloquence and Musick, which are said to have most Power over the Minds of Men, it is certain that very few have a Taste or Judgment of the Excellencies of the two former; and if a Man succeeds in either, it is upon the Authority of those few Judges, that lend their Taste to the Bulk of Readers, who have none of their own. I am told there are as few good Judges in Musick, and that among those who crowd the Opera's, Nine in Ten go thither merely out of Curiosity, Fashion, or Affectation.

But a Taste for Humour is in some Manner fixed to the very Nature of Man, and generally obvious to the Vulgar, except upon Subjects too refined, and superior to their Understanding.

And as this Taste of Humour is purely Natural, so is Humour it self, neither is it a Talent confined to Men of Wit, or Learning; for we observe it sometimes among common Servants, and the Meanest of the People, while the very Owners are often ignorant of the Gift they possess.

I know very well, that this happy Talent is contemptibly treated by Criticks, under the Name of low Humour, or low Comedy; but I know likewise, that the Spaniards and Italians, who are allowed to have the most Wit of any Nation in Europe, do most excel in it, and do most esteem it.

By what Disposition of the Mind, what Influence of the Stars, or what Situation of the Climate this Endowment is bestowed upon Mankind, may be a Question fit for Philosophers to discuss. It is certainly the best Ingredient towards that Kind of Satyr, which is most useful, and give the least Offence; which instead of lashing, laughs Men out of their Follies, and Vices, and is the Character which gives Horace the Preference to Juvenal.

And

And although some Things are too serious, solemn, or sacred to be turned into Ridicule, yet the Abuses of them are certainly not, since it is allowed that Corruption in Religion, Politics, and Law, may be proper Topicks for this Kind of Satyr.

There are two Ends that Men propose in writing Satyr, one of them less Noble than the other, as regarding nothing further than personal Satisfaction, and Pleasure of the Writer, but without any View towards Personal Malice; the other is a Publick Spirit, prompting Men of Genius and Virtue, to mend the World as far as they are able. And as both these Ends are innocent, so the latter is highly commendable. With Regard to the former, I demand whether I have not as good a Title to laugh, as Men have to be ridiculous, and to expose Vice, as another hath to be vicious. If I ridicule the Follies and Corruptions of a Court, a Ministry, or a Senate, are they not amply paid by Pensions, Titles, and Power, while I expect and desire no other Reward, than that of laughing with a few Friends in a Corner? Yet, if those who take Offence, think me in the Wrong, I am ready to change the Scene with them, whenever they please.

But if my Design be to make Mankind better, then I think it is my Duty; at least I am sure it is the Interest of those very Courts and Ministers, whose Follies or Vices I ridicule, to reward me for my good Intentions: For if it be reckoned a high Point of Wisdom to get the Laughers on our Side, it is much more Easy, as well as Wise to get those on our Side, who can make Millions laugh when they please.

My Reason for mentioning Courts, and Ministers, (whom I never think on but with the most profound Veneration) is, because an Opinion obtains that in the *Beggars Opera* there appears to be some Reflection upon Courtiers

Courtiers and Statesmen, whereof I am by no Means a Judge.

It is true indeed, that Mr. Gay, the Author of this Piece, hath been somewhat singular in the Course of his Fortunes; for it hath happened, that after Fourteen Years attending the Court, with a large Stock of real Merit, a modest and agreeable Conversation, a Hundred Promises and Five Hundred Friends, hath failed of Preferment, and upon a very weighty Reason. He lay under the Suspicion of having written a Libel, or Lampoon against a great M——. It is true that great M—— was demonstratively convinced, and publickly owned his Conviction, that Mr. Gay was not the Author; but having lain under the Suspicion, it seemed very just, that he should suffer the Punishment; because in this most reformed Age, the Virtues of a great M—— are no more to be suspected, than the Chastity of Cæsar's Wife.

It must be allowed, That the *Beggars Opera* is not the first of Mr. Gay's Works, wherein he hath been faulty, with Regard to Courtiers and Statesmen. For to omit his other Pieces, even in his Fables, published within two Years past, and dedicated to the Duke of Cumberland, for which he was Promised a Reward, he hath been thought somewhat too bold upon Courtiers. And although it is highly probable, he meant only the Courtiers of former Times, yet he acted unwarily, by not considering that the Malignity of some People might misinterpret what he said to the Disadvantage of present Persons and Affairs.

But I have now done with Mr. Gay as a Politician, and shall consider him henceforward only as Author of the *Beggars Opera*, wherein he hath by a Turn of Humour, entirely New, placed Vices of all Kinds in the strongest and most odious Light; and thereby done eminent

Service

Service, both to Religion and Morality. This appears from the unparallell'd Success he hath met with. All Ranks, Parties and Denominations of Men either crowding to see his Opera, or reading it with Delight in their Closets, even Ministers of State, whom he is thought to have most offended (next to those whom the Actors more immediately represent) appearing frequently at the Theatre, from a Consciousness of their own Innocence, and to convince the World how unjust a Parallel, Malice, Envy and Disaffection to the Government have made.

I am assured that several worthy Clergy-Men in this City, went privately to see the *Beggars Opera* represented; and that the fleering Coxcombs in the Pit, amused themselves with making Discoveries, and spreading the Names of those Gentlemen round the Audience.

I shall not pretend to vindicate a Clergyman, who would appear openly in his Habit at a Theatre, among such a vicious Crew, as would probably stand round him, and at such lewd Comedies, and prophane Tragedies as are often represented. Besides I know very well, that Persons of their Function are bound to avoid the Appearance of Evil, or of giving Cause of Offence. But when the Lords Chancellors, who are Keepers of the King's Conscience; when the Judges of the Land, whose Title is Reverend; when Ladies, who are bound by the Rules of their Sex to the strictest Decency, appear in the Theatre without Censure, I cannot understand, why a young Clergy-man who goes concealed out of Curiosity to see an innocent and moral Play, should be so highly condemned; nor do I much approve the Rigour of a great P——te, who said, he hoped none of his Clergy were there. I am glad to hear there are no weightier Objections against that Reverend Body, planted in this City, and I wish there never may. But I should be very sorry that

any

any of them should be so weak, as to imitate a Court-Chaplain in England, who preached against the *Beggars Opera*, which will probably do more Good than a thousand Sermons of so stupid, so injudicious, and so prostitute a Divine.

In this happy Performance of Mr. Gay's, all the Characters are just, and none of them carried beyond Nature, or hardly beyond Practice. It discovers the whole System of that Common-Wealth, or that Imperium in Imperio of Iniquity, established among us, by which neither our Lives, nor our Properties are secure, either in the High-ways, or in publick Assemblies, or even in our own Houses. It shews the miserable Lives and the constant Fate of those abandoned Wretches; for how little they sell their Lives and Souls; betrayed by their Whores, their Comrades, and the Receivers and Purchasers of these Thefts and Robberies. This Comedy contains likewise a Satyr, which although it doth by no Means affect the present Age, yet might have been useful in the former, and may possibly be so in Ages to come: I mean where the Author takes Occasion of comparing those common Robbers of the Publick, and their several Stratagems of betraying, undermining and hanging each other, to the several Arts of Politicians in Times of Corruption.

This Comedy likewise exposeth with great Justice that unnatural Taste for Italian Musick among us, which is wholly unsuitable to our Northern Climate, and the Genius of the People, whereby we are overrun with Italian-Effeminacy, and Italian Nonsense. An old Gentleman said to me, that many Years ago, when the Practice of an unnatural Vice grew so frequent in London that many were prosecuted for it, he was sure it would be the Fore-runner of Italian Opera's and Singers; and then

we

we should want nothing but stabbing or poysoning, to make us perfect Italians.

Upon the Whole, I deliver my Judgment, That nothing but servile Attachment to a Party, Affectation of Singularity, lamentable Dullness, mistaken Zeal, or studied Hypocrisy, can have the least reasonable Objection against this excellent moral Performance of the Celebrated Mr. Gay.

A LETTER TO A YOUNG GENTLEMAN LATELY ENTERED INTO HOLY ORDERS

In this essay we have Swift divested of irony, writing soberly as a priest of the Church. He does not flatter his fellow clergy in the picture he draws, but nowhere does he belittle their profession. Never blind to the faults of the Church and of the clergy, as *A Tale of a Tub* certifies, he maintains throughout respect and reverence for his vocation. The evidence is too clear to permit any doubt on this point. The fidelity with which Swift discharged his clerical and pastoral duties in remote Irish parishes, his sermons, and the prayers he composed for Stella, not to mention the *Argument Against Abolishing Christianity*, prove him to have been a devout and intelligent Churchman, though not very much of a mystic. When finally his faculties disintegrated and his memory failed, the last bit of intelligible discourse he retained was the Lord's Prayer, which he would repeat often to himself.

There is much more in this letter than evidence for Swift's Anglo-Catholic philosophy. In some respects the most thoughtful and sincere work of his pen, it embodies his clearest ideas about style. Preachers and journalists, teachers and 'popular' lecturers will not readily find a rhetoric marked by sturdier common sense, by which they may cure their own dullness.

The text reproduced is that of the original edition, 1721.

DUBLIN, January 9.

SIR,

ALTHOUGH it was against my Knowledge or Advice that you enter'd into Holy Orders, under the present Disposition of Mankind towards the Church, yet since it is now supposed too late to recede, (at least according to the general Practice and Opinion) I cannot forbear offering my Thoughts to you upon this new Condition of Life you are engaged in.

I could heartily wish that the Circumstances of your Fortune had enabled you to have continued some Years longer in the University, at least, 'till you were ten Years standing; to have laid in a competent Stock of human Learning, and some Knowledge in Divinity, before you attempted to appear in the World: For I cannot but lament the common Course, which at least Nine in Ten of those who enter into the Ministry are obliged to run. When they have taken a Degree, and are consequently grown a Burthen to their Friends, who now think themselves fully discharged; they get into Orders as soon as they can, (upon which I shall make no Remarks) first solicit a Readership, and if they be very fortunate, arrive in Time to a Curacy here in Town, or else are sent to be Assistants in the Country, where they probably continue several Years (many of them their whole Lives) with thirty or forty Pounds a Year for their Support, 'till some Bishop, who happens to be not overstock'd with Relations, or attach'd to Favourites, or is content to supply his Diocese without Colonies from England, bestows upon them some inconsiderable Benefice, when 'tis odds they are already encumber'd with a numerous Family. I would be glad to know what Intervals of Life such Persons can possibly set apart for Improvement of their Minds;

Minds; or which way they could be furnish'd with Books. the Library they brought with them from their College being usually not the most numerous, or judiciously chosen. If such Gentlemen arrive to be great Scholars, it must, I think, be either by means supernatural, or by a Method altogether out of any Road yet known to the Learned. But I conceive the Fact directly otherwise, and that many of them lose the greatest Part of the small Pittance they received at the University.

I take it for granted, that you intend to pursue the beaten Track, and are already desirous to be seen in a Pulpit; only I hope you will think it proper to pass your Quarentine among some of the desolate Churches five Miles round this Town, where you may at least learn to Read and to Speak before you venture to expose your Parts in a City-Congregation; not that these are better Judges, but because, if a Man must needs expose his Folly, it is more safe and discreet to do so, before few Witnesses, and in a scattered Neighbourhood. And you will do well, if you can prevail upon some intimate and judicious Friend to be your constant Hearer, and allow him with the utmost Freedom to give you notice of whatever he shall find amiss, either in your Voice or Gesture; for want of which early Warning, many Clergymen continue defective, and sometimes ridiculous, to the End of their Lives; neither is it rare to observe among excellent and learned Divines, a certain ungracious Manner, or an unhappy Tone of Voice, which they never have been able to shake off.

I could likewise have been glad if you had applied your self a little more to the Study of the English Language, than I fear you have done; the Neglect whereof is one of the most general Defects among the Scholars of this Kingdom, who seem to have not the least Conception of a

Style

Style, but run on in a flat kind of Phraseology, often mingled with barbarous Terms and Expressions, peculiar to the Nation: Neither do I perceive that any Person, either finds or acknowledges his Wants upon this Head, or in the least desires to have them supplied. Proper Words in proper Places, makes the true Definition of a Style. But this would require too ample a Disquisition to be now dwelt on: However, I shall venture to name one or two Faults, which are easy to be remedied with a very small Portion of Abilities.

The first is the frequent Use of obscure Terms, which by the Women are called hard Words, and by the better sort of Vulgar fine Language; than which I do not know a more universal, inexcusable, and unnecessary Mistake among the Clergy of all Distinctions, but especially the younger Practitioners. I have been curious enough to take a List of several hundred Words in a Sermon of a new Beginner, which not one of his Hearers, among a hundred, could possibly understand; neither can I easily call to mind any Clergyman of my own Acquaintance who is wholly exempt from this Error, although many of them agree with me in the Dislike of the Thing. But I am apt to put my self in the Place of the Vulgar, and think many Words difficult or obscure, which they will not allow to be so, because those Words are obvious to Scholars. I believe the Method observed by the famous Lord Falkland, in some of his Writings, would not be an ill one for young Divines: I was assured by an old Person of Quality who knew him well, that when he doubted whether a Word were perfectly intelligible, or no, he used to consult one of his Lady's Chambermaids, (not the Waiting-woman, because it was possible she might be conversant in Romances,) and by her Judgment was guided, whether to receive, or to reject it. And if that great

great Person thought such a Caution necessary in Treatises offered to the learned World, it will be sure, at least as proper in Sermons, where the meanest Hearer is supposed to be concerned, and where very often a Lady's Chambermaid may be allowed to equal half the Congregation, both as to Quality and Understanding. But I know not how it comes to pass, that Professors in most Arts and Sciences are generally the worst qualified to explain their Meanings to those who are not of their Tribe: A common Farmer shall make you understand in three Words, that his Foot is out of Joint, or his Collar-bone broken; wherein a Surgeon, after a hundred Terms of Art, if you are not a Scholar, shall leave you to seek. It is frequently the same Case in Law, Physick, and even many of the meaner Arts.

And upon this Account it is, that among hard Words, I number likewise those which are peculiar to Divinity as it is a Science, because I observed several Clergymen, otherwise little fond of obscure Terms, yet in their Sermons very liberal of all those which they find in Ecclesiastical Writers, as if it were our Duty to understand them; which I am sure it is not. And I defy the greatest Divine to produce any Law either of God or Man, which obliges me to comprehend the Meaning of Omniscience, Omnipresence, Ubiquity, Attribute, Beatifick Vision, with a thousand others so frequent in Pulpits, any more than that of Excentrick, Idiosyncrasy, Entity, and the like. I believe I may venture to insist further, that many Terms used in Holy Writ, particularly by St. Paul, might with more Discretion be changed into plainer Speech, except when they are introduced as part of a Quotation.

I am the more earnest in this Matter, because it is a general Complaint, and the justest in the World. For a Divine has nothing to say to the wisest Congregation of

any

any Parish in this Kingdom, which he may not express in a manner to be understood by the meanest among them. And this Assertion must be true, or else God requires from us more than we are able to perform. However, not to contend whether a Logician might possibly put a Case that would serve for an Exception, I will appeal to any Man of Letters, whether at least nineteen in twenty of those perplexing Words might not be changed into easy ones, such as naturally first occur to ordinary Men, and probably did so at first to those very Gentlemen who are so fond of the former.

We are often reproved by Divines from the Pulpits, on account of our Ignorance in Things sacred, and perhaps with Justice enough: However, it is not very reasonable for them to expect, that common Men should understand Expressions, which are never made use of in common Life. No Gentleman thinks it safe or prudent to send a Servant with a Message, without repeating it more than once, and endeavouring to put it into Terms brought down to the Capacity of the Bearer: Yet after all this Care, it is frequent for Servants to mistake, and sometimes to occasion Misunderstandings among Friends. Although the common Domesticks in a Gentleman's Family have more Opportunities of improving their Minds, than the ordinary sort of Tradesmen.

It is usual for Clergymen who are taxed with this learned Defect, to quote Dr. Tillotson, and other famous Divines, in their Defence, without considering the Difference between elaborate Discourses upon important Occasions, delivered to Princes or Parliaments, written with a View of being made publick, and a plain Sermon intended for the middle or lower Size of People. Neither do they seem to remember the many Alterations, Additions, and Expungings made by great Authors, in those Treatises

Treatises which they prepare for the Publick. Besides, that excellent Prelate above mentioned, was known to preach after a much more popular Manner in the City Congregations: And if in those Parts of his Works he be any where too obscure for the Understandings of many, who may be supposed to have been his Hearers, it ought to be numbred among his Omissions.

The Fear of being thought Pedants hath been of pernicious Consequence to young Divines. This hath wholly taken many of them off from their severer Studies in the University, which they have exchanged for Plays, Poems, and Pamphlets, in order to qualify them for Tea-Tables and Coffee-Houses. This they usually call Polite Conversation, knowing the World, and reading Men instead of Books. These Accomplishments, when applied in the Pulpit, appear by a quaint, terse, florid Style, rounded into Periods and Cadencies, commonly without either Propriety or Meaning. I have listen'd with my utmost Attention for half an Hour to an Orator of this Species, without being able to understand, much less to carry away one single Sentence out of a whole Sermon. Others, to shew that their Studies have not been confined to Sciences, or ancient Authors, will talk in the Style of a Gaming Ordinary, and White Friars, where I suppose the Hearers can be little edified by the Terms of Palming, Shuffling, Biting, Bamboozling, and the like, if they have not been sometimes conversant among Pickpockets and Sharpers. And truly, as they say, a Man is known by his Company, so it should seem, that a Man's Company may be known by his Manner of expressing himself, either in publick Assemblies, or private Conversation.

It would be endless to run over the several Defects of Style among us: I shall therefore say nothing of the Mean and the Paultry, (which are usually attended by the Fustian,)

Fustian,) much less of the Slovenly or Indecent. Two Things I will just warn you against: The First is, the Frequency of flat, unnecessary Epithets; and the other is, the Folly of using old thread-bare Phrases, which will often make you go out of your Way to find and apply them, are nauseous to rational Hearers, and will seldom express your Meaning as well as your own natural Words.

Although, as I have already observed, our English Tongue is too little cultivated in this Kingdom, yet the Faults are Nine in Ten owing to Affectation, and not to the Want of Understanding. When a Man's Thoughts are clear, the properest Words will generally offer themselves first, and his own Judgment will direct him in what Order to place them, so as they may be best understood. Where Men err against this Method, it is usually on purpose, and to shew their Learning, their Oratory, their Politeness, or their Knowledge of the World. In short, that Simplicity, without which no human Performance can arrive to any great Perfection, is no where more eminently useful than in this.

I have been considering that Part of Oratory which relates to the moving of the Passions: This I observe is in Esteem and Practice among some Church Divines, as well as among all the Preachers and Hearers of the Fanatick or Enthusiastick Strain. I will here deliver to you (perhaps with more Freedom than Prudence) my Opinion upon the Point.

The two great Orators of Greece and Rome, Demosthenes and Cicero, though each of them a Leader (or as the Greeks called it, a Demagogue) in a popular State, yet seem to differ in their Practice upon this Branch of their Art: The former, who had to deal with a People of much more Politeness, Learning, and Wit, laid the greatest Weight of his Oratory upon the Strength of his Argu-

ments

ments offered to their Understanding and Reason: Whereas Tully considered the Dispositions of a sincere, more ignorant, and less mercurial Nation, by dwelling almost entirely on the pathetick Part.

But the principal Thing to be remember'd is, that the constant Design of both these Orators in all their Speeches, was to drive some one particular Point, either the Condemnation or Acquittal of an accused Person, a Persuasive to War, the Enforcing of a Law, and the like; which was determined upon the Spot, according as the Oratory on either Side prevailed. And here it was often found of absolute Necessity to enflame or cool the Passions of the Audience; especially at Rome, where Tully spoke. And with those Writings young Divines (I mean those among them who read old Authors) are more conversant than with those of Demosthenes, who by many Degrees excelled the other, at least as an Orator. But I do not see how this Talent of moving the Passions can be of any great Use towards directing Christian Men in the Conduct of their Lives, at least in these Northern Climates, where I am confident, the strongest Eloquence of that kind will leave few Impressions upon any of our Spirits deep enough to last till the next Morning, or rather to the next Meal.

But what hath chiefly put me out of Conceit with this moving Manner of Preaching, is the frequent Disappointment it meets with. I know a Gentleman, who made it a Rule in reading, to skip over all Sentences where he spy'd a Note of Admiration at the End. I believe those Preachers who abound in Epiphonema's, if they look about them, would find one part of their Congregation out of Countenance, and the other asleep, except perhaps an old Female Beggar or two in the Isles, who (if they be sincere) may probably groan at the Sound.

Nor is it a wonder that this Expedient should so often miscarry,

miscarry, which requires so much Art and Genius to arrive at any Perfection in it, as any Man will find, much sooner than learn by consulting Cicero himself.

I therefore entreat you to make use of this Faculty (if you are ever so unfortunate as to think you have it) as seldom, and with as much Caution as you can, else I may probably have occasion to say of you as a great Person said of another upon this very Subject. A Lady ask'd him, coming out of Church, whether it were not a very moving Discourse? 'Yes,' said he, 'I was extreamly sorry, for the Man is my Friend.'

If in Company you offer something for a Jest, and no body seconds you in your own Laughter, nor seems to relish what you said, you may condemn their Taste, if you please, and appeal to better Judgments; but in the mean Time, it must be agreed you make a very indifferent Figure: And it is at least equally ridiculous to be disappointed in endeavouring to make other Folks grieve, as to make them laugh.

A plain convincing Reason may possibly operate upon the Mind both of a learned and ignorant Hearer as long as they live, and will edify a thousand Times more than the Art of wetting the Handkerchiefs of a whole Congregation, if you were sure to attain it.

If your Arguments be strong, in God's Name offer them in as moving a Manner as the Nature of the Subject will probably admit, wherein Reason and good Advice will be your safest Guides; but beware of letting the pathetick Part swallow up the rational: For I suppose, Philosophers have long agreed, that Passion should never prevail over Reason.

As I take it, the two principal Branches of Preaching, are first to tell the People what is their Duty, and then to convince them that it is so. The Topicks for both these,

we

we know are brought from Scripture and Reason. Upon this first, I wish it were often practised to instruct the Hearers in the Limits, Extent, and Compass of every Duty, which requires a good deal of Skill and Judgment: The other Branch is, I think not so difficult. But what I would offer upon both, is this, That it seems to be in the Power of a reasonable Clergyman, if he will be at the Pains to make the most ignorant Man comprehend what is his Duty, and to convince him by Argument drawn to the Level of his Understanding, that he ought to perform it.

But I must remember that my Design in this Paper was not so much to instruct you in your Business either as a Clergyman, or a Preacher, as to warn you against some Mistakes which are obvious to the Generality of Mankind as well as to me; and we who are Hearers, may be allowed to have some Opportunities in the Quality of being Standers by. Only perhaps I may now again transgress, by desiring you to express the Heads of your Divisions in as few and clear Words as you possibly can; otherwise, I and many thousand others will never be able to retain them, nor consequently to carry away a Syllable of the Sermon.

I shall now mention a Particular, wherein your whole Body will be certainly against me, and the Laity, almost to a Man, on my Side. However it came about, I cannot get over the Prejudice of taking some little Offence at the Clergy, for perpetually reading their Sermons; perhaps, my frequent hearing of Foreigners, who never make use of Notes, may have added to my Disgust. And I cannot but think, that whatever is read, differs as much from what is repeated without Book, as a Copy does from an Original. At the same time, I am highly sensible what an extream Difficulty it would be upon you to alter this Method; and that, in such a Case, your Sermons would be

much

much less valuable than they are, for want of Time to improve and correct them. I would therefore gladly come to a Compromise with you in this Matter: I knew a Clergyman of some Distinction, who appeared to deliver his Sermon without looking into his Notes, which when I complimented him upon, he assured me, he could not repeat six Lines; but his Method was to write the whole Sermon in a large plain Hand, with all the Forms of Margin, Paragraph, marked Page, and the like; then on Sunday Morning, took care to run it over five or six Times, which he could do in an Hour; and when he deliver'd it, by pretending to turn his Face from one Side to the other, he would (in his own Expression) pick up the Lines, and cheat his People by making them believe he had it all by Heart. He farther added, that whenever he happened by Neglect to omit any of these Circumstances, the Vogue of the Parish was, 'our Doctor gave us but an indifferent Sermon to Day'. Now among us, many Clergymen act too directly contrary to this Method, that from a Habit of saving Time and Paper, which they acquired at the University, they write in so diminutive a Manner, with such frequent Blots and Interlineations, that they are hardly able to go on without perpetual Hesitations or extemporary Expletives: And I desire to know what can be more inexcusable, than to see a Divine, and a Scholar, at a Loss in reading his own Compositions, which it is supposed he has been preparing with much Pains and Thought for the Instruction of his People. The want of a little more Care in this Article, is the Cause of much ungraceful Behaviour. You will observe some Clergymen with their Heads held down from the Beginning to the End, within an Inch of the Cushion, to read what is hardly legible; which, besides the untoward Manner, hinders them from making the best Advantage

of

of their Voice: Others, again, have a Trick of popping up and down every Moment, from their Paper to the Audience, like an idle School-Boy on a Repetition-Day.

Let me entreat you, therefore, to add one half Crown a Year to the Article of Paper; to transcribe your Sermons in as large and plain a Manner as you can, and either make no Interlineations, or change the whole Leaf; for we your Hearers would rather you should be less correct, than perpetually stammering, which I take to be one of the worst Solecisms in Rhetorick. And lastly, read your Sermon once or twice for a few Days before you preach it: To which you will probably answer some Years hence, 'That it was but just finished when the last Bell rung to Church'; and I shall readily believe, but not excuse you.

I cannot forbear warning you, in the most earnest Manner, against endeavouring at Wit in your Sermons; because, by the strictest Computation, it is very near a Million to one that you have none; and because too many of your Calling have consequently made themselves everlastingly ridiculous by attempting it. I remember several young Men in this Town, who could never leave the Pulpit under half a dozen Conceits; and this Faculty adhered to those Gentlemen a longer or shorter Time, exactly in proportion to their several Degrees of Dulness: Accordingly, I am told that some of them retain it to this Day. I heartily wish the Brood were at an End.

Before you enter into the common unsufferable Cant, of taking all Occasions to disparage the Heathen Philosophers, I hope you will differ from some of your Brethren, by first enquiring what those Philosophers can say for themselves. The System of Morality to be gathered out of the Writings or Sayings of those ancient Sages, falls undoubtedly very short of that delivered in the Gospel, and

and wants, besides, the divine Sanction which our Saviour gave to his. Whatever is further related by the Evangelists, contains chiefly Matters of Fact, and consequently of Faith; such as the Birth of Christ, his being the Messiah, his Miracles, his Death, Resurrection, and Ascension: None of which can properly come under the Appellation of human Wisdom, being intended only to make us wise unto Salvation. And therefore in this Point, nothing can justly be laid to the Charge of the Philosophers further, than that they were ignorant of certain Facts which happened long after their Death. But I am deceived, if a better Comment could be any where collected upon the moral Part of the Gospel, than from the Writings of those excellent Men; even that divine Precept of loving our Enemies, is at large insisted on by Plato, who puts it, as I remember, into the Mouth of Socrates. And as to the Reproach of Heathenism, I doubt they had less of it than the corrupted Jews, in whose Time they lived. For it is a gross Piece of Ignorance among us, to conceive, that in those polite and learned Ages, even Persons of any tolerable Education, much less the wisest Philosophers, did acknowledge or worship any more than one Almighty Power, under several Denominations, to whom they allowed all those Attributes we ascribe to the Divinity: And as I take it, human Comprehension reacheth no further; neither did our Saviour think it necessary to explain to us the Nature of God, because I suppose it would be impossible, without bestowing on us other Faculties than we possess at present. But the true Misery of the Heathen World appears to be what I before mentioned, the want of a divine Sanction, without which the Dictates of the Philosophers failed in the Point of Authority, and consequently the Bulk of Mankind lay indeed under a great Load of Ignorance, even in the

Article

Article of Morality; but the Philosophers themselves did not. Take the Matter in this Light, and it will afford Field enough for a Divine to enlarge on, by shewing the Advantages which the Christian World has over the Heathen, and the absolute Necessity of divine Revelations, to make the Knowledge of the true God, and the Practice of Virtue more universal in the World.

I am not ignorant how much I differ in this Opinion from some ancient Fathers in the Church, who arguing against the Heathens, made it a principal Topick to decry their Philosophy as much as they could: Which, I hope, is not altogether our present Case. Besides, it is to be considered, that those Fathers lived in the Decline of Literature; and in my Judgment, (who should be unwilling to give the least Offence,) appear to be rather most excellent holy Persons, than of transcendant Genius and Learning. Their genuine Writings (for many of them have extremely suffered by spurious Additions) are of admirable Use for confirming the Truth of ancient Doctrines and Discipline, by shewing the State and Practice of the Primitive Church. But among such of them as have fallen in my Way, I do not remember any whose Manner of arguing or exhorting I could heartily recommend to the Imitation of a young Divine, when he is to speak from the Pulpit. Perhaps I judge too hastily; there being several of them, in whose Writings I have made very little Progress, and in others none at all. For I perused only such as were recommended to me, at a Time when I had more Leisure, and a better Disposition to read, than have since fallen to my Share.

To return then to the Heathen Philosophers: I hope you will not only give them Quarter, but make their Works a considerable Part of your Study. To these I will venture to add the principal Orators and Historians, and perhaps

a few

a few of the Poets: By the reading of which, you will soon discover your Mind and Thoughts to be enlarged, your Imagination extended and refined, your Judgment directed, your Admiration lessened, and your Fortitude encreased: All which Advantages must needs be of excellent Use to a Divine, whose Duty it is to preach and practise the Contempt of human Things.

I would say something concerning Quotations, wherein I think you cannot be too sparing, except from Scripture, and the primitive Writers of the Church. As to the former, when you offer a Text as a Proof or an Illustration, we your Hearers expect to be fairly used, and sometimes think we have reason to complain, especially of you younger Divines; which makes us fear, that some of you conceive you have no more to do than to turn over a Concordance, and there having found the principal Word, introduce as much of the Verse as will serve your Turn, though in reality it makes nothing for you. I do not altogether disapprove the Manner of interweaving Texts of Scripture through the Style of your Sermon, wherein, however, I have sometimes observed great Instances of Indiscretion and Impropriety, against which I therefore venture to give you a Caution.

As to Quotations from ancient Fathers, I think they are best brought in, to confirm some Opinion controverted by those who differ from us: In other Cases we give you full Power to adopt the Sentence for your own, rather than tell us, 'as St. Austin excellently observes'. But to mention modern Writers by Name, or use the Phrase of 'a late excellent Prelate of our Church', and the like, is altogether intolerable, and, for what Reason I know not, makes every rational Hearer ashamed. Of no better a Stamp is your 'Heathen Philosopher', and 'famous Poet', and 'Roman Historians', at least in common

mon Congregations, who will rather believe you on your own Word, than on that of Plato or Homer.

I have lived to see Greek or Latin almost entirely driven out of the Pulpit, for which I am heartily glad. The frequent Use of the latter was certainly a Remnant of Popery, which never admitted Scripture in the vulgar Language; and I wonder that Practice was never accordingly objected to us by the Fanaticks.

The mention of Quotations puts me in mind of Common-Place Books, which have been long in use by industrious young Divines, and, I hear, do still continue so; I know they are very beneficial to Lawyers and Physicians, because they are Collections of Facts or Cases, whereupon a great Part of their several Faculties depend; of these I have seen several, but never yet any written by a Clergyman; only from what I am informed, they generally are Extracts of Theological and Moral Sentences, drawn from Ecclesiastical and other Authors, reduced under proper Heads, usually begun, and perhaps finished, while the Collectors were young in the Church, as being intended for Materials, or Nurseries to stock future Sermons. You will observe the wisest Editors of ancient Authors, when they meet a Sentence worthy of being distinguished, take special Care to have the first Word printed in Capital Letters, that you may not overlook it: Such, for Example, as 'the Inconstancy of Fortune, the Goodness of Peace, the Excellency of Wisdom, the Certainty of Death; that Prosperity makes Men insolent, and Adversity humble'; and the like eternal Truths, which every Plowman knew long enough before Aristotle or Plato were born. If Theological common Place-Books be no better filled, I think they had better be laid aside; and I could wish that Men of tolerable Intellectuals would trust their own natural Reason, improved by a general Conversation with

Books

Books, to enlarge on Points which they are suppos'd already to understand. If a rational Man reads an excellent Author with just Application, he shall find himself extreamly improved, and perhaps insensibly led to imitate that Author's Perfections, although in a little Time he should not remember one Word in the Book, nor even the Subject it handled: For Books give the same Turn to our Thoughts and Way of Reasoning, that good and ill Company does to our Behaviour and Conversation; without either loading our Memories, or making us even sensible of the Change. And particularly I have observed in Preaching, that no Men succeed better than those, who trust entirely to the Stock or Fund of their own Reason, advanced indeed, but not overlaid by Commerce with Books: Whoever only reads in order to transcribe wise and shining Remarks, without entring into the Genius and Spirit of the Author, as it is probable he will make no very judicious Extract, so he will be apt to trust to that Collection in all his Compositions, and be misled out of the regular Way of Thinking, in order to introduce those Materials which he has been at the Pains to gather: And the Product of all this will be found a manifest incoherent Piece of Patchwork.

Some Gentlemen abounding in their University Erudition, are apt to fill their Sermons with Philosophical Terms and Notions of the metaphysical or abstracted Kind, which generally have one Advantage, to be equally understood by the Wise, the Vulgar, and the Preacher himself. I have been better entertained, and more informed by a Chapter in the *Pilgrim's Progress*, than by a long Discourse upon the Will and the Intellect, and simple or complex Ideas. Others again, are fond of dilating on Matter and Motion, talk of the fortuitous Concourse of Atoms, of Theories, and Phænomena; directly against the

Advice

Advice of St. Paul, who yet appears to have been conversant enough in those kinds of Studies.

I do not find that you are any where directed in the Canons or Articles, to attempt explaining the Mysteries of the Christian Religion. And indeed, since Providence intended there should be Mysteries, I do not see how it can be agreeable to Piety, Orthodoxy, or good Sense, to go about such a Work. For, to me there seems to be a manifest Dilemma in the Case: If you explain them, they are Mysteries no longer; if you fail, you have laboured to no Purpose. What I should think most reasonable and safe for you to do upon this Occasion, upon solemn Days to deliver the Doctrine as the Church holds it, and confirm it by Scripture. For my part, having considered the Matter impartially, I can see no great Reason which those Gentlemen, you call the Free-Thinkers, can have for their Clamour against religious Mysteries; since it is plain, they were not invented by the Clergy, to whom they bring no Profit, nor acquire any Honour. For every Clergyman is ready, either to tell us the utmost he knows, or to confess that he does not understand them; neither is it strange that there should be Mysteries in Divinity, as well as in the commonest Operations of Nature.

And here I am at a Loss what to say, upon the frequent Custom of preaching against Atheism, Deism, Free-Thinking, and the like, as young Divines are particularly fond of doing, especially when they exercise their Talent in Churches, frequented by the People of Quality; which, as it is but an ill Compliment to the Audience, so I am under some doubt whether it answers the Ends.

Because Persons under those Imputations are generally no great Frequenters of Churches, and so the Congregation is but little edify'd for the sake of three or four Fools who are past Grace: Neither do I think it any Part of Prudence,

Prudence, to perplex the Minds of well-disposed People with Doubts, which probably would never have otherwise come into their Heads. But I am of Opinion, and dare be positive in it, that not one in a hundred of those, who pretend to be Free-Thinkers, are really so in their Hearts. For there is one Observation which I never knew to fail, and I desire you will examine it in the Course of your Life, That no Gentleman of a liberal Education, and regular in his Morals, did ever profess himself a Free-Thinker: Where then are these kinds of People to be found? Among the worst Part of the Soldiery, made up of Pages, younger Brothers of obscure Families, and others of desperate Fortunes; or else among idle Town Fops; and now and then a drunken 'Squire of the Country. Therefore, nothing can be plainer, than that Ignorance and Vice are two Ingredients absolutely necessary in the Composition of those you generally call Free-Thinkers, who, in Propriety of Speech, are no Thinkers at all. And since I am in the Way of it, pray consider one thing farther: As young as you are, you cannot but have already observed, what a violent Run there is among too many weak People against University Education: Be firmly assured, that the whole Cry is made up by those, who were either never sent to a College, or through their Irregularities and Stupidity never made the least Improvement while they were there. I have at least forty of the latter sort now in my Eye; several of them in this Town, whose Learning, Manners, Temperance, Probity, Good-nature, and Politicks, are all of a Piece: Others of them in the Country, oppressing their Tenants, tyrannizing over the Neighbourhood, cheating the Vicar, talking Nonsense, and getting Drunk at the Sessions. It is from such Seminaries as these, that the World is provided with the several Tribes and Denominations of Free-Thinkers,

 who,

who, in my Judgment, are not to be reformed by Arguments offered to prove the Truth of the Christian Religion, because Reasoning will never make a Man correct an ill Opinion, which by Reasoning he never acquired: For in the Course of Things, Men always grow vicious before they become Unbelievers; but if you could once convince the Town or Country Profligate, by Topicks drawn from the View of their own Quiet, Reputation, Health, and Advantage, their Infidelity would soon drop off: This, I confess, is no easy Task, because it is almost in a literal Sense, to fight with Beasts. Now, to make it clear, that we are to look for no other Original of this Infidelity, whereof Divines so much complain, it is allowed on all Hands, that the People of England are more corrupt in their Morals than any other Nation at this Day under the Sun: And this Corruption is manifestly owing to other Causes both numerous and obvious, much more than to the Publication of irreligious Books, which indeed are but the Consequence of the former. For all the Writers against Christianity, since the Revolution, have been of the lowest Rank among Men, in regard to Literature, Wit, and good Sense, and upon that Account wholly unqualified to propagate Heresies, unless among a People already abandoned.

In an Age where every Thing disliked by those who think with the Majority, is called Disaffection, it may perhaps be ill interpreted, when I venture to tell you, that this universal Depravation of Manners, is owing to the perpetual bandying of Factions among us for thirty Years past; when, without weighing the Motives of Justice, Law, Conscience, or Honour, every Man adjusts his Principles to those of the Party he hath chosen, and among whom he may best find his own Account: But by reason of our frequent Vicissitudes, Men who were impatient

patient to be out of Play, have been forced to recant, or at least to reconcile their former Tenets with every new System of Admiration. Add to this, that the old fundamental Custom of annual Parliaments being wholly laid aside, and Elections growing chargeable, since Gentlemen found that their Country Seats brought them in less than a Seat in the House, the Voters, that is to say, the Bulk of the common People have been universally seduced into Bribery, Perjury, Drunkenness, Malice, and Slanders.

Not to be further tedious, or rather invidious, these are a few, among other Causes, which have contributed to the Ruin of our Morals, and consequently to the Contempt of Religion: For, imagine to your self, if you please, a landed Youth, whom his Mother would never suffer to look into a Book, for fear of spoiling his Eyes, got into Parliament, and observing all Enemies to the Clergy heard with the utmost Applause; what Notions he must imbibe; how readily he will join in the Cry; what an Esteem he will conceive of himself; and what a Contempt he must entertain, not only for his Vicar at home, but for the whole Order.

I therefore again conclude, That the Trade of Infidelity hath been taken up only for an Expedient to keep in Countenance that universal Corruption of Morals, which many other Causes first contributed to introduce and to cultivate. And thus, Mr. Hobb's Saying upon Reason, may be much more properly apply'd to Religion: That, if Religion will be against a Man, a Man will be against Religion. Though after all, I have heard a Profligate offer much stronger Arguments against paying his Debts, than ever he was known to do against Christianity; indeed, the Reason was, because in that Juncture he happened to be closer press'd by the Bailiff than the Parson.

Ignorance may perhaps be the Mother of Superstition, but

but Experience hath not proved it to be so of Devotion; for Christianity always made the most easy and quickest Progress in civilized Countries. I mention this, because it is affirmed, that the Clergy are in most Credit where Ignorance prevails, (and surely this Kingdom would be called the Paradise of Clergymen, if that Opinion were true) for which they instance England in the Times of Popery. But whoever knows any thing of three or four Centuries before the Reformation, will find the little Learning then stirring, was more equally divided between the English Clergy and Laity than it is at present. There were several famous Lawyers in that Period, whose Writings are still in the highest Repute, and some Historians and Poets, who were not of the Church. Whereas, now-a-days our Education is so corrupted, that you will hardly find a young Person of Quality with the least Tincture of Knowledge, at the same time that the Clergy were never more learned, or so scurvily treated. Here among us, at least, a Man of Letters, out of the three Professions, is almost a Prodigy. And those few, who have preserved any Rudiments of Learning, are (except perhaps one or two Smatterers) the Clergy's Friends to a Man: And I dare appeal to any Clergyman in this Kingdom, whether the greatest Dunce in his Parish is not always the most proud, wicked, fraudulent, and intractable of his Flock.

I think the Clergy have almost given over perplexing themselves and their Hearers, with abstruse Points of Predestination, Election, and the like, at least, it is time they should; and therefore I shall not trouble you further upon this Head.

I have now said all I could think convenient, with relation to your Conduct in the Pulpit: Your Behaviour in Life is another Scene, upon which I shall readily offer you

my

my Thoughts, if you appear to desire them from me, by your Approbation of what I have here written; if not, I have already troubled you too much.

I am Sir,

Your Affectionate

Friend and Servant.

Jan. 9. 1719–20.

A LETTER TO THE WHOLE PEOPLE OF IRELAND

Swift's political writings have lost more interest for us, in the lapse of time, than any other section of his writings. The fourth of the famous *Drapier Letters* is alone reprinted as a specimen of his vigorous and direct partisanship in Anglo-Irish affairs. This letter, read in conjunction with *A Modest Proposal,* affords an excellent illustration of his command over straightforward exposition, as well as over irony. Both weapons were wielded to good advantage in behalf of the Irish people.

Ever since the reign of Charles II the right to mint and circulate copper coins in Ireland had been a privilege farmed out to private individuals. In dire need of a coinage established by law, as in England and Scotland, the Irish government petitioned Parliament in 1720 to establish copper coins of guaranteed, intrinsic value. The petition was ignored, and a patent to issue the coins was granted to William Wood, a hardware merchant, 12 July 1722, in return for handsome bribes paid by Wood to the king's mistress. Public indignation in Ireland flared high, and was fanned higher by the anonymous *Drapier Letters* written by Swift. The first and fourth letters are the best, though all are well worth reading. The immediate effect of the letters was to unify Irish parties in a solid front against Wood and Walpole, and to make Swift the hero of the hour. The Irish decorated and thronged the streets when the 'Drapier Dean' rode into Dublin. They proposed tearing down the statues of 'military murderers' to erect statues of Swift, the saviour of their country. These *Drapier Letters* explain what so many commentators have understated: the popularity of Swift with the common people of Ireland; and they refute the libel that he was cold to the sufferings of his fellow men. Sentimentalists, like Thackeray, who judge the heart by voice and gesture, will never understand Swift. Thackeray complained of the 'brutality' of the *Modest Proposal,* and said, 'I would rather have a potato from Goldsmith than a guinea from Swift.' The Irish, however, were grateful for the guineas, as well as for the genuine coppers, which fell from the hand of their champion who did not know how to weep instead of helping. Furthermore, he was one of the few men living who could make Walpole look like a fool, and the Irish were human enough to be grateful for that.

The fourth *Letter* appeared 13 October 1724, signed, as the others had been, 'M. B. Drapier'. A proclamation was issued by the Lord-Lieutenant of Ireland, 27 October, offering three hundred pounds reward 'to such person or persons as shall within the specified six months from this date hereof, discover the author of the said pamphlet, so as he be apprehended and convicted thereby'. Swift immediately let it be known that he was the Drapier, and defied arrest. The Lord-Lieutenant discreetly did nothing. To arrest Swift would have been to get himself promptly lynched by the mob.

The text reproduced is that of the original edition, 1724.

My Dear Countrymen,

HAVING already written three Letters, upon so disagreeable a Subject as Mr. Wood and his Half-pence; I conceived my Task was at an End: But, I find that Cordials must be frequently applied to weak Constitutions, Political as well as Natural. A People long used to Hardships, lose by Degrees the very Notions of Liberty; they look upon themselves as Creatures at Mercy; and that all Impositions laid on them by a stronger Hand, are, in the Phrase of the Report legal and obligatory. Hence proceed that Poverty and Lowness of Spirit, to which a Kingdom may be subject, as well as a particular Person. And when Esau came fainting from the Field, at the Point to die, it is no wonder that he sold his Birth-right for a Mess of Pottage.

I thought I had sufficiently shewn to all who could want Instruction, by what Methods they might safely proceed, whenever this Coin should be offered to them: And, I believe, there hath not been, for many Ages, an Example of any Kingdom so firmly united in a Point of great Importance, as this of ours is at present, against that detestable Fraud. But, however, it so happens, that some weak People begin to be alarmed a-new, by Rumours industriously spread. Wood prescribes to the News-Mongers in London, what they are to write. In one of their Papers published here by some obscure Printer, (and certainly with a bad Design) we are told; that the Papists in Ireland, have entered into an Association against his Coin; altho' it be notoriously known, that they never once offered to stir in the Matter: So, that the two Houses of Parliament, the Privy-Council, the great Numbers of Corporations, the Lord Mayor, and Aldermen of Dublin, the Grand-Juries, and principal Gentlemen of several

Counties,

Counties, are stigmatized in a Lump, under the Name of Papists.

This Impostor and his Crew, do likewise give out, that, by refusing to receive his Dross for Sterling, we dispute the King's Prerogative; are grown ripe for Rebellion, and ready to shake off the Dependency of Ireland upon the Crown of England. To Countenance which Reports, he hath published a Paragraph in another News-Paper, to let us know, that the Lord Lieutenant is ordered to come over immediately, to settle his Half-pence.

I intreat you, my dear Countrymen, not to be under the least Concern, upon these and the like Rumours; which are no more than the last Howls of a Dog dissected alive, as I hope he hath sufficiently been. These Calumnies are the only Reserve that is left him. For surely, our continued and (almost) unexampled Loyalty, will never be called in Question, for not suffering our selves to be robbed of all that we have, by one obscure Ironmonger.

As to disputing the King's Prerogative, give me leave to explain to those who are ignorant, what the Meaning of that Word Prerogative is.

The Kings of these Realms enjoy several Powers, wherein the Laws have not interposed: So they can make War and Peace without the Consent of Parliament; and this is a very great Prerogative. But if the Parliament do not approve of the War, the King must bear the Charge of it out of his own Purse; and this is a great Check on the Crown. So, the King hath a Prerogative to coin Money, without Consent of Parliament: But he cannot compel the Subject to take the Money, except it be Sterling, Gold or Silver; because, herein he is limited by Law. Some Princes have, indeed, extended their Prerogative further than the Law allowed them: Wherein, however, the Lawyers of succeeding Ages, as fond as they are of Precedents,

dents, have never dared to justify them. But, to say the Truth, it is only of late Times that Prerogative hath been fixed and ascertained. For, whoever reads the Histories of England, will find, that some former Kings, and those none of the worst, have, upon several Occasions, ventured to controul the Laws, with very little Ceremony or Scruple, even later than the Days of Queen Elizabeth. In her Reign, that pernicious Counsel of sending base Money hither, very narrowly failed of losing the Kingdom; being complained of by the Lord Deputy, the Council, and the whole Body of the English here: So, that soon after her Death, it was recalled by her Successor, and lawful Money paid in Exchange.

Having thus given you some Notion of what is meant by the King's Prerogative, as far as a Tradesman can be thought capable of explaining it, I will only add the Opinion of the great Lord Bacon; that as God governs the World by the settled Laws of Nature, which he hath made, and never transcends those Laws, but upon high important Occasions: So, among earthly Princes, those are the wisest and the best, who govern by the known Laws of the Country, and seldomest make use of their Prerogative.

Now, here you may see, that the vile Accusation of Wood and his Accomplices, charging us with disputing the King's Prerogative, by refusing his Brass, can have no Place; because compelling the Subject to take any Coin, which is not Sterling, is no Part of the King's Prerogative; and I am very confident, if it were so, we should be the last of his People to dispute it; as well from that inviolable Loyalty we have always paid to his Majesty, as from the Treatment we might in such a Case justly expect from some, who seem to think, we have neither common Sense, nor common Senses. But, God be thanked, the best of them are only our Fellow Subjects, and not our Masters.

One

One great Merit I am sure we have, which those of English Birth can have no Pretence to; that our Ancestors reduced this Kingdom to the Obedience of England; for which we have been rewarded with a worse Climate, the Privilege of being governed by Laws, to which we do not consent; a ruined Trade, a House of Peers without Jurisdiction; almost an Incapacity for all Employments, and the Dread of Wood's Half-pence.

But we are so far from disputing the King's Prerogative in coining, that we own he hath Power to give a Patent to any Man, for setting his Royal Image and Superscription upon whatever Materials he pleaseth; and Liberty to the Patentee to offer them in any Country from England to Japan, only attended with one small Limitation, that no Body alive is obliged to take them.

Upon these Considerations, I was ever against all Recourse to England, for a Remedy against the present impending Evil; especially, when I observed, that the Addresses of both Houses, after long Expectance, produced nothing but a Report altogether in Favour of Wood; upon which, I made some Observations in a former Letter; and might at least have made as many more: For, it is a Paper of as singular a Nature, as I ever beheld.

But I mistake; for before this Report was made, his Majesty's most gracious Answer to the House of Lords was sent over, and printed; wherein there are these Words, 'granting the Patent for coining Half-pence and Farthings, Agreeable to the Practice of his Royal Predecessors,' &c. That King Charles II, and King James II, (and they only) did grant Patents for this Purpose, is indisputable, and I have shewn it at large. Their Patents were passed under the great Seal of Ireland, by References to Ireland, the Copper to be coined in Ireland; the Patentee

Patentee was bound, on Demand, to receive his Coin back in Ireland, and pay Silver and Gold in Return. Wood's Patent was made under the Great Seal of England, the Brass coined in England, not the least Reference made to Ireland; the Sum immense, and the Patentee under no Obligation to receive it again, and give good Money for it: This I only mention, because in my private Thoughts, I have sometimes made a Query, whether the Penner of those Words in his Majesty's most gracious Answer, Agreeable to the Practice of his Royal Predecessors, had maturely considered the several Circumstances; which, in my poor Opinion, seem to make a Difference.

Let me now say something concerning the other great Cause of some People's Fear; as Wood hath taught the London News Writer to express it: That his Excellency the Lord Lieutenant is coming over to settle Wood's Half-pence.

We know very well, that the Lords Lieutenants for several Years past, have not thought this Kingdom worthy the Honour of their Residence, longer than was absolutely necessary for the King's Business; which consequently wanted no Speed in the Dispatch. And therefore, it naturally fell into most Men's Thoughts, that a new Governor coming at an unusual Time, must portend some unusual Business to be done; especially, if the common Report be true; that the Parliament prorogued to I know not when, is, by a new Summons (revoking that Prorogation, to assemble soon after his Arrival: For which extraordinary Proceeding, the Lawyers, on t'other Side the Water, have, by great good Fortune, found two Precedents.

All this being granted, it can never enter into my Head, that so little a Creature as Wood could find Credit enough with the King and his Ministers, to have the Lord Lieutenant

tenant of Ireland sent hither in a Hurry, upon his Errand.

For, let us take the whole Matter nakedly, as it lies before us, without the Refinements of some People, with which we have nothing to do. Here is a Patent granted under the great Seal of England, upon false Suggestions, to one William Wood, for coining Copper Half-pence for Ireland: The Parliament here, upon Apprehensions of the worst Consequences from the said Patent, address the King to have it recalled: This is refused, and a Committee of the Privy-Council report to his Majesty, that Wood hath performed the Conditions of his Patent. He then is left to do the best he can with his Half-pence; no Man being obliged to receive them; the People here, being likewise left to themselves, unite as one Man; resolving they will have nothing to do with his Ware. By this plain Account of the Fact, it is manifest, that the King and his Ministry are wholly out of the Case; and the Matter is left to be disputed between him and us. Will any Man therefore attempt to persuade me, that a Lord Lieutenant is to be dispatched over in great Haste, before the ordinary Time, and a Parliament summoned, by anticipating a Prorogation; merely to put an Hundred Thousand Pounds into the Pocket of a Sharper, by the Ruin of a most loyal Kingdom?

But, supposing all this to be true. By what Arguments could a Lord Lieutenant prevail on the same Parliament, which addressed with so much Zeal and Earnestness against this Evil; to pass it into a Law? I am sure their Opinion of Wood and his Project are not mended since their last Prorogation: And supposing those Methods should be used, which, Detractors tell us, have been sometimes put in Practice for gaining Votes; it is well known, that in this Kingdom there are few Employments to be given;

given; and if there were more, it is as well known to whose Share they must fall.

But, because great Numbers of you are altogether ignorant in the Affairs of your Country, I will tell you some Reasons, why there are so few Employments to be disposed of in this Kingdom. All considerable Offices for Life here, are possessed by those, to whom the Reversions were granted; and these have been generally Followers of the Chief Governors, or Persons who had Interest in the Court of England. So, the Lord Berkely of Stratton holds that great Office of Master of the Rolls; the Lord Palmerstown is First Remembrancer, worth near 2,000*l.* per Annum. One Dodington, Secretary to the Earl of Pembroke, begged the Reversion of Clerk of the Pells, worth 2,500*l.* a Year, which he now enjoys by the Death of the Lord Newtown. Mr. Southwell is Secretary of State, and the Earl of Burlington, Lord High-Treasurer of Ireland by Inheritance. These are only a few among many others, which I have been told of, but cannot remember. Nay, the Reversion of several Employments during Pleasure are granted the same way. This among many others, is a Circumstance whereby the Kingdom of Ireland is distinguished from all other Nations upon Earth; and makes it so difficult an Affair to get into a Civil Employ, that Mr. Addison was forced to purchase an old obscure Place, called Keeper of the Records in Bermingham's Tower, of Ten Pounds a Year, and to get a Salary of 400*l.* annexed to it, though all the Records there are not worth half a Crown, either for Curiosity or Use. And we lately saw a Favourite Secretary[1], descend to be Master of the Revels, which by his Credit and Extortion he hath made pretty Considerable. I say nothing of the Under-Treasurership worth about 9000*l.* a Year; nor the Commissioners of the

[1] Mr. Hopkins, Secretary to the Duke of Grafton.

Revenue

Revenue, Four of whom generally live in England: For, I think none of these are granted in Reversion. But the Jest is, that I have known upon Occasion, some of these absent Officers as Keen against the Interest of Ireland, as if they had never been indebted to her for a Single Groat.

I confess, I have been sometimes tempted to wish that this Project of Wood might succeed; because I reflected with some Pleasure, what a Jolly Crew it would bring over among us of Lords and Squires, and Pensioners of Both Sexes, and Officers Civil and Military; where we should live together as merry and sociable as Beggars; only with this one Abatement, that we should neither have Meat to feed, nor Manufactures to cloath us; unless we could be content to Prance about in Coats of Mail; or eat Brass as Ostritches do Iron.

I return from this Digression, to that which gave me the Occasion of making it: And, I believe you are now convinced, that if the Parliament of Ireland were as Temptable as any other Assembly within a Mile of Christendom, (which God forbid) yet the Managers must of Necessity fail for want of Tools to work with. But I will yet go one Step further, by supposing that a Hundred new Employments were erected on Purpose to gratify Compliers: Yet still an insuperable Difficulty would remain. For it happens, I know not how, that Money is neither Whig nor Tory, neither of Town nor Country Party; and it is not improbable, that a Gentleman would rather chuse to live upon his own Estate, which brings him Gold and Silver, than with the Addition of any Employment; when his Rents and Salary must both be paid in Wood's Brass, at above Eighty per Cent. Discount.

For these, and many other Reasons, I am confident you need not be under the least Apprehensions, from the sud-

den

den Expectation of the Lord Lieutenant, while we continue in our present hearty Disposition; to alter which there is no suitable Temptation can possibly be offered: And if, as I have often asserted from the best Authority, the Law hath not left a Power in the Crown to force any Money, except Sterling, upon the Subject; much less can the Crown devolve such a Power upon another.

This I speak with the utmost Respect to the Person and Dignity of his Excellency the Lord Carteret; whose Character was lately given me, by a Gentleman that hath known him from his first Appearance in the World: That Gentleman describes him as a young Man of great Accomplishments, excellent Learning, Regular in his Life, and of much Spirit and Vivacity. He hath since, as I have heard, been employed abroad; was Principal Secretary of State; and is now about the 37th Year of his Age appointed Lord Lieutenant of Ireland. From such a Governor this Kingdom may reasonably hope for as much Prosperity, as under so many Discouragements it can be capable of receiving.

It is true indeed, that within the Memory of Man, there have been Governors of so much Dexterity, as to carry Points of terrible Consequence to this Kingdom, by their Power with those who are in Office; and by their Arts in managing or deluding others with Oaths, Affability, and even with Dinners. If Wood's Brass had, in those Times, been upon the Anvil, it is obvious enough to conceive what Methods would have been taken. Depending Persons would have been told in plain Terms, that it was a Service expected from them, under the Pain of the publick Business being put into more complying Hands. Others would be allured by Promises. To the Country Gentlemen, besides, good Words, Burgundy and Closeting; it might, perhaps, have been hinted, how kindly it would be taken

taken to comply with a Royal Patent, although it were not compulsory. That, if any Inconveniencies ensued, it might be made up with other Graces or Favours hereafter: That, Gentlemen ought to consider, whether it were prudent or safe to disgust England: They would be desired to think of some good Bills for encouraging of Trade, and setting the Poor to work: Some further Acts against Popery, and for uniting Protestants. There would be solemn Engagements, that we should never be troubled with above Forty Thousand Pounds in his Coin, and all of the best and weightiest Sort; for which we should only give our Manufactures in Exchange, and keep our Gold and Silver at home. Perhaps, a seasonable Report of some Invasion would have been spread in the most proper Juncture; which is a great Smoother of Rubs in publick Proceedings: And we should have been told, that this was no Time to create Differences, when the Kingdom was in Danger.

These, I say, and the like Methods, would, in corrupt Times, have been taken to let in this Deluge of Brass among us: And, I am confident, would even then have not succeeded; much less under the Administration of so excellent a Person as the Lord Carteret; and in a Country, where the People of all Ranks, Parties, and Denominations, are convinced to a Man, that the utter undoing of themselves and their Posterity for ever, will be dated from the Admission of that execrable Coin: That, if it once enters, it can be no more confined to a small or moderate Quantity, than the Plague can be confined to a few Families; and that no Equivalent can be given by any earthly Power, any more than a dead Carcase can be recovered to Life by a Cordial.

There is one comfortable Circumstance in this universal Opposition to Mr. Wood, that the People sent over hither

from

from England, to fill up our Vacancies, Ecclesiastical, Civil, and Military, are all on our Side: Money, the great Divider of the World, hath, by a strange Revolution, been the great Uniter of a most divided People. Who would leave a Hundred Pounds a Year in England (a Country of Freedom) to be paid a Thousand in Ireland out of Wood's Exchequer? The Gentleman[1] they have lately made Primate, would never quit his Seat in an English House of Lords, and his Preferments at Oxford and Bristol, worth Twelve Hundred Pounds a Year, for four times the Denomination here, but not half the Value: Therefore, I expect to hear he will be as good an Irishman, at least, upon this one Article, as any of his Brethren; or even of Us, who have had the Misfortune to be born in this Island. For those, who in the common Phrase, do not come hither to learn the Language, would never change a better Country for a worse, to receive Brass instead of Gold.

Another Slander spread by Wood and his Emissaries is, that, by opposing him, we discover an Inclination to shake off our Dependance upon the Crown of England. Pray observe, how important a Person is this same William Wood; and how the publick Weal of two Kingdoms, is involved in his private Interest. First, all those who refuse to take his Coin are Papists; for he tells us, that none but Papists are associated against him. Secondly, they dispute the King's Prerogative. Thirdly, they are ripe for Rebellion. And Fourthly, they are going to shake off their Dependance upon the Crown of England; that is to say, they are going to chuse another King: For there can be no other Meaning in this Expression, however some may pretend to strain it.

And this gives me an Opportunity of explaining, to those who are ignorant, another Point which hath often

[1] Dr. Hugh Boulter.

swelled

swelled in my Breast. Those who come over hither to us from England, and some weak People among ourselves, whenever, in Discourse, we make mention of Liberty and Property, shake their Heads, and tell us, that Ireland is a depending Kingdom; as if they would seem, by this Phrase, to intend, that the People of Ireland are in some State of Slavery or Dependance, different from those of England: Whereas, a depending Kingdom is a modern Term of Art; unknown, as I have heard, to all antient Civilians, and Writers upon Government; and Ireland is, on the contrary, called in some Statutes an Imperial Crown, as held only from God; which is as high a Style, as any Kingdom is capable of receiving. Therefore by this Expression, a depending Kingdom, there is no more understood, than that by a Statute made here, in the 33d Year of Henry VIII, The King and his Successors, are to be Kings Imperial of this Realm, as united and knit to the Imperial Crown of England. I have looked over all the English and Irish Statutes, without finding any Law that makes Ireland depend upon England; any more than England doth upon Ireland. We have, indeed, obliged ourselves to have the same King with them; and consequently they are obliged to have the same King with us. For the Law was made by our own Parliament; and our Ancestors then were not such Fools (whatever they were in the preceding Reign) to bring themselves under I know not what Dependance, which is now talked of, without any Ground of Law, Reason, or common Sense.

Let whoever think otherwise, I M. B. Drapier, desire to be excepted. For I declare, next under God, I depend only on the King my Sovereign, and on the Laws of my own Country: And, I am so far from depending upon the People of England, that, if they should ever rebel against my Sovereign, (which God forbid) I would be ready at the first

first Command from his Majesty, to take Arms against them; as some of my Countrymen did against theirs at Preston. And, if such a Rebellion should prove so successful as to fix the Pretender on the Throne of England; I would venture to transgress that Statute, so far, as to lose every Drop of my Blood, to hinder him from being King of Ireland.

It is true, indeed, that within the Memory of Man, the Parliaments of England, have sometimes assumed the Power of binding this Kingdom, by Laws enacted there; wherein they were, at first, openly opposed (as far as Truth, Reason and Justice, are capable of opposing) by the famous Mr. Molineaux, an English Gentleman born here; as well as by several of the greatest Patriots, and best Whigs in England; but the Love and Torrent of Power prevailed. Indeed, the Arguments on both Sides were invincible. For in Reason, all Government, without the Consent of the Governed, is the very Definition of Slavery: But in Fact, eleven Men well armed, will certainly subdue one single Man in his Shirt. But I have done. For those who have used Power to cramp Liberty, have gone so far as to resent even the Liberty of Complaining; although a Man upon the Rack, was never known to be refused the Liberty of roaring as loud as he thought fit.

And, as we are apt to sink too much under unreasonable Fears, so we are too soon inclined to be raised by groundless Hopes, (according to the Nature of all consumptive Bodies like ours.) Thus, it hath been given for several Days past, that Somebody in England, empowered a second Somebody, to write to a third Somebody here, to assure us, that we should no more be troubled with those Half-pence. And this is reported to have been done by the same Person[1], who was said to have sworn some

[1] Mr. Walpole, now Sir Robert.

Months

Months ago, that he would ram them down our Throats, (though I doubt they would stick in our Stomachs). But, which ever of these Reports is true or false, it is no Concern of ours. For, in this Point, we have nothing to do with English Ministers: And I should be sorry to leave it in their Power to redress this Grievance, or to enforce it: For the Report of the Committee, hath given me a Surfeit. The Remedy is wholly in your own Hands; and therefore I have digressed a little, in order to refresh and continue that Spirit so seasonably raised amongst you; and to let you see, that by the Laws of GOD, of NATURE, of NATIONS, and of your own COUNTRY, you ARE, and OUGHT to be a FREE PEOPLE, as your Brethren in England.

If the Pamphlets published at London by Wood and his Journeymen, in Defence of his Cause, were Reprinted here, and that our Countrymen could be persuaded to read them, they would convince you of his wicked Design, more than all I shall be ever able to say. In short, I make him a perfect Saint, in Comparison of what he appears to be, from the Writings of those whom he hires, to justify his Project. But he is so far Master of the Field (let others guess the Reason) that no London Printer dare publish any Paper written in Favour of Ireland: And here no Body hath yet been so bold, as to publish any Thing in Favour of him.

There was a few Days ago a Pamphlet sent me of near 50 Pages, written in Favour of Mr. Wood and his Coinage; printed in London: It is not worth answering, because probably it will never be published here: But, it gave me an Occasion, to reflect upon an Unhappiness we lie under, that the People of England are utterly ignorant of our Case: Which, however, is no Wonder, since it is a Point they do not in the least concern themselves about; farther then,

then, perhaps, as a Subject of Discourse in a Coffee-house, when they have nothing else to talk of. For I have Reason to believe, that no Minister ever gave himself the Trouble of reading any Papers written in our Defence; because, I suppose their Opinions are already determined, and are formed wholly upon the Reports of Wood and his Accomplices; else it would be impossible, that any Man could have the Impudence, to write such a Pamphlet, as I have mentioned.

Our Neighbours, whose Understandings are just upon a Level with Ours (which perhaps are none of the Brightest) have a strong Contempt for most Nations, but especially for Ireland: They look upon us as a Sort of Savage Irish, whom our Ancestors conquered several Hundred Years ago: And, if I should describe the Britons to you, as they were in Cæsar's Time, when they painted their Bodies, or cloathed themselves with the Skins of Beasts, I should act full as reasonably as they do. However, they are so far to be excused, in Relation to the present Subject, that, hearing only one Side of the Cause, and having neither Opportunity nor Curiosity to examine the other, they believe a Lye, meerly for their Ease; and conclude, because Mr. Wood pretends to have Power, he hath also Reason on his Side.

Therefore, to let you see how this Case is represented in England by Wood and his Adherents, I have thought it proper to extract out of that Pamphlet, a few of those notorious Falshoods, in Point of Fact and Reasoning, contained therein; the Knowledge whereof, will confirm my Countrymen in their own Right Sentiments, when they will see by comparing both, how much their Enemies are in the Wrong.

First, The Writer positively asserts, That Wood's Halfpence were current among us for several Months, with the

universal

universal Approbation of all People, without one single Gain-sayer; and we all to a Man thought our selves Happy in having them.

Secondly, He affirms, That we were drawn into a dislike of them, only by some cunning evil-designing Men among us, who opposed this Patent of Wood, to get another for themselves.

Thirdly, That those who most declared at first against Wood's Patent, were the very Men who intend to get another for their own Advantage.

Fourthly, That our Parliament and Privy-Council, the Lord Mayor and Alderman of Dublin, the Grand Juries and Merchants, and in short the whole Kingdom; nay, the very Dogs, (as he expresseth it) were fond of these Half-pence, till they were inflamed by those few designing Persons aforesaid.

Fifthly, He says directly, That all those who opposed the Half-pence, were Papists, and Enemies to King George.

Thus far I am confident, the most ignorant among you can safely swear from your own Knowledge, that the Author is a most notorious Lyar in every Article; the direct contrary being so manifest to the whole Kingdom, that if occasion required, we might get it confirmed under Five Hundred Thousand Hands.

Sixthly, He would perswade us, That if we sell Five Shillings worth of our Goods or Manufactures for Two Shillings and Four-pence worth of Copper, although the Copper were melted down, and that we could get Five Shillings in Gold and Silver for the said Goods; yet to take the said Two Shillings and Four-pence in Copper, would be greatly for our Advantage.

And, Lastly, He maketh us a very fair Offer, as empowered by Wood, That if we will take off Two Hundred Thousand

Thousand Pounds in his Half-pence for our Goods, and likewise pay him Three per Cent. Interest for Thirty Years, for an Hundred and Twenty Thousand Pounds (at which he computes the Coinage above the intrinsick Value of the Copper) for the Loan of his Coin, he will after that Time give us good Money for what Half-pence will be then left.

Let me place this Offer in as clear a Light as I can, to shew the insupportable Villainy and Impudence of that incorrigible Wretch. First, (says he) I will send Two Hundred Thousand Pounds of my Coin into your Country: The Copper I compute to be in real Value Eighty Thousand Pounds, and I charge you with an Hundred and Twenty Thousand Pounds for the Coinage; so that you see, I lend you an Hundred and Twenty Thousand Pounds for Thirty Years; for which you shall pay me Three per Cent. That is to say, Three Thousand Six Hundred Pounds per Annum, which in Thirty Years, will amount to an Hundred and Eight Thousand Pounds. And when these Thirty Years are expired, return me my Copper, and I will give you good Money for it.

This is the Proposal made to us by Wood, in that Pamphlet, written by one of his Commissioners: And the Author is supposed to be the same infamous Coleby, one of his Under-Swearers at the Committee of Council, who was tryed for Robbing the Treasury here, where he was an Under-Clerk.

By this Proposal he will first receive Two Hundred Thousand Pounds, in Goods or Sterling, for as much Copper as he values at Eighty Thousand Pounds; but in Reality not worth Thirty Thousand Pounds. Secondly, He will receive for Interest an Hundred and Eight Thousand Pounds: And when our Children come Thirty Years hence,

hence, to return his Half-pence upon his Executors, (for before that Time he will be probably gone to his own Place) those Executors will very reasonably reject them as Raps and Counterfeits; which they will be, and Millions of them of his own Coinage.

Methinks, I am fond of such a Dealer as this, who mends every Day upon our Hands, like a Dutch Reckoning; where, if you dispute the Unreasonableness and Exorbitancy of the Bill, the Landlord shall bring it up every Time with new Additions.

Although these and the like Pamphlets, published by Wood in London, be altogether unknown here, where no Body could read them, without as much Indignation as Contempt would allow; yet I thought it proper to give you a Specimen how this Man employs his Time; where he rides alone, without any Creature to contradict him; while our few Friends there, wonder at our Silence: And the English in general, if they think of this Matter at all, impute our Refusal to Wilfulness or Disaffection, just as Wood and his Hirelings are pleased to represent.

But, although our Arguments are not suffered to be printed in England, yet the Consequence will be of little Moment. Let Wood endeavour to persuade the People there, that we ought to receive his Coin; and let Me convince our People here, that they ought to reject it, under Pain of our utter Undoing. And then let him do his best and his worst.

Before I conclude, I must beg Leave in all Humility to tell Mr. Wood, that he is guilty of great Indiscretion, by causing so Honourable a Name as that of Mr. Walpole to be mentioned so often, and in such a Manner, upon this Occasion. A short Paper, printed at Bristol, and reprinted here, reports Mr. Wood to say, that he wonders at the Impudence and Insolence of the Irish, in refusing his

Coin,

Coin, and what he will do when Mr. Walpole comes to Town. Where, by the Way, he is mistaken; for it is the true English People of Ireland, who refuse it; although we take it for granted, that the Irish will do so too, whenever they are asked. In another printed Paper of his contriving, it is roundly expressed, that Mr. Walpole will cram his Brass down our Throats. Sometimes it is given out, that we must either take these Half-pence or eat our Brogues. And, in another News-Letter, but of Yesterday, we read, that the same great Man hath sworn to make us swallow his Coin in Fire-Balls.

This brings to my Mind the known Story of a Scotch Man, who receiving Sentence of Death, with all the Circumstances of Hanging, Beheading, Quartering, Embowelling, and the like; cried out, what needs all this Cookery? And, I think, we have Reason to ask the same Question: For, if we believe Wood, here is a Dinner getting ready for us, and you see the Bill of Fare; and I am sorry the Drink was forgot, which might easily be supplied with melted Lead and flaming Pitch.

What vile Words are these to put into the Mouth of a great Counsellor, in high Trust with his Majesty, and looked upon as a Prime Minister? If Mr. Wood hath no better a Manner of representing his Patrons; when I come to be a Great Man, he shall never be suffered to attend at my Levee. This is not the Style of a Great Minister; it savours too much of the Kettle and the Furnace; and came entirely out of Wood's Forge.

As for the Threat of making us eat our Brogues, we need not be in Pain; for if his Coin should pass, that unpolite Covering for the Feet, would no longer be a National Reproach; because then, we should have neither Shoe nor Brogue left in the Kingdom. But here the Falshood of Mr. Wood is fairly detected; for I am confident,

fident, Mr. Walpole never heard of a Brogue in his whole Life.

As to Swallowing these Half-pence in Fire-Balls, it is a Story equally improbable. For, to execute this Operation, the whole Stock of Mr. Wood's Coin and Metal must be melted down, and molded into hollow Balls, with Wild-Fire, no bigger than a reasonable Throat can be able to swallow. Now, the Metal he hath prepared, and already coined, will amount to at least Fifty Millions of Half-pence, to be swallowed by a Million and a Half of People; so, that allowing Two Half-pence to each Ball, there will be about Seventeen Balls of Wild-Fire a-piece, to be swallowed by every Person in the Kingdom: And to administer this Dose, there cannot be conveniently fewer than Fifty Thousand Operators, allowing one Operator to every Thirty; which, considering the Squeamishness of some Stomachs, and the Peevishness of young Children, is but reasonable. Now, under Correction of better Judgments, I think the Trouble and Charge of such an Experiment, would exceed the Profit; and therefore I take this Report to be spurious; or at least, only a new Scheme of Mr. Wood himself; which, to make it pass the better in Ireland, he would father upon a Minister of State.

But I will now demonstrate, beyond all Contradiction, that Mr. Walpole is against this Project of Mr. Wood, and is an entire Friend to Ireland, only by this one invincible Argument, That he has the Universal Opinion of being a wise Man, an able Minister, and, in all his Proceedings, pursuing the true Interest of the King his Master: And, that as his Integrity is above all Corruption, so is his Fortune above all Temptation. I reckon therefore, we are perfectly safe from that Corner; and shall never be under the Necessity of contending with so Formidable a Power;

Power; but be left to possess our Brogues and Potatoes in Peace, as Remote from Thunder, as we are from Jupiter[1].

I am, my dear Countrymen,
Your Loving Fellow Subject,
Fellow-Sufferer, and
Humble Servant,

Oct. 13.
1724.

M. B.

[1] *Procul à Jove, procul à fulmine.*

THE JOURNAL TO STELLA

These letters were written daily, from 2 September 1710 to 6 June 1713, to the person whom Swift loved above all others, Esther Johnson (reputed to be the natural daughter of his patron, Sir William Temple), fifteen years his junior, to whom he had acted as tutor at Moor Park. The story that Swift married her secretly, though he never lived with her, is probably untrue; but either view of the matter leaves their relationship shrouded in mystery. When she went to live near him in Ireland, she was attended constantly by Mrs. Dingley. Swift addressed them jointly, even when it is clear that his concern is only for Stella, and after her maturity he seldom, if ever, remained with her alone. One point is clear: seldom have a man and a woman remained throughout life so devoted to each other as were Stella and Swift. Her death in 1728 broke his heart, leaving Arbuthnot the only person alive whom he really loved. The affectionate prattle and nursery language with which these letters were full (reproduced only in the last three letters here reprinted) was no doubt a survival of their comradeship when she was a child, learning from him how to speak and write. In these letters we see Swift in the intimate and rather disquieting act of whispering those childlike and silly endearments which are bred by affection and are never intended for the ears of strangers. When Swift died, in his desk was found hung a lock of Stella's hair, wrapped in a well-worn scrap of paper on which was written in Swift's faltering hand, 'Only a woman's hair'. The rest is silence.

No knowledge of Swift is complete without a study of these letters, impudent and presumptuous as that study must ever be. One can hardly conceive the fury Swift would feel, if he knew that strangers were reading these intimate confessions. Writing, propped up in bed, to the one whom he loved and trusted, he exposed sentimental and fantastic qualities elsewhere concealed from us. In making these selections, I have limited the reproduction of his affectionate puerilities, to give greater space to his political ambitions, and his daily routine as dictator to the Tory government.

The letters were first entitled *The Journal to Stella*, in Sheridan's edition of Swift's *Works*, 1784. The originals of letters II to XL, and LIV no longer exist. They were first printed by Deane Swift in vol. xii of the quarto edition of Swift's *Works*, 1768, in a text replete with printer's errors. Selections from these letters have been reproduced here from Deane Swift's revision of this first edition, vols. xxii and xxiii of Swift's *Works*, 1775. Letters XLI to LXV were first printed by Hawkesworth in vol. x of the quarto edition of Swift's *Works*, 1766, in a text not only corrupt, but marred wantonly by omission of all vestiges of the affectionate language. The original form of letters I, XLI to LIII, and LV to LXV, is not a matter of conjecture as the manuscripts of these are preserved in the British Museum. Three of these letters, XLIV, LXIV, and LXV, are here reproduced from vol. xix of Deane Swift's edition of Swift's *Works*, 1775, with the corrections and restorations made from the manuscripts, as these appear in the edition by Frederick Ryland, *Prose Works of Swift*, vol. ii, 1908.

LETTER II

London, Sept. 9, 1710.

I GOT here last Thursday, after five days traveling, weary the first, almost dead the second, tolerable the third, and well enough the rest; and am now glad of the fatigue, which has served for exercise; and I am at present well enough. The Whigs were ravished to see me, and would lay hold on me as a twig while they are drowning, and the great men making me their clumsy apologies, &c. But my lord treasurer[1] received me with a great deal of coldness, which has enraged me so, I am almost vowing revenge. I have not yet gone half my circle; but I find all my acquaintance just as I left them. I hear my lady Giffard[2] is much at Court, and lady Wharton was ridiculing it the other day; so I have lost a friend there. I have not yet seen her, nor intend it; but I will contrive to see Stella's mother[3] some other way. I writ to the bishop of Clogher from Chester; and I now write to the archbishop of Dublin. Every thing is turning upside down; every Whig in great office will, to a man, be infallibly put out; and we shall have such a winter as hath not been seen in England. Every body asks me, how I came to be so long in Ireland, as naturally as if here were my being; but no soul offers to make it so: and I protest I shall return to Dublin, and the Canal at Laracor,[4] with more satisfaction than ever I did in my life. The Tatler[5] expects every day to be turned out of his employment; and the duke of Ormond, they say, will be lieutenant of

[1] The earl of Godolphin.

[2] Lady Giffard was sister to sir William Temple.

[3] She was at that time in lady Giffard's family.

[4] The Doctor's benefice in the diocese of Meath.

[5] Richard Steele, Esq.

Ireland,

Ireland. I hope you are now peaceably in Presto's[1] lodgings; but I resolve to turn you out by Christmas; in which time I shall either do my business, or find it not to be done. Pray be at Trim by the time this letter comes to you; and ride little Johnson, who must needs be now in good case. I have begun this letter unusually, on the post-night, and have already written to the archbishop; and cannot lengthen this. Henceforth I will write something every day to MD, and make it a sort of journal; and when it is full, I will send it whether MD writes or no; and so that will be pretty: and I shall always be in conversation with MD, and MD with Presto. Pray make Parvisol[2] pay you the ten pounds immediately; so I ordered him. They tell me I am grown fatter, and look better; and, on Monday, Jervas is to retouch my picture. I thought I saw Jack Temple and his wife pass by me to-day in their coach; but I took no notice of them. I am glad I have wholly shaken off that family.[3] Tell the provost, I have obeyed his commands to the duke of Ormond; or let it alone, if you please. I saw Jemmey Leigh just now at the Coffee-house, who asked after you with great kindness: he talks of going in a fortnight to Ireland. My service to the dean, and Mrs. Walls, and her archdeacon. Will Frankland's wife is near bringing to-

[1] In these letters, pdfr, stands for Dr. Swift; Ppt, for Stella; D. for Dingley; D. D. generally for Dingley, but sometimes for both Stella and Dingley; and M D generally stands for both these ladies; yet sometimes only for Stella. But, to avoid perplexing the reader, it was thought more adviseable to use the word Presto for Swift, which is borrowed from the duchess of Shrewsbury, who, not recollecting the Doctor's name, called him Dr. Presto, (which is Italian for Swift). Instead of Ppt. Stella is used for Mrs. Johnson, and so for D. Dingley; but as M D stands for both Dingley and Stella, it was thought more convenient to let it remain a cypher in its original state.

[2] The Doctor's agent at Laracor.

[3] It never has yet appeared to the publick what gave rise to this great coolness between the Temple family and Dr. Swift.

bed,

bed, and I have promised to christen the child. I fancy you had my Chester letter the Tuesday after I writ. I presented Dr. Raymond to lord Wharton at Chester. Pray let me know when Joe gets his money. It is near ten, and I hate to send by the bell-man. MD shall have a longer letter in a week, but I send this only to tell I am safe in London; and so farewell, &c.

LETTER VI

London, Oct. 10, 1710.

SO, as I told you just now in the letter I sent half an hour ago, I dined with Mr. Harley to-day, who presented me to the attorney-general sir Simon Harcourt, with much compliment on all sides, &c. Harley told me, 'He had shewn my memorial to the queen, and seconded it very heartily;' and he desires me to dine with him again on Sunday, when he promises to settle it with her majesty, before she names a governor: and I protest I am in hopes it will be done, all but the forms, by that time; for he loves the church. This is a popular thing, and he would not have a governor share in it; and, besides, I am told by all hands, he has a mind to gain me over. But in the letter I writ last post (yesterday) to the archbishop, I did not tell him a syllable of what Mr. Harley said to me last night, because he charged me to keep it secret; so I would not tell it to you, but that, before this goes, I hope the secret will be over. I am now writing my poetical *Description of a shower in London*,[1] and will send it to the *Tatler*. This is the last sheet of a whole quire I have written since I came to town. Pray, now it comes into my head, will you, when you go to Mrs. Walls, contrive to know whether Mrs. Wesley be in town and still at her

[1] Printed in the *Tatler*, No. 238.

brother's,

brother's, and how she is in health, and whether she stays in town. I writ to her from Chester, to know what I should do with her note; and I believe the poor woman is afraid to write to me: so I must go to my business, &c.

11. To-day at last I dined with lord Montrath, and carried lord Mountjoy and sir Andrew Fountain with me; and was looking over them at ombre till eleven this evening like a fool: they played running ombre half crowns; and sir Andrew Fountain won eight guineas of Mr. Coote: so I am come home late, and will say but little to MD this night. I have gotten half a bushel of coals, and Patrick, the extravagant whelp, had a fire ready for me; but I pickt off the coals before I went to-bed. It is a sign London is now an empty place, when it will not furnish me with matter for above five or six lines in a day. Did you smoak in my last how I told you the very day and the place you were playing at ombre? But I interlined and altered a little, after I had received a letter from Mr. Manley, that said you were at it in his house, while he was writing to me; but without his help I guessed within one day. Your town is certainly much more sociable than ours. I have not seen your mother yet, &c.

12. I dined to-day with Dr. Garth and Mr. Addison, at the Devil tavern by Temple-bar, and Garth treated; and it is well I dine every day, else I should be longer making out my letters: for we are yet in a very dull state, only inquiring every day after new elections, where the Tories carry it among the new members six to one. Mr. Addison's election has passed easy and undisputed; and, I believe, if he had a mind to be chosen king, he would hardly be refused. An odd accident has happened at Colchester: one captain Lavallin, coming from Flanders or Spain, found his wife with child by a clerk of Doctors Commons,

whose

whose trade, you know, it is to prevent fornications: and this clerk was the very same fellow that made the discovery of Dyet's counterfeiting the stamp-paper. Lavallin has been this fortnight hunting after the clerk, to kill him; but the fellow was constantly employed at the Treasury, about the discovery he made: the wife had made a shift to patch up the business, alledging that the clerk had told her her husband was dead, and other excuses; but the other day somebody told Lavallin, his wife had intrigues before he married her: upon which he goes down in a rage, shoots his wife through the head, then falls on his sword; and, to make the matter sure, at the same time discharges a pistol through his own head, and died on the spot, his wife surviving him about two hours, but in what circumstances of mind and body is terrible to imagine. I have finished my poem on the Shower, all but the beginning; and am going on with my *Tatler*. They have fixt about fifty things on me since I came: I have printed but three. One advantage I get by writing to you daily, or rather you get, is, that I shall remember not to write the same things twice; and yet, I fear, I have done it often already: but I will mind and confine myself to the accidents of the day; and so get you gone to ombre, and be good girls, and save your money, and be rich against Presto comes, and write to me now and then: I am thinking it would be a pretty thing to hear sometimes from sawcy MD; but do not hurt your eyes, Stella, I charge you.

13. O Lord, here is but a trifle of my letter written yet; what shall Presto do for prittle-prattle, to entertain MD? The talk now grows fresher of the duke of Ormond for Ireland; though Mr. Addison says, he hears it will be in commission, and lord Galloway one. These letters of mine are a sort of journal, where matters open by degrees; and, as I tell true or false, you will find by the event

whether

whether my intelligence be good; but I do not care twopence whether it be or no.——At night. To-day I was all about St. Paul's, and up at the top like a fool, with sir Andrew Fountain and two more; and spent seven shillings for my dinner like a puppy: this is the second time he has served me so; but I will never do it again, though all mankind should persuade me, unconsidering puppies! There is a young fellow here in town we are all fond of, and about a year or two come from the university, one Harrison, a little pretty fellow, with a great deal of wit, good sense, and good-nature; has written some mighty pretty things; that in your 6th *Miscellanea,* about the *Sprig of an Orange*, is his: he has nothing to live on but being governor to one of the duke of Queensberry's sons for forty pounds a year. The fine fellows are always inviting him to the tavern, and make him pay his club. Henley is a great crony of his: they are often at the tavern at six or seven shillings reckoning, and he always makes the poor lad pay his full share. A colonel and a lord were at him and me the same way to-night: I absolutely refused, and made Harrison lag behind, and persuaded him not to go to them. I tell you this, because I find all rich fellows have that humour of using all people without any consideration of their fortunes; but I will see them rot before they shall serve me so. Lord Halifax is always teazing me to go down to his country house, which will cost me a guinea to his servants, and twelve shillings coach-hire; and he shall be hanged first. Is not this a plaguy silly story? But I am vext at the heart; for I love the young fellow, and am resolved to stir up people to do something for him: he is a Whig, and I will put him upon some of my cast Whigs; for I have done with them; and they have, I hope, done with this kingdom for our time. They were sure of the four members for London above

all

all places, and they have lost three in the four. Sir Richard Onslow, we hear, has lost for Surrey; and they are overthrown in most places. Lookee, gentlewomen, if I write long letters, I must write you news and stuff, unless I send you my verses; and some I dare not; and those on the Shower in London I have sent to the *Taller*, and you may see them in Ireland. I fancy you will smoak me in the *Taller* I am going to write; for I believe I have told you the hint. I had a letter sent me to-night from sir Matthew Dudley, and found it on my table when I came in. Because it is extraordinary, I will transcribe it from beginning to end. It is as follows [Is the Devil in you? Oct. 13, 1710]. I would have answered every particular passage in it, only I wanted time. Here is enough for to-night, such as it is, &c.

14. Is that tobacco at the top of the paper,[1] or what? I do not remember I slobbered. Lord, I dreamt of Stella, &c. so confusedly last night, and that we saw dean Bolton and Sterne go into a shop: and she bid me call them to her, and they proved to be two parsons I know not; and I walked without till she was shifting, and such stuff, mixt with much melancholy and uneasiness, and things not as they should be, and I know not how: and it is now an ugly gloomy morning.—At night. Mr. Addison and I dined with Ned Southwell, and walked in the Park; and at the Coffee-house I found a letter from the bishop of Clogher, and a pacquet from MD. I opened the bishop's letter; but put up MD's, and visited a lady just come to town; and am now got into bed, and going to open your little letter: and God send I may find MD well, and happy, and merry, and that they love Presto as they do fires. Oh, I will not open it yet! yes I will! no I will not! I am

[1] The upper part of the letter was a little besmeared with some such stuff; the mark is still on it.

going;

going; I cannot stay till I turn over.[1] What shall I do? My fingers itch; and now I have it in my left hand; and now I will open it this very moment.—I have just got it, and am cracking the seal, and cannot imagine what is in it; I fear only some letter from a bishop, and it comes too late, I shall employ nobody's credit but my own. Well, I see though—Pshaw, it is from sir Andrew Fountain. What, another! I fancy this is from Mrs. Barton; she told me, she would write to me; but she writes a better hand than this: I wish you would inquire; it must be at Dawson's office at the Castle. I fear this is from Patty Rolt, by the scrawl. Well, I will read MD's letter. Ah, no; it is from poor lady Berkeley, to invite me to Berkeley-castle this winter; and now it grieves my heart: she says, 'she hopes my lord is in a fair way of recovery'; poor lady! Well, now I go to MD's letter: faith, it is all right; I hoped it was wrong. Your letter, N. 3, that I have now received, is dated Sept. 26; and Manley's letter, that I had five days ago, was dated Oct. 3, that is a fortnight difference: I doubt it has lain in Steele's office, and he forgot. Well, there is an end of that: he is turned out of his place; and you must desire those who send me pacquets, to inclose them in a paper directed to Mr. Addison, at St. James's Coffee-house: not common letters, but pacquets: the bishop of Clogher may mention it to the archbishop when he sees him. As for your letter, it makes me mad: slidikins, I have been the best boy in Christendom, and you come with your two eggs a penny.—Well; but stay, I will look over my book: adad, I think there was a chasm between my N. 2. and N. 3. Faith, I will not promise to write to you every week; but I will write every night, and when it is full I will send it; that

[1] That is, to the next page; for he is now within three lines of the bottom of the first.

will

will be once in ten days, and that will be often enough: and if you begin to take up the way of writing to Presto, only because it is Tuesday, a Monday bedad it will grow a task; but write when you have a mind.——No, no, no, no, no, no, no, no—Agad, agad, agad, agad, agad, agad; no, poor Stellakins. Slids, I would the horse were in your —chamber! Have not I ordered Parvisol to obey your directions about him? And have not I said in my former letters, that you may pickle him, and boil him, if you will? What do you trouble me about your horses for? Have I any thing to do with them?—Revolutions a hindrance to me in my business? Revolutions to me in my business? If it were not for the revolutions, I could do nothing at all; and now I have all hopes possible, though one is certain of nothing; but to-morrow I am to have an answer, and am promised an effectual one. I suppose I have said enough in this and a former letter how I stand with new people; ten times better than ever I did with the old; forty times more caressed. I am to dine to-morrow at Mr. Harley's; and if he continues as he has begun, no man has been ever better treated by another. What you say about Stella's mother, I have spoken enough to it already. I believe she is not in town; for I have not yet seen her. My lampoon is cried up to the skies; but nobody suspects me for it, except sir Andrew Fountain: at least they say nothing of it to me. Did not I tell you of a great man who received me very coldly?[1] That's he; but say nothing; it was only a little revenge. I will remember to bring it over. The bishop of Clogher has smoaked my *Tatler*,[2] about shortening of words, &c. But, God so![3] &c.

15. I will write plainer if I can remember it; for Stella

[1] Lord Godolphin. [2] No. 230.

[3] This appears to be an interjection of surprize at the length of his journal.

must

must not spoil her eyes, and Dingley cannot read my hand very well; and I am afraid my letters are too long: then you must suppose one to be two, and read them at twice. I dined to-day with Mr. Harley: Mr. Prior dined with us. He has left my memorial with the queen, who has consented to give the First Fruits and Twentieth Parts, and will, we hope, declare it to-morrow in the cabinet. But I beg you to tell it to no person alive; for so I am ordered, till in publick: and I hope to get something of greater value. After dinner came in lord Peterborow: we renewed our acquaintance, and he grew mightily fond of me. They began to talk of a paper of verses called Sid Hamet. Mr. Harley repeated part, and then pulled them out, and gave them to a gentleman at the table to read, though they had all read them often: lord Peterborow would let nobody read them but himself: so he did; and Mr. Harley bobbed me at every line, to take notice of the beauties. Prior raillied lord Peterborow for author of them; and lord Peterborow said, he knew them to be his; and Prior then turned it upon me, and I on him. I am not guessed at all in town to be the author; yet so it is: but that is a secret only to you. Ten to one whether you see them in Ireland; yet here they run prodigiously. Harley presented me to lord president of Scotland, and Mr. Benson, lord of the treasury. Prior and I came away at nine, and sat at the Smyrna till eleven, receiving acquaintance.

16. This morning early I went in a chair, and Patrick before it, to Mr. Harley, to give him another copy of my memorial, as he desired; but he was full of business, going to the queen, and I could not see him; but he desired I would send up the paper, and excused himself upon his hurry. I was a little baulkt; but they tell me it is nothing. I shall judge by next visit. I tipt his porter with half a crown; and so I am well there for a time at least. I dined

at

at Stratford's in the city, and had Burgundy and Tokay: came back afoot like a scoundrel: then went with Mr. Addison and supt with lord Mountjoy, which made me sick all night. I forgot that I bought six pounds of chocolate for Stella, and a little wooden box: and I have a great piece of Brazil tobacco for Dingley, and a bottle of palsy water for Stella: all which, with the two handkerchiefs that Mr. Sterne has bought, and you must pay him for, will be put in the box, directed to Mrs. Curry's, and sent by Dr. Hawkshaw, whom I have not seen; but Sterne has undertaken it. The chocolate is a present, madam, for Stella. Don't read this, you little rogue, with your little eyes; but give it to Dingley, pray now; and I will write as plain as the skies: and let Dingley write Stella's part, and Stella dictate to her, when she apprehends her eyes, &c.

17. This letter should have gone this post, if I had not been taken up with business, and two nights being late out; so it must stay till Thursday. I dined to-day with your Mr. Sterne, by invitation, and drank Irish wine[1]; but, before we parted, there came in the prince of puppies, colonel Edgworth; so I went away. This day came out the *Tatler*, made up wholly of my *Shower*, and a preface to it. They say it is the best thing I ever writ, and I think so too. I suppose the bishop of Clogher will shew it you. Pray tell me how you like it. Tooke is going on with my *Miscellany*. I would give a penny the letter to the bishop of Killala was in it: it would do him honour. Could not you contrive to say, you hear they are printing my Things together; and that you wish the bookseller had that letter among the rest: but don't say any thing of it as from me. I forget whether it was good or no; but only having heard it much commended, perhaps it may deserve it.

[1] Claret.

Well,

Well, I have to-morrow to finish this letter in, and then I will send it next day. I am so vext that you should write your third to me, when you had but my second, and I had written five, which now I hope you have all: and so I tell you, you are sawcy, little, pretty, dear rogues, &c.

18. To-day I dined, by invitation, with Stratford and others, at a young merchant's in the city, with Hermitage and Tokay, and staid till nine, and am now come home. And that dog Patrick is abroad, and drinking, and I cannot get my night-gown. I have a mind to turn that puppy away: he has been drunk ten times in three weeks. But I have not time to say more; so good night, &c.

19. I am come home from dining in the city with Mr. Addison, at a merchant's; and just now, at the Coffee-house, we have notice that the duke of Ormond was this day declared lord lieutenant at Hampton-court, in council. I have not seen Mr. Harley since; but hope the affair is done about First Fruits. I will see him, if possible, to-morrow morning; but this goes to-night. I have sent a box to Mr. Sterne, to send to you by some friend: I have directed it for Mr. Curry, at his house; so you have warning when it comes, as I hope it will soon. The handkerchiefs will be put in some friend's pocket, not to pay custom. And so here ends my sixth, sent when I had but three of MD's: now I am beforehand, and will keep so; and God Almighty bless dearest MD, &c.

LETTER XIII

London, January 4, 1710–11.

I WAS going into the city (where I dined) and put my 12th, with my own fair hands, into the post-office as I came back, which was not till nine this night. I dined with people that you never heard of, nor is it worth your while

while to know; an authoress[1] and a printer. I walked home for exercise, and at eleven got to bed; and, all the while I was undressing myself, there was I speaking monkey things in air, just as if MD had been by, and did not recollect myself till I got into bed. I writ last night to the archbishop, and told him, the warrant was drawn for the First Fruits; and I told him, lord Peterborow was set out for his journey to Vienna; but, it seems, the lords have addressed to have him stay, to be examined about Spanish affairs, upon this defeat there, and to know where the fault lay, &c. So I writ to the archbishop a lie; but I think it was not a sin.

5. Mr. secretary St. John sent for me this morning so early, that I was forced to go without shaving, which put me quite out of method. I called at Mr. Ford's, and desired him to lend me a shaving; and so made a shift to get into order again. Lord! here is an impertinence: sir Andrew Fountain's mother and sister are come above a hundred miles, from Worcester, to see him before he died. They got here but yesterday; and he must have been past hopes, or past fears, before they could reach him. I fell a scolding when I heard they were coming; and the people about him wondered at me; and said, what a mighty content it would be on both sides to die when they were with him! I knew the mother; she is the greatest Overdo upon earth; and the sister, they say, is worse; the poor man will relapse again among them. Here was the scoundrel brother always crying in the outer room till sir Andrew was in danger; and the dog was to have all his estate if he died; and it is an ignorant, worthless, scoundrel-rake: and the nurses were comforting him, and desiring he would not take on so. I dined to-day the first time with Ophy Butler and his wife; and you supped with

[1] Mrs. Manley, writer of the *Atalantis.*

the dean, and lost two and twenty pence at cards. And so Mrs. Walls is brought-to-bed of a girl, who died two days after it was christened; and, betwixt you and me, she is not very sorry: she loves her ease and diversions too well to be troubled with children. I will go to bed.

6. Morning. I went last night to put some coals on my fire after Patrick was gone to bed; and there I saw in a closet a poor linnet he has bought to bring over to Dingley: it cost him six pence, and is as tame as a dormouse. I believe he does not know he is a bird: where you put him, there he stands, and seems to have neither hope nor fear; I suppose in a week he will die of the spleen. Patrick advised with me before he bought him. I laid fairly before him the greatness of the sum, and the rashness of the attempt; shewed how impossible it was to carry him safe over the salt sea: but he would not take my counsel; and he will repent it. It is very cold this morning in bed; and I hear there is a good fire in the room without (what do you call it?), the dining-room. I hope it will be good weather, and so let me rise, sirrahs, do so.—At night. I was this morning to visit the dean, or Mr. Prolocutor, I think you call him, don't you? Why should not I go to the dean's as well as you? A little, black man, of pretty near fifty? Aye, the same. A good pleasant man? Aye, the same. Cunning enough? Yes. One that understands his own interests? As well as any body. How comes it MD and I do not meet there sometimes? A very good face, and abundance of wit? Do you know his lady? O Lord![1] whom do you mean? I mean Dr. Atterbury, dean of Carlisle and Prolocutor. Pshaw, Presto, you are a fool: I thought you had meant our dean of St. Patrick's.—Silly, silly, silly, you are silly, both are silly, every kind

[1] Dr. Sterne, dean of St. Patrick's, was not a married man; which seems to have been the cause of this surprize in MD.

of

of thing is silly. As I walked into the city, I was stopped with clusters of boys and wenches buzzing about the cake-shops like flies. There had the fools let out their shops two yards forward into the streets, all spread with great cakes frothed with sugar, and stuck with streamers of tinsel. And then I went to Bateman's the bookseller, and laid out eight and forty shillings for books. I bought three little volumes of Lucian in French for our Stella, and so and so. Then I went to Garraway's, to meet Stratford and dine with him; but it was an idle day with the merchants, and he was gone to our end of the town: so I dined with sir Thomas Frankland at the post office, and we drank your Manley's health. It was in a news-paper that he was turned out; but secretary St. John told me it was false: only that news-writer is a plaguy Tory. I have not seen one bit of Christmas merriment.

7. Morning. Your new lord chancellor sets out to-morrow for Ireland: I never saw him. He carries over one Trap a parson as his chaplain, a sort of pretender to wit, a second-rate pamphleteer for the cause, whom they pay by sending him to Ireland. I never saw Trap neither. I met Tighe and your Smyth of Lovet's yesterday by The Exchange. Tighe and I took no notice of each other; but I stopped Smyth, and told him of the box that lies for you at Chester, because he says he goes very soon to Ireland, I think this week: and I will send this morning to Sterne, to take measures with Smyth; so good-morrow, sirrahs, and let me rise, pray. I took up this paper when I came in at evening, I mean this minute, and then said I, 'No, no, indeed, MD, you must stay'; and then was laying it aside, but could not for my heart, though I am very busy, till I just ask you how you do since morning; bye and bye we shall talk more, so let me leave you: softly down, little paper, till then; so there—now to business;

business; there, I say, get you gone; no, I will not push you neither, but hand you on one side—So—Now I am got into bed, I will talk with you. Mr. secretary St. John sent for me this morning in all haste; but I would not lose my shaving, for fear of missing church. I went to Court, which is of late always very full; and young Manley and I dined at sir Matthew Dudley's.—I must talk politicks. I protest, I am afraid we shall all be embroiled with parties. The Whigs, now they are fallen, are the most malicious toads in the world. We have had now a second misfortune, the loss of several Virginia ships. I fear people will begin to think that nothing thrives under this ministry: and, if the ministry can once be rendered odious to the people, the parliament may be chosen Whig or Tory as the queen pleases. Then I think our friends press a little too hard on the duke of Marlborough. The country members[1] are violent to have past faults inquired into, and they have reason; but I do not observe the ministry to be very fond of it. In my opinion, we have nothing to save us but a Peace; and I am sure we cannot have such a one as we hoped; and then the Whigs will bawl what they would have done, had they continued in power. I tell the ministry this as much as I dare: and shall venture to say a little more to them, especially about the duke of Marlborough, who, as the Whigs give out, will lay down his command; and I question whether ever any wise state laid aside a general who had been successful nine years together; whom the enemy so much dread; and his own soldiers cannot but believe must always conquer; and you know that in war opinion is nine parts in ten. The ministry hear me always with appearance of regard, and much kindness; but I doubt they let personal quarrels mingle too much with

[1] Those were afterwards called The October Club.

their

their proceedings. Mean time, they seem to value all this as nothing, and are as easy and merry as if they had nothing in their hearts or upon their shoulders; like physicians, who endeavour to cure, but feel no grief, whatever the patient suffers.—Pshaw, what is all this? Do you know one thing, that I find I can write politicks to you much easier than to any body alive? But I swear my head is full; and I wish I were at Laracor, with dear charming MD, &c.

8. Morning. Methinks, young women, I have made a great progress in four days, at the bottom of this side already, and no letter yet come from MD (that word interlined is morning). I find I have been writing state-affairs to MD. How do they relish it? Why, any thing that comes from Presto is welcome; though really, to confess the truth, if they had their choice, not to disguise the matter, they had rather, &c. Now, Presto, I must tell you, you grow silly, says Stella. That is but one body's opinion, madam. I promised to be with Mr. secretary St. John this morning; but I am lazy, and will not go, because I had a letter from him yesterday, to desire I would dine there to-day. I shall be chid; but what care I?—Here has been Mrs. South with me, just come from sir Andrew Fountain, and going to market. He is still in a fever, and may live or die. His mother and sister are now come up, and in the house; so there is a lurry. I gave Mrs. South half a pistole for a New-year's-gift. So good-morrow, dears both, till anon.—At night. Lord! I have been with Mr. Secretary from dinner till eight; and, though I drank wine and water, I am so hot! Lady Stanley came to visit Mrs. St. John, and sent up for me, to make up a quarrel with Mrs. St. John, whom I never yet saw; and do you think that devil of a secretary would let me go, but kept me by main force, though I told him,

'I was

'I was in love with his lady, and it was a shame to keep back a lover, &c.?' But all would not do; so at last I was forced to break away, but never went up, it was then too late; and here I am, and have a great deal to do to-night, though it be nine o'clock; but one must say something to these naughty MDs, else there will be no quiet. . . .

LETTER XV

London, Jan. 31, 1710–11.

I AM to send you my fourteenth to-morrow; but my head, having some little disorders, confounds all my journals. I was early this morning with Mr. secretary St. John about some business, so I could not scribble my morning lines to MD. They are here intending to tax all little printed penny papers a half-penny every half-sheet, which will utterly ruin Grub-street, and I am endeavouring to prevent it. Besides, I was forwarding an impeachment against a certain great person; that was two of my businesses with the secretary, were they not worthy ones? It was Ford's Birth-day, and I refused the secretary, and dined with Ford. We are here in as smart a frost for the time as I have seen; delicate walking weather, and the Canal and Rosamond's Pond full of the rabble sliding and with skates, if you know what those are. Patrick's bird's water freezes in the gally-pot, and my hands in bed.

Feb. 1. I was this morning with poor lady Kerry, who is much worse in her head than I. She sends me bottles of her bitter; and we are so fond of one another, because our ailments are the same; don't you know that, Madam Stella? Have not I seen you conning ailments with Joe's wife,[1] and some others, sirrah? I walked into the city to dine, because of the walk, for we must take care of Presto's health; you know, because of poor little MD.

[1] Mrs. Beaumont.

But

But I walked plaguy carefully, for fear of sliding against my will; but I am very busy.

2. This morning Mr. Ford came to me to walk into the city, where he had business, and then to buy books at Bateman's; and I laid out one pound five shillings for a Strabo and Aristophanes, and I have now got books enough to make me another shelf, and I will have more, or it shall cost me a fall; and so as we came back, we drank a flask of right French wine at Ben Tooke's chamber; and when I got home, Mrs. Vanhomrigh sent me word her eldest daughter was taken suddenly very ill, and desired I would come and see her; I went, and found it was a silly trick of Mrs. Armstrong, lady Lucy's sister, who, with Moll Stanhope, was visiting there; however, I rattled off the daughter.

3. To-day I went and dined at lady Lucy's, where you know I have not been this long time; they are plaguy Whigs, especially the sister Armstrong, the most insupportable of all women, pretending to wit, without any taste. She was running down the last *Examiner*, the prettiest I had read, with a character of the present ministry.—I left them at five, and came home. But I forgot to tell you, that this morning my cousin Dryden Leach the printer, came to me with a heavy complaint, that Harrison the new *Tatler* had turned him off, and taken the last *Tatler's* printers again. He vowed revenge; I answered gravely, and so he left me, and I have ordered Patrick to deny me to him from henceforth: and at night comes a letter from Harrison, telling me the same thing, and excused his doing it without my notice, because he would bear all the blame; and in his *Tatler* of this day he tells you the story, how he has taken his old officers, and there is a most humble letter from Morphew and Lilly to beg his pardon, &c. And lastly, this morning Ford sent me

me two letters from the Coffee-house (where I hardly ever go) one from the archbishop of Dublin, and the other from —— Who do you think the other was from?—I will tell you, because you are friends; why then it was, faith it was from my own dear little MD, N. 10. Oh, but will not answer it now, no, noooooh, I will keep it between the two sheets; here it is, just under; oh, I lifted up the sheet and saw it there: lie still, you shall not be answered yet, little letter; for I must go to bed, and take care of my head.

I avoid going to church yet, for fear of my head, though it has been much better these last five or six days, since I have taken lady Kerry's bitter. Our frost holds like a dragon. I went to Mr. Addison's, and dined with him at his lodgings; I had not seen him these three weeks, we are grown common acquaintance; yet what have not I done for his friend Steele? Mr. Harley reproached me the last time I saw him, that to please me he would be reconciled to Steele, and had promised and appointed to see him, and that Steele never came. Harrison, whom Mr. Addison recommended to me, I have introduced to the secretary of state, who has promised me to take care of him; and I have represented Addison himself so to the ministry, that they think and talk in his favour, though they hated him before.——Well; he is now in my debt, and there is an end; and I never had the least obligation to him, and there is another end. This evening I had a message from Mr. Harley, desiring to know whether I was alive, and that I would dine with him to-morrow. They dine so late, that since my head has been wrong I have avoided being with them.—Patrick has been out of favour these ten days; I talk dry and cross to him, and have called him Friend three or four times. But, sirrahs, get you gone.

5. Morning.

5. Morning. I am going this morning to see Prior, who dines with me at Mr. Harley's; so I cannot stay fiddling and talking with dear little brats in a morning, and it is still terribly cold.—I wish my cold hand was in the warmest place about you, young women, I would give ten guineas upon that account with all my heart, faith; oh, it starves my thigh; so I will rise and bid you good morrow, my ladies both, good morrow. Come, stand away, let me rise: Patrick, take away the candle. Is there a good fire?—So—up-a-dazy.—At night. Mr. Harley did not sit down till six, and I staid till eleven; henceforth I will chuse to visit him in the evenings, and dine with him no more if I can help it. It breaks all my measures, and hurts my health; my head is disorderly, but not ill, and I hope it will mend.

6. Here has been such a hurry with the Queen's Birth-day, so much fine cloaths, and the Court so crowded that I did not go there. All the frost is gone. It thawed on Sunday, and so continues, yet ice is still on the Canal (I did not mean that of Laracor, but St. James's Park) and boys sliding on it. Mr. Ford pressed me to dine with him in his chamber.—Did not I tell you Patrick has got a bird, a linnet, to carry over to Dingley? It was very tame at first, and it is now the wildest I ever saw. He keeps it in a closet, where it makes a terrible litter; but I say nothing: I am as tame as a clout. When must we answer our MD's letter? One of these oddcome-shortlies. This is a week old, you see, and no further yet. Mr. Harley desired I would dine with him again to-day; but I refused him, for I fell out with him yesterday, and will not see him again till he makes me amends: and so I go to-bed....

9. Morning. After I had been a-bed an hour last night, I was forced to rise and call to the landlady and maid to have the fire removed in a chimney below stairs, which made

made my bed-chamber smoke, though I had no fire in it. I have been twice served so. I never lay so miserable an hour in my life. Is it not plaguy vexatious?—It has snowed all night, and rains this morning.——Come, where is MD's letter? Come, Mrs. Letter, make your appearance. Here am I, says she, answer me to my face.—Oh, faith, I am sorry you had my twelfth so soon; I doubt you will stay longer for the rest. I am so afraid you have got my fourteenth while I am writing this; and I would always have one letter from Presto reading, one traveling, and one writing. As for the box, I now believe it lost. It is directed for Mr. Curry, at his house in Capel-street, &c. I had a letter yesterday from Dr. Raymond in Chester, who says, 'He sent his man every where, and cannot find it'; and God knows whether Mr. Smyth will have better success. Sterne spoke to him, and I writ to him with the bottle of palsey-water; that bottle, I hope, will not miscarry: I long to hear you have it. Oh, faith, you have too good an opinion of Presto's care. I am negligent enough of every thing but MD, and I should not have trusted Sterne.—But it shall not go so: I will have one more tug for it.—As to what you say of goodman Peasly and Isaac, I answer as I did before. Fye, child, you must not give yourself the way to believe any such thing: and afterwards, only for curiosity, you may tell me how these things are approved, and how you like them; and whether they instruct you in the present course of affairs, and whether they are printed in your town, or only sent from hence.—Sir Andrew Fountain is recovered; so take your sorrow again, but do not keep it, fling it to the dogs. And does little MD walk indeed?—I am glad of it at heart.—Yes, we have done with the plague here: it was very saucy in you to pretend to have it before your betters. Your intelligence that the story is is false about the officers forced to sell, is admirable. You may see them all three here every day, no more in the army than you. Twelve shillings for mending the strong box; that is, for putting a farthing's worth of iron on a hinge, and gilding it; give him six shillings, and I will pay it, and never employ him or hers again.—No—indeed, I put off preaching as much as I can. I am upon another foot: nobody doubts here whether I can preach, and you are fools.—The account you give of that weekly paper[1] agrees with us here. Mr. Prior was like to be insulted in the street for being supposed the author of it; but one of the last papers cleared him. Nobody knows who it is, but those few in the secret, I suppose the ministry and the printer.—Poor Stella's eyes! God bless them, and send them better. Pray spare them, and write not above two lines a day in broad day-light. How does Stella look, madam Dingley? Pretty well, a handsome young woman still. Will she pass in a crowd? Will she make a figure in a country church?—Stay a little, fair ladies. I this minute sent Patrick to Sterne: he brings back word that your box is very safe with one Mr. Earl's sister in Chester, and that colonel Edgeworth's widow goes for Ireland on Monday next, and will receive the box at Chester, and deliver it you safe: so there are some hopes now.—Well, let us go on to your letter.——The warrant is passed for the First-Fruits. The queen does not send a letter; but a patent will be drawn here, and that will take up time. Mr. Harley of late has said nothing of presenting me to the queen:—I was overseen when I mentioned it to you. He has such a weight of affairs on him, that he cannot mind all; but he talked of it three or four times to me, long before I dropped it to you. What, is not Mrs. Wall's business over yet? I had hopes she was

[1] The *Examiner*.

up

up and well, and the child dead before this time.—You did right, at last, to send me your accompts; but I did not stay for them, I thank you. I hope you have your bill sent in my last, and there will be eight pounds interest soon due from Hawkeshaw: pray look at his bond. I hope you are good managers; and that, when I say so, Stella will not think I intend she should grudge herself wine. But going to those expensive lodgings requires some fund. I wish you had staid till I came over, for some reasons. That Frenchwoman will be grumbling again in a little time: and if you are invited any where to the country, it will vex you to pay in absence; and the country may be necessary for poor Stella's health: but do as you like, and do not blame Presto.—Oh, but you are telling your reasons.—Well, I have read them; do as you please.—Yes, Raymond says, he must stay longer than he thought, because he cannot settle his affairs. M—— is in the country at some friend's, comes to town in Spring, and then goes to settle in Herefordshire. Her husband is a surly ill-natured brute, and cares not she should see any body. O Lord, see how I blundered, and left two lines short; it was that ugly score in the paper[1] that made me mistake.——I believe you lie about the story of the fire, only to make it more odd. Bernage must go to Spain; and I will see to recommend him to the duke of Argyle, his general, when I see the duke next: but the officers tell me, 'it would be dishonourable in the last degree for him to sell now, and he would never be preferred in the army'; so that, unless he designs to leave it for good and all, he must go. Tell him so, and that I would write if I knew where to direct to him; which I have said four-score times already. I had rather any thing almost than that you should strain yourselves to send a letter when it is in-

[1] A crease in the sheet.

convenient;

convenient; we have settled that matter already. I will write when I can, and so shall MD; and upon occasions extraordinary I will write, though it be a line; and when we have not letters soon, we agree that all things are well; and so that is settled for ever, and so hold your tongue.—Well, you shall have your pins; but for candles ends, I cannot promise, because I burn them to the stumps; besides, I remember what Stella told Dingley about them many years ago, and she may think the same thing of me.—And Dingley shall have her hinged spectacles.—Poor dear Stella, how durst you write those two lines by candle-light? bang your bones! Faith, this letter shall go to-morrow, I think, and that will be in ten days from the last, young women; that is too soon of all conscience: but answering yours has filled it up so quick, and I do not design to use you to three pages in folio, no, nooooh. All this is one morning's work in bed;—and so good morrow, little sirrahs; that is for the rhyme.[1] You want politicks: faith, I cannot think of any; but may be at night I may tell you a passage. Come, sit off the bed, and let me rise, will you?—At night. I dined to-day with my neighbour Vanhomrigh; it was such dismal weather I could not stir further. I have had some threatenings with my head, but no fits. I still drink Dr. Radcliffe's bitter, and will continue it.

10. I was this morning to see the secretary of state, and have engaged him to give a memorial from me to the duke of Argyle in behalf of Bernage. The duke is a man that distinguishes people of merit, and I will speak to him myself; but the secretary backing it will be very effectual, and I will take care to have it done to purpose. Pray tell Bernage so, and that I think nothing can be luckier for

[1] In the original it was, *good mallows, little sollahs*. But in these words, and many others, he writes constantly *ll* for *rr*.

him,

him, and that I would have him go by all means. I will order it that the duke shall send for him when they are in Spain; or, if he fails, that he shall receive him kindly when he goes to wait on him. Can I do more? Is not this a great deal?—I now send away this letter, that you may not stay.—I dined with Ford upon his Opera-day, and am now come home, and am going to study; do not you presume to guess, sirrahs, impudent saucy dear boxes. Towards the end of a letter I could not say saucy boxes without putting dear between. En't that right now? Farewel. *This* should *be* longer, *but* that *I* send *it* to-*night*.[1]

O silly, silly loggerhead! . . .

LETTER XVII

Feb. 24–*Mar.* 10, 1710–11.

. . . zoo[2] must cly Lele and Hele, and Hele aden. Must loo mimitate pdfr, pay? Iss, and so la shall. And so leles fol ee rettle. Dood mollow.—At night. Mrs. Barton sent this morning to invite me to dinner; and there I dined, just in that genteel manner that MD used when they would treat some better sort of body than usual.

8. O dear MD, my heart is almost broken. You will hear the thing before this comes to you. I writ a full account of it this night to the archbishop of Dublin; and the dean may tell you the particulars from the archbishop. I was in a sorry way to write, but thought it might be proper to send a true account of the fact; for

[1] Those letters which are in Italicks, in the original are of a monstrous size, which occasioned his calling himself a loggerhead.

[2] Here is just one specimen given of his way of writing to Stella in these journals. The reader, I hope, will excuse my omitting it in all other places where it occurs. The meaning of this pretty language is; 'And you must cry There, and Here, and Here again. Must you imitate Presto, pray? Yes, and so you shall. And so there's for your letter. Good morrow.'

you

you will hear a thousand lying circumstances. It is of Mr. Harley's being stabbed this afternoon, at three o'clock, at a committee of the council. I was playing lady Catharine Morris's cards, where I dined, when young Arundel came in with the story. I ran away immediately to the secretary, which was in my way: no one was at home. I met Mrs. St. John in her chair; she had heard it imperfectly. I took a chair to Mr. Harley, who was asleep, and they hope in no danger; but he has been out of order, and was so when he came abroad to-day, and it may put him in a fever: I am in mortal pain for him. That desperate French villain, marquis De Guiscard, stabbed Mr. Harley. Guiscard was taken up by Mr. secretary St. John's warrant for high treason, and brought before the lords to be examined; there he stabbed Mr. Harley. I have told all the particulars already to the archbishop. I have now, at nine, sent again, and they tell me he is in a fair way. Pray pardon my distraction; I now think of all his kindness to me.—The poor creature now lies stabbed in his bed by a desperate French Popish villain. Good night, and God preserve you both, and pity me; I want it. . . .

LETTER XVIII

Mar. 10–24, 1710–11.

. . . 15. I was this morning at Mr. secretary St. John's for all my shin; and he has given me for young Harrison, the *Tatler*, the prettiest employment in Europe; secretary to my lord Raby, who is to be ambassador extraordinary at The Hague, where all the great affairs will be concerted; so we shall lose the Tatlers in a fortnight. I will send Harrison to-morrow morning to thank the secretary. Poor Biddy Floyd has got the small-pox. I called this morning to see lady Betty Germaine, and when she told

me

me so, I fairly took my leave. I have the luck of it;[1] for about ten days ago I was to see lord Carteret; and my lady was entertaining me with telling of a young lady, a cousin, who was then ill in the house of the small-pox, and is since dead: it was near lady Betty's, and I fancy Biddy took the fright by it.[2] I dined with Mr. Secretary; and a physician came in just from Guiscard, who tells us he is dying of his wounds, and can hardly live till to-morrow. A poor wench that Guiscard kept, sent him a bottle of sack; but the keeper would not let him touch it, for fear it was poison. He had two quarts of old clotted blood come out of his side to-day, and is delirious. I am sorry he is dying; for they had found out a way to hang him. He certainly had an intention to murder the queen.

16. I have made but little progress in this letter for so many

[1] Dr. Swift never had the small-pox.

[2] Dr. Goldsmith, in his Life of Parnell, has given this anecdote: 'The Scriblerus club, when the members were in town, were seldom asunder; and they often made excursions together into the country, and generally on foot. Swift was usually the butt of the company; and, if a trick was played, he was always the sufferer. The whole party once agreed to walk down to the house of lord B——, who is still living, and whose seat is about twelve miles from town. As every one agreed to make the best of his way, Swift, who was remarkable for walking, soon left all the rest behind him; fully resolved, upon his arrival, to chuse the very best bed for himself, for that was his custom. In the mean time, Parnell was determined to prevent his intentions; and, taking horse, arrived at lord B——'s, by another way, long before him. Having apprized his lordship of Swift's design, it was resolved at any rate to keep him out of the house; but how to do this, was the question. Swift never had the small-pox, and was much afraid of catching it: as soon, therefore, as he appeared striding along at some distance from the house, one of his lordship's servants was dispatched, to inform him, that the small-pox was then making great ravages in the family; but that there was a summer-house with a field-bed at his service, at the end of the garden. There the disappointed Dean was obliged to retire, and take a cold supper that was sent out to him, while the rest were feasting within. However, at last, they took compassion on him; and, upon his promising never to chuse the best bed again, they permitted him to make one of the company.'—There is something satisfactory (as Dr. Goldsmith observes) in these accounts of the follies of the wise: they give a natural air to the picture, and reconcile us to our own. N.

many days, thanks to Guiscard and Mr. Harley; and it would be endless to tell you all the particulars of that odious fact. I do not yet hear that Guiscard is dead, but they say it is impossible he should recover. I walked too much yesterday for a man with a broken shin; to-day I rested, and went no further than Mrs. Vanhomrigh's, where I dined; and lady Betty Butler coming in about six, I was forced in good manners to sit with her till nine; then I came home, and Mr. Ford came in to visit my shin, and sat with me till eleven: so I have been very idle and naughty. It vexes me to the pluck that I should lose walking this delicious day. Have you seen the *Spectator* yet, a paper that comes out every day? It is written by Mr. Steele, who seems to have gathered new life, and have a new fund of wit; it is in the same nature as his Tatlers, and they have all of them had something pretty. I believe Addison and he club. I never see them; and I plainly told Mr. Harley and Mr. St. John, ten days ago, before my lord keeper and lord Rivers, 'That I had been foolish enough to spend my credit with them in favour of Addison and Steele; but that I would engage and promise never to say one word in their behalf, having been used so ill for what I had already done.'—So, now I am got into the way of prating again, there will be no quiet for me.

When Presto begins to prate,
Give him a rap upon the pate.

O Lord, how I blot! it is time to leave off, &c.

LETTER XXVII

July 19–*Aug*. 11, 1711.

...8. There was a drawing-room to-day at Court; but so few company, that the queen sent for us into her bed-chamber, where we made our bows, and stood about twenty

twenty of us round the room, while she looked at us round with her fan in her mouth, and once a minute said about three words to some that were nearest her, and then she was told dinner was ready, and went out. I dined at the green-cloth, by Mr. Scarborow's invitation, who is in waiting. It is much the best table in England, and costs the queen a thousand pounds a month while she is at Windsor or Hampton-Court; and is the only mark of magnificence or hospitality I can see in the queen's family: it is designed to entertain foreign ministers, and people of quality, who come to see the queen, and have no place to dine at.

9. Mr. Coke, the vice-chamberlain, made me a long visit this morning, and invited me to dinner; but the toast, his lady, was unfortunately engaged to lady Sunderland. Lord treasurer stole here last night, but did not lie at his lodgings in the Castle; and, after seeing the queen, went back again. I just drank a dish of chocolate with him. I fancy I shall have reason to be angry with him very soon: but what care I; I believe I shall die with ministries in my debt.—This night I received a certain letter from a place called Wexford, from two dear naughty girls of my acquaintance; but, faith, I will not answer it here, no in troth. I will send this to Mr. Reading, supposing it will find you returned; and I hope better for the waters.

10. Mr. vice-chamberlain lent me his horses to ride about and see the country this morning. Dr. Arbuthnot, the queen's physician and favourite, went out with me to shew me the places: we went a little after the queen, and overtook miss Forester, a maid of honour, on her palfry, taking the air; we made her go along with us. We saw a place they have made for a famous horse-race to-morrow, where the queen will come. We met the queen coming back,

back, and miss Forester stood, like us, with her hat off while the queen went by. The doctor and I left the lady where we found her, but under other conductors; and we dined at a little place he has taken, about a mile off.—When I came back, I found Mr. Scarborow had sent all about to invite me to the green cloth, and lessened his company, on purpose to make me easy. It is very obliging, and will cost me thanks. Much company is come to town this evening, to see to-morrow's race. I was tired with riding a trotting mettlesome horse a dozen miles, having not been on horseback this twelvemonth. And miss Forester did not make it easier; she is a silly true maid of honour, and I did not like her, although she be a toast, and was dressed like a man.

11. I will send this letter to-day. I expect the secretary by noon. I will not go to the race, unless I can get room in some coach. It is now morning. I must rise, and fold up and seal my letter. Farewell, and God preserve dearest MD.

I believe I shall leave this town on Monday.

LETTER XXVIII

Aug. 11–25, 1711.

. . . 23. Dilly and I dined to-day with lord Abercorn, and had a fine fat haunch of venison, that smelt rarely on one side: and after dinner Dilly won half a crown of me at backgammon at his lodgings, to his great content. It is a scurvy empty town this melancholy season of the year; but I think our weather begins to mend. The roads are as deep as in Winter. The grapes are sad things; but the peaches are pretty good, and there are some figs. I sometimes venture to eat one, but always repent it. You say nothing of the box sent half a year ago. I wish you would

pay

pay me for Mrs. Walls's tea. Your mother is in the country, I suppose. Pray send me the account of MD, madam Dingley, as it stands since November, that is to say, for this year (excluding the twenty pounds lent Stella for Wexford), for I cannot look in your letters. I think I ordered that Hawkshaw's interest should be paid to you. When you think proper, I will let Parvisol know you have paid that twenty pounds, or part of it; and so go play with the dean, and I will answer your letter to-morrow. Good night, sirrahs, and love Presto, and be good girls.

24. I dined to-day with lord treasurer, who chid me for not dining with him yesterday, for it seems I did not understand his invitation: and their Club of the ministry dined together, and expected me. Lord Radnor and I were walking the Mall this evening; and Mr. secretary met us, and took a turn or two, and then stole away, and we both believed it was to pick up some wench; and to-morrow he will be at the cabinet with the queen: so goes the world! Prior has been out of town these two months, nobody knows where, and is lately returned. People confidently affirm he has been in France, and I half believe it. It is said, he was sent by the ministry, and for some overtures towards a peace. The secretary pretends he knows nothing of it. I believe your parliament will be dissolved. I have been talking about the quarrel between your lords and commons with lord treasurer; and did, at the request of some people, desire that the queen's answer to the commons address might express a dislike of some principles, &c.; but was answered dubiously.—And so now to your letter, fair ladies. I know drinking is bad; I mean writing is bad in drinking the waters; and was angry to see so much in Stella's hand. But why Dingley drinks them, I cannot imagine; but truly she will drink waters

as

as well as Stella: why not? I hope you now find the benefit of them since you are returned; pray let me know particularly. I am glad you are forced upon exercise, which, I believe, is as good as the waters for the heart of them. It is now past the middle of August; so by your reckoning you are in Dublin. It would vex me to the dogs that letters should miscarry between Dublin and Wexford, after scaping the salt seas. I will write no more to that nasty town in haste again, I warrant you. I have been four Sundays together at Windsor, of which a fortnight together; but I believe I shall not go to-morrow; for I will not, unless the secretary asks me. I know all your news about the mayor: it makes no noise here at all, but the quarrel of your parliament does; it is so very extraordinary, and the language of the commons so very pretty. The *Examiner* has been down this month, and was very silly the five or six last papers; but there is a pamphlet come out, in answer to a letter to the seven lords who examined Gregg. The Answer is by the real author of the *Examiner*, as I believe; for it is very well written. We had Trap's poem on the duke of Ormond printed here, and the printer sold just eleven of them. It is a dull piece, not half so good as Stella's; and she is very modest to compare herself with such a poetaster. I am heartily sorry for poor Mrs. Parnell's death; she semed to be an excellent good-natured young woman, and I believe the poor lad is much afflicted; they appeared to live perfectly well together. Dilly is not tired at all with England, but intends to continue here a good while: he is mighty easy to be at distance from his two sisters-in-law. He finds some sort of scrub acquaintance; goes now and then in disguise to a play; smoaks his pipe; reads now and then a little trash, and what else the Lord knows. I see him now and then; for he calls here, and the town

 being

being thin, I am less pestered with company than usual. I have got rid of many of my solicitors, by doing nothing for them: I have not above eight or nine left, and I will be as kind to them. Did I tell you of a knight, who desired me to speak to lord treasurer to give him two thousand pounds, or five hundred pounds a year, until he could get something better? I honestly delivered my message to the treasurer, adding, 'The knight was a puppy, whom I would not give a groat to save from the gallows.' Cole Reading's father-in-law has been two or three times at me, to recommend his Lights to the ministry; assuring me, that a word of mine would, &c. Did not that dog use to speak ill of me, and profess to hate me? He knows not where I lodge, for I told him I lived in the country; and I have ordered Patrick to deny me constantly to him.—Did the bishop of London die in Wexford? poor gentleman! Did he drink the waters? were you at his burial? was it a great funeral? so far from his friends? But he was very old: we shall all follow. And yet it was a pity, if God pleased. He was a good man; not very learned: I believe he died but poor. Did he leave any charity legacies? who held up his pall? was there a great sight of clergy? do they design a tomb for him? are you sure it was the bishop of London? because there is an elderly gentleman here that we give the same title to: or did you fancy all this in your water, as others do strange things in their wine? They say, these waters trouble the head, and make people imagine what never came to pass. Do you make no more of killing a bishop? are these your Whiggish tricks?—Yes, yes, I see you are in a fret. Oh faith, says you, saucy Presto, I will break your head; what, cannot one report what one hears, without being made a jest and a laughing-stock? Are these your English tricks, with a murrain? And Sacheverell will be the next bishop?

bishop? He would be glad of an addition of two hundred pounds a year to what he has; and that is more than they will give him, for aught I see. He hates the new ministry mortally, and they hate him, and pretend to despise him too. They will not allow him to have been the occasion of the late change; at least some of them will not: but my lord keeper owned it to me the other day. No, Mr. Addison does not go to Ireland this year: he pretended he would; but he is gone to Bath with Pastoral Philips, for his eyes.—So now I have run over your letter; and I think this shall go to-morrow, which will be just a fortnight from the last, and bring things to the old form again, after your rambles to Wexford, and mine to Windsor. Are there not many literal faults in my letters? I never read them over, and I fancy there are. What do you do then? do you guess my meaning; or are you acquainted with my manner of mistaking? I lost my handkerchief in the Mall to-night with lord Radnor: but I made him walk with me to find it, and find it I did not. Tisdall (that lodges with me) and I have had no conversation, nor do we pull off our hats in the streets. There is a cousin of his (I suppose), a young parson, that lodges in the house too; a handsome genteel fellow. Dick Tighe and his wife lodged over-against us; and he has been seen, out of our upper windows, beating her two or three times: they are both gone to Ireland, but not together; and he solemnly vows, never to live with her. Neighbours do not stick to say, that she has a tongue: in short, I am told, she is the most urging provoking devil that ever was born; and he a hot whiffling puppy, very apt to resent. I will keep this bottom till to-morrow: I am sleepy.

LETTER

LETTER XXX

Sept. 8–25, 1711.

. . . 19. The queen designs to have cards and dancing here next week, which makes us think she will stay here longer than we believed. Mrs. Masham is not well after her lying-in: I doubt she got some cold; she is lame in one of her legs with a rheumatic pain. Dr. Arbuthnot and Mrs. Hill go to-morrow to Kensington to see her, and return the same night. Mrs. Hill and I dined with the Doctor to-day. I rode out this morning with the Doctor to see Cranburn, a house of lord Ranelagh's, and the duchess of Marlborough's lodge, and the Park; the finest places they are, for nature and plantations, that ever I saw; and the finest riding upon artificial roads, made on purpose for the queen. Arbuthnot made me draw up a sham subscription for a book, called *A History of the Maids of honour since Harry the Eighth*, shewing they make the best wives, with a list of all the maids of honour since, &c.; to pay a crown in hand, and the other crown upon delivery of the book; and all in common forms of those things. We got a gentleman to write it fair, because my hand is known; and we sent it to the maids of honour, when they came to supper. If they bite at it, it will be a very good court jest; and the queen will certainly have it; we did not tell Mrs. Hill.

20. To-day I was invited to the green-cloth by colonel Godfrey, who married the duke of Marlborough's sister, mother to the duke of Berwick by king James: I must tell you those things that happened before you were born. But I made my excuses, and young Harcourt (lord keeper's son) and I dined with my next neighbour Dr. Adams. Mrs. Masham is better, and will be here in three

or

or four days. She had need; for the duchess of Somerset is thought to gain ground daily.—We have not sent you over all your bills; and I think we have altered your money-bill. The duke of Ormond is censured here, by those in power, for very wrong management in the affair of the mayoralty. He is governed by fools; and has usually much more sense than his advisers, but never proceeds by it. I must know how your health continues after Wexford. Walk and use exercise, sirrahs both; and get somebody to play at shuttlecock with you, madam Stella, and walk to the dean's and Donnybroke.

21. Colonel Godfrey sent to me again to-day; so I dined at the green-cloth, and we had but eleven at dinner, which is a small number there, the Court being always thin of company till Saturday night.—This new ink and pen make a strange figure; *I must write larger, yes I must, or Stella will not be able to read this.*[1] S. S. S. there is your S s for you, Stella. The maids of honour are bit, and have all contributed their crowns, and are teazing others to subscribe for the book. I will tell lord keeper and lord treasurer to-morrow; and I believe the queen will have it. After a little walk this evening, I squandered away the rest of it in sitting at Lewis's lodging, while he and Dr. Arbuthnot played at piquet. I have that foolish pleasure, which I believe nobody has beside me, except old lady Berkeley. But I fretted when I came away; I will loiter so no more, for I have a plaguy deal of business upon my hands, and very little time to do it. The pamphleteers begin to be very busy against the ministry: I have begged Mr. secretary to make examples of one or two of them; and he assures me he will. They are very bold and abusive.

22. This being the day the ministry come to Windsor,

[1] These words in Italicks are written enormously large.

I ate

I ate a bit or two at Mr. Lewis's lodgings, because I must sup with lord treasurer; and at half an hour after one, I led Mr. Lewis a walk up the avenue, which is two miles long: we walked in all about five miles; but I was so tired with his slow walking, that I left him here, and walked two miles towards London, hoping to meet lord treasurer, and return with him; but it grew darkish, and I was forced to walk back, so I walked nine miles in all; and lord treasurer did not come till after eight; which is very wrong, for there was no Moon, and I often tell him how ill he does to expose himself so; but he only makes a jest of it. I supped with him, and staid till now, when it is half an hour after two. He is as merry and careless and disengaged as a young heir at one and twenty. It is late indeed. . . .

LETTER XXXII

London, October 9, 1711.

I WAS forced to lie down at twelve to-day, and mend my night's sleep: I slept till after two, and then sent for a bit of mutton and pot of ale from the next cook's shop, and had no stomach. I went out at four, and called to see Biddy Floyd, which I had not done these three months: she is something marked, but has recovered her complexion quite, and looks very well. Then I sat the evening with Mrs. Vanhomrigh, and drank coffee, and ate an egg. I likewise took a new lodging to-day, not liking a ground floor, nor the ill smell, and other circumstances. I lodge, or shall lodge, by Leicester-Fields, and pay ten shillings a week; that will not hold out long, faith. I shall lie here but one night more. It rained terribly till one o'clock today. I lie, for I shall lie here two nights, till Thursday, and then remove. Did I tell you that my friend Mrs. Barton has a brother drowned, that went on the expedition

tion with Jack Hill? He was a lieutenant-colonel, and a coxcomb; and she keeps her chamber in form, and the servants say, she receives no messages.—Answer MD's letter, Presto, d'ye hear? No, says Presto, I will not yet, I am busy: you are a saucy rogue. Who talks?

10. It cost me two shillings in coach-hire to dine in the city with a printer. I have sent, and caused to be sent, three pamphlets out in a fortnight. I will ply the rogues warm; and whenever any thing of theirs makes a noise, it shall have an answer. I have instructed an under-spur-leather to write so, that it is taken for mine. A rogue that writes a news-paper called *The Protestant Post-boy*, has reflected on me in one of his papers; but the secretary has taken him up, and he shall have a squeeze extraordinary. He says, 'That an ambitious Tantivy, missing of his towering hopes of preferment in Ireland, is come over, to vent his spleen on the late ministry, &c.' I will Tantivy him with a vengeance. I sat the evening at home and am very busy, and can hardly find time to write, unless it were to MD. I am in furious haste.

11. I dined to-day with lord treasurer. Thursdays are now his days when his choice company comes, but we are too much multiplied. George Granville sent his excuses upon being ill; I hear he apprehends the apoplexy, which would grieve me much. Lord treasurer calls Prior nothing but Monsieur Baudrier, which was the feigned name of the Frenchman that writ his journey to Paris. They pretend to suspect me; so I talk freely of it, and put them out of their play. Lord treasurer calls me now Dr. Martin, because Martin[1] is a sort of a swallow, and so is a Swift.

[1] From this pleasantry of my lord Oxford, the appellative Martinus Scriblerus took its rise.—[Dr. Goldsmith (in his Life of Parnell) supposes the Scriblerus society to have commenced soon after 1706, and to have ceased at the death of Parnell in 1718.—From the circumstance here mentioned of Mr. Harley, who was occasionally a member of the club, as

When

When he and I came last Monday from Windsor, we were reading all the signs on the road. He is a pure trifler; tell the bishop of Clogher so. I made him make two lines in verse for the Bell and Dragon, and they were rare bad ones. I suppose Dilly is with you by this time: what could his reason be of leaving London, and not owning it? It was plaguy silly. I believe his natural inconstancy made him weary: I think he is the king of inconstancy. I stayed with lord treasurer till ten; we had five lords and three commoners. Go to ombre, sirrahs.

12. Mrs. Vanhomrigh has changed her lodging as well as I. She found she had got with a bawd, and removed: I dined with her to-day; for though she boards, her landlady does not dine with her. I am grown a mighty lover of

appears by his humourous verses in vol. XX. p. 23, it seems probable that the Society was not formed sooner than 1710–11; and, in proof of this, it actually appears that Swift was newly acquainted with Arbuthnot in March that year. The lighter publications of this friendly knot of wits seem to begin in 1712, and to end in 1714. But their *Art of Sinking in Poetry* appeared not till 1727, the last year of the dean's being in England, when the foundation was laid for *The Memoirs of Scriblerus*, the first book of which is printed in Mr. Pope's Works, whose learned Commentator has favoured the publick with the following curious particulars on that subject: 'Mr. Pope, Dr. Arbuthnot, and Dr. Swift, projected to write a satire, in conjunction, on the abuses of human learning; and, to make it the better received, they proposed to do it in the manner of Cervantes (the original author of this species of satire) under the history of some feigned adventures.—But the separation of our Author's friends, which soon after happened, with the death of one, and the infirmities of the other, put a final stop to their project, when they had only drawn out an imperfect essay towards it, under the title of *The First Book of the Memoirs of Scriblerus*.—Polite letters never lost more than in the defeat of this scheme, in which, each of this illustrious triumvirate would have found exercise for his own peculiar talent; besides constant employment for that they all had in common. Dr. Arbuthnot was skilled in every thing which related to science; Mr. Pope was a master in the fine arts; and Dr. Swift excelled in the knowledge of the World. Wit they had all in equal measure; and this so large, that no age perhaps ever produced three men, to whom Nature had more beautifully bestowed it, or Art brought it to higher perfection.'—The Travels of Gulliver, The Treatise of the Profound, of Literary Criticisms on Virgil, and the Memoirs of a Parish-clerk, are only so many detached parts and fragments of this Work. N.]

of herrings; but they are much smaller here than with you. In the afternoon I visited an old major-general, and eat six oysters; then sat an hour with Mrs. Colledge, the joiner's daughter that was hanged; it was the joiner was hanged, and not his daughter; with Thompson's wife, a magistrate. There was the famous Mrs. Floyd of Chester, who, I think, is the handsomest woman (except MD) that ever I saw. She told me, that twenty people had sent her the verses upon Biddy,[1] as meant to her: and indeed, in point of handsomeness, she deserves them much better. I will not go to Windsor to-morrow, and so I told the secretary to-day. I hate the thoughts of Saturday and Sunday suppers with lord treasurer. Jack Hill is come home from his unfortunate expedition, and is, I think, now at Windsor: I have not yet seen him. He is privately blamed by his own friends, for want of conduct. He called a council of war, and therein it was determined to come back. But they say, a general should not do that, because the officers will always give their opinion for returning, since the blame will not lie upon them, but the general: I pity him heartily. Bernage received his commission to-day.

13. I dined to-day with colonel Crowe, late governor of Barbadoes; he is a great acquaintance of your friend Sterne, to whom I trusted the box. Lord treasurer has refused Sterne's business; and I doubt he is a rake; Jemmy Leigh stays for him, and nobody knows where to find him. I am so busy now, I have hardly time to spare to write to our little MD; but in a fortnight I hope it will be over. I am going now to be busy, &c.

14. I was going to dine with Dr. Cockburn; but Sir Andrew Fountain met me, and carried me to Mrs. Van's, where I drank the last bottle of Raymond's wine, admirable good, better than any I get among the ministry. I

[1] Mrs. Floyd, Lord Berkeley's housekeeper. N.

must

must pick up time to answer this letter of MD's; I will do it in a day or two for certain.—I am glad I am not at Windsor, for it is very cold, and I will not have a fire till November. I am contriving how to stop up my grate with bricks. Patrick was drunk last night; but did not come to me, else I should have given him the other cuff. I sat this evening with Mrs. Barton, it is the first day of her seeing company: but I made her merry enough, and we were three hours disputing upon Whig and Tory. She grieved for her brother only for form, and he was a sad dog. Is Stella well enough to go to church, pray? no numbings left? no darkness in your eyes? do you walk and exercise? Your exercise is ombre.—People are coming to town; the queen will be at Hampton-court in a week. Lady Betty Germaine, I hear, is come, and lord Pembroke is coming: his new wife is as big with child as she can tumble.

15. I sat at home till four this afternoon to-day writing, and ate a roll and butter; then visited Will Congreve an hour or two, and supped with lord treasurer, who came from Windsor to-day, and brought Prior with him. The queen has thanked Prior for his good service in France, and promised to make him a commissioner of the customs. Several of that commission are to be out; among the rest, my friend Sir Matthew Dudley; I can do nothing for him, he is so hated by the ministry. Lord treasurer kept me till twelve, so I need not tell you it is now late. . . .

LETTER XL

London, *Jan*. 26, 1711–12.

I HAVE no gilt paper left of this size, so you must be content with plain. Our Society dined together to-day; for it was put off, as I told you, upon lord Marlborough's business,

business, on Thursday. The duke of Ormond dined with us to-day, the first time; we were thirteen at table; and lord Lansdown came in after dinner, so that we wanted but three. The secretary proposed the duke of Beaufort, who desires to be one of our Society; but I stopt it, because the duke of Ormond doubts a little about it, and he was gone before it was proposed. I left them at seven, and sat this evening with poor Mrs. Wesley, who has been mighty ill to-day with a fainting fit: she has often convulsions too; she takes a mixture with *assa fœtida*, which I have now in my nose; and every thing smells of it. I never smelt it before, it is abominable. We have eight pacquets, they say, due from Ireland.

27. I could not see prince Eugene at Court to-day, the crowd was so great. The Whigs contrive to have a crowd always about him, and employ the rabble to give the word, when he sets out from any place. When the duchess of Hamilton came from the queen after church, she whispered me, 'that she was going to pay me a visit': I went to lady Oglethorp's, the place appointed; for ladies always visit me in third places, and she kept me till near four: she talks too much, is a plaguy detractor, and I believe I shall not much like her. I was engaged to dine with lord Masham; they staid as long as they could, yet had almost dined, and were going in anger to pull down the brass peg for my hat, but lady Masham saved it. At eight I went again to lord Masham's; lord treasurer is generally there at night: we sat up till almost two. Lord treasurer has engaged me to contrive some way to keep the archbishop of York from being seduced by lord Nottingham. I will do what I can in it to-morrow. It is very late, so I must go sleep.

28. Poor Mrs. Manley the author is very ill of a dropsy and sore leg; the printer tells me, 'he is afraid she cannot

live

live long'. I am heartily sorry for her; she has very generous principles for one of her sort; and a great deal of good sense and invention: she is about forty, very homely, and very fat. Mrs. Van made me dine with her to-day. I was this morning with the duke of Ormond and the prolocutor, about what lord treasurer spoke to me yesterday; I know not what will be the issue. There is but a slender majority in the house of lords; and we want more. We are sadly mortified at the news of the French taking the town in Brasil from the Portuguese. The sixth edition of three thousand of the *Conduct of the Allies* is sold, and the printer talks of a seventh: eleven thousand of them have been sold; which is a most prodigious run. The little two-penny *Letter of Advice to the October Club* does not sell; I know not the reason; for it is finely written, I assure you; and, like a true author, I grow fond of it, because it does not sell: you know that is usual to writers, to condemn the judgement of the world: if I had hinted it to be mine, every body would have bought it; but it is a great secret.

26. I borrowed one or two idle books of *Contes de Fees*, and have been reading them these two days, although I have much business upon my hands. I loitered till one at home: then went to Mr. Lewis at his office; and the vice chamberlain told me, 'That lady Ryalton had yesterday resigned her employment of lady of the bed-chamber, and that lady Jane Hyde, lord Rochester's daughter, a mighty pretty girl, is to succeed'; he said too, 'That lady Sunderland would resign in a day or two.' I dined with Lewis, and then went to see Mrs. Wesley, who is better to-day. But you must know, that Mr. Lewis gave me two letters, one from the bishop of Cloyne, with an inclosed from lord Inchiquin to lord treasurer; which he desires I would deliver and recommend. I am told, that lord was much

much in with lord Wharton, and I remember he was to have been one of the lords justices by his recommendation; yet the bishop recommends him as a great friend to the church, &c. I'll do what I think proper. The other letter was from little saucy MD, N. 26. O Lord, never saw the like, under a cover too, and by way of journal; we shall never have done. Sirrahs; how durst you write so soon, sirrahs? I won't answer it yet.

30. I was this morning with the secretary, who was sick, and out of humour: he would needs drink Champagne some days ago, on purpose to spite me, because I advised him against it, and now he pays for it. Stella used to do such tricks formerly; he put me in mind of her. Lady Sunderland has resigned her place too. It is lady Catharine Hyde that succeeds lady Ryalton; and not lady Jane. Lady Catharine is the late earl of Rochester's daughter. I dined with the secretary, then visited his lady; and sat this evening with lady Masham; the secretary came to us: but lord treasurer did not; he dined with the master of the rolls, and staid late with him. Our Society does not meet till to-morrow sevennight, because we think the parliament will be very busy to-morrow upon the state of the war; and the secretary, who is to treat as president, must be in the house. I fancy my talking of persons and things here must be very tedious to you, because you know nothing of them; and I talk as if you did. You know Kevin's-street, and Werburgh-street, and (what do you call the street where Mrs. Walls lives?) and Ingoldsby, and Higgins, and lord Santry; but what care you for lady Catharine Hyde? Why do you say nothing of your health, sirrah? I hope it is well.

31. Trimnel, bishop of Norwich, who was with this lord Sunderland at Moore park in their travels, preached yesterday before the house of lords; and to-day the question

tion was put to thank him, and print his sermon; but passed against him; for it was a terrible Whig sermon. The Bill to repeal the Act for naturalizing Protestant foreigners passed the house of lords to-day by a majority of twenty, though the Scotch lords went out, and would vote neither way, in discontent about duke Hamilton's patent, if you know any thing of it. A poem is come out to-day inscribed to me, by way of a flirt; for it is a Whiggish poem, and good for nothing. They plagued me with it in the court of requests. I dined with lord treasurer at five alone, only with one Dutchman. Prior is now a commissioner of the customs. I told you so before, I suppose. When I came home to-night, I found a letter from Dr. Sacheverell, thanking me for recommending his brother to lord treasurer and Mr. secretary for a place. Lord treasurer sent to him about it: so good a solicitor was I, although I once hardly thought I should be a solicitor for Sacheverell.

Feb. 1. Has not your dean of St. Patrick's received my letter? You say nothing of it, although I writ above a month ago. My printer has got the gout, and I was forced to go to him to-day, and there I dined. It was a most delicious day; why don't you observe whether the same days be fine with you? To-night at six Dr. Atterbury, and Prior, and I, and Dr. Freind, met at Dr. Robert Freind's house at Westminster, who is master of the school: there we sat till one, and were good enough company. I here take leave to tell politic Dingley, that the passage in the *Conduct of the Allies* is so far from being blameable, that the secretary designs to insist upon it in the house of commons, when the Treaty of Barrier is debated there, as it now shortly will, for they have ordered it to be laid before them. The pamphlet of *Advice to the October Club* begins now to sell; but I believe it's fame

will

will hardly reach Ireland: it is finely written, I assure you. I long to answer your letter; but won't yet; you know it is late, &c.

2. This day ends Christmas; and what care I? I have neither seen, nor felt, nor heard any Christmas this year. I passed a lazy dull day: I was this morning with lord treasurer, to get some papers from him, which he will remember as much as a cat, although it be his own business. It threatened rain, but did not much; and Prior and I walked an hour in the Park, which quite put me out of my measures. I dined with a friend hard by; and in the evening sat with lord Masham till twelve. Lord treasurer did not come; this is an idle dining day usually with him. We want to hear from Holland how our peace goes on; for we are afraid of those scoundrels the Dutch, lest they should play us tricks. Lord Marr, a Scotch earl, was with us at lord Masham's; I was arguing with him about the stubbornness and folly of his countrymen; they are so angry about the affair of duke Hamilton, whom the queen has made a duke of England, and the house of lords will not admit him: he swears, 'he would vote for us, but dare not; because all Scotland would detest him if he did; he should never be chosen again, nor be able to live there.'

3. I was at Court to-day to look for a dinner; but did not like any that were offered me; and I dined with lord Mountjoy. The queen has the gout in her knee, and was not at chapel. I hear we have a Dutch mail; but I know not what news, although I was with the secretary this morning. He shewed me a letter from the Hanover envoy, M. Bothmar, complaining that the Barrier Treaty is laid before the house of commons; and desiring that no infringement may be made in the Guarantee of the Succession; but the secretary has written him a peppering answer. I fancy you understand all this, and are able

state-

state-girls, since you have read the *Conduct of the Allies.* We are all preparing against the birth-day, I think it is Wednesday next. If the queen's gout increases, it will spoil sport. Prince Eugene has two fine suits made against it: and the queen is to give him a sword worth four thousand pounds, the diamonds set transparent.

4. I was this morning soliciting at the house of commons' door for Mr. Vesey, a son of the archbishop of Tuam, who has petitioned for a Bill, to relieve him in some difficulty about his estate; I secured him about fifty members. I dined with lady Masham. We have no pacquet from Holland, as I was told yesterday; and this wind will hinder many people from appearing at the birth-day, who expected cloaths from Holland. I appointed to meet a gentleman at the secretary's to-night, and they both failed. The house of commons have this day made many severe votes about our being abused by our allies. Those who spoke, drew all their arguments from my book, and their votes confirm all I writ; the Court had a majority of a hundred and fifty: all agree, that it was my book that spirited them to these resolutions; I long to see them in print. My head has not been so well as I could wish it for some days past; but I have not had any giddy fit, and I hope it will go over.

5. The secretary turned me out of his room this morning, and shewed me fifty guineas rolled up, which he was going to give to some French spy. I dined with four Irishmen at a tavern to-day; I thought I had resolved against it before, but I broke it. I played at cards this evening at lady Masham's, but I only played for her while she was writing; and I won her a pool; and supt there. Lord treasurer was with us, but went away before twelve. The ladies and lords have all their cloaths ready against to-morrow: I saw several mighty fine; and I hope there will

be

be a great appearance, in spite of that spiteful French fashion of the Whiggish ladies not to come, which they have all resolved to a woman; and I hope it will more spirit the queen against them for ever.

6. I went to dine at lord Masham's at three, and met all the company just coming out of Court; a mighty crowd; they staid long for their coaches: I had an opportunity of seeing several lords and ladies of my acquaintance in their fineries. Lady Ashburnham looked the best in my eyes. They say, the Court was never fuller nor finer. Lord treasurer, his lady, and two daughters, and Mrs. Hill, dined with lord and lady Masham; the five ladies were monstrous fine. The queen gave prince Eugene the diamond sword to-day; but nobody was by when she gave it, except my lord chamberlain. There was an entertainment of Opera songs at night; and the queen was at all the entertainment, and is very well after it. I saw lady Wharton, as ugly as the Devil, coming out in the crowd all in an undress; she had been with the Marlborough daughters and lady Bridgewater in St. James's, looking out of the window, all undressed, to see the sight. I do not hear that one Whig lady was there, except those of the bed-chamber. Nothing has made so great a noise as one Kelson's chariot, that cost nine hundred and thirty pounds, the finest was ever seen. The rabble huzzaed him as much as they did prince Eugene. This is birth-day chat.

7. Our Society met to-day, the duke of Ormond was not with us; we have lessened our dinners, which were grown so extravagant, that lord treasurer and every body else cried shame. I left them at seven, visited for an hour, and then came home, like a good boy. The queen is much better after yesterday's exercise: her friends wish she would use a little more. I opposed lord Jersey's election into

into our Society, and he is refused: I likewise opposed the duke of Beaufort; but I believe he will be chosen in spite of me: I don't much care; I shall not be with them above two months; for I resolve to set out for Ireland the beginning of April next (before I treat them again), and see my willows.

8. I dined to-day in the city; this morning a scoundrel dog, one of the queen's musick, a German, whom I had never seen, got access to my chamber by Patrick's folly, and gravely desired me to get an employment in the customs for a friend of his, who would be very grateful; and likewise to forward a project of his own, for raising ten thousand pounds a year upon Operas: I used him civiler than he deserved; but it vexed me to the pluck. He was told, 'I had a mighty interest with lord treasurer, and one word of mine, &c.'—Well; I got home early, on purpose to answer MD's letter, N. 26; for this goes to-morrow.—Well; I never saw such a letter in all my life; so saucy, so journalish, so sanguine, so pretending, so every thing.—I satisfied all your fears in my last. All is gone well, as you say; yet you are an impudent slut, to be so positive; you will swagger so upon your sagacity, that we shall never have done. Pray don't mislay your reply; I would certainly print it, if I had it here: how long is it? I suppose, half a sheet: was the Answer written in Ireland? Yes, yes, you shall have a letter when you come from Baligall. I need not tell you again who 's out and who 's in: we can never get out the duchess of Somerset.—So, they say Presto writ the Conduct, &c. Do they like it? I don't care whether they do or no; but the Resolutions printed the other day in the Votes are almost quotations from it; and would never have passed, if that book had not been written. I will not meddle with the *Spectator*, let him fair-sex it to the world's end. My disorder

order is over, but blood was not from the p—les.—Well, madam Dingley, the frost; why we had a great frost, but I forget how long ago; it lasted above a week or ten days: I believe about six weeks ago; but it did not break so soon with us, I think, as December 29; yet I think it was about that time, on second thoughts. MD can have no letter from Presto, says you; and yet four days before you own you had my thirty-seventh, unreasonable sluts! The bishop of Gloucester is not dead, and I am as likely to succeed the duke of Marlborough as him if he were; there's enough for that now. It is not unlikely that the duke of Shrewsbury will be your governor; at least I believe the duke of Ormond will not return.—Well, Stella again: why really three editions of the Conduct, &c. is very much for Ireland; it is a sign you have some honest among you.—Well; I will do Mr. Manley all the service I can: but he will ruin himself. What business had he to engage at all about the city? cannot he wish his cause well, and be quiet, when he finds that stirring will do it no good, and himself a great deal of hurt? I cannot imagine who should open my letter; it must be done at your side.—If I hear of any thoughts of turning out Mr. Manley, I will endeavour to prevent it. I have already had all the gentlemen of Ireland here upon my back often, for defending him. So now I have answered your saucy letter. My humble service to goody Stoyte and Catharine; I will come soon for my dinner.

9. Morning. My cold goes off at last; but I think I have got a small new one. I have no news since last. They say, 'We hear, by the way of Calais, that peace is very near concluding.' I hope it may be true. I'll go and seal up my letter, and give it myself to-night into the post-office; and so I bid my dearest MD farewell to-night. I heartily wish myself with them, as hope saved. My willows,

lows, and quicksets, and trees, will be finely improved, I hope, this year. It has been fine hard frosty weather yesterday and to-day. Farewell, &c. &c. &c.

LETTER XLIV

London, *March*, 22, 1711–12.

UGLY, nasty weather. I was in the city to-day with Mrs. Wesley and Mrs. Percival, to get money from a banker for Mrs. Wesley, who goes to Bath on Thursday. I left them there, and dined with a friend, and went to see lord treasurer; but he had people with him I did not know: so I went to lady Masham's, and lost a crown with her at picquet, and then sate with lord Masham and lord treasurer, &c. there till past one; but I had my man with me, to come home. I gave in my forty-third, and one for the bishop of Clogher, to the post-office, as I came from the city; and so oo know 'tis late now, and I have nothing to say for this day. Our Mohocks are all vanished; however, I shall take care of my person. Nite my own two deelest nautyas MD.

23. I was this morning, before church, with the secretary, about lord Abercorn's business, and some others. My soliciting season is come, and will last as long as the session. I went late to court, and the company was almost gone. The court serves me for a coffee-house; once a week I meet acquaintance there, that I should not otherwise see in a quarter. There is a flying report, that the French have offered a cessation of arms, and to give us Dunkirk, and the Dutch Namur, for security, till the peace is made. The duke of Ormond, they say, goes in a week. Abundance of his equipage is already gone. His friends are afraid the expence of this employment will ruin him, since he must lose the government of Ireland.

I dined

I dined privately with a friend, and refused all dinners offered me at court; which, however, were but two, and I did not like either. Did I tell you of a scoundrel about the court, that sells employments to ignorant people, and cheats them of their money? He lately made a bargain for the vice-chamberlain's place, for seven thousand pounds, and had received some guineas earnest; but the whole thing was discovered tother day, and examination taken of it by lord Dartmouth, and I hope he will be swinged. The vice-chamberlain told me several particulars of it last night at lord Masham's. Can DD play at ombre yet, enough to hold the cards while Ppt steps into the next room? Nite deelest sollahs.[1]

24. This morning I recommended Newcomb again to the duke of Ormond, and left Dick Stewart to do it farther. Then I went to visit the duchess of Hamilton, who was not awake. So I went to the duchess of Shrewsbury, and sat an hour at her toilet. I talked to her about the duke's being lord-lieutenant. She said she knew nothing of it; but I rallied her out of that, and she resolves not to stay behind the duke. I intend to recommend the bishop of Clogher to her for an acquaintance. He will like her very well: she is, indeed, a most agreeable woman, and a great favourite of mine. I know not whether the ladies in Ireland will like her. I was at the Court of Requests, to get some lords to be at a committee to-morrow, about a friend's bill: and then the duke of Beaufort gave me a poem, finely bound in folio, printed at Stamford, and writ by a country squire. Lord Exeter desired the duke to give it the queen, because the author is his friend; but the duke desired I would let him know whether it was good for any thing. I brought it home, and will return it to-morrow, as the dullest thing I ever read; and advise

[1] All after 'yet' is partially obliterated. (R.)

the

the duke not to present it. I dined with Domville at his lodgings, by invitation; for he goes in a few days for Ireland. Nite dee MD.

25. There is a mighty feast at a Tory sheriff's to-day in the city: twelve hundred dishes of meat.—Above five lords, and several hundred gentlemen, will be there, and give four or five guineas a-piece, according to custom. Dr. Coghill and I dined, by invitation, at Mrs. Van's. It has rained or mizzled all day, as my pockets feel. There are two new answers come out to the Conduct of the Allies. The last year's *Examiners*, printed together in a small volume, go off but slowly. The printer over-printed himself by at least a thousand; so soon out of fashion are party papers, however so well writ. The Medleys are coming out in the same volume, and perhaps may sell better. Our news about a cessation of arms begins to flag, and I have not these three days seen any body in business to ask them about it. We had a terrible fire last night in Drury-Lane, or thereabouts, and three or four people destroyed. One of the maids of honour has the small-pox: but the best is, she can lose no beauty; and we have one new handsome maid of honour. Nite MD.

26. I forgot to tell you, that on Sunday last, about seven at night, it lightened above fifty times as I walked the Mall, which I think is extraordinary at this time of the year, and the weather was very hot. Had you any thing of this in Dublin? I intended to dine with lord treasurer to-day; but lord Mansel and Mr. Lewis made me dine with them at Kit Musgrave's. I sate the evening with Mrs. Wesley, who goes to-morrow morning to the Bath. She is much better than she was. The news of the French desiring a cessation of arms, &c. was but town talk. We shall know in a few days, as I am told, whether there will be a peace or not. The duke of Ormond will go

in

in a week for Flanders, they say. Our Mohocks go on still, and cut people's faces every night, fais, they shan't cut mine. I like it better as it is. The dogs will cost me at least a crown a-week in chairs. I believe the souls of your houghers of cattle have got into them, and now they don't distinguish between a cow and a Christian. I forgot to wish you yesterday a happy new-year. You know the twenty-fifth of March is the first day of the year, and now you must leave off cards, and put out your fire. I'll put out mine the first of April, cold or not cold. I believe I shall lose credit with you, by not coming over at the beginning of April; but I hoped the session would be ended, and I must stay till then; yet I would fain be at the beginning of my willows growing. Percival tells me, that the quicksets upon the flat in the garden do not grow so well as those famous ones on the ditch. They want digging about them. The cherry trees, by the river side, my heart is set upon. Nite MD.

27. Society day. You know that, I suppose. Dr. Arthburnett [Arbuthnot] was president. His dinner was dressed in the queen's kitchen, and was mighty fine. We eat it at Ozinda's Chocolate-house, just by St. James's. We were never merrier, nor better company, and did not part till after eleven. I did not summon lord Lansdown: he and I are fallen out. There was something in an *Examiner* a fortnight ago, that he thought reflected on the abuses in his office, (he is secretary-at-war,) and he writ to the secretary, that he heard I had inserted that paragraph. This I resented highly, that he should complain of me before he spoke to me. I sent him a peppering letter, and would not summon him by a note, as I did the rest; nor ever will have any thing to say to him, till he begs my pardon. I met lord treasurer to-day, at lady Masham's. He would fain have carried me home to dinner,

but

but I begged his pardon. What! upon a Society day! No, no. 'Tis rate, sollahs. I a'nt dlunk.—Nite MD.

28. I was with my friend Lewis to-day, getting materials for a little mischief; and I dined with lord treasurer, and three or four fellows I never saw before. I left them at seven, and came home, and have been writing to the archbishop of Dublin, and cousin Deane, in answer to one of his of four months old, that I spied by chance, routing among my papers. I have a pain these two days exactly upon the top of my left shoulder. I fear it is something rheumatic; it winches now & then. Shall I put flannel to it? Domville is going to Ireland; he came here this morning to take leave of me, but I shall dine with him to-morrow. Does the bishop of Clogher talk of coming for England this summer? I think lord Molesworth told me so about two months ago. The weather is bad again; rainy and very cold this evening. Do you know what the longitude is? A projector has been applying himself to me, to recommend him to the ministry, because he pretends to have found out the longitude. I believe he has no more found it out than he has found out mine ****.[1] However, I will gravely hear what he says, and discover him a knave or fool. Nite MD.

29. I am plagued with these pains in my shoulder; I believe it is rheumatic; I will do something for it to-night. Mr. Lewis and I dined with Mr. Domville, to take our leave of him. I drank three or four glasses of champagne by perfect teasing, though it is bad for my pain; but if it continue, I will not drink any wine without water till I am well. The weather is abominably cold and wet. I am got into bed, and have put some old flannel, for want of new, to my shoulder; and rubbed it with Hungary water. It is plaguy hard. I never would drink any wine, if it

[1] Word obliterated.

were

were not for my head, and drinking has given me this pain. I will try abstemiousness for a while. How does MD do now; how does DD, and Ppt? You must know I hate pain, as the old woman said. But I'll try to go seep. My flesh sucks up Hungary water rarely. My man is an awkward rascal, and makes me peevish. Do you know that t' other day he was forced to beg my pardon, that he could not shave my head, his hand shook so? He is drunk every day, and I design to turn him off soon as ever I get to Ireland. I'll write no more now, but go to sleep, and see whether sleep and flannel will cure my shoulder. Nite deelest MD.

30. I was not able to go to church or court to-day for my shoulder. The pain has left my shoulder, and crept to my neck and collar-bone. It makes me think of poor Ppt's bladebone. Urge, urge, urge; dogs gnawing. I went in a chair at two, and dined with Mrs. Van, where I could be easy, and came back at seven. My Hungary water is gone; and to-night use spirits of wine; which my landlady tells me is very good. It has rained terribly hard all day long, and is extremely cold. I am very uneasy, and such cruel twinges every moment! Nite deelest MD.

31. April 1, 2, 3, 4, 5, 6, 7, 8. All these days I have been extremely ill; though I twice crawled out a week ago; but am now recovering, though very weak. The violence of my pain abated the night before last: I will just tell you how I was, and then send away this letter, which ought to have gone Saturday last. The pain increased with mighty violence in my left shoulder and collar-bone, and that side my neck. On Thursday morning appeared great red spots in all those places where my pain was, and the violence of the pain was confined to my neck behind, a little on the left side; which was so violent, that I had not a minute's ease, nor hardly a minute's sleep in three days and

and nights. The spots increased every day, and bred red little pimples, which are now grown white, and full of corruption, though small. The red still continues too, and most prodigious hot and inflamed. The disease is the shingles. I eat nothing but water-gruel; am very weak; but out of all violent pain. The doctors say it would have ended in some violent disease if it had not come out thus. I shall now recover fast. I have been in no danger of life, but miserable torture. I must not write too much. So adieu, deelest MD MD MD FW FW, ME ME ME, Lele. I can say yet lele, oo see. Fais. I don't conceal a bit, as hope saved.

I must purge and clyster after this; and my next letter will not be in the old order of journal, till I have done with physic. An't oo surprised to see a letter want half a side?

LETTER LXIV

London, *May* 16, [1713.]

I HAD yours, N. 40, yesterday. Your new bishop acts very ungratefully. I cannot say so bad of it as he deserved. I begged at the same post his warrant and mine went over, that he would leave those livings to my disposal. I shall write this post to him to let him know how ill I take it. I have letters to tell me, that I ought to think of employing somebody to set the tithes of the deanery. I know not what to do at this distance. I cannot be in Ireland under a month. I will write two orders; one to Parvisol, and t'other to Parvisol, and a blank for whatever fellow it is whom the last dean employed; and I would desire you to advise with friends, which to make use of: and if the latter, let the fellow's name be inserted, and both act by commission. If the former, then speak to Parvisol, and know whether he can undertake it. I

doubt

doubt it is hardly to be done by a perfect stranger alone, as Parvisol is. He may perhaps venture at all, to keep up his interest with me; but that is needless, for I am willing to do him any good, that will do me no harm. Pray advise with Walls and Raymond, and a little with bishop Sterne for form. Tell Raymond I cannot succeed for him to get that living of Moimed. It is represented here as a great sinecure. Several chaplains have solicited for it; and it has vexed me so, that, if I live, I will make it my business to serve him better in something else. I am heartily sorry for his illness, and that of the other two. If it be not necessary to let the tithes till a month hence, you may keep the two papers, and advise well in the mean time; and whenever it is absolutely necessary, then give that paper which you are most advised to. I thank Mr. Walls for his letter. Tell him, that must serve for an answer, with my service to him and her. I shall buy Bishop Sterne's hair as soon as his household goods. I shall be ruined, or at least sadly cramped, unless the queen will give me a thousand pounds. I am sure she owes me a great deal more. Lord treasurer rallies me upon it, and I believe intends it; but, *quando*? I am advised to hasten over as soon as possible, and so I will, and hope to set out the beginning of June. Take no lodging for me. What? at your old tricks again? I can lie somewhere after I land, and I care not where, nor how. I will buy your eggs and bacon, DD **** your caps and Bible; and pray think immediately, and give me some commissions, and I will perform them as far as poor Pdfr can. The letter I sent before this was to have gone a post before; but an accident hindered it: and, I assure oo, I wam vely akklee MD did not write to Dean Pdfr, and I think oo might have had a dean under your girdle for the superscription. I have just finished my Treatise, and must be ten days correcting

recting it. Farewell, deelest MD, MD, MD, FW, FW, FW, MD, MD, MD, Lele, MD, FW, ME, Lele.

LETTER LXV

Chester, *June* 6, 1713.

I AM come here after six days. I set out on Monday last, and got here to-day about eleven in the morning. A noble rider, fais! and all the ships and people went off yesterday with a rare wind. This was told me, to my comfort, upon my arrival. Having not used riding these three years, made me terrible weary; yet I resolve on Monday to set out for Holyhead, as weary as I am. 'Tis good for my health, mun. When I came here, I found MD's letter of the 26th of May, sent down to me. Had you written a post sooner, I might have brought some pins: but you were lazy, and would not write your orders immediately, as I desired you. I will come, when God pleases; perhaps I may be with you in a week. I will be three days going to Holyhead; I cannot ride faster, say hat oo will. I am upon Stay-behind's mare. I have the whole inn to myself. I would fain 'scape this Holyhead journey; but I have no prospect of ships, and it will be almost necessary I should be in Dublin before the 25th instant, to take the others [oaths]; otherwise I must wait to a quarter sessions. I will lodge as I can; therefore take no lodgings for me, to pay in my absence. The poor dean can't afford it. I spoke again to the duke of Ormond about Moimed for Raymond, and hope he may yet have it, for I laid it strongly to the duke, and gave him the bishop of Meath's memorial. I am sorry for Raymond's fistula; tell him so. I will speak to lord treasurer about Mrs. South to-morrow.—Odso! I forgot; I thought I had been in London. Mrs. Tisdall is very big, ready to lie down.

Her

Her husband is a puppy. Do his feet stink still? The letters to Ireland go at so uncertain an hour, that I am forced to conclude. Farewell, MD MD MD FW FW FW ME ME ME ME

Lele lele
lele logues and
Ladies bose fair
and slender.

[*On flyleaf.*]

I mightily approve Ppt's project of hanging the blind parson. When I read that passage upon Chester walls, as I was coming into town, and just received your letter, I said aloud—Agreeable B—tch.

PRAYERS FOR STELLA

These prayers, composed by Swift and used by him at Stella's bedside during her fatal illness, attest at once the quality of his devotion to her, of his religion, and of his most personal style.

The first prayer is reproduced from the original edition, vol. viii of the quarto edition of Swift's *Works*, 1765.

The second and third prayers first appeared in Faulkner's edition of Swift's *Works*, vol. viii, 1746. They have been reproduced from the reprint of this edition, vol. viii, 1752.

ALMIGHTY and most gracious Lord God, extend, we beseech thee, thy pity and compassion towards this thy languishing servant: Teach her to place her hope and confidence entirely in thee; give her a true sense of the emptyness and vanity of all earthly things; make her truly sensible of all the infirmities of her life past, and grant to her such a true sincere repentance as is not to be repented of. Preserve her, O Lord, in a sound mind and understanding, during this thy visitation; keep her from both the sad extremes of presumption and despair. If thou shalt please to restore her to her former health, give her grace to be ever mindful of that mercy, and to keep those good resolutions she now makes in her sickness, so that no length of time, nor prosperity, may entice her to forget them. Let no thought of her misfortunes distract her mind, and prevent the means towards her recovery, or disturb her in her preparations for a better life. We beseech thee also, O Lord, of thy infinite goodness to remember the good actions of this thy servant; that the naked she hath clothed, the hungry she hath fed, the sick and the fatherless whom she hath relieved, may be reckoned according to thy gracious promise, as if they had been done unto thee. Hearken, O Lord, to the prayers offered up by the friends of this thy servant in her behalf, and especially those now made by us unto thee. Give thy blessing to those endeavours used for her recovery; but take from her all violent desire, either of life or death, further than with resignation to thy holy will. And now, O Lord, we implore thy gracious favour towards us here met together; grant that the sense of this thy servant's weakness may add strength to our faith, that we, considering the infirmities of our nature, and the uncertainty of life, may, by this example, be drawn to repentance before it shall please Thee to visit us in the like manner. Accept these prayers, we beseech Thee, for the sake of thy dear Son Jesus Christ, our Lord; who, with Thee and the Holy Ghost, liveth and reigneth ever one God world without end. Amen.

A prayer used by the dean for Mrs. Johnson, in her last sickness, written October 17, 1727.

MOST merciful Father, accept our humblest Prayers in Behalf of this thy languishing Servant: Forgive the Sins, the Frailties, and Infirmities of her Life past. Accept the good Deeds she hath done in such a Manner, that at whatever Time Thou shalt please to call her, she may be received into Everlasting Habitations. Give her Grace to continue sincerely thankful to Thee for the many Favours thou hast bestowed upon her; The Ability and Inclination, and Practice to do Good, and those Virtues, which have procured the Esteem and Love of her Friends, and a most unspotted Name in the World. O God, thou dispensest thy Blessings and thy Punishments, as it becometh infinite Justice and Mercy; and, since it was thy Pleasure to afflict her with a long, constant, weakly State of Health, make her truly sensible, that it was for very wise Ends, and was largely made up to her in other Blessings more valuable and less common. Continue to her, O Lord, that Firmness and Constancy of Mind, wherewith thou hast most graciously endowed her, together with that Contempt of worldly Things and Vanities, that she hath shewn in the whole Conduct of her Life. O All-powerful Being, the least motion of whose Will can create or destroy a World; pity us the mournful Friends of thy distressed Servant, who sink under the Weight of her present Condition, and the Fear of losing the

the most valuable of our Friends: Restore her to us, O Lord, if it be thy gracious Will, or inspire us with Constancy and Resignation, to support ourselves under so heavy an Affliction. Restore her, O Lord, for the Sake of those Poor, who by losing her, will be desolate; and those Sick, who will not only want her Bounty, but her Care and Tending; or else, in thy Mercy, raise up some other in her Place, with equal Disposition and better Abilities. Lessen, O Lord, we beseech thee, her bodily Pains, or give her a double Strength of Mind to support them. And if thou wilt soon take her to thyself, turn our Thoughts rather upon that Felicity which we hope she shall enjoy, than upon that unspeakable Loss we shall endure. Let her Memory be ever dear unto us; and the Example of her many Virtues, as far as human Infirmity will admit, our constant Imitation. Accept, O Lord, these Prayers, poured from the Bottom of our Hearts, in thy Mercy, and for the Merits of our Blessed Saviour. Amen.

Another, written Nov. 6, 1727.

O MERCIFUL Father, who never afflictest thy Children, but for their own Good, and with Justice, over which thy Mercy always prevaileth, either to turn them to Repentance, or to punish them in the present Life in order to reward them in a better; take Pity, we beseech thee, upon this thy poor afflicted Servant, languishing so long and so grievously under the Weight of thy Hand. Give her strength, O Lord, to support her Weakness; and Patience to endure her Pains, without repining at thy Correction. Forgive every rash and inconsiderate Expression, which her Anguish may at any Time force from her Tongue, while her Heart continueth in an entire Submission to thy Will. Suppress in her, O Lord, all eager Desires

Desires of Life, and lessen her Fears of Death, by inspireing into her an humble, yet assured, Hope of thy Mercy. Give her a sincere Repentance for all her Transgressions and Omissions, and a firm Resolution to pass the Remainder of her Life in endeavouring to her utmost to observe all thy Precepts. We beseech thee, likewise, to compose her Thoughts; and preserve to her the Use of her Memory and Reason during the course of her Sickness. Give her a true Conception of the Vanity, Folly, and Insignificancy of all human Things; and strengthen her so as to beget in her a sincere Love of thee in the Midst of her Sufferings. Accept, and impute, all her good Deeds; and forgive her all those Offences against thee, which she hath sincerely repented of, or through the Frailty of Memory hath forgot. And now, O Lord, we turn to thee, in Behalf of ourselves and the rest of her sorrowful Friends. Let not our Grief afflict her Mind, and thereby have an ill Effect on her present Distempers. Forgive the Sorrow and Weakness of those among us, who sink under the Grief and Terror of losing so dear and useful a Friend. Accept and pardon our most earnest Prayers and Wishes for her longer Continuance in this evil World, to do what thou art pleased to call thy Service, which is only her bounden Duty; that she may be still a Comfort to us, and to all others who will want the benefit of her Conversation, her Advice, her good Offices, or her Charity. And since thou hast promised, that where two or three are gathered together in thy Name, thou wilt be in the midst of them, to grant their Request; O gracious Lord, grant to us, who are here met in thy Name, that those Requests, which, in the utmost Sincerity and Earnestness of our Hearts we have now made in behalf of this thy distressed Servant and of ourselves, may effectually be answered; through the Merits of Jesus Christ our Lord. Amen.

ON THE DEATH OF MRS. JOHNSON

Swift received the news of Stella's death while he was entertaining friends at dinner, Sunday evening, January 28, 1728. As soon as he was alone, he commenced writing this tribute, which he continued on several succeeding evenings. His emotion may be read in and between the lines. The estimate of Stella's virtues given is not exaggerated by sentiment. All records of her confirm Swift's praise. Her modesty and kindliness; her patient devotion to the interests of Swift, who for reasons that have been buried with them never made her the full partner of his life that she longed to be; her self-forgetfulness in relieving the distresses of others; were noted by all who knew her. One can read history for a long time without encountering another woman who surpassed Stella in gentleness and heroism.

Not a line of all that she wrote to Swift has been preserved. While she carefully kept his letters to her, after her death he destroyed everything she had written to him. They were put beyond the reach of editors for ever.

The text reproduced is that of the original edition, vol. viii of the quarto edition of Swift's *Works*, 1765.

THIS day, being Sunday, January 28th, 1727–8, about eight o'clock at night a servant brought me a note, with an account of the death of the truest, most virtuous, and valuable friend, that I or perhaps any other person ever was blessed with. She expired about six in the evening of this day; and, as soon as I am left alone, which is about eleven at night, I resolve, for my own satisfaction, to say something of her life and character.

She was born at Richmond in Surrey on the thirteenth day of March, in the year 1681. Her father was a younger brother of a good family in Nottinghamshire, her mother of a lower degree; and indeed she had little to boast of her birth. I knew her from six years old, and had some share in her education, by directing what books she should read, and perpetually instructing her in the principles of honour and virtue; from which she never swerved in any one action or moment of her life. She was sickly from her childhood until about the age of fifteen: But then grew into perfect health, and was looked upon as one of the most beautiful, graceful, and agreeable young women in London, only a little too fat. Her hair was blacker than a raven, and every feature of her face in perfection. She lived generally in the country, with a family, where she contracted an intimate friendship with another lady of more advanced years. I was then (to my mortification) settled in Ireland; and, about a year after, going to visit my friends in England, I found she was a little uneasy upon the death of a person on whom she had some dependance. Her fortune, at that time, was in all not above fifteen hundred pounds, the interest of which was but a scanty maintenance, in so dear a country, for one of her spirit. Upon this consideration, and indeed very much for my own satisfaction, who had few friends or ac-

quaintance

quaintance in Ireland, I prevailed with her and her dear friend and companion, the other lady,[1] to draw what money they had into Ireland, a great part of their fortune being in annuities upon funds. Money was then at ten per cent. in Ireland besides the advantage of turning it, and all necessaries of life at half the price. They complied with my advice, and soon after came over; but, I happening to continue some time longer in England, they were much discouraged to live in Dublin, where they were wholly strangers. She was at that time about nineteen years old, and her person was soon distinguished. But the adventure looked so like a frolic, the censure held, for some time as if there were a secret history in such a removal; which, however, soon blew off by her excellent conduct. She came over with her friend on the
in the year 170–; and they both lived together until this day, when death removed her from us. For some years past, she had been visited with continual ill-health: and several times, within these two years her life was despaired of. But, for this twelve-month past, she never had a day's health; and properly speaking, she hath been dying six months, but kept alive, almost against nature, by the generous kindness of two physicians, and the care of her friends. Thus far I writ the same night between eleven and twelve.

Never was any of her sex born with better gifts of the mind, or more improved them by reading and conversation. Yet her memory was not of the best, and was impaired in the latter years of her life. But I cannot call to mind that I ever once heard her make a wrong judgment of persons, books, or affairs. Her advice was always the best, and with the greatest freedom, mixed with the greatest decency. She had a gracefulness somewhat more

[1] Mrs. Dingley.

than

than human in every motion, word, and action. Never was so happy a conjunction of civility, freedom, easiness and sincerity. There seemed to be a combination among all that knew her, to treat her with a dignity much beyond her rank: Yet people of all sorts were never more easy than in her company. Mr. Addison, when he was in Ireland, being introduced to her, immediately found her out; and if he had not soon after left the kingdom, assured me he would have used all endeavours to cultivate her friendship. A rude or conceited coxcomb passed his time very ill, upon the least breach of respect; for in such a case she had no mercy, but was sure to expose him to the contempt of the standers by; yet in such a manner as he was ashamed to complain, and durst not resent. All of us, who had the happiness of her friendship, agreed unanimously, that, in an afternoon or evening's conversation, she never failed before we parted of delivering the best thing that was said in the company. Some of us have written down several of her sayings, or what the French call *Bon Mots*, wherein she excelled almost beyond belief. She never mistook the understanding of others; nor ever said a severe word, but where a much severer was deserved.

Her servants loved and almost adored her at the same time. She would, upon occasions, treat them with freedom, yet her demeanour was so awful, that they durst not fail in the least point of respect. She chid them seldom, but it was with severity, which had an effect upon them for a long time after.

January 29th, My head aches, and I can write no more.

January 30th, Tuesday.

This is the night of the funeral, which my sickness will not suffer me to attend. It is now nine at night, and I am removed into another apartment, that I may not see the light

light in the church, which is just over against the window of my bed-chamber.

With all the softness of temper that became a lady, she had the personal courage of a hero. She and her friend having removed their lodgings to a new house, which stood solitary, a parcel of rogues, armed, attempted the house, where there was only one boy: She was then about four and twenty: And, having been warned to apprehend some such attempt, she learned the management of a pistol; and the other women and servants being half-dead with fear, she stole softly to her dining-room window, put on a black hood, to prevent being seen, primed the pistol fresh, gently lifted up the sash; and, taking her aim with the utmost presence of mind, discharged the pistol loaden with the bullets, into the body of one villain, who stood the fairest mark. The fellow, mortally wounded, was carried off by the rest, and died the next morning, but his companions could not be found. The Duke of Ormond hath often drank her health to me upon that account, and had always an high esteem of her. She was indeed under some apprehensions of going in a boat, after some danger she had narrowly escaped by water, but she was reasoned thoroughly out of it. She was never known to cry out, or discover any fear, in a coach or on horseback, or any uneasiness by those sudden accidents with which most of her sex, either by weakness or affectation, appear so much disordered.

She never had the least absence of mind in conversation, nor given to interruption, or appeared eager to put in her word by waiting impatiently until another had done. She spoke in a most agreeable voice, in the plainest words, never hesitating, except out of modesty before new faces, where she was somewhat reserved; nor, among her nearest friends, ever spoke much at a time. She was

but

but little versed in the common topics of female chat; scandal, censure, and detraction, never came out of her mouth: Yet, among a few friends, in private conversation, she made little ceremony in discovering her contempt of a coxcomb, and describing all his follies to the life; but the follies of her own sex she was rather inclined to extenuate or to pity.

When she was once convinced by open facts of any breach of truth or honour, in a person of high station, especially in the church, she could not conceal her indignation, nor hear them named without shewing her displeasure in her countenance; particularly one or two of the latter sort, whom she had known and esteemed, but detested above all mankind, when it was manifest that they had sacrificed those two precious virtues to their ambition, and would much sooner have forgiven them the common immoralities of the laity.

Her frequent fits of sickness, in most parts of her life, had prevented her from making that progress in reading which she would otherwise have done. She was well versed in the Greek and Roman story, and was not unskilled in that of France and England. She spoke French perfectly, but forgot much of it by neglect and sickness. She had read carefully all the best books of travels, which serve to open and enlarge the mind. She understood the Platonic and Epicurean philosophy, and judged very well of the defects of the latter. She made very judicious abstracts of the best books she had read. She understood the nature of government, and could point out all the errors of Hobbes, both in that and religion. She had a good insight into physic, and knew somewhat of anatomy; in both which she was instructed in her younger days by an eminent physician, who had her long under his care, and bore the highest esteem for her person and understanding.

standing. She had a true taste of wit and good sense, both in poetry and prose, and was a perfect good critic of style: Neither was it easy to find a more proper or impartial judge, whose advice an author might better rely on, if he intended to send a thing into the world, provided it was on a subject that came within the compass of her knowledge. Yet, perhaps, she was sometimes too severe, which is a safe and pardonable error. She preserved her wit, judgment, and vivacity to the last, but often used to complain of her memory.

Her fortune, with some accession, could not, as I have heard say, amount to much more than two thousand pounds, whereof a great part fell with her life, having been placed upon annuities in England, and one in Ireland. In a person so extraordinary, perhaps it may be pardonable to mention some particulars, although of little moment, further than to set forth her character. Some presents of goldpieces being often made to her while she was a girl, by her mother and other friends, on promise to keep them, she grew into such a spirit of thrift, that, in about three years, they amounted to above two hundred pounds. She used to shew them with boasting; but her mother, apprehending she would be cheated of them, prevailed, in some months, and with great importunities, to have them put out to interest: When the girl lost the pleasure of seeing and counting her gold, which she never failed of doing many times in a day, and despaired of heaping up such another treasure, her humour took the quite contrary turn: She grew careless and squandering of every new acquisition, and so continued till about two and twenty; when, by advice of some friends, and the fright of paying large bills of tradesmen, who enticed her into their debt, she began to reflect upon her own folly, and was never at rest until she had

discharged

discharged all her shop-bills, and refunded herself a considerable sum she had run out. After which, by the addition of a few years and a superior understanding, she became, and continued all her life a most prudent oeconomist; yet still with a strong bent to the liberal side, wherein she gratified herself by avoiding all expence in cloaths, (which she ever despised) beyond what was merely decent. And, although her frequent returns of sickness were very chargeable, except fees to physicians, of which she met with several so generous that she could force nothing on them, (and indeed she must otherwise have been undone;) yet she never was without a considerable sum of ready money. Insomuch that, upon her death, when her nearest friends thought her very bare, her executors found in her strong box about a hundred and fifty pounds in gold. She lamented the narrowness of her fortune in nothing so much, as that it did not enable her to entertain her friends so often, and in so hospitable a manner as she desired. Yet they were always welcome; and, while she was in health to direct, were treated with neatness and elegance: So that the revenues of her and her companion, passed for much more considerable than they really were. They lived always in lodgings, their domesticks consisting of two maids and one man. She kept an account of all the family-expences, from her arrival in Ireland to some months before her death; and she would often repine, when looking back upon the annals of her houshold bills, that every thing necessary for life was double the price, while interest of money was sunk almost to one half; so that the addition made to her fortune was indeed grown absolutely necessary.

[I since writ as I found time.]

But her charity to the poor was a duty not to be diminished, and therefore became a tax upon those

tradesmen

tradesmen who furnish the fopperies of other ladies. She bought cloaths as seldom as possible, and those as plain and cheap as consisted with the situation she was in; and wore no lace for many years. Either her judgment or fortune was extraordinary, in the choice of those on whom she bestowed her charity; for it went further in doing good than double the sum from any other hand. And I have heard her say, she always met with gratitude from the poor: Which must be owing to her skill in distinguishing proper objects, as well as her gracious manner in relieving them.

But she had another quality that much delighted her, although it may be thought a kind of check upon her bounty; however it was a pleasure she could not resist: I mean that of making agreeable presents, wherein I never knew her equal, although it be an affair of as delicate a nature as most in the course of life. She used to define a present, That it was a gift to a friend of something he wanted or was fond of, and which could not be easily gotten for money. I am confident, during my acquaintance with her, she hath, in these and some other kinds of liberality, disposed of to the value of several hundred pounds. As to presents made to herself, she received them with great unwillingness, but especially from those to whom she had ever given any; being on all occasions the most disinterested mortal I ever knew or heard of.

From her own disposition, at least as much as from the frequent want of health, she seldom made any visits; but her own lodgings, from before twenty years old, were frequented by many persons of the graver sort, who all respected her highly, upon her good sense, good manners, and conversation. Among these were the late Primate Lindsay, Bishop Lloyd, Bishop Ashe, Bishop Brown, Bishop Stearne, Bishop Pulleyn, with some others of later

date;

date; and indeed the greatest number of her acquaintance was among the clergy. Honour, truth, liberality, good nature, and modesty, were the virtues she chiefly possessed, and most valued in her acquaintance; and where she found them, would be ready to allow for some defects, nor valued them less, although they did not shine in learning or in wit; but would never give the least allowance for any failures in the former, even to those who made the greatest figure in either of the two latter. She had no use of any person's liberality, yet her detestation of covetous people made her uneasy if such a one was in her company; upon which occasion she would say many things very entertaining and humorous.

She never interrupted any person who spoke; she laught at no mistakes they made, but helped them out with modesty; and if a good thing were spoken, but neglected, she would not let it fall, but set it in the best light to those who were present. She listened to all that was said, and had never the least distraction, or absence of thought.

It was not safe nor prudent, in her presence, to offend in the least word against modesty; for she then gave full employment to her wit, her contempt, and resentment, under which even stupidity and brutality were forced to sink into confusion; and the guilty person, by her future avoiding him like a bear or a satyr, was never in a way to transgress a second time.

It happened one single coxcomb, of the pert kind, was in her company, among several other ladies; and, in his flippant way, began to deliver some double meanings: The rest flapt their fans, and used the other common expedients practised in such cases, of appearing not to mind or comprehend what was said. Her behaviour was very different, and perhaps may be censured. She said thus

thus to the man: 'Sir, all these ladies and I understand your meaning very well, having, in spite of our care, too often met with those of your sex who wanted manners and good sense. But, believe me, neither virtuous nor even vicious women love such kind of conversation. However, I will leave you, and report your behaviour: And, whatever visit I make, I shall first enquire at the door whether you are in the house, that I may be sure to avoid you.' I know not whether a majority of ladies would approve of such a proceeding; but I believe the practice of it would soon put an end to that corrupt conversation, the worst effect of dulness, ignorance, impudence, and vulgarity, and the highest affront to the modesty and understanding of the female sex.

By returning very few visits, she had not much company of her own sex, except those whom she most loved for their easiness, or esteemed for their good sense; and those, not insisting on ceremony, came often to her. But she rather chose men for her companions, the usual topics of ladies' discourse being such as she had little knowledge of, and less relish. Yet no man was upon the rack to entertain her, for she easily descended to any thing that was innocent and diverting. News, politics, censure, family-management, or town-talk, she always diverted to something else; but these indeed seldom happened, for she chose her company better: And therefore many, who mistook her and themselves, having solicited her acquaintance, and finding themselves disappointed after a few visits, dropt off; and she was never known to enquire into the reason, or ask what was become of them.

She was never positive in arguing, and she usually treated those who were so, in a manner which well enough gratified that unhappy disposition; yet in such a sort as

made

made it very contemptible, and at the same time did some hurt to the owners. Whether this proceeded from her easiness in general, or from her indifference to certain persons, or from her despair of mending them, or from the same practice which she much liked in Mr. Addison, I cannot determine; but when she saw any of the company very warm in a wrong opinion, she was more inclined to confirm them in it than oppose them. The excuse she commonly gave when her friends asked the reason, was, That it prevented noise, and saved time. Yet I have known her very angry with some whom she much esteemed for sometimes falling into that infirmity.

She loved Ireland much better than the generality of those who owe both their birth and riches to it; and, having brought over all the fortune she had in money, left the reversion of the best part of it, one thousand pounds, to Dr. Stephens's Hospital. She detested the tyranny and injustice of England, in their treatment of this kingdom. She had indeed reason to love a country, where she had the esteem and friendship of all who knew her, and the universal good-report of all who ever heard of her, without one exception, if I am told the truth by those who keep general conversation. Which character is the more extraordinary, in falling to a person of so much knowledge, wit, and vivacity, qualities that are used to create envy, and consequently censure; and must be rather imputed to her great modesty, gentle behaviour, and inoffensiveness, than to her superior virtues.

Although her knowledge, from books and company, was much more extensive than usually falls to the share of her sex; yet she was so far from making a parade of it, that her female visitants, on their first acquaintance, who expected to discover it, by what they call hard words and deep discourse, would be sometimes disappointed, and

say,

say, they found she was like other women. But wise men, through all her modesty, whatever they discoursed on, could easily observe that she understood them very well, by the judgment shewn in her observations as well as in her questions.

THOUGHTS

While walking together one day in the country, Swift and Pope agreed that chance thoughts are often as true and as useful to a writer as the conclusions reached through painstaking study. Acting on this theory, each proceeded to keep a commonplace book in which he noted down without any plan all sorts of fugitive ideas and impressions.

A man's life is to be judged (we have been warned by good authority) not merely by work completed but by 'instincts immature', by 'fancies that broke through language and escaped', as well. These thoughts of Swift are too fragmentary and incomplete to serve as the basis for any far-reaching conclusions about his philosophy. They represent opinions which he held, some for a lifetime, others for perhaps an hour. They are invaluable to the student of Swift's mind not as final statements but as tentative queries, as seeds from which brilliant essays might have grown, as sentences from chapters which he never wrote. With the exception of the resolutions for old age, they would seem to have been unstudied observations, lacking both the polish and the insincerity of the epigrams of a Congreve and a La Rochefoucauld.

'Resolutions When I Come to Be Old' is reproduced by photostat from the manuscript at South Kensington.

'Thoughts on Various Subjects' is reproduced from Swift's *Miscellanies*, vol. i, 1728.

'Thoughts on Religion' is reproduced from the original edition by Deane Swift, vol. viii of the quarto edition of Swift's *Works*, 1765.

RESOLUTIONS WHEN I COME TO BE OLD

NOT to marry a young Woman.

Not to keep young Company, unless they really desire it.

Not to be peevish, or morose, or suspicious.

Not to scorn present Ways, or Wits, or Fashions, or Men, or War, &c.

Not to be fond of children.[1]

Not to tell the same Story over and over to the same People.

Not to be covetous.

Not to neglect decency, or cleanliness, for fear of falling into Nastiness.

Not to be over severe with young People, but give allowances for their youthful follys and weaknesses.

Not to be influenced by, or give ear to knavish tattling servants, or others.

Not to be too free of advice, nor trouble any but those that desire it.

To desire[2] some good Friends to inform me which of these Resolutions I break, or neglect, & wherein; and reform accordingly.

Not to talk much, nor of myself.

Not to boast of my former beauty, or strength, or favour with ladies, &c.

Not to hearken to Flatteries, nor conceive I can be beloved by a young woman; *et eos qui hæreditatem captant, odisse ac vitare.*

Not to be positive or opiniative.

Not to set up for observing all these Rules, for fear I should observe none.

[1] *MS. has here, and deletes:* or let them come near me hardly,
[2] *MS. has* covet *corrected to* desire.

THOUGHTS ON VARIOUS SUBJECTS

WE have just enough Religion to make us hate, but not enough to make us love one another.

Reflect on Things past, as Wars, Negotiations, Factions, &c. We enter so little into those Interests, that we wonder how Men could possibly be so busy and concerned for Things so transitory: Look on the present Times, we find the same Humour, yet wonder not at all.

A wise Man endeavours, by considering all Circumstances, to make Conjectures, and form Conclusions, but the smallest Accident intervening, (and in the Course of Affairs it is impossible to foresee all) does often produce such Turns and Changes, that at last he is just as much in doubt of Events, as the most ignorant and unexperienced Person.

Positiveness is a good Quality for Preachers and Orators, because he that would obtrude his Thoughts and Reasons upon a Multitude, will convince others the more, as he appears convinced himself.

How is it possible to expect that Mankind will take Advice, when they will not so much as take Warning?

I forget whether Advice be among the lost Things which, Ariosto says, are to be found in the Moon; That and Time ought to have been there.

No Preacher is listened to but Time, which gives us the same Train and Turn of Thought that elder People have tried in vain to put into our Heads before.

When we desire or solicite any Thing, our Minds run wholly on the good Side or Circumstances of it; when 'tis obtained, our Minds run wholly on the bad Ones.

In a Glass-House, the Workmen often fling in a small Quantity of fresh Coals, which seems to disturb the Fire, but very much enlivens it. This seems to allude to a gentle

gentle stirring of the Passions, that the Mind may not languish.

Religion seems to have grown an Infant with Age, and requires Miracles to nurse it, as it had in its Infancy.

All Fits of Pleasure are ballanced by an equal Degree of Pain or Languor; 'tis like spending this Year, part of the next Year's Revenue.

The latter Part of a wise Man's Life is taken up in curing the Follies, Prejudices, and false Opinions he had contracted in the former.

Would a Writer know how to behave himself with relation to Posterity, let him consider in old Books, what he finds, that he is glad to know, and what Omissions he most laments.

Whatever the Poets pretend, 'tis plain they give Immortality to none but themselves: 'Tis Homer and Virgil we reverence and admire, not Achilles or Æneas. With Historians it is quite the contrary; our Thoughts are taken up with the Actions, Persons, and Events we read, and we little regard the Authors.

When a true Genius appears in the World, you may know him by this Sign, that the Dunces are all in confederacy against him.

Men who possess all the Advantages of Life, are in a State where there are many Accidents to disorder and discompose, but few to please them.

'Tis unwise to punish Cowards with Ignominy; for if they had regarded that, they would not have been Cowards: Death is their proper Punishment, because they fear it most.

The greatest Inventions were produced in the Times of Ignorance; as the Use of the Compass, Gunpowder, and Printing; and by the dullest Nation, as the Germans.

One Argument to prove that the common Relations of

Ghosts

Ghosts and Spectres are generally false, may be drawn from the Opinion held, that Spirits are never seen by more than one Person at a Time, that is to say, it seldom happens to above one Person in a Company to be possest with any high Degree of Spleen or Melancholy.

I am apt to think, that in the Day of Judgment there will be small Allowance given to the Wise for their Want of Morals, nor to the Ignorant for their Want of Faith, because both are without Excuse. This renders the Advantages equal of Ignorance and Knowledge. But some Scruples in the Wise, and some Vices in the Ignorant, will perhaps be forgiven upon the Strength of Temptation to each.

The Value of several Circumstances in Story lessens very much by Distance of Time, though some minute Circumstances are very valuable, and it requires great Judgment in a Writer to distinguish.

'Tis grown a Word of Course for Writers to say, this critical Age, as Divines say, this sinful Age.

'Tis pleasant to observe, how free the present Age is in laying Taxes on the next. Future Ages shall talk of this; this shall be famous to all Posterity; whereas their Time and Thoughts will be taken up about present Things, as ours are now.

The Camelion, who is said to feed upon nothing but Air, hath of all Animals the nimblest Tongue.

When a Man is made a Spiritual Peer, he loses his Sirname; when a Temporal, his Christian Name.

It is in Disputes as in Armies, where the weaker Side sets up false Lights, and makes a great Noise to make the Enemy believe them more numerous and strong than they really are.

Some Men, under the Notions of weeding out Prejudices, eradicate Virtue, Honesty, and Religion.

In

In all well-instituted Commonwealths, Care has been taken to limit Men's Possessions; which is done for many Reasons, and among the rest, for one which perhaps is not often considered, That when Bounds are set to Men's Desires, after they have acquired as much as the Laws will permit them, their private Interest is at an End, and they have nothing to do but to take care of the Publick.

There are but three Ways for a Man to revenge himself of the Censure of the World; to despise it, to return the like, or to endeavour to live so as to avoid it: The first of these is usually pretended, the last is almost impossible, the universal Practice is for the second.

Herodotus tells us, that in cold Countries Beasts very seldom have Horns, but in hot they have very large ones. This might bear a pleasant Application.

I never heard a finer Piece of Satyr against Lawyers, than that of Astrologers, when they pretend by Rules of Art to tell when a Suit will end, and whether to the Advantage of the Plaintiff or Defendant; thus making the Matter depend entirely upon the Influence of the Stars, without the least Regard to the Merits of the Cause.

The Expression in Apocrypha about Tobit, and his Dog following him, I have often heard ridiculed; yet Homer has the same Words of Telemachus more than once, and Virgil says something like it of Evander. And I take the Book of Tobit to be partly Poetical.

I have known some Men possessed of good Qualities, which were very serviceable to others, but useless to themselves; like a Sun-Dial on the Front of a House, to inform the Neighbours and Passengers, but not the Owner within.

If a Man would register all his Opinions upon Love, Politicks, Religion, Learning, &c. beginning from his Youth,

Youth, and so go on to old Age, what a Bundle of Inconsistencies and Contradictions would appear at last?

What they do in Heaven we are ignorant of; what they do not we are told expressly, That they neither marry, nor are given in Marriage.

When a Man observes the Choice of Ladies now-a-days, in the dispensing of their Favours, can he forbear paying some Veneration to the Memory of those Mares mentioned by Xenophon, who, while their Manes were on, that is, while they were in their Beauty, would never admit the Embraces of an Ass.

De re equestri,

'Tis a miserable Thing to live in Suspence; it is the Life of a Spider. *Vive quidem, pende tamen, improba, dixit.* Ovid. Metam.

The Stoical Scheme of supplying our Wants, by lopping off our Desires, is like cutting off our Feet when we want Shoes.

Physicians ought not to give their Judgment of Religion, for the same Reason that Butchers are not admitted to be Jurors upon Life and Death.

The Reason why so few Marriages are happy, is, because young Ladies spend their Time in making Nets, not in making Cages.

If a Man will observe as he walks the Streets, I believe he will find the merriest Countenances in Mourning Coaches.

Nothing more unqualifies a Man to act with Prudence, than a Misfortune that is attended with Shame and Guilt.

The Power of Fortune is confest only by the Miserable; for the Happy impute all their Success to Prudence or Merit.

Ambition often puts Men upon doing the meanest Offices; so Climbing is performed in the same Posture with Creeping.

Ill

Ill Company is like a Dog, who dirts those most whom he loves best.

Censure is the Tax a Man pays to the Publick for being eminent.

Although Men are accus'd for not knowing their own Weakness, yet perhaps as few know their own Strength. It is in Men as in Soils, where sometimes there is a Vein of Gold, which the Owner knows not of.

Satyr is reckon'd the easiest of all Wit; but I take it to be otherwise in very bad Times: For it is as hard to satyrize well a Man of distinguish'd Vices, as to praise well a Man of distinguish'd Virtues. It is easy enough to do either to People of moderate Characters.

Invention is the Talent of Youth, and Judgment of Age; so that our Judgment grows harder to please, when we have fewer Things to offer it: This goes through the whole Commerce of Life. When we are old, our Friends find it difficult to please us, and are less concern'd whether we be pleas'd or no.

No wise Man ever wished to be younger.

An idle Reason lessens the Weight of the good Ones you gave before.

The Motives of the best Actions will not bear too strict an Enquiry. It is allow'd, that the Cause of most Actions, good or bad, may be resolved into the Love of our selves: But the Self-Love of some Men inclines them to please others; and the Self-Love of others is wholly employ'd in pleasing themselves. This makes the great Distinction between Virtue and Vice. Religion is the best Motive of all Actions, yet Religion is allow'd to be the highest Instance of Self-Love.

When the World has once begun to use us ill, it afterwards continues the same Treatment with less Scruple or Ceremony, as Men do to a Whore.

Old

Old Men view best at distance with the Eyes of their Understanding, as well as with those of Nature.

Some People take more Care to hide their Wisdom than their Folly.

Arbitrary Power is the natural Object of Temptation to a Prince, as Wine or Women to a young Fellow, or a Bribe to a Judge, or Avarice to old Age, or Vanity to a Woman.

Anthony Henly's Farmer dying of an Asthma, said, Well, if I can get this Breath once out, I'll take care it shall never get in again.

The Humour of exploding many Things under the Names of Trifles, Fopperies, and only imaginary Goods, is a very false Proof either of Wisdom or Magnanimity, and a great Check to virtuous Actions. For instance, with regard to Fame: There is in most People a Reluctance and Unwillingness to be forgotten. We observe, even among the Vulgar, how fond they are to have an Inscription over their Grave. It requires but little Philosophy to discover and observe that there is no intrinsick Value in all this; however, if it be founded in our Nature, as an Incitement to Virtue, it ought not to be ridicul'd.

Complaint is the largest Tribute Heaven receives, and the sincerest Part of our Devotion.

The common Fluency of Speech in many Men, and most Women, is owing to a Scarcity of Matter, and Scarcity of Words; for whoever is a Master of Language, and hath a Mind full of Ideas, will be apt, in speaking, to hesitate upon the Choice of both; whereas common Speakers have only one Sett of Ideas, and one Sett of Words to cloath them in; and these are always ready at the Mouth: So People come faster out of a Church when it is almost empty, than when a Crowd is at the Door.

Few are qualified to shine in Company; but it is in

most

most Men's Power to be agreeable. The Reason, therefore, why Conversation runs so low at present, is not the Defect of Understanding, but Pride, Vanity, ill Nature, Affectation, Singularity, Positiveness, or some other Vice, the Effect of a wrong Education.

To be vain, is rather a Mark of Humility than Pride. Vain Men delight in telling what Honours have been done them, what great Company they have kept, and the like; by which they plainly confess, that these Honours were more than their Due, and such as their Friends would not believe if they had not been told: Whereas a Man truly proud, thinks the greatest Honours below his Merit, and consequently scorns to boast. I therefore deliver it as a Maxim, that whoever desires the Character of a proud Man, ought to conceal his Vanity.

Law, in a free Country, is, or ought to be, the Determination of the Majority of those who have Property in Land.

One Argument used to the Disadvantage of Providence, I take to be a very strong One in its defence. It is objected, that Storms and Tempests, unfruitful Seasons, Serpents, Spiders, Flies, and other noxious or troublesome Animals, with many more Instances of the like kind, discover an Imperfection in Nature, because human Life would be much easier without them: But the Design of Providence may clearly be perceived in this Proceeding. The Motions of the Sun and Moon; in short, the whole System of the Universe, as far as Philosophers have been able to discover and observe, are in the utmost Degree of Regularity and Perfection; but wherever God hath left to Man the Power of interposing a Remedy by Thought or Labour, there he hath plac'd Things in a State of Imperfection, on Purpose to stir up human Industry, without which Life would stagnate, or indeed rather could not subsist at all: *Curis acuunt mortalia corda.*

Praise

Praise is the Daughter of present Power.

How inconsistent is Man with himself!

I have known several Persons of great Fame for Wisdom in publick Affairs and Counsels, govern'd by foolish Servants.

I have known great Ministers, distinguish'd for Wit and Learning, who prefer'd none but Dunces.

I have known Men of great Valour Cowards to their Wives.

I have known Men of the greatest Cunning perpetually cheated.

I knew three great Ministers, who could exactly compute and settle the Accounts of a Kingdom, but were wholly ignorant of their own Œconomy.

The Preaching of Divines helps to preserve well-inclin'd Men in the Course of Virtue, but seldom or never reclaims the Vicious.

Princes usually make wiser Choices than the Servants whom they trust for the Disposal of Places: I have known a Prince, more than once, chuse an able Minister; but I never observ'd that Minister to use his Credit in the Disposal of an Employment to a Person whom he thought the fittest for it. One of the greatest in this Age own'd and excus'd the Matter from the Violence of Parties, and the Unreasonableness of Friends.

Small Causes are sufficient to make a Man uneasy, when great Ones are not in the Way: For want of a Block he will stumble at a Straw.

Dignity, high Station, or great Riches, are in some sort necessary to old Men, in order to keep the younger at a Distance, who are otherwise too apt to insult them upon the Score of their Age.

Every Man desires to live long; but no Man would be old.

Love of Flattery in most Men proceeds from the mean Opinion

Opinion they have of themselves; in Women from the contrary.

If Books and Laws continue to increase as they have done for fifty Years past, I am in some Concern for future Ages, how any Man will be Learned, or any Man a Lawyer.

Kings are commonly said to have long Hands; I wish they had as long Ears.

Princes in their Infancy, Childhood, and Youth, are said to discover prodigious Parts and Wit, to speak Things that surprize and astonish: Strange, so many hopeful Princes, and so many shameful Kings! If they happen to die young, they would have been Prodigies of Wisdom and Virtue: If they live, they are often Prodigies indeed, but of another sort.

Politicks, as the Word is commonly understood, are nothing but Corruptions, and consequently of no Use to a good King, or a good Ministry, for which Reason Courts are so over-run with Politicks.

Silenus, the Foster-Father of Bacchus, is always carried by an Ass, and has Horns on his Head. The Moral is, that Drunkards are led by Fools, and have a great Chance to be Cuckolds.

Venus, a beautiful good-natur'd Lady, was the Goddess of Love; Juno, a terrible Shrew, the Goddess of Marriage; and they were always mortal Enemies.

Those who are against Religion, must needs be Fools; and therefore we read that, of all Animals, God refus'd the First-born of an Ass.

A very little Wit is valued in a Woman, as we are pleas'd with a few Words spoken plain by a Parrot.

A Nice Man is a Man of nasty Ideas.

Apollo was held the God of Physick, and Sender of Diseases: Both were originally the same Trade, and still continue.

Old

Old Men and Comets have been reverenc'd for the same Reason; their long Beards, and Pretences to foretel Events.

A Person was ask'd at Court, what he thought of an Ambassador, and his Train, who were all Embroidery and Lace, full of Bows, Cringes, and Gestures? He said, it was Solomon's Importation, Gold and Apes.

There is a Story in Pausanias, of a Plot for betraying of a City, discover'd by the Braying of an Ass: The Cackling of Geese sav'd the Capitol; and Cataline's Conspiracy was discover'd by a Whore. These are the only three Animals, as far as I remember, famous in History for Evidences and Informers.

Most Sorts of Diversion in Men, Children, and other Animals, are an Imitation of Fighting.

Augustus meeting an Ass with a lucky Name, foretold himself good Fortune. I meet many Asses, but none of them have lucky Names.

If a Man makes me keep my Distance, the Comfort is, he keeps his at the same Time.

Who can deny that all Men are violent Lovers of Truth, when we see them so positive in their Errors, which they will maintain out of their Zeal to Truth, although they contradict themselves every Day of their Lives?

That was excellently observ'd, say I, when I read a Passage in an Author, where his Opinion agrees with mine. When we differ, there I pronounce him to be mistaken.

Very few Men, properly speaking, live at present, but are providing to live another Time.

As universal a Practice as Lying is, and as easy a one as it seems, I do not remember to have heard three good Lyes in all my Conversation, even from those who were most celebrated in that Faculty.

THOUGHTS ON RELIGION

I AM in all opinions to believe according to my own impartial reason; which I am bound to inform and improve, as far as my capacity and opportunities will permit.

It may be prudent in me to act sometimes by other men's reason, but I can think only by my own.

If another man's reason fully convinceth me, it becomes my own reason.

To say a man is bound to believe, is neither truth nor sense.

You may force men, by interest or punishment, to say or swear they believe, and to act as if they believed: You can go no further.

Every man, as a member of the common wealth, ought to be content with the possession of his own opinion in private, without perplexing his neighbour or disturbing the public.

Violent zeal for truth hath an hundred to one odds to be either petulancy, ambition, or pride.

There is a degree of corruption wherein some nations, as bad as the world is, will proceed to an amendment; till which time particular men should be quiet.

To remove opinions fundamental in religion is impossible, and the attempt wicked, whether those opinions be true or false; unless your avowed design be to abolish that religion altogether. So, for instance, in the famous doctrine of Christ's divinity, which hath been universally received by all bodies of Christians, since the condemnation of Arianism under Constantine and his successors: Wherefore the proceedings of the Socinians are both vain and unwarrantable; because they will be never able to

advance

advance their own opinion, or meet any other success than breeding doubts and disturbances in the world. *Qui ratione suâ disturbant mœnia mundi.*

The want of belief is a defect that ought to be concealed when it cannot be overcome.

The Christian religion, in the most early times, was proposed to the Jews and Heathens without the article of Christ's divinity; which, I remember, Erasmus accounts for, by its being too strong a meat for babes. Perhaps, if it were now softened by the Chinese missionaries, the conversion of those infidels would be less difficult: And we find by the Alcoran, it is the great stumbling-block of the Mahometans. But, in a country already Christian, to bring so fundamental a point of faith into debate, can have no consequences that are not pernicious to morals and public peace.

I have been often offended to find St. Paul's allegories, and other figures of Grecian eloquence, converted by divines into articles of faith.

God's mercy is over all his works, but divines of all sorts lessen that mercy too much.

I look upon myself, in the capacity of a clergyman, to be one appointed by providence for defending a post assigned me, and for gaining over as many enemies as I can. Although I think my cause is just, yet one great motion is my submitting to the pleasure of Providence, and to the laws of my country.

I am not answerable to God for the doubts that arise in my own breast, since they are the consequence of that reason which he hath planted in me, if I take care to conceal those doubts from others, if I use my best endeavours to subdue them, and if they have no influence on the conduct of my life.

I believe that thousands of men would be orthodox enough

enough in certain points, if divines had not been too curious, or too narrow, in reducing orthodoxy within the compass of subtleties, niceties, and distinctions, with little warrant from Scripture and less from reason or good policy.

I never saw, heard, nor read, that the clergy were beloved in any nation where Christianity was the religion of the country. Nothing can render them popular but some degree of persecution.

Those fine gentlemen who affect the humour of railing at the clergy, are, I think, bound in honour to turn parsons themselves, and shew us better examples.

Miserable mortals! can we contribute to the honour and glory of God? I could wish that expression were struck out of our Prayer-books.

Liberty of conscience, properly speaking, is no more than the liberty of possessing our own thoughts and opinions, which every man enjoys without fear of the magistrate: But how far he shall publicly act in pursuance of those opinions, is to be regulated by the laws of the country. Perhaps, in my own thoughts, I prefer a well-instituted commonwealth before a monarchy; and I know several others of the same opinion. Now, if, upon this pretence, I should insist upon liberty of conscience, form conventicles of republicans, and print books preferring that government and condemning what is established, the magistrate would, with great justice, hang me and my disciples. It is the same case in religion, although not so avowed, where liberty of conscience, under the present acceptation, equally produces revolutions, or at least convulsions and disturbances in a state; which politicians would see well enough, if their eyes were not blinded by faction, and of which these kingdoms, as well as France, Sweden, and other countries, are flaming instances. Cromwell's

Cromwell's notion upon this article was natural and right; when, upon the surrender of a town in Ireland, the Popish governor insisted upon an article for liberty of conscience, Cromwell said, he meddled with no man's conscience; but, if by liberty of conscience, the governor meant the liberty of the Mass, he had express orders from the parliament of England against admitting any such liberty at all.

It is impossible that any thing so natural, so necessary, and so universal as death, should ever have been designed by providence as an evil to mankind.

Although reason were intended by providence to govern our passions, yet it seems that, in two points of the greatest moment to the being and continuance of the world, God hath intended our passions to prevail over reason. The first is, the propagation of our species, since no wise man ever married from the dictates of reason. The other is, the love of life, which, from the dictates of reason, every man would despise, and wish it at an end, or that it never had a beginning.

LETTERS

Judged by his correspondence, Swift would rank as a prose writer above Pope but still far below Chesterfield. His virtues and his faults as a letter writer are those of his age. Indeed, it would seem as though he adapted himself to the style of others in his letters more than in his other writings, and this is, perhaps, what we should expect of a correspondent. To the coarseness of Walls and Thomas Sheridan, he replied in kind. To Gay he wrote with paternal affection, recommending to his young friend those sycophantic avenues for advancement which as author of *Gulliver* he despised for himself. The most revealing letters are to Pope and Arbuthnot, with whom of all men he had most in common; but for the most part we learn more about his friends than about his own intimate thoughts. We read much of Swift's discontent with politics; of his literary projects; of the penurious circumstances in which he kept house. He admits that he is lonely and that life in Ireland is dull; but the strength of his attachments or the depth of his disappointments is not revealed. These friends are not Stella! They are a part of the public from whom Swift ever screened his heart. It is foolish, however, to expect an author to be 'significant' whenever he writes a letter in an hour of relaxation. It is enough that we have him conversing freely with his friends.

The earliest editions of Swift's letters are incomplete. The text of most of the letters reproduced is that of Deane Swift's edition of Swift's *Works,* 1775, supplemented by and collated with the definitive edition of Swift's *Correspondence,* by F. E. Ball, London, 1910, 6 vols., which I have followed in dating the letters.

To THOMAS SWIFT

December 6, 1693.

Your letter speaks of so many choices of employment, that one would think you too busy to be very unhappy; though the pinch of a present uneasiness makes one a very ill reasoner; and he that lies ill on one side, though the posture may help to his health, is very hardly dissuaded from turning on the other. This is enough to say on that score, in the place this letter finds you. For the rest, I think the advice of a friend is very far from being disinterested, and to avoid that was the chief reason I forbore it. I cannot at this distance give a judgement near enough upon your other hopes, but if they be not certain, I think there is no avoiding the choice of what is; this I told you, or something like it before. I protest I cannot much pity your present circumstances, which keep your mind and your body in motion, and myself was never very miserable while my thoughts were in a ferment, for I imagine a dead calm to be the troublesomest part of our voyage through the world. If that curacy were not disposed of which I once mentioned to you, I think I should say it was, for it fits your present prospects almost as ill as it did your merit then.

Though you are so crammed with business I must needs desire your assistance in paying forty-five shillings for Nan Swift and Matt. Rooke and me, for our Dictionary which is about this time to be delivered, or else my bookseller (Sympson) may perhaps be careless in the choice of the copies, in which there is difference enough...

Yours

J. Swift.

To thwart business with rhyme, to spoil its witchcraft, and

and my letter to cousin Rooke and Matt: she must find money for those dictionaries, but to show how rich I am I will send her my share myself.

To JOHN GAY

June 12, 1714.

I wonder how you could have the impudence to know where I am. I have this post writ to Mr. Harley,[1] who is just come from Hanover, to desire he would give you a letter. I have described you to him, and told him I would write to you to wait on him, which will do you no hurt about your affair in the Treasury. You begin to be an able courtier, which I know from two instances: first for giving me thanks for your preferment, to which I only contributed by saying to Dr. Arbuthnot and Mr. Lewis that I wished it; secondly for wheedling my Lord Treasurer with an epigram, which I like very well, and so I am sure will he, and I reckon you will succeed. But pray learn to be a manager, and pick up language as fast as you can, and get Aristotle upon politics, and read other books upon government, Grotius de Jure Belli et Pacis, and accounts of negotiations and treaties, &c.; and be a perfect master of the Latin, and be able to learn everything of the Court where you go; and keep correspondence with Mr. Lewis, who if you write letters worth showing, will make them serviceable to you with Lord Treasurer; and take Mr. Lewis's advice in all things, and do not despise mine, and so God bless you, and make you able to make my fortunes. I am glad Mr. Pope has made so much despatch. My service to him and the Parnellian.

[1] Thomas Harley, cousin of Lord Oxford.

To

To JOHN ARBUTHNOT

June 16, 1714.

Dear Brother,

My stomach is prouder than you imagine, and I scorned to write till I was writ to. I have already half lost the ideas of Courts and Ministers. I dine between twelve and one, and the whole house is abed by ten and up at six. I drink no wine, and see but one dish of meat. I pay a guinea a week for dieting and lodging myself and man with an honest clergyman of my old acquaintance, and my paying is forced, for he has long invited me. I did not know till last night that the Princess Sophia was dead, when my landlord and I chanced to pay a visit to a farmer in a neighbouring village, and was told so over a mug of ale, by a brisk young fellow just come from London, who talked big and looked on us with great contempt. I thank you for your kindness to poor Gay. Was the money paid, or put off till the day after he went? I reckon by what you tell me that it is now a high season to be very merry in Lady Fair's[1] lodgings. I heartily pity you in particular. Look after your mistress and yourself, grow rich, and since nothing better can be done, let the world *vadere*.

I have a mind to live in Yorkshire for a year, in order to put myself out of memory and debt. The fashion of this world passeth away: however, I am angry at those who disperse us sooner than there was need. I have a mind to be very angry, and to let my anger break out in some manner that will not please them at the end of a pen. I wish you could get Lady M—— to give you those hints[2] we have often spoke of, and to muster up your own;

[1] Alice Hill, sister of Lady Masham who intrigued with the Tories to oust the Whig ministry.

[2] Swift was collecting materials about back-stairs court history for use in his history of the last four years of Queen Anne's reign.

for

for the Dragon,[1] I despair he will do that any more than anything else, and indeed you are all of you Dragons more or less, for I am sure it is above three years since I have spoke to Lady M—— and you about this. My humble service to my Lord and her, whom I love as much as you do, though I have greater obligations to them, and my humble services and thanks to the Qu—— of Prudes for remembering me.

You are a set of people drawn almost to the dregs; you must try another game; this is at an end. Your Ministry is fourscore and ten years old, and all you can endeavour at is an euthanasia, or rather it is in a deep consumption at five-and-twenty. I approve Lady M——'s conduct, and think all she can now do in relation to the Dragon is to be passive; for the rest to cultivate her own credit to the utmost. Writing to you much would make me stark mad; judge his condition who has nothing to keep him from being miserable but endeavouring to forget those for whom he has the greatest value, love, and friendship. But you are a philosopher and a physician, and can overcome by your wisdom and your faculty those weaknesses which other men are forced to reduce by not thinking on them. Adieu, and love me half so well as I do you.

To JOHN ARBUTHNOT

July 3, 1714.

I reckoned you would have held up for one letter and so have given over; this is the usual way I treat my best absent friends when I am in London. Did I describe myself in a happy state here? Upon my faith you read wrong: I have no happiness but being so far out of the way of the Dragon and the rest. Lewis reproaches me as

[1] Lord Oxford.

one

one who still has an itch to the Court, only because I asked him how the *summa rerum* went. Was not that unjust? And quotes upon me, *quae lucis miseris tam dira cupido.* I do assert that living near a Court with some circumstances is a most happy life, and would be so still if the Dragon did not spoil it. I find the triumvirate of honest counsellors is at an end; I am gone, Lewis says he lives in ignorance in his castle, and you meddle as little as you can. One thing still lies upon you, which is to be a constant adviser to Lady Masham. The game will of course be played into her hand. She has very good sense, but may be imposed upon. And I had a whisper, that the Squire[1] plies there again. It is as you say, if the Dragon speaks kindly of Parnell, he is gone. It is the Ossorys that get the Derrys and the Chesters the Yorks.

To talk of Martin in any hands but yours is a folly. You every day give better hints than all of us together could do in a twelve-month; and to say the truth, Pope who first thought of the hint has no genius at all to it, in my mind. Gay is too young; Parnell has some ideas of it, but is idle; I could put together, and lard, and strike out well enough, but all that relates to the sciences must be from you. I am a vexed unsettled vagabond, and my thoughts are turned towards some papers I have, and some other things I would fain get from you and Lady Masham and would have had from the Dragon, but that is impossible till he is out and then I will go to him to Herefordshire and make him give me hints. I have got my History from Secretary Bromley; and they shall never have it again; and it shall be an altered thing if I live. . . .

But country politics are doubly insupportable, and so I have done, and retire to lament with my neighbours the

[1] Bolinbroke.

want

want of rain, and dryness of hay. Farmer Tyler says, the white mead at Chawdry has not been so bad in the memory of man, and the summer barley is quite dried up; but we hope to have a pretty good crop of wheat. Parson Hunsdon it is thought must stick to his bargain, but all the neighbours say the attorney was an arrant rogue. We cannot get a bit of good butter for love or money. I could tell you more of the state of our affairs, but doubt your taste is not refined enough for it.

To Alexander Pope

September 29, 1725.

Sir,

I cannot guess the reason of Mr. Stopford's management, but impute it at a venture to either haste or bashfulness, in the latter of which he is excessive to a fault, although he had already gone the tour of Italy and France to harden himself. Perhaps this second journey, and for a longer time, may amend him. He treated you just as he did Lord Carteret, to whom I recommended him.

My letter you saw to Lord Bolinbroke has shown you the situation I am in, and the company I keep, if I do not forget some of its contents, but I am now returning to the noble scene of Dublin, into the *grand monde*, for fear of burying my parts, to signalise myself among curates and vicars, and correct all corruptions crept in relating to the weight of bread and butter, through those dominions where I govern.[1] I have employed my time, besides ditching, in finishing, correcting, amending, and transcribing my Travels, in four parts complete, newly augmented, and intended for the press, when the world

[1] The grounds about St. Patrick's Cathedral, over which, as Dean, Swift had civil control.

shall

shall deserve them, or rather when a printer shall be found brave enough to venture his ears. I like the scheme of our meeting after distresses and dispersions; but the chief end I propose to myself in all my labours is to vex the world rather than divert it; and if I could compass that design, without hurting my own person or fortune, I would be the most indefatigable writer you have ever seen, without reading. I am exceedingly pleased that you have done with translations. Lord Treasurer Oxford often lamented that a rascally world should lay you under a necessity of mis-employing your genius for so long a time. But since you will now be so much better employed, when you think of the world give it one lash the more at my request. I have ever hated all nations, professions, and communities, and all my love is toward individuals: for instance, I hate the tribe of lawyers, but I love Counsellor Such-a-one, and Judge Such-a-one: so with physicians—I will not speak of my own trade—soldiers, English, Scotch, French, and the rest. But principally I hate and detest that animal called man, although I heartily love John, Peter, Thomas, and so forth. This is the system upon which I have governed myself many years, but do not tell, and so I shall go on till I have done with them. I have got materials toward a treatise, proving the falsity of that definition *animal rationale*, and to show it would be only *rationis capax*. Upon this great foundation of misanthropy, though not in Timon's manner, the whole building of my travels is erected; and I never will have peace of mind till all honest men are of my opinion. By consequence you are to embrace it immediately, and procure that all who deserve my esteem may do so too. The matter is so clear that it will admit of no dispute; nay, I will hold a hundred pounds that you and I agree in the point.

I did

I did not know your Odyssey was finished, being yet in the country, which I shall leave in three days. I shall thank you kindly for the present, but shall like it three-fourths the less, from the mixture you mention of another hand; however, I am glad you saved yourself so much drudgery. I have long been told by Mr. Ford of your great achievements in building and planting, and especially of your subterranean passage to your garden, whereby you turned a blunder into a beauty, which is a piece of *ars poetica.*

I have almost done with harridans, and shall soon become old enough to fall in love with girls of fourteen. The lady whom you describe to live at court, to be deaf, and no party woman, I take to be mythology, but know not how to moralize it. She cannot be Mercy, for Mercy is neither deaf, nor lives at court. Justice is blind, and perhaps deaf, but neither is she a Court lady. Fortune is both blind and deaf, and a Court lady, but then she is a most damnable party woman, and will never make me easy, as you promise. It must be Riches, which answers all your description. I am glad she visits you, but my voice is so weak that I doubt she will never hear me.

Mr. Lewis sent me an account of Dr. Arbuthnot's illness which is a very sensible affliction to me, who, by living so long out of the world, have lost that hardness of heart contracted by years and general conversation. I am daily losing friends, and neither seeking nor getting others. Oh! if the world had but a dozen Arbuthnots in it, I would burn my Travels. But, however, he is not without fault. There is a passage in Bede highly commending the piety and learning of the Irish in that age, where, after abundance of praises, he overthrows them all, by lamenting that, alas! they kept Easter at a wrong time

time of the year. So our Doctor has every quality and virtue that can make a man amiable or useful; but, alas! he has a sort of slouch in his walk. I pray God protect him, for he is an excellent Christian, though not a Catholic, and as fit a man either to live or die as ever I knew.

I hear nothing of our friend Gay, but I find the Court keeps him at hard meat. I advised him to come over here with a Lord Lieutenant. Mr. Tickell is in a very good office. I have not seen Philips, though formerly we were so intimate. He has got nothing and by what I find will get nothing, though he writes little flams, as Lord Leicester called those sorts of verses, on Miss Carteret. It is remarkable, and deserves recording that a Dublin blacksmith, a great poet, has imitated his manner in a poem to the same Miss. Philips is a complainer, and on this occasion I told Lord Carteret that complainers never succeed at Court, though railers do.

Are you altogether a country gentleman, that I must address to you out of London, to the hazard of your losing this precious letter, which I will now conclude, although so much paper is left. I have an ill name, and therefore shall not subscribe it, but you will guess it comes from one who esteems and loves you about half as much as you deserve, I mean as much as he can.

I am in great concern, at what I am just told is in some of the newspapers, that Lord Bolinbroke is much hurt by a fall in hunting. I am glad he has so much youth and vigour left, of which he has not been thrifty, but I wonder he has no more discretion.

'THE

'The Prince of Lilliput' *to* 'Stella'

March 11, 1726–7.

The high and mighty Prince Egroego,[1] born
to the most puissant empire of the East,
Unto
Stella, the most resplendent glory of the Western
hemisphere, sendeth health and happiness.

Brightest Princess,

That invincible hero, the Man Mountain,[2] fortunately arriving at our coasts some years ago, delivered us from ruin by conquering the fleets and armies of our enemies, and gave us hopes of a durable peace and happiness. But now the martial people of Blefuscu, encouraged from his absence, have renewed the war, to revenge upon us the loss and disgrace they suffered by our valiant champion.

The fame of your super excellent person and virtue, and the huge esteem which that great general has for you, urged us in this our second distress to sue for your favour. In order to which, we have set our able and trusty Nardac Koorbnilob,[3] requesting, that if our general does yet tread upon the terrestrial globe, you, in compassion to us, would prevail upon him to take another voyage for our deliverance.

And lest any apprehensions of famine among us should render Nardac Mountain averse to the undertaking, we signify to you, that we have stored our folds, our coops, our granaries and cellars with plenty of provision for a long supply of the wastes to be made by his capacious stomach.

And furthermore, because as we hear you are not so

[1] An anagram for 'O'George'.
[2] Swift himself.
[3] Bolinbroke.

well as we could wish, we beg you would complete our happiness by venturing your most valuable person along with him into our country; where, by the salubrity of our finer air and diet, you will soon recover your health and stomach.

In full assurance of your complying goodness, we have sent you some provision for your voyage, and we shall with impatience wait for your safe arrival to our kingdom. Most illustrious lady, farewell.

Prince Egroego.

The 11 th day of the 6 th moon, in the 2001 year of the Lilliputian era.

To L'Abbé des Fontaines

July, 1727.

Il y a plus d'un mois que j'ay recûe vôtre lettre du 4 de Juin, Monsieur; mais l'exemplaire de la seconde edition de vôtre ouvrage ne m'a pas été encore remis. J'ay lû la preface de la premiere; et vous me permettrez de vous dire, que j'ay été fort surpris d'y voir, qu'en me donnant pour patrie un pais, dans lequel je ne suis pas né, vous ayez trouvé a propos de m'attribuer un livre, qui porte le nom de son auteur, qui a eu le malheur de deplaire a quelques uns de nos ministres, et que je n'ay jamais avoué. Cette plainte, que je fais de vôtre conduite a mon egard, ne m'empeche pas de vous rendre justice. Les traducteurs donnent pour la plupart des louanges excessives aux ouvrages qu'ils traduisent, et s'imaginent peut-etre, que leur reputation depend en quelque façon de celles des auteurs, qu'ils ont choisis. Mais vous avez senti vos forces, qui vous mettent au dessus de pareilles precautions. Capable de corriger un mauvais livre, entreprise plus difficile que celle d'en composer un bon, vous n'avez n'avez pas craint de donner au public la traduction d'un ouvrage, que vous assurez etre plein de polisoneries, de sottises, de puerilités, &c. Nous convenons icy, que le goût des nations n'est pas toujours le meme. Mais nous sommes portés a croire, que le bon goût est le même par tout, ou il y a des gens d'esprit, de jugement, et de scavoir. Si donc les livres du sieur Gulliver ne sont calculés que pour les isles Britanniques, ce voyageur doit passer pour un tres pitoyable ecrivain. Les memes vices et les memes folies regnent par tout; du moins, dans tous les pays civilisés de l'Europe: et l'auteur, qui n'ecrit que pour une ville, une province, un royaume, ou meme un siecle, merite si peu d'être traduit, qu'il ne merite pas d'etre lû. . . .

To BENJAMIN MOTTE

December 28, 1727.

I had yours of the 16th from Mr. Hyde, and desire that henceforth you will write directly to me, without scrupling to load me with the postage. My head is so confused with the returns of my deafness to a very great degree—which left me after a fortnight, and then returned with more violence—that I am in an ill way to answer a letter which requires some thinking.

As to having cuts in Gulliver's Travels, you will consider how much it will raise the price of the book. The world glutted itself with that book at first, and now it will go off but soberly; but I suppose will not be soon worn out. The part of the little men will bear cuts much better than that of the great. I have not the book by me, but will speak by memory. Gulliver in his carriage to the metropolis, his extinguishing the fire, the ladies in their coaches driving about his table, his rising up out of his carriage when he is fastened to his horse, his drawing the

fleet,

fleet, the troop upon his handkerchief, the army marching between his legs, his hat drawn by eight horses, seem the fittest to be represented, and perhaps two adventures may be sometimes put in one print.

It is difficult to do anything in the great men, because Gulliver makes so diminutive a figure, and he is but one in the whole kingdom. Among some cuts I bought in London, he is shown taken out of the bowl of cream; but the hand that holds him hides the whole body. He would appear best wedged in the marrow-bone up to the middle, or in the monkey's arms upon the roof, or left upon the ridge, and the footman on the ladder going to relieve him, or fighting with the rats on the farmer's bed, or in the spaniel's mouth, which being described as a small dog, he might look as large as a duck in one of ours. One of the best would be, I think, to see his chest just falling into the sea, while three eagles are quarreling with one another; or the monkey hauling him out of his box. Mr. Wootton, the painter who draws landscapes and horses, told Mr. Pope and me that the graver did wrong in not making the big folks bear something [large], and enormous in their shapes, for, as drawn by those gravers, they look only like common human creatures. Gulliver being alone, and so little, cannot make the contrast appear.

The Flying Island might be drawn at large as described in the book, and Gulliver drawing up into it, and some fellows with flappers. I know not what to do with the Projectors. Nor what figure the Island of Ghosts would make, or any passage related in it, because I do not well remember it.

The Country of Horses, I think, would furnish many. Gulliver brought to be compared with the Yahoos; the family at dinner and he waiting; the grand council of horses, assembled, sitting, one of them standing with a

hoof

hoof extended, as if he were speaking; the she-Yahoos embracing Gulliver in the river, who turns away his head in disgust; the Yahoos got into a tree, to infest him under it; the Yahoos drawing carriages, and driven by a horse with a whip in his hoof. I can think of no more, but Mr. Gay will advise you, and carry you to Mr. Wootton and some other skilful people.

As to the poetical volume of Miscellany, I believe five parts in six, at least, are mine. Our two friends,[1] you know, have printed their works already, and we could expect nothing but slight loose papers. There is all the poetry I ever writ worth printing. Mr. Pope rejected some I sent him, for I desired him to be as severe as possible, and I will take his judgement. He writ to me, that he intended a pleasant discourse on the subject of poetry[2] should be printed before the volume, and says that discourse is ready[3] . . . I am as weary with writing as I fear you will be with reading. I am, Yours, &c.

To JOHN GAY

February 26, 1727–8.

Now why does not Mr. Pope publish his Dulness? The rogues he mauls will die of themselves in peace, and so will his friends, and so there will be neither punishment nor reward. Pray inquire how my Lord St. John does? There is no man's health in England I am more concerned about than his. I wonder whether you begin to taste the pleasure of independency; or whether you do not sometimes leer upon the Court, *oculo retorto*? Will you now think of an annuity, when you are two years older, and

[1] Pope and Gay.

[2] One of the Scriblerus essays, *Bathos, or, The Art of Sinking in Poetry*. See Pope's *Works*.

[3] The manuscript is torn here and the following lines are defective.

have

have doubled your purchase money? Have you dedicated your opera, and got the usual dedication fee of twenty guineas? How is the Doctor? Does he not chide that you never called upon him for hints? Is my Lord Bolinbroke, at the moment I am writing, a planter, a philosopher, or a writer? Is Mr. Pulteney in expectation of a son, or my Lord Bathurst of an employment, or my Lord Oxford of a new old manuscript?

Ask Mrs. Howard if she will take the remedy with which I twice perfectly cured my deafness, though I am again relapsed, and I will send her the receipt. I said something of this to Mr. Pope. Does Walpole think you intended an affront to him in your opera? Pray God he may, for he has held the longest hand at hazard that ever fell to any sharper's share, and keeps his run when the dice are charged. Present my most humble service to the deliverer of this letter, for so he must be, and not Dr. Delany, who stole away without it, by an accident. It is probable that I have forgot something of more moment than anything here. My service to Mr. Pope and all friends. Adieu.

I bought your opera to-day for sixpence, a cursed print. I find there is neither dedication nor preface, both which wants I approve; it is in the *grand goût*.

To ALEXANDER POPE

July 16, 1728.

I have often run over the Dunciad, in an Irish edition —I suppose full of faults—which a gentleman sent me. The notes I could wish to be very large, in what relates to the persons concerned; for I have long observed that twenty miles from London nobody understands hints, initial letters, or town facts and passages, and in a few years not even those who live in London. I would have

the

the names of those scribblers printed indexically at the beginning or end of the poem, with an account of their works, for the reader to refer to. I would have all the parodies, as they are called, referred to the author they imitate. When I began this long paper, I thought I should have filled it with setting down the several passages I had marked in the edition I had, but I find it unnecessary, so many of them falling under the same rule. After twenty times reading the whole, I never in my life saw so much good satire, or more good sense, in so many lines. How it passes in Dublin, I know not yet, but I am sure it will be a great disadvantage to the poem, that the persons and facts will not be understood till an explanation comes out, and a very full one. I imagine it not to be published till towards winter, when folks begin to gather in town. Again I insist, you must have your asterisks filled up with some real names of real dunces. . . .

As to yourself, I doubt you want a spurrer-on to exercise and to amusements; but to talk of decay at your season of life is a jest. But you are not so regular as I. You are the most temperate man God-ward, and the most intemperate yourself-ward, of most I have known. I suppose Mr. Gay will return from the Bath with twenty pounds more flesh, and two-hundred less in money. Providence never designed him to be above two-and-twenty, by his thoughtlessness and cullibility. He has as little foresight of age, sickness, poverty, or loss of admirers, as a girl of fifteen. By the way, I must observe, that my Lord Bolinbroke, from the effects of his kindness to me, argues most sophistically. The fall from a million to a hundred thousand pounds is not so great as from eight hundred pounds a year to one: besides he is a controller of fortune, and poverty dares not look a great Minister in the face under his lowest declension. I never

knew

knew him live so greatly and expensively as he has done since his return from exile; such mortals have resources that others are not able to comprehend. But God bless you, whose great genius had not transported you as to leave you to the courtesy of mankind; for wealth is liberty, and liberty is a blessing fittest for a philosopher, and Gay is a slave just by two thousand pounds too little, and Horace was of my mind, and let my Lord contradict him if he dares.

To Viscount Bolinbroke

March 21, 1729-30.

You tell me you have not quitted the design of collecting, writing, &c. This is the answer of every sinner who defers his repentance. I wish Mr. Pope were as great an urger as I, who long for nothing more than to see truth, under your hands, laying all detraction in the dust. I find myself disposed every year, or rather every month, to be more angry and revengeful; and my rage is so ignoble, that it descends even to resent the folly and baseness of the enslaved people among whom I live. I knew an old Lord in Leicestershire, who amused himself with mending pitchforks and spades for his tenants gratis. Yet I have higher ideas left, if I were nearer to objects on which I might employ them; and contemning my private fortune, would gladly cross the channel and stand by while my betters were driving the boars out of the garden, if there be any probable expectation of such an endeavour. When I was of your age I often thought of death, but now, after a dozen years more, it is never out of my mind, and terrifies me less. I conclude that Providence has ordered our fears to decrease with our spirits; and yet I love *la bagatelle* better than ever, for, finding it troublesome to read at night, and the company

here

here growing tasteless, I am always writing bad prose, or worse verses, either of rage or raillery, whereof some few escape to give offence, or mirth, and the rest are burnt. They print some Irish trash in London, and charge it on me, which you will clear me of to my friends, for all are spurious except one paper,[1] for which Mr. Pope very lately chid me.

I remember your Lordship used to say, that a few good speakers would in time carry any point that was right; and that the common method of a majority, by calling to the question, would never hold long when reason was on the other side. Whether politics do not change like gaming, by the invention of new tricks, I am ignorant; but I believe in your time you would never, as a Minister, have suffered an Act to pass through the House of Commons, only because you were sure of a majority in the House of Lords to throw it out, because it would be unpopular, and consequently a loss of reputation. Yet this, we are told, has been the case in the Qualification Bill relating to Pensioners. It would seem to me that corruption, like avarice, has no bounds. I had opportunities to know the proceedings of your Ministry better than any man of my rank; and having not much to do, I have often compared it with these last sixteen years of a profound peace all over Europe, and we running seven millions in debt. I am forced to play at small game, to set the beasts here a-madding merely for want of better game. *Tentanda via est qua me quoque possim*, &c. The d— take those politics, where a dunce might govern for a dozen years together. I will come in person to England if I am provoked, and send for the dictator from the plough. I disdain to say, *O mihi praeteritos*, but *cruda deo viridisque senectus*.

[1] The poem, *A Libel on Dr. Delany*.

Pray,

Pray, my Lord, how are the gardens? Have you taken down the mount, and removed the yew hedges? Have you not bad weather for the spring corn? Has Mr. Pope gone farther in his ethic poems? And is the headland sown with wheat? And what says Polybius? And how does my Lord St. John, which last question is very material to me, because I love Burgundy, and riding between Twickenham and Dawley? I built a wall five years ago, and when the masons played the knaves, nothing delighted me so much as to stand by while my servants threw down what was amiss. I have likewise seen a monkey overthrow all the dishes and plates in a kitchen, merely for the pleasure of seeing them tumble, and hearing the clatter they made in their fall. I wish you would invite me to such another entertainment; but you think, as I ought to think, that it is time for me to have done with the world, and so I would if I could get into a better before I was called into the best, and not die here in a rage, like a poisoned rat in a hole. I wonder you are not ashamed to let me pine away in this kingdom, while you are out of power.

I come from looking over the *mélange* above-written, and declare it to be a true copy of my present disposition, which must needs please you, since nothing was ever more displeasing to myself. I desire you to present my most humble respects to my Lady.

To JOHN ARBUTHNOT

November, 1734.

My Dear Friend,

I never once suspected your forgetfulness or want of friendship, but very often dreaded your want of health, to which alone I imputed every delay longer than ordinary in hearing from you. I should be very ungrateful, indeed,

if

if I acted otherwise to you, who are pleased to take such generous constant care of my health, my interests, and my reputation, who represented me so favourably to that blessed Queen your mistress, as well as to her Ministers, and to all your friends. The letters you mention, which I did not answer, I cannot find, and yet I have all that ever came from you, for I constantly endorse yours and those of a few other friends, and date them; only if there be anything particular, though of no consequence, when I go to the country I send them to some friends among other papers for fear of accidents in my absence. I thank you kindly for your favour to the young man who was bred in my choir. The people of skill in music represent him to me as a lad of virtue, and hopeful and endeavouring in his way. It is your own fault if I give you trouble, because you never refused me anything in your life.

You tear my heart with the ill account of your health; yet if it should please God to call you away before me, I should not pity you in the least, except on the account of what pains you might feel before you passed into a better life. I should pity none but your friends, and among them chiefly myself, although I never can hope to have health enough to leave this country till I leave the world. I do not know among mankind any person more prepared to depart from us than yourself, not even the Bishop of Marseilles, if he be still alive; for among all your qualities that have procured you the love and esteem of the world, I ever most valued your moral and Christian virtues, which were not the product of years or sickness, but of reason and religion, as I can witness after above five-and-twenty years' acquaintance. I except only the too little care of your fortune; upon which I have been so free as sometimes to examine and to chide you, and the consequence of which hath been to confine you to London, when

when you are under a disorder for which I am told, and know, that the clear air of the country is necessary.

The great reason that hinders my journey to England, is the same that drives you from Highgate. I am not in circumstances to keep horses and servants in London. My revenues by the miserable oppressions of this kingdom are sunk three hundred pounds a year, for tithes are become a drug, and I have but little rents from the deanery lands, which are my only sure payments. I have here a large convenient house; I live at two-thirds cheaper here than I could there; I drink a bottle of French wine myself every day, though I love it not, but it is the only thing that keeps me out of pain; I ride every fair day a dozen miles, on a large strand or turnpike roads. You in London have no such advantages. I can buy a chicken for a groat, and entertain three or four friends, with as many dishes, and two or three bottles of French wine, for ten shillings. When I dine alone, my pint and chicken with the appendixes cost me about fifteen pence. I am thrifty in everything but wine, of which though I be not a constant housekeeper, I spend between five and six hogshead a year. When I ride to a friend a few miles off, if he be not richer than I, I carry my bottle, my bread and chicken, that he may be no loser.

I talk thus foolishly to let you know the reasons which, joined to my ill-health, make it impossible for me to see you and my other friends; and perhaps this domestic tattle may excuse me and amuse you. I could not live with my Lord Bolinbroke or Mr. Pope: they are both too temperate and too wise for me, and too profound and too poor. And how could I afford horses? And how could I ride over their cursed roads in winter, and be turned into a ditch by every carter or hackney-coach? Every parish minister of this city is governor of all carriages, and so are

the

the two Deans, and every carrier should make way for us at their peril. Therefore, like Caesar, I will be one of the first here rather than the last among you. I forget that I am so near the bottom. I am now with one of my Prebendaries, five miles in the country, for five days. I brought with me eight bottles of wine, with bread and meat for three days, which is my club; he is a bachelor, with three hundred pounds a year. May God preserve you, my dear friend.

Entirely yours,
J. Swift.

To Alexander Pope

February 7, 1735–6.

It is some time since I dined at the Bishop of Derry's, where Mr. Secretary Carey told me, with great concern, that you were taken very ill. I have heard nothing since, only I have continued in great pain of mind, yet for my own sake and the world's more than for yours; because I know well how little you value life, both as a philosopher, and a Christian, particularly the latter, wherein hardly one in a million of us heretics can equal you. If you are well recovered, you ought to be reproached for not putting me especially out of pain, who could not bear the loss of you; although we must be forever distant as much as if I were in the grave, for which my years and continual indisposition are preparing me every season. I have stayed too long from pressing you to give me some ease by an account of your health. Pray do not use me so ill any more. I look upon you as an estate from which I receive my best annual rents, although I am never to see it. Mr. Tickell was at the same meeting under the same real concern, and so were a hundred others of this town who had never seen you.

I read

I read to the Bishop of Derry the paragraph in your letter which concerned him, and his Lordship expressed his thankfulness in a manner that became him. He is esteemed here as a person of learning, and conversation, and humanity; but he is beloved by all people. He is a most excessive Whig, but without any appearing rancour, and his idol is King William; besides, three thousand a year is an invincible sweetener.

I have nobody now left but you. Pray be so kind as to outlive me, and then die as soon as you please, but without pain; and let us meet in a better place, if my religion will permit, but rather my virtue, although much unequal to yours. Pray let my Lord Bathurst know how much I love him. I still insist on his remembering me, although he is too much in the world to honour an absent friend with his letters. My state of health is not to boast of; my giddiness is more or less too constant; I have not an ounce of flesh between skin and bone; I sleep ill, and have a poor appetite. I can as easily write a poem in the Chinese language as my own. I am as fit for matrimony as invention; and yet I have daily schemes for innumerable essays in prose, and proceed sometimes to no less than half a dozen lines, which the next morning become waste paper. What vexes me most is, that my female friends, who could bear me very well a dozen years ago, have now forsaken me, although I am not so old in proportion to them, as I formerly was, which I can prove by arithmetic, for then I was double their age, which now I am not.

Pray put me out of fear as soon as you can, about that ugly report of your illness; and let me know who this Cheselden is, that has so lately sprung up in your favour. Give me also some account of your neighbour who writ to me from Bath. I hear he resolves to be strenuous for

taking

taking off the Test, which grieves me extremely, from all the unprejudiced reasons I ever was able to form, and against the maxims of all wise Christian governments, which always had some established religion, leaving at best a toleration to others. Farewell, my dearest friend, ever, and upon every account that can create friendship and esteem.

To Mrs. Whiteway

October 3, 1738.

Mr. Swift's gimcracks of cups and balls,[1] in order to my convenient shaving with ease and dispatch, together with the prescription on half a sheet of paper, was exactly followed, but some inconveniences attended; for I cut my face once or twice, was just twice as long in the performance, and left twice as much hair behind as I have done this twelvemonth past. I return him therefore all his implements, and my own compliments, with abundance of thanks, because he hath fixed me during life in my old humdrum way. Give me a full and true account of all your healths, and so adieu. I am ever, &c.

J. Swift.

October 3rd or 4th, or rather,
as the butler says, the 2nd,
on Tuesday, 1738.

To ———

January 9, 1739–40.

Whereas the bearer served me the space of one year, during which time he was an idler and a drunkard, I then discharged him as such; but how far his having been five years at sea may have mended his manners, I leave to the penetration of those who may hereafter choose to employ him.

Jon. Swift.

[1] A shaving set sent as a gift by Deane Swift.

To

To Mrs. Whiteway

April 29, 1740.

Dear Madam,

I find that you and I are fellow sufferers almost equally in our healths, although I am more than twenty years older; but I am and have been these two days in so miserable a way, and so cruelly tortured, that can hardly be conceived. The whole of last night I was equally struck as if I had been in Phalaris's brazen bull, and roared as loud for eight or nine hours. I am at this instant unable to move without excessive pain, although not the one-thousandth part of what I suffered all last night and this morning. This you will now style the gout. I continue still very deaf. Doctor Wilson's left eye is still disordered, and very uneasy. You have now your family at home; I desire to present them with my kind and hearty service. I am,

Ever entirely yours, &c.

J. Swift.

POEMS

Swift's general characteristics and limitations as a writer of verse have been discussed in the Introduction. The selection of poems to be included in this volume is not representative of the complete list. Much of Swift's poetry would not pass the censor, and is, in any case, not fit for reading. Another large section of his verse consists of rubbish which he wrote in his old age: puns, riddles, jumbles of Latin and English, echoes, and double acrostics. The remainder, however, includes much that is of interest, and is represented here by one or two trifles, some verses to Stella, a few really effective satires, the verses in which Swift discusses his favourite weapon, irony, and (above all) the famous verses on his own death. The darkest hours of his scepticism, when distrust of reason and of religion alike led him to the borders of insanity, is reflected in *The Day of Judgment.*

The early printings of Swift's verse are unsatisfactory. The texts reproduced are those of Faulkner's first edition of Swift's *Works*, 1735, vol. ii, collated carefully with the edition of Swift's *Poems*, by W. E. Browning, London, 1910, 2 vols.

Verses Wrote on a Lady's Ivory Table-Book, 1698

PERUSE my leaves thro' ev'ry part,
And think thou seest my owner's heart,
Scrawl'd o'er with trifles thus, and quite
As hard, as senseless, and as light;
Expos'd to ev'ry coxcomb's eyes,
But hid with Caution from the wise.
Here you may read (*Dear charming saint*)
Beneath (*A new receipt for paint:*)
Here in beau-spelling (*tru tel deth,*)
There in her own (*for an el breth.*)
Here (*lovely nymph pronounce my doom,*)
There (*a safe way to use perfume;*)
Here a page fill'd with billets-doux;
On t'other side (*laid out for shoes:*)
(*Madam, I die without your grace,*)
(Item, *for half a yard of lace*).
Who that had wit would place it here,
For ev'ry peeping fop to jeer?
In power of spittle, and a clout,
Whene'er he please to blot it out;
And then, to heighten the disgrace,
Clap his own nonsense in the place.
Whoe'er expects to hold his part
In such a book, and such a heart,
If he be wealthy, and a fool,
Is in all points the fittest tool;
Of whom it may be justly said,
He's a gold pencil tipp'd with lead.

A Description

A Description of the Morning, 1709[1]

NOW hardly here and there an hackney coach
Appearing, shew'd the ruddy morn's approach.
Now Betty from her master's bed had flown,
And softly stole to discompose her own.
The slipshod 'prentice from his master's door
Had par'd the dirt, and sprinkled round the floor.
Now Moll had twirl'd her mop with dext'rous airs,
Prepar'd to scrub the entry and the stairs.
The youth with broomy stumps began to trace
The Kennel-edge, where wheels had worn the place.
The small-coal man was heard with cadence deep,
'Till drown'd in shriller notes of chimney-sweep.
Duns at his lordship's gate began to meet;
And brick-dust Moll had scream'd thro' half the street.
The turnkey now his flock returning sees,
Duly let out a-nights to steal for fees.
The watchful bailiffs take their silent stands;
And school-boys lag with satchels in their hands.

A Description of a City Shower, 1710[2]

CAREFUL observers may foretell the hour
(By sure prognosticks) when to dread a show'r.
While rain depends, the pensive cat gives o'er
Her frolicks, and pursues her tail no more;
Returning home at night, you'll find the sink
Strike your offended sense with double stink.
If you be wise, then go not far to dine,
You'll spend in coach-hire more than save in wine.

[1] First printed in the *Tatler*, No. 9.
[2] First printed in the *Tatler*, No. 238.

A coming

A coming show'r your shooting corns presage,
Old achés throb, your hollow tooth will rage.
Saunt'ring in coffee-house is Dulman seen;
He damns the climate, and complains of spleen.
  Meanwhile the South, rising with dabbled wings,
A sable cloud athwart the welkin flings,
That swill'd more liquor than it could contain,
And like a drunkard gives it up again.
Brisk Susan whips her linen from the rope,
While the first drizzling show'r is born aslope;
Such is that sprinkling which some careless quean
Flirts on you from her mop, but not so clean.
You fly, invoke the gods; then turning, stop
To rail; she singing, still whirls on her mop.
Not yet the dust had shunn'd th' unequal strife,
But aided by the wind, fought still for life,
And wafted with its foe by violent gust,
'Twas doubtful which was rain, and which was dust.
Ah, where must needy poet seek for aid,
When dust and rain at once his coat invade?
His only coat, where dust confus'd with rain
Roughen the nap, and leave a mingled stain.
  Now in contiguous drops the flood comes down,
Threat'ning with deluge this devoted town.
To shops in crowds the daggled females fly,
Pretend to cheapen goods, but nothing buy.
The Templar spruce, while ev'ry spout's abroach,
Stays till 'tis fair, yet seems to call a coach.
The tuck'd-up sempstress walks with hasty strides,
While streams run down her oil'd umbrella's sides.
Here various kinds by various fortunes led,
Commence acquaintance underneath a shed.
Triumphant Tories, and desponding Whigs,
Forget their feuds, and join to save their wigs.

Box'd

Box'd in a chair the beau impatient sits,
While spouts run clatt'ring o'er the roof by fits;
And ever and anon, with frightful din
The leather sounds; he trembles from within.
So when Troy chairmen bore the wooden steed,
Pregnant with Greeks, impatient to be freed;
(Those bully Greeks, who, as the Modern do,
Instead of paying chairmen, run them thro'.)
Laocoon struck the outside with his spear,
And each imprison'd hero quaked for fear.
Now from all parts the swelling kennels flow,
And bear their trophies with them as they go:
Filth of all hues and odours, seem to tell
What street they sail'd from, by their sight and smell.
They, as each torrent drives, with rapid force
From Smithfield, or St. Pulchre's shape their course,
And in huge confluence join at Snow-hill ridge,
Fall from the conduit prone to Holbourn bridge.
Sweepings from butchers' stalls, dung, guts, and blood,
Drown'd puppies, stinking sprats, all drench'd in mud,
Dead cats, and turnip-tops, come tumbling down the flood.

Phyllis; or, The Progress of Love, 1716

DESPONDING Phyllis was endu'd
With ev'ry talent of a prude:
She trembled when a man drew near;
Salute her, and she turn'd her ear;
If o'er against her you were plac'd,
She durst not look above your waste:
She'd rather take you to her bed
Than let you see her dress her head;
In church you'd hear her, thro' the crowd,
Repeat the Absolution loud;

In

In church, secure behind her fan,
She durst behold that monster, man;
There practis'd how to place her head,
And bite her lips to make them red;
Or, on the mat devoutly kneeling,
Would lift her eyes up to the ceiling,
And heave her bosom, unaware,
For neighb'ring beaux to see it bare.
At length, a lucky lover came,
And found admittance to the dame.
Suppose all parties now agreed,
The writings drawn, the lawyer fee'd,
The vicar and the ring bespoke;
Guess, how could such a match be broke?
See then what mortals place their bliss in!
Next morn, betimes, the bride was missing.
The mother scream'd, the father chid;
Where can this idle wench be hid?
No news of Phil! The bridegroom came,
And thought his bride had skulk'd for shame;
Because her father us'd to say,
The girl had such a bashful way.
Now John the butler must be sent,
To learn the road that Phyllis went.
The groom was wish'd to saddle Crop;
For John must neither light nor stop,
But find her wheresoe'er she fled,
And bring her back, alive or dead.
See here again, the devil to do!
For truly, John was missing too.
The horse and pillion both were gone!
Phyllis, it seems, was fled with John.
Old Madam, who went up to find
What papers Phil had left behind,

A letter on the toilet sees,
'To my much honour'd father—these—'
('Tis always done, romances tell us,
When daughters run away with fellows,)
Fill'd with the choicest common-places,
By others us'd in the like cases.
'That, long ago, a fortune-teller
Exactly said what now befell her;
And in a glass had made her see
A serving-man of low degree.
It was her fate, must be forgiven;
For marriages were made in heaven:
His pardon begg'd; but, to be plain,
She'd do't if 'twere to do again.
Thank God, 'twas neither shame nor sin,
For John was come of honest kin.
Love never thinks of rich or poor,
She'd beg with John from door to door.
Forgive her, if it be a crime,
She'll never do't another time.
She ne'er before in all her life
Once disobey'd him, maid nor wife.'
One argument she summ'd up all in,
'The thing was done, and past recalling;
And therefore hop'd she should recover
His favour when his passion's over.
She valued not what others thought her,
And was—his most obedient daughter.'

Fair maidens all, attend the Muse,
Who now the wand'ring pair pursues.
Away they rode in homely sort,
Their journey long, their money short;
The loving couple well bemir'd;
The horse and both the riders tir'd;

Their

Their victuals bad, their lodging worse:
Phil cry'd, and John began to curse;
Phil wish'd that she had strained a limb.
When first she ventur'd out with him;
John wish'd that he had broke a leg,
When first for her he quitted Peg.
But what adventures more befell 'em.
The Muse hath now no time to tell 'em;
How Johnny wheedled, threaten'd, fawn'd,
'Till Phyllis all her trinkets pawn'd;
How oft she broke her marriage vows,
In kindness, to maintain her spouse,
'Till swains unwholesome spoil'd the trade;
For now the surgeon must be pay'd,
To whom those perquisites are gone,
In Christian justice due to John.
When food and raiment now grew scarce,
Fate put a period to the farce,
And with exact poetic justice;
For John is landlord, Phyllis hostess;
They keep, at Staines, the Old Blue Boar,
Are cat and dog, and rogue and whore.

To a Lady

(Who Desired the Author to Write Some Verses upon Her in the Heroic Style)

AFTER venting all my spite,
Tell me, what have I to write?
Every error I could find
Through the mazes of your mind,
Have my busy Muse employ'd,
Till the company was cloy'd.

Are

Are you positive and fretful,
Heedless, ignorant, forgetful?
Those, and twenty follies more,
I have often told before.
  Hearken what my lady says:
'Have I nothing then to praise?
Ill it fits you to be witty,
Where a fault should move your pity.
If you think me too conceited,
Or to passion quickly heated;
If my wandering head be less
Set on reading than on dress;
If I always seem too dull t'ye;
I can solve the diffi-culty.
  You would teach me to be wise;
Truth and honour how to prize;
How to shine in conversation,
And with credit fill my station
How to relish notions high;
How to live and how to die.
  But it was decreed by Fate—
Mr. Dean, you come too late.
Well I know, you can discern,
I am now too old to learn;
Follies, from my youth instill'd,
Have my soul entirely fill'd;
In my head and heart they centre,
Nor will let your lessons enter.
  Bred a fondling and an heiress;
Drest like any lady mayoress;
Cocker'd by the servants round,
Was too good to touch the ground;
Thought the life of every lady
Should be one continued play-day:

Balls,

Balls, and masquerades, and shows,
Visits, plays, and powder'd beaux.
  Thus you have my case at large,
And may now perform your charge.
Those materials I have furnish'd,
When by you refined and burnish'd,
Must, that all the world may know 'em,
Be reduced into a poem.
  But, I beg, suspend a while
That same paltry, burlesque style;
Drop for once your constant rule,
Turning all to ridicule;
Teaching others how to ape you;
Court nor parliament can 'scape you;
Treat the public and your friends
Both alike, while neither mends.
Sing my praise in strain sublime;
Treat me not with dogg'rel rhyme.
'Tis but just you should produce,
With each fault, each fault's excuse;
Not to publish every trifle,
And my few perfections stifle.
With some gifts at least endow me,
Which my very foes allow me.
Am I spiteful, proud, unjust?
Did I ever break my trust?
Which of all our modern dames
Censures less, or less defames?
In good manners am I faulty?
Can you call me rude or haughty?
Did I e'er my mite withhold
From the impotent and old?
When did ever I omit
Due regard for men of wit?

When

When have I esteem express'd
For a coxcomb gaily dress'd?
Do I, like the female tribe,
Think it wit to fleer and gibe?
Who with less designing ends
Kindlier entertains her friends;
With good words and countenance sprightly,
Strives to treat them more politely?
Think not cards my chief diversion;
'Tis a wrong, unjust aspersion;
Never knew I any good in 'em,
But to dose my head like laudanum.
We, by play, as men, by drinking,
Pass our nights to drive out thinking.
From my ailments give me leisure,
I shall read and think with pleasure;
Conversation learn to relish,
And with books my mind embellish.'
  Now, methinks, I hear you cry,
Mr. Dean, you must reply:
  Madam, I allow 'tis true,
All these praises are your due.
You, like some acute philosopher,
Every fault have drawn a gloss over;
Placing in the strongest light
All your virtues to my sight.
  Though you lead a blameless life,
Are a humble prudent wife,
Answer all domestic ends;
What is this to us your friends?
Though your children by a nod
Stand in awe without a rod;
Though, by your obliging sway,
Servants love you, and obey;

Though

Though you treat us with a smile;
Clear your looks, and smooth your style;
Load our plates from every dish;
This is not the thing we wish.
Colonel . . . may be your debtor;
We expect employment better.
You must learn, if you would gain us,
With good sense to entertain us.
Scholars, when good sense describing,
Call it tasting and imbibing;
Metaphoric meat and drink
Is to understand and think;
We may carve for others thus,
And let others carve for us;
To discourse, and to attend,
Is to help yourself and friend.
Conversation is but carving;
Carve for all, yourself is starving;
Give no more to every guest,
Than he's able to digest;
Give him always of the prime,
And but little at a time.
Carve to all but just enough;
Let them neither starve nor stuff.
And, that you may have your due,
Let your neighbours carve for you.
This comparison will hold,
Could it well in rhyme be told,
How conversing, listening, thinking,
Justly may resemble drinking;
For a friend a glass you fill,
What is this but to instil?
To conclude this long essay;
Pardon if I disobey,

Nor

Nor against my natural vein,
Treat you in heroic strain.
I, as all the parish knows,
Hardly can be grave in prose.
Still to lash, and lashing smile,
Ill befits a lofty style.
From the planet of my birth
I encounter vice with mirth.
Wicked ministers of state
I can easier scorn than hate;
And I find it answers right;
Scorn torments them more than spight.
All the vices of a court
Do but serve to make me sport.
Were I in some foreign realm,
Which all vices overwhelm,
Should a monkey wear a crown,
Must I tremble at his frown?
Could I not, through all his ermine,
'Spy the strutting chattering vermin;
Safely write a smart lampoon,
To expose the brisk baboon?
When my Muse officious ventures
On the nation's representers;
Teaching by what golden rules
Into knaves they turn their fools;
How the helm is ruled by Walpole,
At whose oars, like slaves, they all pull;
Let the vessel split on shelves;
With the freight enrich themselves.
Safe within my little wherry,
All their madness makes me merry.
Like the waterman of Thames,
I row by, and call them names;

Like

Like the ever-laughing sage,[1]
In a jest I spend my rage.
(Though it must be understood,
I would hang them if I could.)
I can but fill up my niche,
I attempt no higher pitch;
Leave to d'Anvers and his mate
Maxims wise to rule the state.
Pulteney deep, accomplish'd St. Johns,
Scourge the villains with a vengeance;
Let me, though the smell be noisome,
Strip their bums; let Caleb hoise 'em;
Then apply Alecto's[2] whip
Till they wriggle, howl, and skip.
'Deuce is in you, Mr. Dean;
What can all this passion mean?
Mention courts, you'll ne'er be quiet
On corruptions running riot.
End as it befits your station;
Come to use and application;
Nor with senates keep a fuss.'
I submit; and answer thus:
If the machinations brewing,
To complete the public ruin,
Never once could have the power
To affect me half an hour;
Sooner would I write in buskins,
Mournful elegies on Blueskins.[3]
If I laugh at Whig and Tory;
I conclude *à fortiori*,
All your eloquence will scarce

[1] Democritus.
[2] One of the three avenging Furies of Greek mythology.
[3] A criminal who stabbed Jonathan Wild at the Old Bailey.

Drive

Drive me from my favourite farce.
This I must insist on; for, as
It is well observed by Horace,[1]
Ridicule has greater power
To reform the world than sour.
Horses thus, (let jockeys judge else)
Switches better guide than cudgels.
Bastings heavy, dry, obtuse,
Only dulness can produce;
While a little gentle jerking
Sets the spirits all a-working.
  Thus, I find it by experiment,
Scolding moves you less than merriment.
I may storm and rage in vain;
It but stupifies your brain.
But with raillery to nettle,
Sets your thoughts upon their mettle;
Gives imagination scope;
Never lets your mind elope;
Drives out brangling and contention.
Brings in reason and invention.
For your sake as well as mine,
I the lofty style decline.
I should make a figure scurvy,
And your head turn topsy-turvy.
  I who love to have a fling
Both at senate-house and king;
That they might some better way tread,
To avoid the public hatred;
Thought no method more commodious,
Than to show their vices odious;
Which I chose to make appear,
Not by anger but by sneer.

[1] *Satires*, i. x. 14–15.

As

As my method of reforming,
Is by laughing, not by storming,
(For my friends have always thought
Tenderness my greatest fault,)
Would you have me change my style?
On your faults no longer smile;
But, to patch up all our quarrels,
Quote you texts from Plutarch's Morals,
Or from Solomon produce
Maxims teaching Wisdom's use?

If I treat you like a crown'd head,
You have cheap enough compounded;
Can you put in higher claims,
Than the owners of St. James?
You are not so great a grievance,
As the hirelings of St. Stephen's.
You are of a lower class
Than my friend Sir Robert Brass.
None of these have mercy found;
I have laugh'd, and lashed them round.

Have you seen a rocket fly?
You would swear it pierced the sky.
It but reach'd the middle air,
Bursting into pieces there;
Thousand sparkles falling down
Light on many a coxcomb's crown.
See what mirth the sport creates!
Singes hair, but breaks no pates.
Thus, should I attempt to climb,
Treat you in a style sublime,
Such a rocket is my Muse:
Should I lofty numbers choose,
Ere I reach'd Parnassus' top,
I should burst, and bursting drop;

All

All my fire would fall in scraps.
Give your head some gentle raps;
Only make it smart a while;
Then could I forbear to smile,
When I found the tingling pain
Entering warm your frigid brain;
Make you able upon sight
To decide of wrong and right;
Talk with sense whate'er you please on;
Learn to relish truth and reason!

Thus we both shall gain our prize;
I to laugh, and you grow wise.

A Satirical Elegy

On the Death of a Late Famous General, 1722[1]

HIS Grace! impossible! what, dead!
Of old age too, and in his bed!
And could that mighty warrior fall,
And so inglorious, after all?
Well, since he's gone, no matter how,
The last loud trump must wake him now;
And, trust me, as the noise grows stronger,
He'd wish to sleep a little longer.
And could he be indeed so old
As by the newspapers we're told?
Threescore, I think, is pretty high;
'Twas time in conscience he should die!
This world he cumber'd long enough;
He burnt his candle to the snuff;
And that's the reason, some folks think,
He left behind so great a stink.

[1] The Duke of Marlborough.

Behold

Behold his funeral appears,
Nor widows' sighs, nor orphans' tears,
Wont at such times each heart to pierce,
Attend the progress of his hearse.
And what of that? his friends may say,
He had those honours in his day.
True to his profit and his pride,
He made them weep before he died.
  Come hither, all ye empty things.
Ye bubbles raised by breath of kings!
Who float upon the tide of state;
Come hither, and behold your fate.
Let Pride be taught by this rebuke,
How very mean a thing's a duke;
From all his ill-got honours flung,
Turn'd to that dirt from whence he sprung.

Verses

On the Revival of the Order of the Bath, during Walpole's Administration, 1725

QUOTH King Robin, our ribbons I see are too few
Of St. Andrew's the green, and St. George's the blue.
I must find out another of colour more gay,
That will teach all my subjects with pride to obey.
Though the exchequer be drain'd by prodigal donors,
Yet the king ne'er exhausted his fountain of honours.
Men of more wit than money our pensions will fit,
And this will fit men of more money than wit.
Thus my subjects with pleasure will obey my commands,
Though as empty as Younge, and as saucy as Sandes.
And he who'll leap over a stick for the king,
Is qualified best for a dog in a string.[1]

[1] Cf. *Gulliver's Travels*, i, ch. 3.

On

On the Vowels

We are little airy creatures,
All of different voice and features;
One of us in *glass* is set,
One of us you'll find in *jet*.
T'other you may see in *tin*,
And the fourth a *box* within.
If the fifth you should pursue,
It can never fly from *you*.

Verses made for Fruit-Women

Apples

Come buy my fine wares,
Plums, apples, and pears.
A hundred a penny,
In conscience too many.
Come, will you have any?
My children are seven,
I wish them in heaven;
My husband a sot,
With his pipe and his pot,
Not a farthing will gain them,
And I must maintain them.

Oysters

Charming oysters I cry:
My masters, come buy,
So plump and so fresh,
So sweet is their flesh,
No Colchester oyster
Is sweeter and moister.

Your

Your stomach they settle,
And rouse up your mettle.
They'll make you a dad
Of a lass or a lad;
And madam your wife
They'll please to the life.
Be she barren, be she old,
Be she slut, or be she scold,
Eat my oysters, and lie near her,
She'll be fruitful, never fear her.

Oranges

Come buy my fine oranges, sauce for your veal,
And charming, when squeezed in a pot of brown ale;
Well roasted, with sugar and wine in a cup,
They'll make a sweet bishop when gentlefolk sup.

To Dr. Delany

On the Libels Written Against Him, 1729

AS some raw youth in country bred,
To arms by thirst of honour led,
When at a skirmish first he hears
The bullets whistling round his ears,
Will duck his head, aside will start,
And feel a trembling at his heart;
Till, 'scaping oft without a wound
Lessens the terror of the sound;
Fly bullets now as thick as hops,
He runs into a cannon's chops.
An author thus who pants for fame
Begins the world with fear and shame;
When first in print, you see him dread
Each pot-gun levell'd at his head.

The

The lead yon critic's quill contains,
Is destined to beat out his brains;
As if he heard loud thunders roll,
Cries, Lord have mercy on his soul;
Concluding, that another shot
Will strike him dead upon the spot.
But, when with squibbing, flashing, popping,
He cannot see one creature dropping;
That, missing fire, or missing aim,
His life is safe, I mean his fame,
The danger past, takes heart of grace,
And looks a critic in the face.
  Though splendour gives the fairest mark
To poison'd arrows from the dark,
Yet, *in yourself when smooth and round*,
They glance aside without a wound.
  'Tis said, the gods tried all their art,
How pain they might from pleasure part
But little could their strength avail,
Both still are fasten'd by the tail.
Thus, fame and censure with a tether
By fate are always link'd together.
  Why will you aim to be preferr'd
In wit before the common herd?
And yet, grow mortify'd and vext,
To pay the penalty annext?
  'Tis eminence makes envy rise,
As fairest fruits attract the flies.
Should stupid libels grieve your mind,
You soon a remedy may find;
Lie down obscure like other folks
Below the lash of snarlers' jokes.
Their faction is five hundred odds,
For, ev'ry coxcomb lends them rods;

And

And sneers as learnedly as they,
Like females o'er their morning tea.
  You say, the Muse will not contain,
And write you must, or break a vein.
Then, if you find the terms too hard,
No longer my advice regard;
But raise your fancy on the wing;
The Irish senate's praises sing:
How jealous of the nation's freedom,
And, for corruptions, how they weed 'em;
How each the public good pursues,
How far their hearts from private views;
Make all true patriots up to shoe-boys,
Huzza their brethren at the Blue-boys.
And dread no more the rage of Grub,
You then may soon be of the Club.
  How oft am I for rhyme to seek?
To dress a thought, I toil a week;
And then how thankful to the town,
If all my pains will earn a crown.
Whilst ev'ry critic can devour
My work and me in half an hour.
Would men of genius cease to write,
The rogues must die for want of spight;
Must die for want of food and raiment,
If scandal did not find them payment.
How cheerfully the hawkers cry
A satire, and the gentry buy!
While my hard-labour'd poem pines
Unsold upon the printer's lines.
  A genius in the reverend gown,
Must ever keep its owner down;
'Tis an unnatural conjunction,
And spoils the credit of the function.

Round

Round all your brethren cast your eyes,
Point out the surest men to rise:
That club of candidates in black,
The least deserving of the pack,
Aspiring, factious, fierce, and loud,
With grace and learning unendow'd,
Will sooner coin a thousand lies,
Than suffer men of parts to rise;
They crowd about preferment's gate,
And press you down with all their weight.
For as of old mathematicians
Were by the vulgar thought magicians;
So academic dull ale-drinkers
Pronounce all men of wit, free-thinkers.
Wit, as the chief of virtue's friends,
Disdains to serve ignoble ends.
Observe what loads of stupid rhymes
Oppress us in corrupted times;
What pamphlets in a court's defence
Shew reason, grammar, truth, or sense?
For, though the Muse delights in fiction,
She ne'er inspires against conviction.
Then keep your virtue still unmixt,
And let not faction come betwixt.
By party-steps no grandeur climb at,
Though it should make you England's primate;
First learn the science to be dull,
You then may soon your conscience lull;
If not, however seated high,
Your genius in your face will fly.
When Jove was, from his teeming head,
Of Wit's fair goddess brought to bed,
There follow'd at his lying-in
For after-birth a sooterkin;

Which,

Which, as the nurse pursued to kill,
Attain'd by flight the Muses' hill;
There in the soil began to root,
And litter'd at Parnassus' foot.
From hence the critic vermin sprung,
With harpy claws and poisonous tongue;
Who fatten on poetic scraps;
Too cunning to be caught in traps.
Dame Nature, as the learned shew,
Provides each animal its foe:
Hounds hunt the hare, the wily fox
Devours your geese, the wolf your flocks;
Thus Envy pleads a natural claim
To persecute the Muse's fame;
On poets in all times abusive,
From Homer down to Pope inclusive.
  Yet what avails it to complain?
You try to take revenge in vain.
A rat your utmost rage defies
That safe behind the wainscot lies.
Say, did you ever know by sight
In cheese an individual mite?
Shew me the same numeric flea,
That bit your neck but yesterday.
You then may boldly go in quest
To find the Grub-Street poet's nest.
What spunging-house, in dread of jail,
Receives them while they wait for bail;
What alley they are nestled in,
To flourish o'er a cup of gin;
Find the last garret where they lay,
Or cellar where they starve today.
Suppose you have them all trepann'd,
With each a libel in his hand,

What

What punishment would you inflict?
Or call 'em rogues, or get 'em kickt?
These they have often tried before;
You but oblige them so much more;
Themselves would be the first to tell,
To make their trash the better sell.
  You have been libell'd—Let us know,
What senseless coxcomb told you so?
Will you regard the hawker's cries,
Who in his titles always lies?
Whate'er the noisy scoundrel says
It might be something in your praise.
And praise bestow'd in Grub-Street rhymes,
Would vex me more a thousand times.
Till blockheads blame, and judges praise,
The poet cannot claim his bays.
On me, when dunces are satiric,
I take it for a panegyric.
Hated by fools, and, *Fools to hate*,
Be that my motto, and my fate.

Stella's Birth-Day, March 13, 1718–19

STELLA this day is thirty-four,
(We shan't dispute a year or more)
However, Stella, be not troubled,
Although thy size and years are doubled,
Since first I saw thee at sixteen,
The brightest virgin on the green;
So little is thy form declin'd;
Made up so largely in thy mind.
  Oh, would it please the gods to split
Thy beauty, size, and years, and wit,

No

No age could furnish out a pair
Of nymphs so graceful, wise, and fair;
With half the lustre of your eyes,
With half your wit, your years and size.
And then, before it grew too late,
How should I beg of gentle fate,
(That either nymph might have her swain,)
To split my worship too in twain.

Stella's Birth-Day, March 13, 1726–7

THIS day, whate'er the Fates decree,
Shall still be kept with joy by me;
This day then let us not be told,
That you are sick, and I grown old;
Nor think on our approaching ills,
And talk of spectacles and pills;
Tomorrow will be time enough
To hear such mortifying stuff.
Yet, since from reason may be brought
A better and more pleasing thought,
Which can, in spite of all decays,
Support a few remaining days;
From not the gravest of divines
Accept for once some serious lines.
Although we now can form no more
Long schemes of life, as heretofore;
Yet you, while time is running fast,
Can look with joy on what is past.
Were future happiness and pain
A mere contrivance of the brain;
As atheists argue, to entice
And fit their proselytes for vice;

(The

(The only comfort they propose,
To have companions in their woes;)
Grant this the case; yet sure 'tis hard
That virtue, styled its own reward,
And by all sages understood
To be the chief of human good,
Should acting die; nor leave behind
Some lasting pleasure in the mind,
Which, by remembrance will assuage
Grief, sickness, poverty, and age;
And strongly shoot a radiant dart
To shine through life's declining part.
Say, Stella, feel you no content,
Reflecting on a life well spent?
Your skilful hand employ'd to save
Despairing wretches from the grave;
And then supporting with your store
Those whom you dragg'd from death before?
(So Providence on mortals waits,
Preserving what it first creates.)
Your generous boldness to defend
An innocent and absent friend;
That courage which can make you just
To merit humbled in the dust;
The detestation you express
For vice in all its glittering dress;
That patience under torturing pain,
Where stubborn stoics would complain;
Must these like empty shadows pass,
Or forms reflected from a glass?
Or mere chimeras in the mind,
That fly, and leave no marks behind?
Does not the body thrive and grow
By food of twenty years ago?

And,

And, had it not been still supplied,
It must a thousand times have died.
Then who with reason can maintain
That no effects of food remain?
And is not virtue in mankind
The nutriment that feeds the mind;
Upheld by each good action past,
And still continued by the last?
Then, who with reason can pretend
That all effects of virtue end?
  Believe me, Stella, when you show
That true contempt for things below,
Nor prize your life for other ends,
Than merely to oblige your friends;
Your former actions claim their part,
And join to fortify your heart.
For Virtue, in her daily race,
Like Janus, bears a double face;
Looks back with joy where she has gone
And therefore goes with courage on.
She at your sickly couch will wait,
And guide you to a better state.
  O then, whatever Heaven intends,
Take pity on your pitying friends!
Nor let your ills affect your mind,
To fancy they can be unkind.
Me, surely me, you ought to spare,
Who gladly would your suffering share;
Or give my scrap of life to you,
And think it far beneath your due;
You, to whose care so oft I owe
That I'm alive to tell you so.

The

The Day of Judgment[1]

WITH a whirl of thought oppress'd,
I sunk from reverie to rest.
An horrid vision seized my head;
I saw the graves give up their dead!
Jove arm'd with terrors, bursts the skies,
And thunder roars and lightning flies!
Amaz'd, confus'd, its fate unknown,
The world stands trembling at his throne!
While each pale sinner hung his head,
Jove, nodding, shook the heavens, and said:
'Offending race of human kind,
By nature, reason, *learning*, blind;
You who, through frailty, stepp'd aside;
And you, who never fell—*through pride*;
You who in different sects were shamm'd,
And come to see each other damn'd;
(So some folk told you, but they knew
No more of Jove's designs than you;)
—The world's mad business now is o'er,
And I resent these pranks no more.
—I to such blockheads set my wit!
I damn such fools!—Go, go, you're *bit*.

On the Death of Dr. Swift, 1731

AS Rochefoucauld his maxims drew
From nature, I believe 'em true:
They argue no corrupted mind
In him; the fault is in mankind.

[1] This poem was not published during Swift's lifetime. It was sent to Voltaire by Lord Chesterfield in a letter, August 27, 1752, with the following comment: 'Je vous envoie ci-jointe une pièce par le feu Docteur Swift, laquelle je crois ne vous déplaira pas. Elle n'a jamais été imprimée, vous en dévinerez bien la raison, mais elle est authentique. J'en ai l'original, écrit de sa propre main.'

This

This maxim more than all the rest
Is thought too base for human breast:
'In all distresses of our friends,
We first consult our private ends;
While nature, kindly bent to ease us,
Points out some circumstance to please us.'
If this perhaps your patience move,
Let reason and experience prove.
We all behold with envious eyes
Our *equal* raised above our *size.*
Who would not at a crowded show
Stand high himself, keep others low?
I love my friend as well as you;
But why should he obstruct my view?
Then let me have the higher post,
Suppose it but an inch at most.
If in a battle you should find
One whom you love of all mankind,
Had some heroic action done,
A champion kill'd, or trophy won;
Rather than thus be overtopt,
Would you not wish his laurels cropt?
Dear honest Ned is in the gout,
Lies rackt with pain, and you without:
How patiently you hear him groan.
How glad the case is not your own.
What poet would not grieve to see
His breth'ren write as well as he?
But rather than they should excel,
He'd wish his rivals all in hell.
Her end when Emulation misses,
She turns to Envy, stings and hisses;
The strongest friendship yields to pride,
Unless the odds be on our side.

Vain

Vain human kind! fantastic race!
Thy various follies who can trace?
Self-love, ambition, envy, pride,
Their empire in our hearts divide.
Give others riches, power, and station.
'Tis all on me an usurpation.
I have no title to aspire;
Yet when you sink, I seem the higher.
In Pope I cannot read a line,
But with a sigh I wish it mine;
Yet he can in one couplet fix
More sense than I can do in six;
It gives me such a jealous fit,
I cry, 'Pox take him and his wit!'
I grieve to be outdone by Gay
In my own hum'rous biting way.
Arbuthnot is no more my friend,
Who dares to irony pretend,
Which I was born to introduce,
Refin'd it first, and shew'd its use.
St. John, as well as Pultney, knows
That I had some repute for prose;
And, till they drove me out of date
Could maul a minister of state.
If they have mortify'd my pride,
And made me throw my pen aside;
If with such talents Heav'n has blest 'em,
Have I not reason to detest 'em?
To all my foes, dear Fortune, send
Thy gifts; but never to my friend.
I tamely can endure the first;
But this with envy makes me burst.
Thus much may serve by way of proem,
Proceed we therefore to our poem.

The

The time is not remote, when I
Must by the course of nature die;
When, I foresee, my special friends
Will try to find their private ends;
Tho' it is hardly understood
Which way my death can do them good,
Yet thus, methinks, I hear 'em speak:
'See, how the Dean begins to break!
Poor gentleman, he droops apace!
You plainly find it in his face.
That old vertigo in his head
Will never leave him till he's dead.
Besides, his memory decays;
He recollects not what he says;
He cannot call his friends to mind;
Forgets the place where last he din'd;
Plyes you with stories o'er and o'er;
He told them fifty times before.
How does he fancy we can sit
To hear his out-of-fashion'd wit?
But he takes up with younger folks,
Who for his wine will bear his jokes.
Faith, he must make his stories shorter,
Or change his comrades once a quarter;
In half the time he talks them round,
There must another set be found.
For poetry he's past his prime;
He takes an hour to find a rhyme;
His fire is out, his wit decay'd,
His fancy sunk, his Muse a jade.
I'd have him throw away his pen;—
But there's no talking to some men.'
And then their tenderness appears,
By adding largely to my years;

'He's older than he would be reckon'd,
And well remembers Charles the Second.
He hardly drinks a pint of wine;
And that, I doubt, is no good sign.
His stomach too begins to fail;
Last year we thought him strong and hale;
But now he's quite another thing;
I wish he may hold out till spring.'
Then hug themselves, and reason thus:
'It is not yet so bad with us.'
  In such a case they talk in tropes,
And by their fears express their hopes;
Some great misfortune to portend,
No enemy can match a friend.
With all the kindness they profess,
The merit of a lucky guess
(When daily how d'ye's come of course,
And servants answer, '*Worse and worse.*')
Wou'd please 'em better, than to tell,
That, 'God be prais'd, the Dean is well.'
Then he, who prophecy'd the best,
Approves his foresight to the rest:
'You know I always fear'd the worst,
And often told you so at first.'
He'd rather chuse that I should die,
Than his prediction prove a lie.
Not one foretells I shall recover;
But all agree to give me over.
  Yet, shou'd some neighbour feel a pain
Just in the parts where I complain;
How many a message would he send.
What hearty prayers that I should mend.
Inquire what regimen I kept;
What gave me ease, and how I slept?

And

And more lament when I was dead,
Than all the sniv'llers round my bed.
My good companions, never fear;
For though you may mistake a year,
Though your prognostics run too fast,
They must be verify'd at last.
Behold the fatal day arrive.
'How is the Dean?'—'He's just alive.'
Now the departing prayer is read;
'He hardly breathes.'—'The Dean is dead.'
Before the Passing-bell begun,
The news thro' half the town has run.
'O! may we all for death prepare.
What has he left? and who's his heir?'—
'I know no more than what the news is;
'Tis all bequeath'd to public uses.'
'To public use! a perfect whim.
What had the public done for him?
Mere envy, avarice and pride:
He gave it all—but first he died.
And had the Dean, in all the nation
No worthy friend, no poor relation?
So ready to do strangers good,
Forgetting his own flesh and blood.'
Now, Grub-Street wits are all employ'd;
With elegies the town is cloy'd.
Some paragraph in ev'ry paper
To curse the Dean, or bless the Drapier.
The doctors, tender of their fame,
Wisely on me lay all the blame:
'We must confess, his case was nice;
But he would never take advice.
Had he been ruled, for aught appears,
He might have lived these twenty years;

For,

For, when we open'd him, we found,
That all his vital parts were sound.'
  From Dublin soon to London spread,
'Tis told at court, 'the Dean is dead.'
Kind Lady Suffolk,[1] in the spleen,
Runs laughing up to tell the queen.
The queen, so gracious, mild, and good,
Cries, 'Is he gone! 'tis time he shou'd.
He's dead, you say; why, let him rot;
I'm glad the medals were forgot.
I promis'd him, I own; but when?
I only was a princess then;
But now, as consort of a king,
You know 'tis quite a different thing.'
Now Chartres,[2] at Sir Robert's levee,
Tells with a sneer the tidings heavy:
'Why, is he dead without his shoes,'
Cries Bob, 'I'm sorry for the news;
O, were the wretch but living still,
And in his place my good friend Will![3]
Or had a mitre on his head,
Provided Bolinbroke were dead!'
Now Curll his shop from rubbish drains;
Three genuine tomes of Swift's remains!
And then, to make them pass the glibber,
Revised by Tibbalds, Moore, and Cibber.
He'll treat me as he does my betters,
Publish my will, my life, my letters;
Revive the libels born to die;
Which Pope must bear, as well as I.

[1] Mrs. Howard, lady-in-waiting to the Queen, a friend and correspondent of Swift.

[2] A filthy but fashionable lecher, who at the age of seventy was tried for rape.

[3] William Pulteney, formerly the friend, later the enemy, of Robert Walpole.

Here

Here shift the scene, to represent
How those I love my death lament.
Poor Pope will grieve a month, and Gay
A week, and Arbuthnot a day.
St. John himself will scarce forbear
To bite his pen, and drop a tear.
The rest will give a shrug, and cry,
'I'm sorry—but we all must die!'
Indifference, clad in Wisdom's guise,
All fortitude of mind supplies.
For how can stony bowels melt
In those who never pity felt!
When *we* are lash'd, *they* kiss the rod,
Resigning to the will of God.
The fools, my juniors by a year,
Are tortur'd with suspense and fear;
Who wisely thought my age a screen,
When death approach'd, to stand between.
The screen removed, their hearts are trembling;
They mourn for me without dissembling.
My female friends, whose tender hearts,
Have better learn'd to act their parts,
Receive the news in doleful dumps:
'The Dean is dead: (and what is trumps?)
Then, Lord have mercy on his soul!
(Ladies, I'll venture for the vole.[1])
Six deans, they say, must bear the pall;
(I wish I knew what king to call.)
Madam your husband will attend
The funeral of so good a friend.
No, madam, 'tis a schocking sight;
And he's engaged tomorrow night;

[1] A play on which the player risks losing all tricks in an attempt for a 'grand slam'.

My

My Lady Club would take it ill,
If he shou'd fail her at quadrille.
He loved the Dean—(I lead a heart,)
But dearest friends, they say, must part.
His time was come: he ran his race;
We hope he's in a better place.'
Why do we grieve that friends should die?
No loss more easy to supply.
One year is past; a different scene!
No further mention of the Dean;
Who now, alas! no more is miss'd,
Than if he never did exist.
Where's now this fav'rite of Apollo!
Departed:—and his works must follow;
Must undergo the common fate;
His kind of wit is out of date.
Some country squire to Lintot goes,
Inquires for 'Swift in Verse and Prose'.
Says Lintot, 'I have heard the name;
He died a year ago.'—'The same.'
He searches all the shop in vain.
'Sir, you may find them in Duck-lane;
I sent them with a load of books,
Last Monday to the pastry-cook's.
To fancy they could live a year!
I find you're but a stranger here.
The Dean was famous in his time,
And had a kind of knack at rhyme.
His way of writing now is past;
The town has got a better taste;
I keep no antiquated stuff,
But spick and span I have enough.
Pray do but give me leave to show 'em;
Here's Colley Cibber's birth-day poem.

This

This ode you never yet have seen,
By Stephen Duck,[1] upon the queen.
Then here's a letter finely penned
Against the Craftsman and his friend;
It clearly shows that all reflection
On ministers is disaffection.
Next, here's Sir Robert's vindication,
And Mr. Henley's last oration.
The hawkers have not got them yet:
Your honour please to buy a set?
Here's Woolston's tracts, the twelfth edition;
'Tis read by every politician;
The country members, when in town,
To all their boroughs send them down;
You never met a thing so smart;
The courtiers have them all by heart;
Those maids of honour (who can read),
Are taught to use them for their creed.
The rev'rend author's good intention
Has been rewarded with a pension.
He does an honour to his gown,
By bravely running priestcraft down;
He shows, as sure as God's in Gloucester,
That Moses was a grand imposter;
That all his miracles were cheats,
Perform'd as jugglers do their feats;
The church had never such a writer;
A shame he has not got a mitre!'
Suppose me dead; and then suppose
A club assembled at the Rose;
Where, from discourse of this and that,

[1] The 'poetical thresher', whom Queen Caroline subsidized in the belief that he would immortalize rustic life and manual labour in poetry. He pined away at court and finally drowned himself in the Thames.

I grow

I grow the subject of their chat.
And while they toss my name about,
With favour some, and some without,
One, quite indifferent in the cause,
My character impartial draws:
'The Dean, if we believe report,
Was never ill receiv'd at court.
As for his works in verse and prose
I own myself no judge of those;
Nor can I tell what critics thought 'em;
But this I know, all people bought 'em.
As with a moral view design'd
To cure the vices of mankind.
And, if he often miss'd his aim,
The world must own it, to their shame,
The praise is his, and theirs the blame.'—
'Sir, I have heard another story;
He was a most confounded Tory,
And grew, or he is much belied,
Extremely dull, before he died.'—
'Can we the Drapier then forget?
Is not our nation in his debt?
'Twas he that writ the Drapier's letters!—
'He should have left them for his betters,
We had a hundred abler men,
Nor need depend upon his pen.'—
'Say what you will about his reading,
You never can defend his breeding;
Who in his satires running riot,
Could never leave the world in quiet;
Attacking, when he took the whim,
Court, city, camp—all one to him.'—
'But why should he, except he slobber't,
Offend our patriot, great Sir Robert,

Whose

Whose counsels aid the sov'reign power
To save the nation every hour?
What scenes of evil he unravels
In satires, libels, lying travels!
Not sparing his own clergy-cloth,
But eats into it, like a moth!'—
'His vein, ironically grave,
Exposed the fool, and lash'd the knave.
To steal a hint was never known,
But what he writ was all his own.
'He never thought an honour done him,
Because a duke was proud to own him,
Would rather slip aside and chuse
To talk with wits in dirty shoes;
Despised the fools with stars and garters,
So often seen caressing Chartres.
He never courted men in station,
Nor persons held in admiration;
Of no man's greatness was afraid,
Because he sought for no man's aid.
Though trusted long in great affairs
He gave himself no haughty airs.
Without regarding private ends,
Spent all his credit for his friends;
And only chose the wise and good;
No flatterers; no allies in blood;
But succour'd virtue in distress,
And seldom fail'd of good success;
As numbers in their hearts must own,
Who, but for him, had been unknown.
'With princes kept a due decorum,
But never stood in awe before 'em.
He follow'd David's lesson just:
In princes never put thy trust.

And

And would you make him truly sour,
Provoke him with a slave in power.
The Irish senate if you named,
With what impatience he declaim'd!
Fair LIBERTY was all his cry,
For her he stood prepared to die;
For her he boldly stood alone;
For her he oft exposed his own.
Two kingdoms, just as faction led,
Had set a price upon his head;
But not a traitor could be found
To sell him for six hundred pound.
'Had he but spared his tongue and pen
He might have rose like other men;
But power was never in his thought,
And wealth he valued not a groat.
Ingratitude he often found,
And pities those who meant the wound.
But kept the tenor of his mind,
To merit well of human kind.
Nor made a sacrifice of those
Who still were true, to please his foes.
He labour'd many a fruitless hour,
To reconcile his friends in power;
Saw mischief by a faction brewing,
While they pursued each other's ruin.
But finding vain was all his care,
He left the court in mere despair.
'And oh! how short are human schemes!
Here ended all our golden dreams.
What St. John's skill in state affairs,
What Ormond's valour, Oxford's cares,
To save their sinking country lent,
Was all destroy'd by one event.

Too

Too soon that precious life was ended.
On which alone our weal depended.
When up a dangerous faction starts,
With wrath and vengeance in their hearts;
By solemn League and Cov'nant bound,
To ruin, slaughter, and confound;
To turn religion to a fable,
And make the government a Babel;
Pervert the laws, disgrace the gown,
Corrupt the senate, rob the crown;
To sacrifice old England's glory,
And make her infamous in story.
When such a tempest shook the land,
How could unguarded Virtue stand!
With horror, grief, despair, the Dean
Beheld the dire destructive scene.
His friends in exile, or the tower,
Himself within the frown of power,
Pursued by base envenom'd pens,
Far to the land of slaves and fens;[1]
A servile race in folly nursed,
Who truckle most when treated worst.

'By innocence and resolution,
He bore continual persecution;
While numbers to preferment rose,
Whose merits were, to be his foes;
When *ev'n his own familiar friends,*
Intent upon their private ends,
Like renegadoes now he feels,
Against him lifting up their heels.

'The Dean did, by his pen, defeat
An infamous destructive cheat;[2]

[1] Ireland.

[2] Wood's copper half-pence. Cf. M. B. Drapier's *Letter to the Whole People of Ireland*, above.

Taught

Taught fools their int'rest how to know,
And gave them arms to ward the blow.
Envy has own'd it was his doing,
To save that hapless land from ruin;
While they who at the steerage stood,
And reap'd the profit, sought his blood.
'To save them from their evil fate,
In him was held a crime of state,
A wicked monster on the bench,
Whose fury blood could never quench;
As vile and profligate a villain,
As modern Scroggs, or old Tresilian;
Who long all justice had discarded,
Nor fear'd he God, nor man regarded;
Vow'd on the Dean his rage to vent,
And make him of his zeal repent.
But Heaven his innocence defends,
The grateful people stand his friends;
Not strains of law, nor judge's frown,
Nor topics brought to please the crown,
Nor witness hired, nor jury pick't,
Prevail to bring him in convict.
'In exile, with a steady heart,
He spent his life's declining part;
Where folly, pride, and faction sway,
Remote from St. John, Pope, and Gay.
Alas, poor Dean! his only scope
Was to be held a misanthrope.
This into gen'ral odium drew him,
Which if he liked, much good may't do him.
His zeal was not to lash our crimes,
But discontent against the times;
For had we made him timely offers
To raise his post, or fill his coffers,

Perhaps

Perhaps he might have truckled down,
Like other brethren of his gown.
For party he would scarce have bled;
I say no more—because he's dead.
What writings has he left behind?
I hear, they're of a different kind;
A few in verse; but most in prose—
Some high-flown pamphlets, I suppose;—
All scribbled in the worst of times,
To palliate his friend Oxford's crimes,
To praise Queen Anne, nay more, defend her,
As never fav'ring the Pretender;
Or libels yet conceal'd from sight,
Against the court to show his spite;
Perhaps his Travels, part the third;
A lie at every second word—
Offensive to a royal ear;
But not one sermon, you may swear.'
'His friendships there, to few confined,
Were always of the middling kind;
No fools of rank, a mongrel breed,
Who fain would pass for lords indeed;
Where titles give no right or power,
And peerage is a wither'd flower;
He would have held it a disgrace,
If such a wretch had known his face.
On rural squires, that kingdom's bane,
He vented oft his wrath in vain;
[Biennial] squires to market brought;
Who sell their souls and [votes] for nought;
The [nation stripped] go joyful back,
To . . . the church, their tenants rack,
Go snacks with [rogues and rapparees,[1]]

[1] Ex-soldiers turned highwaymen.

And

And keep the peace to pick up fees;
In every job to have a share,
A goal or barrack to repair;
And turn the tax for public roads,
Commodious to their own abodes.
'Perhaps I may allow the Dean,
Had too much satire in his vein;
And seem'd determined not to starve it,
Because no age could more deserve it.
Yet malice never was his aim;
He lash'd the vice, but spared the name;
No individual could resent,
Where thousands equally were meant;
His satire points at no defect,
But what all mortals may correct;
For he abhorr'd that senseless tribe
Who call it humour when they gibe.
He spared a hump, or crooked nose,
Whose owners set not up for beaux.
True genuine dulness moved his pity,
Unless it offer'd to be witty.
Those who their ignorance confest,
He ne'er offended with a jest;
He laugh'd to hear an idiot quote
A verse from Horace learn'd by rote.
'Vice, if it e'er can be abash'd,
Must be or ridiculed or lash'd.
If you resent it, who's to blame?
He neither knew you nor your name.
Should vice expect to 'scape rebuke,
Because its owner is a duke?
'He knew an hundred pleasant stories,
With all the turns of Whigs and Tories.

Was

Was cheerful to his dying day;
And friends would let him have his way.
'He gave what little wealth he had
To build a house for fools and mad;
And show'd by one satiric touch,
No nation wanted it so much.
That kingdom he hath left his debtor,
I wish it soon may have a better.'—
And, since you dread no farther lashes,
Methinks you may forgive his ashes.

ALPHABETICAL INDEX

(*The titles of poems are printed in italics.*)

SET IN
GREAT BRITAIN
AT THE
UNIVERSITY PRESS
OXFORD
PRINTED BY
LATIMER TREND AND CO. LTD.
PLYMOUTH